# ILLUSTRATIONS

# MEMOIRS
# OF WILLIAM HICKEY

## CHAPTER I

### THE VOYAGE FROM LISBON

WE stood out to sea in company with the *Expedition* packet, commanded by Captain Dashwood. This vessel was considered one of the fastest sailers in the service of Government ; it was therefore very gratifying to us on board the *Raynha De Portugal* to see that we rather had the heels of her. At dusk we had got a good offing ; the *Expedition* then left us, bending her course towards England, while we stood to the south-west, at the rate of eight knots an hour.

I soon perceived several peculiarities in the Portuguese mode of managing their ships, some of which appeared to me extremely awkward, such, for instance, as the commanding officer of the watch always walking on the lee side of the deck, whilst the carpenters, sailmakers, or other workmen executed their business to windward, thus reversing the practice of the British Navy, and I believe of every other European power, nor could they give any reason for so doing, replying to my questions upon it exactly as the Chinese did as to some of their uncouth practices, "that it had always been the Portuguese custom."

The 24th[1] we saw two strange sail standing to the southward ; the 25th a schooner to the east-north-east which hoisted Russian colours ; the 26th in the evening saw the Island of Madeira, distant about fourteen

[1] 24th June, 1782.   Ed.

# CONTENTS

# EDITOR'S NOTE

At the time of the publication of the second volume of these Memoirs it was thought that a third volume only would be needed to bring them to a conclusion. The unpublished portion has, however, been found to be much more interesting than was expected, with the result that a fourth volume will be required to complete the work. This is now being prepared and will be published with the least possible delay.

Now that the famous picture of Thais, by Sir Joshua Reynolds, has been proved to be a portrait of Emily Warren (Bob Pott's Emily), although it has been described as a picture of Emily Bertie or Coventry, the Editor is glad to reproduce it in the present volume with a portrait of Bob Pott himself by Romney, owned by the Rev. Alfred Percivall Pott, who has very kindly given permission to the Editor to use it.

Many unsuccessful efforts have been made to obtain a portrait of the author of the Memoirs and one of Charlotte Barry. The present volume mentions several pictures which were painted of them, and in addition there is towards the end of the Memoirs a reference to a portrait of the author painted by Mr. George Chinnery in Calcutta in 1807 or 1808, and presented by him to Sir Henry Russell, the then Chief Justice of Bengal. There appears also to have been an engraved portrait of the author, probably a private plate, of which a copy was sold at the sale of Thomas Haviland Burke's engravings at Christie's, 21–28 June, 1852. It is hoped that some of these portraits will yet be traced and the Editor would be thankful for any information that may be thought likely to assist him in his search for them.

Made and printed in Great Britain at
*The Mayflower Press, Plymouth.* William Brendon & Son, Ltd.

# MEMOIRS OF WILLIAM HICKEY

### EDITED BY
### ALFRED SPENCER

### Vol. III
### (1782–1790)

WITH TWO PHOTOGRAVURE PORTRAITS

### LONDON
### HURST & BLACKETT, LTD.
### PATERNOSTER HOUSE, E.C.

ISBN: 978129022660


Published by:
HardPress Publishing
8345 NW 66TH ST #2561
MIAMI FL 33166-2626

Email: info@hardpress.net
Web: http://www.hardpress.net

leagues, at which we were to complete the cargo with wine :
at eleven at night hove to.   The wind blowing fresh had
raised a high sea, which made the ship roll and tumble about
dreadfully, so that we passed a wretched night.   This was
our first sample of what we might expect in bad weather,
convincing us of the probability of Mr. Moore's prediction
being verified.   At daylight of the 27th made sail; at six
passed the east end of the island, and at eight anchored in
the roads of Funchal ;   found only three small vessels there,
but soon after we anchored a large ship came in having been
only thirteen days on her passage from Portsmouth.

Mrs. Aldus having asked us to reside at her house during
our stay, we gladly accepted the obliging invitation.   At
ten o'clock her husband came on board, to whom she introduced us.   We accompanied them on shore to an excellent
house of Mr. Aldus's.   After dinner he took us to Mr.
Murray's, the British Consul, to Mr. Murdoch's, Mr. Ach-
muty's, and two or three other gentlemen of the island.
Mr. Murray engaged us to pass the whole of the following
day with him at his country seat about four miles distance,
up a mountain immediately above the town.   In the evening
we visited two monasteries, purchasing from the recluses
their ingenious productions ;   from whence we went to a
neat theatre where a comedy was very tolerably performed.
My poor Charlotte was sadly annoyed by lizards, an animal
with which Madeira is overrun, some of them of a larger
kind than I ever saw in any other part of the world.

The next day, being the 28th, at seven in the morning we
set off for Mr. Murray's, the gentlemen of our party mounted
upon small horses, the ladies carried by negroes in a sort of
hammock slung upon a long pole, a safe and pleasant sort
of conveyance, indeed the only fit one for females, the road
in many parts being extremely steep, very rough, and awful
to the sight, one side having nothing between the traveller
and inevitable destruction if the horse made a false step so
as to fall, in which case the rider would be precipitated many
hundred feet upon hard rocks at the bottom.

When at the summit of the mountain the danger of getting

to it is entirely forgotten in the sublimity of the scenery. Mr. Murray's premises are beautiful and romantic. Mr. Aldus told us he had expended between fifteen and twenty thousand pounds upon the house and grounds, a heavy expence having been incurred by conveying water for several miles through leaden pipes to his grounds, which had no springs upon them. Altogether it was as pretty a spot as I ever beheld. Mr. Murray and his lady entertained us admirably. After spending a very pleasant day we crossed the top of the mountain between two and three miles to Mr. Aldus's country house, where notwithstanding excessive hot weather we slept cool and comfortable.

The 29th we returned to Funchal to dine with Donna Guiamara, a Portuguese woman of rank to whom we had been introduced by Mr. Barretto. After a very good dinner she treated us to several sorts of delicious wine, particularly some malmsey, which she assured us was as old as herself, that is seventy years, having been made by her father from his own vintages, and precious liquor it undoubtedly was.

On the 30th Mr. Barretto informed us he had shipped two hundred and forty pipes of madeira, being the quantity he intended to take, and requested we would all be on board early the following morning as he proposed proceeding to sea at noon. We dined at Mr. Murdoch's, a convivial fellow who made us drink a great deal too much claret. At night we had a concert, at which two Portuguese gentlemen sung some of the sweetest duets I ever heard. We likewise had capital catches and glees.

On the 1st of July after breakfast, bidding adieu to our hostess, her husband conveyed us on board our ship in a commodious boat of his own, constructed for encountering the surf, which is sometimes tremendously high at Madeira. When we embarked it was so nearly calm the ship dared not get under way lest the swell of the sea should drive her upon the rocks, but about three in the afternoon, a fine breeze springing up from the land, we weighed anchor and made sail, running from the island rapidly. Charlotte and myself were in perfect health, and her favourite maid, Harriet, had benefited materially at Madeira from the climate, as well as from Mrs. Aldus's nursing. I endeavoured to persuade her to remain there, Mrs. Aldus kindly promising to take care of her until she was quite restored to health, but no arguments of mine or Mrs. Hickey's could induce her to forsake her mistress whom, let the consequence be what it would, she was resolved to follow while life remained.

In a few days after we were at sea I observed a materia alteration for the worse in poor Harriet, her cough increased, her spirits flagged, and her appetite totally failed. Thus she continued gradually sinking to the grave.

The pipes of wine received on board at Madeira not only impeded the ship's progress by making her too deep in the water but greatly increased her motion; at times we rolled so dreadfully deep it was with the utmost difficulty we preserved our seats at meal-time.

While at Madeira Mr. Barretto called upon Mr. Bateman and me to say Messieurs Kemp and Brown found messing with the officers of the ship so disagreeable that he should consider it as a great favour if we would allow them to join our table, which, if we kindly consented to, he would take care to furnish with an ample addition of live-stock and liquors for them. To this we readily acceded, both young men being perfectly correct and well behaved. From Madeira, therefore, they became our messmates, their company proving a great acquisition to us.

Nothing material occurred until the 10th of the month, when it blew hard, with an immense sea, which occasioned the ship to roll so deep we were in momentary expectation of the masts going over her side. The wind being right aft, we ran in these twenty-four hours two hundred and thirty miles.

The 13th we had abundance of vivid lightning, immense numbers of grampus blowing the water up to a considerable height in different directions, some of them being within a quarter of a mile of the ship. At 3 p.m. we saw a sail from the mast-head bearing east.

The 15th a snow upon our beam steering the same course as us. At noon she shewed Portuguese colours, at six she was out of sight astern. Our ship, from constant deep rolling and labouring very heavily, made several inches of water every watch. This rendered it necessary to pump her twice a day.

On the 18th they discovered that the foretop-mast was sprung. In the act of getting it down a man fell off the fore yard upon the spars and booms, being sadly maimed and bruised. The weather was exceedingly squally, and in a severe gust the main and main-topsails both split. A good deal of time was lost in shifting them.

During the rest of the month of July the weather continued boisterous and unpleasant ; an immense high sea made the motion so violent and quick it was impossible to walk the deck and difficult to keep one's feet at all. Not a day passed without some accident of splitting sails or carrying parts of the rigging.

Mrs. Hickey's servant, Harriet Hammersly, became so reduced and weak that she was unable to rise from her bed, and was evidently dying, of which she seemed conscious herself, but she was quite resigned, and the most patient sufferer that could be, never uttering a complaint or even a murmur. Her melancholy and desperate situation gave my dearest girl great affliction, she being much attached to her.

On the 1st of August we got the south-east Trade, very fresh, which drove us at a great rate. On the 3rd the gentle Harriet was suddenly seized with a succession of fainting fits, in one of which she breathed her last, expiring without the slightest struggle or even a sigh. In the evening her corpse was committed to the deep, the burial service being read by Mr. Bateman, the whole ship's crew with their priest attending with the utmost gravity and decorum. The body was enclosed in a plain neat coffin made by the carpenters on board.

This was a cruel blow upon Mrs. Hickey, who was so affected by the death of her favourite and faithful attendant that for several days I could not prevail on her to join us at table or to leave her cabin. The loss was in every way irreparable.

I found the Portuguese strangely perverse in their manner of navigating. Although the Trade wind favoured us exceedingly, seldom being to the southward of east-south-east, instead of availing themselves of so unusual a circumstance by going free, thereby letting the ship have fresh way through the water as English seamen certainly would have done, they kept her constantly close hauled, the sails every minute half aback, thereby not only impeding her progress but unnecessarily tearing both rigging and hull to pieces, one evil consequence of which was the great increase of leakage. The weather becoming still worse, we, on the 18th, being then in the latitude of thirty south, with a threatening sky and every indication of a gale, a large head sea making us pitch dreadfully, began to prepare for it by clinching in the ports fore and aft by fixing dead lights to the great cabin windows, so reducing us to the unpleasant necessity of burning candles all day.

The 19th an albatross made its appearance, an immense bird, I believe unknown in every part of the world except the high southern latitude. Some of them measure five-and-twenty feet from the tip of one wing to the other. I once saw one of twenty-three feet.

On the 21st a seaman fell from the main-topsail yard when reefing the sail into the sea and was lost.

Our fellow-passenger, the Frenchman, whom I have already mentioned, proved a valuable acquisition to us, being a man of general knowledge, deep learning, and abounding in anecdote.

The 22nd saw a vessel, snow-rigged, upon our bow, standing as we did. When about three miles distant we hoisted an English ensign, which she answered with Portuguese. The three or four following days we saw a number of Mother Cary's chickens flying about. There was an immense swell from the westward.

On the 1st of September our latitude by reckoning was

thirty-five, sixteen south ; dismal, dark, threatening sky ; hard squalls, rain, with an immense sea running, which made the ship labour very much. Immense numbers of albatrosses were flying about the ship. By the Captain's Journal we were now upon the edge of the bank of Cape Lagullas ; hove to, and sounded, but got no bottom with a hundred and eighty fathoms of line. As the water continued much discoloured we sounded every watch, but without finding bottom until the 4th, on which morning we saw a gannet, a bird that seamen suppose never goes off soundings, an idea that was verified with us, for upon heaving the lead we got ground at sixty fathoms ; a yellow sand.

On the 5th so heavy a sea run we apprehended being pooped every minute. The ship laboured dreadfully, tumbling about so that we split the main-sail from the violent jerks, and soon after both main and foretop-sails, after which we ran under the fore-sail alone. The 6th, 7th and 8th it blew strong, with at times severe squalls, rain and a sea that seemed disposed to overwhelm us. The motion was quite horrid. On the 8th one of the main chain plates broke, which endangered the mast ; all hands were busily occupied replacing it, a difficult job from the violent motion. Mother Cary's chickens in every quarter.

On the 9th it blew still stronger, with uncommonly black sky, the same high sea running, but more confused, the ship being sometimes struck with great violence. In the evening the gale increased, attended by severe squalls. At 8 p.m. Mrs. Hickey, Mr. Bateman, Mr. Kemp, Mr. Brown, Mr. Barretto and the priest, whom we had invited to supper, and myself, had just seated ourselves, the chairs being made fast to the table, and the latter as we thought so well secured that nothing could move it, when we heard a dreadful crash upon deck. In the same moment too the vessel took so desperate a lurch as to tear the table at which we were sitting from its lashings, and the whole party, chairs, dishes, plates and all the etceteras were dashed in one promiscuous heap against the lee side of the cabin. Providentially none of us received any material personal injury.

Sad screaming and more noise prevailing upon deck, I went up to enquire the cause of it. The night was so dismally dark that to discover anything by the eye was utterly impossible, but I learnt from one of the midshipmen, a young friend of mine, that in a sudden gust of wind the fore yard had snapped in two in the slings, the consequence of which was that the foretop-sail yard gave way and both sails were blown into ribbons. During my stay upon deck the main-topmast with all its rigging went over the side, being immediately followed by the foretop-mast, the main tack at the same time breaking. These complicated misfortunes I heard of from the people, for seeing was entirely out of the question.

The dreadful crash of falling masts, with the flapping of the split sails and melancholy cries of the people struck a general panic throughout the ship ; nothing but confusion and despair prevailed, increased not a little by a piercing cry from below that the pumps were choked and would not work. A more truly terrible scene could not be ; in fact, we expected nothing short of going to the bottom. The greater part of the crew, as I understand is always the case with Portuguese sailors in times of imminent danger, abandoned their duty to assemble round their priest, with whom they joined at the altar, screeching out supplicatory prayers to their patron saint Antonio, and all the other saints in the calendar, to have mercy upon them. A few, however, who possessed more firmness of mind, at the head of whom was the boatswain, never ceased to exert themselves with constancy and firmness. It was by some of them ascertained upon examination that the alarm relative to the pumps was without foundation, arising from the carpenter's fright being so great upon finding the well full of water that he forgot to pull out a stopper or plug, the omission of which prevented them from working. We nevertheless had still evils enough to render our situation very precarious. In less than one hour the ship, from being in good order, became an absolute wreck. Not a sail was left to the yards ; all three top-masts gone and lower rigging torn to pieces ; a dismally dark, blowing night, with a tremendous sea ; in a high southern latitude and tempestuous part of the ocean ; an increasing leak, and the ship labouring in such a manner. as to excite a reasonable apprehension of its becoming still worse, formed such a complication of evils as to make our bearing up against them a very doubtful matter.

The error about the pumps being rectified, they were both kept at work without intermission, affording us the consolation of finding they decreased the water. This had the further good effect of doing away with the panic that prevailed among three-fourths of the crew.

Upon mustering the people it was discovered that two were missing, supposed to have been carried away by some of the heavy seas that broke over the deck. The miserable men lost were one of the mates to the boatswain and a common seaman. The voice of the former was distinguished in the height of the confusion crying for assistance, but none could be afforded where everybody thought only of his own preservation. Two other seamen were carried overboard when the main-topmast fell, but fortunately keeping their hold on some of the ropes they regained a footing in the ship, thus being almost miraculously saved from drowning.

The roaring of the wind and sea, our cabin quite wet, and the natural anxiety from our situation put sleep entirely out of the question. During the first gust nearly every article in the great cabin and mine fetched way ; we had considerable difficulty in again securing them, being employed therein all the latter part of the night. At daybreak I again went upon deck, where I beheld the forlorn state we were reduced to. It still blew strong, the appearance of the sky bearing as threatening an aspect as the preceding day, the wind at north-north-west, with a mountainous sea, the deck strewed with broken rigging, which, with bits of torn sails hung ·about the lower masts, the only ones standing. Altogether it made a wretched exhibition. Upon examination they discovered that the mizzen-mast was sprung. All hands were busily employed clearing the wrecks of masts, yards, sails and cordage, which occupied them the whole day. There we lay in nearly the same spot tumbling about like a log upon the water, one pump being constantly at work night and day. Fortunately we were strongly manned in point of number, having one hundred and forty sailors. The next misfortune was finding both the caps of the main and fore-mast injured by the top-masts being wrenched when going, that of the fore-mast materially.

Towards evening the weather moderated, which enabled the people, who were greatly fatigued, to get some rest and sleep. Early on the 11th their labours were renewed with fresh vigour, the first thing being to get a main-sail set and a top-gallant sail for a fore-sail, which gave her a little way through the water, thereby lessening the violence of the motion. This day Mr. Barretto called a council of his officers to deliberate upon the most prudent measure to be adopted in our critical and dangerous situation, when, after mature consideration, they were unanimously of opinion the best thing we could do would be to steer for the Mauritias as the nearest port. This determination being communicated to the boatswain, he condemned it as highly imprudent, observing they might reach India almost as soon as Mauritias. Besides, the approach to the French islands at that time of the year was extremely dangerous, and should we meet with one of the hurricanes so common in approaching the land it must prove the loss of the ship in her disabled state and, consequently, of every person on board. This opinion had no weight with any one of the officers, who all treated it with vast contempt, but in a very different way did Mr. Barretto view it. He thought it founded in good sense and fair reasoning.

I own that what the boatswain said carried conviction to my mind. My Charlotte considered only what she had understood to be the nearest port, therefore earnestly wished for the Mauritias, and as the boatswain was not one of her favourites her dislike to him greatly increased by this advice of his. In vain I argued in his favour. She was sure he was a ferocious, horrid man. The fact is that though of

stern countenance he possessed a mild and benevolent disposition, blended with the utmost degree of fortitude in the
execution of the duties of his perilous profession, of which
merit we had subsequently undeniable proof.  He proved
our preserver by his zeal and example.

The 12th proved a day of wonderful progress in getting
the ship into some sort of sailing trim.  They got up an old
sprung main-topmast, which by reefing it above the injured
part answered tolerably.  Before dusk a new sail was bent
to a spare yard, and we began to move through the water
four or five knots an hour.  This day they discovered that
another man was lost overboard on the 9th.

The 13th the weather again became very bad ; violent
gusts of wind, rain, hail, thunder and lightning, all of the
severest kind.  A short, irregular sea made the motion of
the ship very distressing and considerably increased the
leak, nor could anything be done in the repairs of rigging
or making more sail.  This squally, disagreeable weather
continued four days.  The carpenter, however, contrived
during it to prepare a new fore-topmast and to fish the
mizzen-mast, so that on the 20th we had once more a tolerable quantity of sail set.  The captain and officers then began
to come round to the boatswain's opinion and admit that he
was right in proposing to stand on for India in preference
to making for the French Islands.  The 21st, 22nd, 23rd
and 24th we had a fresh breeze and fair weather.  The 25th
it increased to a gale, veering backward and forward sixteen
or eighteen points of the compass, which made a very ugly
cross sea, sometimes breaking over and sweeping all before
it.  The leak increased so much as to make it necessary to
keep both pumps at work.  The gale continued until the
30th, but being mostly fair we run very fast, which consoled
us for the abominable rolling.

On the 1st of October a large leak was discovered by the
ship's steward in the bread room, which was about two
feet under water, the sea pouring in with an immense rush.
This being immediately stopped, sanguine hopes were entertained that we might do with one pump.  We were, however,

disappointed, not finding the least difference in the quantity of water every hour. The 7th the wind became moderate and the sea much smoother. The 13th an immense swell annoyed us, though without increase of wind. The ship rolled so dreadfully nothing could remain in its place, and we were most uncomfortable. The leak became more alarming, making fourteen inches of water an hour. The 21st, the weather appearing settled, the dead lights were withdrawn and our cabin once more received the cheerful light of day.

The 29th at noon we were exactly under the Line, a circumstance that few persons have experienced. In the night a great deal of thunder and lightning. At daylight an amazing number of tropic birds flying round us ; at ten in the morning a hawk after fluttering about for some time, apparently exhausted, alighted in the foretop, where one of the seamen caught it. This was considered a very extraordinary circumstance, as we were not by reckoning within many hundred leagues of land.

On the 1st of November at one in the morning we were taken aback in a sudden squall of wind and rain. Soon afterwards it fell almost calm, the sea remarkably smooth, heat intense. Mr. Kemp, whose cabin in the steerage was small and confined, not being able to sleep, arose from his cot and went to sit in the quarter gallery for the sake of air. Whilst looking out of the window he saw something that appeared very like land upon the lee bow. Going immediately upon deck, he pointed it out to the officer of the watch, who was so satisfied of its actually being land that he directly caused the yards to be braced up, hauled close upon a wind, and sent to awaken the captain and Mr. Barretto. At daylight we were close in with two small islands, very low, being nearly level with the water and covered over with trees. The nearest to us was within a short mile, bearing south-east and by south, another somewhat larger about three miles off bearing south-east and by east. Upon referring to the charts we found they could be no other than the Cocos and Hog Island, only a few leagues from the Island of Sumatra! We were just *eleven degrees* to the eastward of the reckoning, which made them in the meridian of Ceylon, for which island, as our captain imagined, we were standing direct.

Fortunate indeed were we in there being so little wind during the night, for had the weather been such as we had experienced during the preceding month the ship would inevitably have plumped on shore, no look-out being kept from supposing themselves such an immense distance as eleven degrees of longitude from land and not having the remotest idea of being upon the eastern coast. So much for Portuguese navigation and Portuguese reckonings!

At eight in the morning it became very thick, smart squalls, excessive heavy rain, accompanied by thunder and lightning. At noon of the same day it cleared up—nothing to be seen of the islands. At two in the afternoon let the hawk that was caught on the 30th of November at liberty. At first it seemed weak and unable to leave the ship, but after hovering about near an hour it flew off with great velocity in the direction the land lay. Soon after the hawk was released another land bird alighted on one of the yards, which the people called a king'sfisher. This day we ran through an immense quantity of seaweed. At sunset very high land was seen from the masthead, bearing east. Several flights of birds went by in different directions.

The serious mistake as to the situation of the ship was a sad disappointment to us passengers, as we had flattered ourselves with the hope of reaching Columbo in a few days, whereas we might now be many weeks ere we got into port, all the directories stating light airs and calms of long duration as being prevalent off the coast of Sumatra in the months of November and December. We were the more uneasy at this from our stock of provisions and the ship's water being nearly expended. For a wonder the precaution of bending a cable to an anchor was taken.

On the 2nd it was quite calm, and we were in terror lest it should continue. The 3rd the same, with extreme sultry weather. We endeavoured to beguile the anxious hours by fishing, such shoals of fish were close round us that with baskets lowered into the sea we caught a vast number of small ones, some of which were beautifully marked and of the most brilliant colours.

On the 4th our captain was seized with a violent fever, supposed to have been brought on by anxiety of mind and fretting at finding himself so egregiously out in point of longitude. It soon affected his brain, and he became so outrageous that it was necessary to tie him down in his bed, sentries constantly watching to see that he did not break loose. In his frenzy he threatened death and destruction to every person that approached him. The strength he showed was quite wonderful, for he was a very slight-made man. Three different times he freed himself from the straps that bound him, when it was quite as much as four powerful fellows could do to hold him.

Our latitude on the 4th was three forty-four north. Soon after daylight of the 5th a drift was discovered about three miles off, which had the appearance of a ship's mast or lower yard : got out our yawl and rowed to it, when it was found to be the trunk of a large tree that must have been long in the water, being much decayed and entirely covered with barnacles and different kinds of shell-fish. In the afternoon saw two more drifts which we passed close to and perceived them likewise to be trees. Caught a beautiful sea-snake.

The 6th we had light airs of wind, an appearance of strong current from great rippling of the water ; calm in the night, the heat quite overcoming and oppressive. The 7th a light air again. At six in the morning saw the land from east to north and by east distant about eight leagues : from the form and height knew it to be part of the Island of Sumatra, and supposed it not far from Acheen Head. This showed that we must have had a great set to the northward and eastward ; remarkably strong rippling at times. The sea for many days had been smooth as a river, but now a high swell suddenly assailed us from the south-west, which indicated its having blown hard in that direction. The ship tumbled about sadly, making a great deal of water. Caught two snakes which made excellent broth. This day a look-out was kept, being the first time of such a precaution the whole voyage.

The 8th light winds but squally ; thunder and lightning : part of Sumatra bearing from east-south-east to east ; the Island of Pulo Brasse, north-east, distant seven leagues. In the afternoon it fell calm, continuing so all night. The 9th light airs ; Pulo Way, east-south-east, seven leagues : find the current still sets to the eastward. At noon saw the Grand Nicobar, bearing from north-north-west to north-west, distant twelve leagues. At sunset we were within six leagues of it, which determined Mr. Barretto to put in there for water and poultry. We hoped to effect it the following morning. At dusk it fell calm, the sea roaring and in particular parts breaking as if over a sand or shoal. The appearance was exceedingly alarming. In one of these ripplings the ship was turned round several times as if in a whirlpool, which indeed I conclude we were. Sounded twice, but did not find bottom with an hundred and twenty fathom of line. Our latitude this day, by observation, was six twenty-nine north.

The 10th, instead of having the harbour of the Grand Nicobar open and we ready to anchor within it, as we fully expected, we had the mortification to learn that the current during the night had set us so violently to the westward that we were at least five leagues to leeward of the island we had the evening before been abreast of. At noon sounded, found a bottom of grey sand at forty fathoms. The wind was baffling, sometimes being so favourable as to encourage the endeavour to work up to the harbour.

Thus we continued the whole day. In the evening we were once more well in with the land when it again fell calm, the current proving as hostile as it had been the preceding night. In the morning we were at least seven leagues to leeward. Another day was lost in fruitless attempts to work up to windward ; we gained not a mile. Mr. Barretto therefore resolved no longer to attempt getting into the

Nicobar, but stand directly across the bay for Point de Galle, or if we failed making that to put into Columbo, which was at the southern point of the Island of Ceylon. Directions were accordingly given for that purpose to the chief mate, the captain being still confined to his cabin from weakness, though he had recovered his senses.

The moment I heard the order given, and found that the ship was put before the wind, I felt a presentiment of the evils that awaited us. At dinner that day I observed it was highly probable we might encounter the breaking up of the monsoon, as we unfortunately were at the critical time when such a thing might be expected every hour, added to which it was near the change of moon. For delivering this opinion I was laughed at by all my messmates except Mrs. Hickey, who, having been in the habit of relying upon whatever I said, became alarmed and uneasy. Mr. Brown was particularly smart in his comments, called me a croaker, and added, "Suppose we have a storm, what matter ? We have already experienced more than one, yet here we are still, and why not surmount half a dozen more ? " This speech was greatly applauded by his friend Kemp and by Mr. Bateman. I then showed Mr. Brown the accounts of the most remarkable hurricanes that had occurred in those seas, as recorded in the *East India Directory*, and the dreadful consequences of some of them, at which he again scoffed, pronounced those records to be either fabrications or preposterously exaggerated, and that he did not believe a word of them. I merely observed that the *Directory* was published under the sanction and authority of the Court of Directors, therefore not likely to misrepresent facts, besides which the lamented loss which the British fleet under Admiral Pocock sustained in ships and men, also that of the French commander, Bourdonnois, was too well known to admit of a doubt. Equally notorious was the more recent loss of the *Chatham* East Indiaman in Madras roads, where every soul on board perished.

For six succeeding days after we bore away from the Nicobars we had gloomy, threatening weather, sometimes blowing strong in squalls, then suddenly falling quite calm, remaining so only a few minutes, when a violent gust succeeded ; heavy showers of rain fell, which was very acceptable, furnishing an abundant supply of water, of which all hands were greatly in want.

# CHAPTER II

## TERRIBLE TIMES ABOARD

AT daylight on Sunday the 17th of November (a memorable day to me), finding as I lay in bed the motion of the ship particularly uneasy, I got up to look out, and never to the last day of my existence shall I forget the shock I experienced at what I beheld. The horizon all round was of a blackish purple, above which rolled great masses of cloud of a deep copper colour, moving in every direction with uncommon rapidity ; vivid lightning in every quarter, thunder awfully roaring at a distance, though evidently approaching us ; a short, irregular sea breaking with a tremendous surf, as if blowing furiously hard though then but moderate, the wind, however, whistling shrill as a boatswain's pipe through the blocks and rigging. The scene altogether was such as to appal the bravest men on board. Going upon deck I found a dead silence prevailing, not a syllable uttered by anyone, all looking in stupid amazement. Not a single precaution was taken, no dead lights to the great cabin or quarter gallery windows, not even a top-gallant yard down ; on the contrary, every sail set, notwithstanding they reckoned themselves within a few leagues of Ceylon, for which they were standing direct, and all this strange neglect at a time when a British vessel would have struck everything that could be and made all snug as possible in order to be the better able to receive the shock that was so perceptibly coming upon us.

In great tribulation I returned to my cabin, telling Mrs. Hickey to secure anything she was particularly anxious about and prepare herself to undergo severe trials. I had a small strong mahogany escritoire in which I kept my letters, papers of consequence and a few trinkets and valuable articles I had. This I jammed in between two of the projecting knees in my cabin in such a manner that until the ship went to pieces it could not be thrown out of its place. At seven we each of us swallowed a dish of tea, being the last and only refreshment we had for many subsequent sorrowful hours.

Although all violent tempests are in a great measure alike, partaking of the same circumstances and consequences as those I have already had occasion to attempt a description of, yet this was so peculiarly dreadful, and our escape with life so wonderful, that I am led to relate the melancholy particulars. At eight in the morning it began to blow hard, torrents of rain pouring down, rendering it almost dark as night. Then was an order first given to take in top-gallant sails and reef topsails. The order was too late ; the instant the sails were lowered they were blown to atoms, being torn from their respective yards in shreds. The sea suddenly increased to an inconceivable height, the wind roaring to such a degree that the officers upon deck could not make themselves heard by the crew with the largest speaking-trumpets. Between nine and ten it blew an absolute hurricane, far surpassing what I had any idea of. As it veered all round the compass so did the sea increase infinitely beyond imagination, one wave encountering another from every direction, and by their mutual force in thus meeting ran up apparently to a sharp point, there breaking at a height that is actually incredible but to those who unhappily saw it. The entire ocean was in a foam white as soap-suds. At a quarter before eleven the fore-topmast, yard rigging and all went over the side, the noise of it being imperceptible amidst the roaring of wind and sea. In a few minutes it was followed by the mizzen-mast, which snapped like a walking-stick about eight feet above the quarter-deck ; part of the wreck of it unfortunately got foul of the rudder chains and every moment struck the ship's bottom with excessive violence. At half-past eleven the fore-mast went, being shivered into splinters quite down to the gun-deck.  The fall of it drew the main-mast forward, whereby the levers upon which the pumps worked (as they do in all ships built in the East Indies) were totally destroyed, putting an end to our pumping.  Before noon the main-mast and bolt-sprit both went at the same instant. Thus in the short space of four hours was this noble vessel reduced to such a state of distress as few have ever been in. Our situation seemed hopeless, not a creature on board but thought every minute would be the last of their lives.  When the masts were gone she immediately began to roll with unparalleled velocity from side to side, each gunwale, with half the quarter-deck, being submerged in water each roll, so that we every moment expected she would be bottom uppermost or roll her sides out.

Thus buffeted about on the angry ocean, I told my poor Charlotte, whom I had secured in the best way I could and was endeavouring to support, that all must soon be over, it being quite impossible that wood and iron could long sustain such extraordinary and terrific motion, and such were my real sentiments.  The dear woman, with a composure and serenity that struck me most forcibly, mildly replied, " God's will be done, to that I bend with humble resignation, blessing a benevolent providence for permitting me, my dearest William, to expire with you, whose fate I am content to share, but oh ! my dearest love, let us in the agonies of death be not separated," and she clasped me in her arms.

Mr. Bateman, at the commencement of the gale, had gone upon deck, from whence he dared not again venture to stir, but was obliged to lay himself down under the wheel and there remain.  Mr. Kemp and Mr. Brown had lashed themselves to the gun rings of the aftermost part in the great cabin to prevent their being dashed from side to side. Whilst thus situated, three out of the five stern windows, frames and all, suddenly burst inward from the mere force of the wind, the noise attending which was such that I conceived the last scene of the tragedy was arrived, but awful as that moment was, the recollection of the way in which Mr. Brown had doubted the facts stated in the *Directory* relative to the hurricanes at the breaking up of the monsoon recurred so forcibly that I could not help saying to him, " Now, Mr. Brown, I think you can no longer entertain a belief that the accounts in the *Directory* are fabricated or exaggerated." He made me no answer, but raising his hands clasped together looked the very image of despair.

The ship was apparently full of water, and seemed to be so completely overwhelmed that we all thought she was fast settling downward. Nevertheless the velocity and depth of her rolling abated nothing, tearing away every article that could be moved ; not a bureau, chest or trunk but broke loose and was soon demolished, the contents, from the quickness and constant splashing from one side to the other of the ship, becoming a perfect paste, adhering to the deck between the beams, many inches in thickness, so as near the sides actually to fill up the space to the deck. Amongst the furniture destroyed was a large bureau with a book-case top belonging to Mr. Barretto, in which were deposited the whole of his ship's papers and his own private ones, scarce a remnant of any one of which was saved.

During the severity of the hurricane about twenty noble fellows, such as would not have disgraced the British Navy, at the head of whom stood the boatswain, acted with the same determined spirit they had shown on the 9th of September, doing all that could be performed by men, while the rest of the crew gave themselves up to despair, clinging round their priest and screeching out prayers for pardon and mercy in such dismal and frantic yells as was horrible to hear. So eager were the miserable enthusiasts to embrace the image of Jesus Christ upon the Cross (which the priest held in his hand) in the instant of their dissolution that they in their endeavours so to do actually tore it to pieces.

By two in the afternoon every bulkhead between decks, except that of my cabin, had fallen from the violent labouring of the ship. The altar also being demolished, an end was thereby put to the functions of the despairing priest. The reason of my cabin standing when every other yielded was that being the state room it partook of the general strength of the vessel, being erected at the time of her building and as firmly fixed as her decks, but the folding door that opened into the great cabin was soon torn off its hinges and broken to pieces, exposing to our view the foaming surges through the great cabin's stern windows. My darling girl sat like patience itself, though drenched to the skin and covered with filth from the washings that burst into our cabin.

At this awful hour did it occur to me what I had somewhere read that death by shipwreck is the most terrible of deaths. The spectacle of a field of battle is lofty and imposing—its glittering apparel, its martial music, its waving banners and floating standards, its high chivalric air and character elevate the soul and conceal from us the dangers of our situation : stretched on our death-bed, enfeebled by sickness, our sensibility becomes enfeebled also, and, while heavy shocks shake the body and make it to the bystander seem to suffer, nature throws over the soul the kindly shroud of a happy insensibility, while the closed shutter, the tiptoe tread and whispered attendance shut out the world we are so soon to leave. But in a storm at sea the scene is not more terrible than disgusting, in a miserable cabin, on a filthy wet bed, in a confined and putrid air, where it is as impossible to think as to breathe freely, the fatigue, the motion, the want of rest and food, give a kind of hysteric sensibility to the frame, which makes it alive to the slightest danger. No wonder, therefore, it should be so to the greatest of all. If we look round the miserable group that surround us no eye beams comfort, no tongue speaks consolation, and when we throw our imagination beyond—to the death-like darkness, the howling blast, the raging and merciless element, expected every moment to become our horrid habitation—surely, surely it is the most terrible of deaths !

It is a remarkable circumstance that upon the fore-mast's going and the confusion and panic that ensued the captain, who had for so many days been confined in a delirium and so reduced that he could not without assistance turn in his bed, on being told what had happened, and that the ship was sinking, instantaneously recovered vigour both of body and mind sufficient to allow not only of his jumping from his cot but going upon deck, where he issued his orders with as much, or perhaps more, precision and skill than he had done during any part of the voyage. The first order he gave was by every possible means to lighten the ship. The sea indeed had already done much towards it for us by carrying off the whole of the masts, yards, rigging and everything that was upon the upper deck. An attempt was therefore made to throw the guns overboard, but only five were so disposed of, and those at the imminent risk of the lives of the men from the excessive motion. An attempt was like-wise made to start the madeira wine. The two first men that went into the hold for that purpose were immediately jammed in between two pipes and killed, after which no other would try. After exerting himself in a wonderful manner the captain, by one of the violent jerks from a tre-mendous sea breaking on board, was thrown down with such force as to break his right arm and receive a severe contusion on his head, which rendered him insensible. The chief mate, an active, clever seaman, was early in the gale carried away by a sea, washed forward, but luckily brought up in the galley under the forecastle, where he remained covered with wounds and bruises. The second mate was not seen after eight o'clock, it was therefore concluded that he had been carried overboard and lost. It, however, did not turn out so. He, apprehending nothing could save the ship, had shut himself up in a small booby hutch, or cabin, just abaft the helm upon the upper deck, where he spent the day between the brandy bottle and prayer book. The third officer had throughout showed the utmost fortitude and energy, sinking at last completely overcome by fatigue, and remained secured by a rope on the spot where he fell.

One of the most active persons on board was the French passenger of whom I have before made mention. He betrayed equal skill and resolution, suggesting and helping to carry into effect several things that proved of material use. This unfortunate man was particularly forward in the endeavours to throw the guns overboard, in doing which one of them grazed his shin, making a slight wound in appearance, the skin being a little broke, which neither he himself nor any one else that saw it considered of consequence. It, however, caused his death, as I shall hereafter state.

Mr. Barretto, as I have already observed, was no seaman ; he, however, much to his credit, resolved to set his people an example by exposing his person to the raging element. He therefore remained upon the quarter-deck, lashed to the side, endeavouring to cheer and encourage the few sailors that were ready to do all in their power to prevent the ship from foundering. Thus he remained until two in the afternoon, when he fainted away, whereupon the people cast off the rope with which he was secured and were about to convey him between decks when at the moment an enormous wave came over the stern, sweeping them all away. Two of the poor fellows were irrecoverably lost, and for some time everybody thought Mr. Barretto had shared the same fate. He was, however, found amongst part of the broken rigging upon the forecastle in a state of insensibility, from whence he was with extreme difficulty carried between decks. Thus hour after hour passed with us in utter despair, but still to our amazement we remained afloat, which seemed to us little short of a miracle for a ship in such a state as ours was, so tossed about at the mercy of such a sea as never was seen, so involved in ruin and desolation on every side, making too, as she did before the hurricane commenced, thirty inches of water every hour, and not a single stroke of a pump after half-past eleven in the morning ; nor could anybody account for her not going to the bottom but by supposing she actually rolled the water out of her as fast as it came in.

At six in the evening the fury of the storm had somewhat abated, though not sufficiently to afford us a hope of ever seeing another day ; our surprise only was at surviving from hour to hour without the least expectation of escaping finally from a watery grave.

At eight at night the gale had evidently subsided or, to use a seaman's language, it had broken up. This encouraged the few men who had throughout behaved themselves like heroes to further exertions. At the imminent risk of their lives some of them went over the stern and ultimately succeeded in cutting away considerable quantities of the rigging, sails and yards that got so entangled with the rudder and rudder chains as totally to prevent the ship's steering, by which our danger of foundering from the overwhelming sea was greatly increased. They also afterwards accomplished the throwing overboard fourteen more of her guns besides much lumber from between decks, by which the ship was importantly benefited, the rolling being less rapid and not so deep. By midnight the sea had gone down a great deal, and the people were enabled to keep their legs enough to rig out one pump and set it at work. This being kept constantly going, the water did not gain upon us, which gave everybody fresh spirits, and for the first time since the commencement of the tempest we began to entertain a hope of preservation. At break of day the clouds moved with great velocity, but were light in comparison to what we had seen. It still blew very strong, and there was a large confused sea, yet when we thought of what it had been it appeared as nothing, besides it was hourly getting more moderate.

Upon going upon deck, oh, what a lamentable sight was there! The first object I saw was the boatswain and some of the seamen bringing Mr. Barretto aft in a hammock they had put him into. It was an arduous task as the ship was still rolling very deep, and he so sore that he cried out upon the least pressure or anything touching him. They at last got him into the great cabin, in the centre of which they hung the hammock with him in it.

Mr. Bateman spoke of the conduct of the boatswain in terms of enthusiastic panegyric, adding that he was perfectly sure we owed our preservation solely to his extraordinary powers, superior skill and persevering labour. He declared that he appeared to him to be more than human ;

notwithstanding the rapidity and the violence of the motion he was everywhere encouraging by his laudable example those men that were disposed to lend their aid. At the commencement of the hurricane the boatswain, finding none of the people could govern the helm, took it himself, nor quitted it for an instant while the ship would steer, but upon the wreck of the masts entangling with the rudder, thereby rendering it useless, he turned his thoughts to other points of duty. At two in the afternoon (of the 17th) this valuable man was given up for lost. He had managed to get forward and had just entered the door of his cabin, which was erected upon the small deck forming the forecastle, and directly over the galley, having gone there for the purpose of recruiting his strength by drinking some brandy, when one of those huge seas of which so many had before broken on board came bursting over her quarter in such a prodigious body as to carry the cabin entire as it stood overboard. The boatswain, however, appeared a few moments after saying that having observed the approach of the wave which he was aware would break over the ship, upon its actually doing so he threw himself off the forecastle to the galley, letting the sea pass above him, and so escaping the rush of it that must otherwise have carried him with it.

By ten in the morning (of the 18th) a bright sun shone forth, the sea became less agitated, and we began to entertain confident hopes. But to counteract this unexpected good fortune I found my dearest Charlotte much indisposed and feverish, nor could that be wondered at considering what she had suffered, drenched in wet for such a length of time, and not having a single change of clothes or an article of dress left, all being destroyed, as were mine also, in the common ruin.

Amidst such complicated and general distress it was scarcely to be expected that any particular attention would be paid to a single individual, although that individual was a female, but so great a favourite had my darling girl made herself throughout the ship by the peculiar gentleness and suavity of her manners that from the moment a chance of escape from drowning appeared she became the first object and immediate care of, I may safely say, everybody on board. Before nine o'clock in the morning (of the 18th) the carpenter, with three men to assist him, were at work in our cabin ; by noon they had repaired the bed and got the whole apartment into some sort of order with a canvas to roll up as a substitute for a door, whereby she could once more be in private. Whilst this was going forward Mr. Bateman entered, having in his hand a tin pot of madeira wine, made hot, which he had contrived to get prepared, and, what I considered of still more consequence, a pair of blankets *only half wet*, which he had procured from the gunner. He advised me to make Mrs. Hickey directly swallow the wine and then lay down between the blankets and endeavour to get that rest she stood so much in need of. This advice was too prudent not to be adopted, but with all my influence I could not persuade her to touch the madeira until I took the half of it myself, when she cheerfully drank the remainder of the comfortable beverage, declaring it to be the most reviving and grateful draught she had ever tasted, nor can that be wondered at when it is recollected that, added to all our other miseries, we had been from two o'clock in the afternoon of Saturday until Monday noon, a period of forty-six hours, without the least particle of nourishment passing our lips, except one wretched dish of tea on Sunday morning. After she had swallowed the wine I made her lay down between the blankets, where she fell into a profuse perspiration, soon dropped asleep for a couple of hours, and then awoke greatly refreshed.

Having thus contributed all in my power towards her relief, I joined in searching amongst the heap of rubbish in the great cabin for anything worth preserving. We soon collected from thence a parcel of six-and-thirty shilling pieces, or half Joes as they are called in Portugal, two watches and various bits of gold and silver ornaments and trinkets. After ransacking in a mass of dirt so blended together that it was difficult to separate for a long time, I got hold of a small tin case, much bruised but unbroken. This I took to Mr. Barretto as he lay in his hammock, who joyfully exclaimed it was the ship's papers. He requested I would carefully open it, and, should they be wet, get them dried, as they were of the utmost importance to him. I directly set about it, but alas! they were totally useless, the ink being entirely effaced although written upon parchment, most of the papers separating into pieces in attempting to unfold them. The only one that was at all legible, and that only partially, was Mr. Barretto's Portuguese naturalization.

Having lent my aid for the service of my friends, I next thought of my own concerns, and accordingly went to look after my escritoire, which I found in the spot I had placed it, and so firmly wedged in that I was obliged to have recourse to the carpenter to extricate it. Upon opening it and examining the contents I found that everything in the way of paper was completely destroyed except three letters that I had received after all the others, and put into a leather pocket-book. My watch had sustained no other injury than what arose from the salt water which ruined the works or, as boys call it, " the guts." What I lamented above everything else, though of no intrinsic value, was the loss of a large book in which I had copied the journals of every voyage I had made, and the remarkable circumstances that had occurred. This was utterly destroyed, as well as my admission as an Attorney of the Court of King's Bench and Solicitor of the Court of Chancery which were in it.

The boatswain upon going over the ship's side to examine her condition found she was more than three feet lighter than when we sailed from the Island of Madeira, this great difference arising from the loss of the masts, yards, sails and rigging, also from the guns and other heavy things that were thrown overboard. In consequence of her being so much more buoyant the leaks decreased to nineteen inches of water an hour, a quantity that was easily cleared by the pumps, the other being put in order as soon as the storm ceased.

Thirteen of the crew lost their lives, the greater part of them, as was conjectured, being washed overboard. Besides the two persons killed by the pipes of wine, three other bodies were found in different places, two of them under the beams upon which the boats had been stowed, the third between the coppers and ship's side, a space of only a few inches wide. It was a shocking spectacle, for being so jammed in by the working of the ship the intestines were squeezed out and the head forced completely round, the face being towards the back. These miserable corpses were committed to the deep in the afternoon.

Nothing in the way of eating could be found except ship's provisions of salt beef and damaged rice, which had been wetted by the sea water ; yet such as it was we were glad to partake of it, making at least a plentiful meal. We were reduced to the necessity of eating with our fingers, for not a knife was to be found the first day. We afterwards procured two from the seamen. After our salt meat and rice we took a good quantity of brandy and water, and at seven in the evening lay down upon our bed, both of us sleeping sound for several hours, and that, too, in spite of an eighteen-pounder which was fired every half-hour through the night as a signal of distress to any vessel that might chance to be within hearing. They had considerable difficulty in making the gun go off, the sea having found its way into the magazine, as it had into every part of the ship.

I rose at five on the morning of the 19th much refreshed ; my Charlotte was also better than I expected. It was a beautiful morning, little wind and the sea gone down. While looking out I was very agreeably surprised at seeing Mr. Barretto come up, assisted by his servant. He complained of violent pains all over him, but said he could not remain in the hammock, it was so intensely hot.

Mr. Brown looked very pitiful upon my just hinting at the dreadful scene we had all witnessed. He said, " Dreadful indeed, past all belief, never can I in future doubt the power of wind, of which until now I had not the least idea. Pray God I never may experience such another instance of it ;

indeed, one such is surely enough for a man's life." It was, however, this poor young man's lot to meet with a second hurricane, in which he perished. About two years after he had been at Bombay he was attacked with the liver, which so reduced him that he was ordered to sea, and embarked in a very fine ship for Bengal, two others sailing at the same time and keeping company. When off Point Palmiras in the Bay of Bengal the south-west monsoon broke upon them with such irresistible force that in four hours after it commenced the ship he was in foundered, every soul being lost, nor could the other ships afford the smallest assistance, themselves expecting a similar fate every moment.

To return to the woeful *Raynha de Portugal.* Every creature on board was busily and earnestly engaged in endeavouring to get some sail set upon her so as to give her way through the water. Part of her cargo consisting of canvas and cordage, the after hatches were opened to get at them, for circumstanced as we were the underwriters could not with propriety object thereto, it being for the pre- servation of both ship and cargo. The gunner happened to have two small spars which he had stowed away in the gun- room as part of his own private trade. These were got out at the gun-room port, which was opened for the purpose. One of them was soon set up in the place of the fore-mast, the other lashed to the stump of the mizzen-mast. In about five hours two small square sails were roughly put together. The wind being at east-north-east, we set our canvas, standing direct for Ceylon, from which it was supposed we could not be far distant. During the afternoon we went through the water at the rate of half a knot an hour. Our latitude this day, by observation, was eight three north.

In the afternoon I saw our French passenger, whose leg had been hurt by one of the guns when throwing it over- board in the hurricane, sitting upon the deck in the steerage bathing the injured part with a mixture of vinegar and brandy, afterwards covering it with coarse brown paper made wet with the same composition. Observing a considerable degree of inflammation round the wound, I took the liberty unasked of advising him to consult the surgeon of the ship, as I had always understood it to be dangerous to neglect such things in a hot climate. He civilly thanked me for my solicitude on his account, but wholly declined applying to the surgeon, whom he considered an ignoramus in his profession, adding, " I am too old a campaigner, sir, and have been too often cut up and maimed in every part of my body, where no surgical aid was procurable, not to know how to treat myself in a much worse case than this. Be assured, sir, my recipe is better than any of the nonsense the faculty would apply. Brandy, vinegar and brown paper do wonders." Whether it was that the bone itself was seriously injured or his habit of body from living long upon salt provisions operated, the wound became daily worse, so much so that I predicted bad consequences.

Through the 19th nothing material occurred. The morning of the 20th I was awoke by the sound of boat's oars. Rising and looking out of the quarter gallery window, I had the pleasure to see a boat just coming alongside and a large brig close to us. Going upon deck, I learnt that it was the *Governor Hermsfelt*, a Danish vessel bound from Serampore in Bengal to Anjingo. She had been drawn to us by our guns. They had not felt any of the hurricane, but from a dreadfully high and confused sea and threatening sky knew there must have been bad weather near them, and therefore bore up upon hearing a gun several times, concluding it came from some vessel in distress. She supplied us with some articles of the utmost consequence for navigating our ship, that is three large spars and three lesser ones to make into yards, which proved of great use, also with an anchor and cable, of which we had only one, the rest having been cut away to ease the ship in the hurricane and the cables thrown overboard with other things to lighten her. Comforts she had none to bestow, having no live-stock at all. She, however, sent us a small barrel of pickled pork and a bag of biscuit, the latter a great treat, although old and full of insects. They also gave us the bearings of the land according to their reckoning, but they had not seen any since Point Palmiras.

Upon consulting with the commander of this vessel he advised Mr. Barretto not to go to the southward, but to steer for Trincomalay, which was nearly under our lee, and by much the nearest port, for as the current now set to the northward we should make a bad hand in such a crippled state by attempting to make for Point de Galle or Columbo. Having given us all the assistance in his power, he proceeded on his voyage. According to his account we were nineteen leagues from the land, thrice the distance we supposed.

The 21st continued moderate and fair. This day one of the large Danish spars was fixed as a main-mast, another as a bolt-sprit, the smaller ones being used as yards, and having made two tolerable-sized sails we ran forty miles during the twenty-four hours. The 22nd the weather still fine, we ran forty-seven miles. If, therefore, the reckoning of the Danish captain had been correct we ought to have seen the land.

It now struck me as not a little extraordinary that we never heard a prayer. Upon leaving Lisbon we had them regularly five times daily, which continued until our disaster off the Cape on the 9th of September, after which they only had them morning and evening, and from the time of the hurricane prayers were altogether dropped. This was very curious in so bigoted a people as the Portuguese are known to be.

The 23rd and 24th were nearly calm. On the latter day the last cask of provisions was broached, and abominably bad it proved, for the pickle having leaked out the meat was become rotten. We had only four butts of rain-water remaining, and they were so strongly impregnated with tar as to be scarce drinkable, making us all very sick. Thus situated, without a single shift of linen or any other article of clothing, it may easily be imagined how anxiously the land was looked for.

In the night the people on deck, observing a strong rippling on the water, they hove a cast of the lead and were surprised to find we were in twelve fathoms ; at daybreak of the 25th we were close to the land, with breakers within a mile of us, and as the current was driving us towards them very fast we came to with the Danish anchor and cable. As the 26th was a dead calm we remained fast, firing a gun every half-hour. The morning of the 27th the same, but in the afternoon a light breeze springing up from the south-east we got under way and ran along shore. We saw smoke rising from two different places a little way inland, but not a living creature appeared though we were within three miles of the beach. At sunset an extremely heavy shower of rain furnished a seasonable supply of water, which we stood in great need of.

The 28th was a mixture of calms and hard squalls. We got under way and anchored three different times ; there was a very heavy black sky, having a windy appearance, that excited our fears of another gale. Happily, however, it turned to torrents of rain accompanied by violent thunder and lightning. On the 29th we had fair weather but scarce any wind. All hands now began to despond, no kind of provision being left except damaged rice, and but a small quantity of that, so that we thought of starving instead of drowning. This day Mr. Barretto broached the madeira wine, serving out a pint to each man in the ship, which recruited their strength greatly, and indeed they stood in need of it, not having had a drop of spirits since the hurricane.

# CHAPTER III

## IN THE HANDS OF THE FRENCH

ON Saturday the 30th we had a charming breeze from the eastward ; at daylight saw high land bearing north-west, which some of the people declared they knew from its form was near Trincomalay. By our latitude at noon we found it must be so, as we were in eight degrees thirty-nine minutes north. We therefore stood boldly into a bay that appeared open before us, and soon after discovered the entrance to the harbour. We fired a gun every ten minutes, and made the best display we could of an ensign with the arms reversed as signals of distress, though the appearance our ship made must have sufficiently indicated that.

At one in the afternoon we plainly discovered the French flag flying in a fort upon the summit of a hill. Mr. Barretto imagined this to be a deception on the part of the English, not thinking it possible they could have suffered so important a place to be wrested from them by an enemy, but at 3 p.m. we were convinced such was the case by a French and a Dutch pilot coming on board and taking charge of the ship. They informed us that the place had been taken in the preceding month of September by Admiral Suffren, the British garrison having surrendered upon the French troops landing.

Before we could get into the harbour it fell calm ; we therefore let go the anchor, soon after which a French officer came on board, who expressed the utmost astonishment at the dreadful situation he saw the ship in, his attention being particularly drawn to the sort of paste I have already mentioned formed by the splashing from side to side, as the ship rolled, of the contents of chests, trunks, et cetera, and which had completely filled up the space between the beams on each side, gradually decreasing in quantity towards the centre of the cabin. He enquired what occasioned so extraordinary an appearance. Being told, he smiled incredulously, but being assured such was the fact he again expressed his surprise that any vessel could have outlived a gale that had produced effects as marvellous as unprecedented. He said he would immediately report the lamentable state we were in to the Chevalier Des Roys, the acting Governor, who he was certain would give us all the assistance in his power, and which our unparalleled misfortunes so well entitled us to. He, however, observed that they were themselves very badly off with respect to fresh provisions, their only certain food being salted meat and rice. He likewise told us there was only one ship of war at present there, the *Consolante* frigate and a Dutch Indiaman.

The following morning, being Sunday the 1st of December, our ill-fated *Raynha de Portugal* was warped into the harbour, one of the finest in the world, of extent enough to receive secure from all danger all the ships of war of Great Britain, being completely landlocked, with excellent anchorage and deep water close to the shore.

Mr. Barretto, although by no means recovered from the effects of his accident, the hour the ship was safely secured went on shore to pay his compliments to Mr. Des Roys. I availed myself of the opportunity to write to the Governor, representing to him the uncomfortable state we were in on board, in want of even the common necessaries of life, both as to food and clothing, and that Mrs. Hickey was much indisposed, for all which reasons I requested we might be permitted to reside on shore. In a couple of hours Mr. Barretto returned with a very gloomy countenance, telling me nothing was to be expected from Mr. Des Roys, who had received him with the utmost hauteur, and behaved insolently ; that so far from fulfilling the promise of the officer by affording us assistance, he said he entertained such strong suspicions respecting the ship's being English property, as well as the cargo, that he was determined to detain her until the arrival of the *General* (the title the French always gave Monsieur Suffren) or of General De Bussy, who was daily expected from France. After such bad success on his own business he presented my letter, which the Governor, seeing it was written in English, threw upon his table. Of course, I had no answer.

Whilst speaking to Mr. Barretto upon this inhuman conduct and telling him I would go in person and state my case to the savage chief, we saw two boats approaching from the frigate, one filled with sailors the other with military men. They all came on board and took possession of the ship, placing a sentry with his musket and bayonet fixed at each gangway, with orders not to allow any person whomsoever to pass without the sanction of the French officer on board. The seamen then unhung our rudder, which they towed on shore. My blood boiled with rage at this unworthy treatment, but complaints were of no avail.

The French commanding officer on board was a very gentlemanlike young man, lieutenant in the regiment of the Isle of France, his name L'Anglade. He was quite shocked at the situation in which he found Mrs. Hickey, without food, without clothing, or the common comfort of a female attendant. After expressing his concern thereat in very feeling terms, he said something must and should be done for the poor lady's relief, it being a disgrace to Frenchmen to permit a female to remain an hour in so unbecoming a state ; that the whole of the passengers ought also to be relieved. Asking for pen, ink and paper, he sat down and wrote two letters, one to Monsieur Mallè, the captain of the *Consolante*, the other to Monsieur Chevillard De Montesson, the Port Captain, or, as the English would call him, Master Attendant. Having dispatched these letters, he observed privately to me that Monsieur Des Roys was universally disliked on account of his unaccommodating temper and unsociable manners, but was known to be an officer of merit and one of the ablest engineers in the service, having been very instrumental in the capture of the place, for which Monsieur Suffren had rewarded him with the temporary government ; that he had acted with such tyranny in the office as to leave himself without a single friend. This was bad news for us.

Captain Mallè upon receipt of Monsieur L'Anglade's letter immediately got into his barge and came to our ship, bringing with him tea, coffee, sugar, chocolate, biscuits, liqueurs and various other articles for the table, also some pieces of white cloth, which, though rather coarse, proved very acceptable. A capital meal was prepared, being the first we had seen for a fortnight, to which we did justice by eating very heartily. Whilst at this repast Mr. Chevillard came alongside with a quantity of fruit and eggs, a few fowls, some fish, and, what was more acceptable than all, a small loaf of excellent bread. Upon seeing the miserable state we were in he was as indignant as Mr. L'Anglade had been, swearing he would go to Mr. Des Roys and in the name of the King call upon him to act more like one of his liberal nation. No one could be more attentive and kind than these three gentlemen, by whose benevolent care my darling girl's sufferings were greatly alleviated.

On the 2nd before ten o'clock in the morning Mr. Chevillard was again with us to say he had been ungraciously received by the Governor, who at first peremptorily refused to allow any passenger to leave the ship until he had Mr. Suffren's sanction for it, but upon his (Chevillard's) remonstrating against such brutal treatment towards an unfortunate female stranger, he consented to let her land. " If, therefore," continued this good man, " you will put Mrs. Hickey under my care she shall be treated like a daughter and receive every accommodation the miserable hovel I inhabit will admit of. I will, if you please, take her and her servant on shore immediately." How his surprize was increased upon my telling him Mrs. Hickey's female attendant had died on board ship soon after we left Madeira, and that she had ever since been without a servant ! He expressed his concern at what she had undergone in the most feeling language. Truly grateful for his good intentions, I said I would speak to Mrs. Hickey, but apprehended she would not consent to leave me, and so it proved, for upon mentioning what Mr. Chevillard proposed she declared she would rather die on board ship than go on shore without me.

During Mr. Chevillard's visit the *Consolante's* barge came alongside, bringing ladies' shoes and stockings, with a variety of different sorts of cloth and four tailors, who forthwith began to cut out and sew, so that by the following morning Mrs. Hickey was very comfortably rigged. They then set to making some shirts, etc., for me. Not satisfied with these munificent acts, the generous Captain Mallè presented Mrs. Hickey with a trunk, which having seen deposited in her cabin, he instantly departed to avoid our grateful thanks. Upon opening the trunk we found it contained two complete suits of woman's apparel which the considerate and kind-hearted man had procured from Mrs. Vansenden, the Dutch chief's wife, who being about Mrs. Hickey's size her clothes answered admirably well without alteration. From this lady, as well as her husband, we afterwards received innumerable instances of kindness.

Not a day passed without Mr. Chevillard's visiting us, always bringing some little matter that he thought might prove acceptable, especially bread, of which very small quantities were made, owing to a scarcity of flour. A few of the French officers by every means in their power did all they could to correct the ferocity of Mr. Des Roys, all of them assuring us the restraint would cease the hour any line of battleship came in, and that one was daily expected.

Amongst those who showed us the most marked attention was Captain Gautier, who had a company of grenadiers in the regiment of Pondicherry. He early became greatly attached to both Mrs. Hickey and me, which he testified in various ways. He was indefatigable in his endeavours to obtain Mr. Des Roys' leave to let us reside on shore, and would have succeeded had it not been for the violence of Mr. Bateman, who addressed several intemperate and disrespectful letters to Mr. Des Roys, which so offended that haughty man that he withdrew his half-given consent.

Captain Gautier in the first instance requested that I would let him be my banker, an offer I availed myself of with gratitude.

Captain Mallè, upon seeing Mrs. Hickey and myself clad more to our satisfaction than when we arrived, made us promise to pass the following day with him on board his frigate, observing at the time he gave the invitation that although he had not the power of controlling Mr. Des Roys in what related to matters on shore, he could act independently of him upon the water. The 10th was therefore spent very agreeably on board the *Consolante*, where we met several military gentlemen. The company very considerately and like well-bred men avoided speaking upon politics before me and Mrs. Hickey, but while walking the deck in the evening I learnt from one of the junior lieutenants that there had been four hard-fought engagements between Monsieur Suffren and Sir Edward Hughes's fleets, in every one of which the English had been defeated ; that Madras was at the time he was speaking closely invested by a well-appointed, well-disciplined French army, while, on the other hand, the miserable garrison pent up within the walls of Fort St. George were daily dying in scores from disease and famine ; that they were in hourly expectation of hearing the place had surrendered, and only waited the arrival of a reinforcement of men, then on its way from the Isle of France, under the command of that brave and experienced general, Monsieur De Bussy, to extend their conquests to Bengal, there being no doubt but that in a few months the English would be routed out of all their Eastern possessions. This was a melancholy history for me, and from the fall of Trincomalay, as well as Suffren's fleet appearing to ride triumphant and unopposed in those seas, I really feared it was but too true, and that the British sun was near setting in the East !

One of the guests who sat next to me at dinner informed me that the Governor was rendered more inexorable than he otherwise would have been towards us by a very insolent letter that Mr. Bateman had addressed to him, wherein after many rude things he charged him in plain terms with showing an interested partiality in my favour, I being allowed to visit about, going when and where I pleased, whilst he was most unjustly kept a close prisoner on board a wreck of a filthy Portuguese ship. Surprized and irritated at this intelligence, on returning to the *Raynha de Portugal* I asked Mr. Bateman whether what I had heard was true. He answered that it was, impudently insinuating it was the charms of Mrs. Hickey (though perhaps unintentional on her part) that had occasioned such evident and unjust partiality to us. This was more than I could patiently submit to ; a violent quarrel ensued in which I did not spare him, giving my opinion of his behaviour in the strongest language. From the best friends we became inveterate enemies.

I thought it right, in consequence of what I had heard, to write Mr. Des Roys to assure him I had never been out of my ship except the one day to dine on board the *Consolante*, to which letter I received an immediate and polite answer lamenting that he had not the possibility of granting lodgings on shore to all the English passengers, and that he considered it cruel in Mr. Bateman to insult him because he so cautiously avoided partiality to any person.

Captain Gautier from his fondness of everything English had made himself tolerably well acquainted with our language, indeed wonderfully so considering he had no parole instruction whatsoever, acquiring all he knew from books. The following letters from him to me will show his proficiency as a self-taught scholar.

" DEAR SIR,

Having no possibility to procure a loaf to Mrs. Hickey to-day I pray Mrs. Hickey to engage her to accept some biscuits, part from this country and part from the Island of Bourbon. To-morrow afternoon without fail I will send to Mrs. Hickey some good loaves, but as our baker does not make bread every day, that is the reason for which I cannot get to-day for sending on board ship. Here are joined some lemons, the only I can find on the market, and a little pot of candy sugar for the use of Mrs. Hickey when she will take her tea. I pray Mr. Hickey to present my duty to his amiable lady and be convinced of my desire to be useful to him. With these sentiments I am of Mr. Hickey the most humble and most obedient servant.

GAUTIER."

"I would be very grateful if Mrs. Hickey was good enough to give me the two songs she had so agreeably sung two days ago. I hope I will have the honour to see her to-morrow. Soldiers' manœuvres engages my less agreeable hours through the current day."

Another as follows :

" DEAR SIR,

I did not answer your letter yesterday because it was delivered me up by a Mr. Vansenden's black servant. I send you this morning two hundred and fifty rix-dollars by a sure envoy. That sum is within a small matter of equal value as that you are wanting for the payment of your debts. I am very glad of finding that opportunity to be useful to you, and would have heartily desired to have sent you a more considerable sum, and to offer the same relief to your fellow-countrymen, but as I am to make war in India and to depart perhaps in a few months for beginning the campaign, I cannot divest myself of a greater quantity of money. As for the payment, I pray you to send me a bill to my order, of which bill I will make no use but in those bad circumstances which the war can procure me. It is only a provisional care against the events of this world. If you arrive at your destination without further misfortune, of which already you have endured so too large share, you will bethink yourself on the means fit for my payment. I only assure you that I would be very sorry if it ever was chargeable to you. I pray you to present my respects to Mrs. Hickey. I send her a loaf. She will receive more to-morrow. I have the honour to be, dear sir, your most humble and most obedient servant.

GAUTIER."

"I would have desired to find an English saddle to buy on your ship if possible ; you will oblige me to procure it for me."

A third is in these words :

" DEAR SIR,

    With the greatest pleasure I have heard of the better health of Mrs. Hickey. Monsieur Mallè, that I have had the pleasure to see yesterday, told me that she was perfectly recovered, and that she showed the day before yesterday all the gaiety of her humour when she is well. I cannot express you how much I have been concerned about her bad situation. The last time I have had the honour to pay my duty to her I was very less affected with her sickness than with the grief she appeared to me troubled with. Her distemper was a little tribute payed to a new climate, but her grief was caused by the bad circumstances which she and you are lying under. I beg to hear that she is low spirited no more. I hoped some days past that I could inform you of the grant of going ashore at Mr. Chevillard's, but an impolite remonstrance from Mr. Bateman to Mr. Des Roys has been an obstacle for his goodwill to procure to Mrs. Hickey the satisfaction of breathing the land air. What is to be done on the matter, dear sir ? Nothing but patience. Were you with Mrs. Hickey alone on board a ship you would have received that permission, but the difficulty to give proper lodgings to other passengers and the fear to do an injustice about your countrymen are the only causes of your detaining. I pray you, my dear sir, not to speak at all about the matter, because I should be very sorry to be mingled any way in Mr. Bateman's letters. My character as a military man hinders me to act according my desires. I have sent to Mr. Mallè some pounds of coffee from Bourbon. I hope Mrs. Hickey will be good enough as receive them from me. It is a trifling thing, and she never will be persuaded how much I would desire to render her situation the less hard possible. I desire my humble respects to her. And I am with the greatest sincerity of friendship, dear sir, your most humble and most obedient servant.

GAUTIER."

    The day after our entertainment on board the *Consolante* Mrs. Hickey complained of violent headache, sickness at her stomach, with an acute pain in her back and limbs. I found by the languor and quickness of her pulse she had a considerable degree of fever. I therefore expressed my extreme uneasiness to Mr. L'Anglade, enquiring whether medical assistance was procurable. He answered they fortunately had a gentleman of first-rate abilities, Mr. De Boissieres, their surgeon-major, who had the chief super-intendence of the hospital in which were a great number of sick and of badly wounded officers and private men, and he would write a note to request his immediate attendance. He accordingly did so, and before noon that gentleman came on board. He was a man of excellent address, with the appearance of a person of fashion. After seeing Mrs. Hickey he told me her disorder was a bilious fever, then very prevalent, by which he had lost many people in the hospital, but as he found no particularly bad symptom about her, and the disease was met at so early a stage, he trusted, and had little doubt, but he should be able to check its progress. He directly wrote a prescription, giving it to the surgeon of the *Consolante*, who was present, to make up. He stayed not only until Mrs. Hickey took it but to see the effect, which having completely answered his wish he went on shore, saying he would return by five or six o'clock. Upon his return in the evening he appeared surprized and alarmed at the great increase of fever. He remained by her bedside the whole night, administering the medicines himself.

Early in the morning Mr. De Boissieres was obliged to attend some surgical operations at the hospital, but came to us again at eleven, bringing with him a Malay woman, one of Mrs. Vansenden's servants, to wait upon my poor invalid. This was a prodigious acquisition, for although she spoke not a word of English she perfectly understood attending a sick chamber, was indefatigable in administer-ing the different medicines to a minute as directed by the doctor, and in every other point attentive as the most assiduous European could have been.

On the third morning Mr. De Boissieres told me he was under serious apprehensions, for notwithstanding every medicine completely answered its object still the fever did not yield in the least, preying so much upon the general system that she was visibly sinking, and that unless a favourable change took place before the following morning, of which he had scarce a hope, I must prepare for the worst.

These were sad tidings, attached as I was to my revered companion. With an aching heart I watched through another night without a glimmering of hope to cheer me. As long as her intellect remained perfect she in the most placid yet tender language endeavoured to console me, assuring me she should do well, conjuring me not to fret and to take some rest. Although too evidently labouring under agonizing pain, she allowed no complaint, not even a sigh, to escape her lest it should increase my misery.

Two more days passed in this manner, when she became delirious, whereupon Mr. De Boissieres with great tenderness told me he feared a very few hours would finally close the scene. He nevertheless continued his exertions with the utmost assiduity and kindness. Anxious to watch any favourable moment that might offer, he directed the surgeon of the *Consolante* to attend the sick and wounded in the hospital while he took his former station by my poor favourite's bedside, with his fingers upon her pulse, administering restoratives as the vibrations fluttered through the day. In the evening she lay in a state of torpidity. The doctor, however, said as she still respired faintly he would continue to apply stimulants as the forlorn hope. Every five or ten minutes he poured a glass of red wine down her throat, so that by midnight she had swallowed a bottle and a half, then falling into a quiet slumber. Before morning she opened her eyes, when looking earnestly towards me who was standing by her side she feebly took hold of my hand and endeavoured, but in vain, to put it to her lips.

Mr. De Boissieres having retired just before to get a little sleep, I instantly summoned him. The moment he saw and felt her pulse he pronounced the crisis favourably past and that she was safe unless a relapse occurred, to avoid which she must be kept quite free from agitation or noise. The event confirmed his opinion ; in four days I had once more the extreme felicity to clasp my adored girl to my bosom with no other remains of her disease than the languor and weakness consequent on so severe an attack in such a climate. To the very eminent abilities and unwearied attendance of Mr. De Boissieres I certainly was indebted for the life of my Charlotte. This worthy and excellent man unfortunately took an active part in the abominable and bloody revolution, to which he finally fell a sacrifice, being one of the many who fell under the stroke of the fatal and destructive guillotine in Paris.

By the 23rd my dearest love being perfectly recovered, we again accepted an invitation of Captain Mallè's and dined on board the *Consolante*.

The 24th the Dutch Indiaman sailed with a cargo of rice for Cuddalore, which the French had also recently taken from us, aided by the native powers hostile to Great Britain, and where both garrison and inhabitants were in the utmost distress for food, the famine which raged along the coast of Coromandel having extended to that part of the country, making dreadful havoc amongst the wretched natives.

On Christmas Day a signal was made from Osnaburgh Fort of the approach of two large ships ; at ten in the morning the *Vengeur*, a sixty-four, commanded by Captain Cuverville, and the *Pourvoyeuse*, a forty-four gun frigate, commanded by Captain Trommelin, anchored in the harbour, having left the remainder of Mr. Suffren's fleet at Acheen completing their stock of poultry and other necessaries.

Our steady and zealous friends of Trincomalay representing the harsh treatment the English passengers of the *Raynha de Portugal* had experienced from Mr. Des Roys, at which Mr. Cuverville seemed much hurt, he, as his rank in the Navy made him superior to Mr. Des Roys, forthwith issued an order for our being allowed to go whithersoever we pleased, an order Monsieur Chevillard politely brought to us himself, conducting Mrs. Hickey, her Malay girl, who Mrs. Vansenden insisted should attend Mrs. Hickey while she remained at Trincomalay, myself and Nabob in his own boat to his *house*, if such a title could be applied to the wretched hovel. It had thentofore been the residence of a Dutch pilot, and consisted of a hall or centre apartment, having a small one at each corner, the walls quite bare, not even plastered, neither roof nor sides being watertight : certainly my poultry in Calcutta were far better lodged ; such as it was, however, it was generously given. Two of the corner rooms were allotted to Mrs. Hickey and me.

No such thing as gauze being procurable to make curtains of, and there being myriads of mosquitoes, some defence against the stings of those tormenting little insects was absolutely requisite. Our attentive host therefore caused two large English flags to be sewed together, which was fixed over our bed, answering the intended purpose but keeping us dreadfully hot. Although at the very edge of the sea, we scarcely ever got any fish, which I never could account for. Our richest dish at table was wild hog, a delicate though high-flavoured meat, of which we had great abundance.

Captains Cuverville and Trommelin came to visit us as soon as their respective ships were moored. Both were men of family, the former about fifty years of age, the other quite young. Captain Cuverville was an uncommonly pleasing-mannered man, who soon became a favourite of Charlotte's, and not less so with me. Indeed, we should have been ungrateful had it been otherwise, as he always treated us with the most marked and polite attention.

The day after the arrival of the two ships I received the following letter from Captain Gautier :

" DEAR SIR,

Yesterday I received by Mr. Touris the kind remembrance of Mrs. Hickey, and I was informed by the same way that you have at last been landed with the grant of living at Mr. Chevillard's. I heartily congratulate you both upon so agreeable an event, and I would have been to dine with you if I was not obliged to receive Mr. Cuverville and other officers who ought to come to dine with us to-day. It would have been a very pleasant thing to me to pray you to come and increase the good company which I am to meet with, but as it is impossible, no more of that. To-morrow without fail, if the weather is not rainy, I will go to pay my duty to Mrs. Hickey and dine with our common friend, Chevillard. If I can be useful to you, or to your charming consort, I pray you both very truly to let me know your wants or desires. You cannot imagine the pleasure with which I would desire to find some opportunity to convince you of the sincerity with which I am,

Dear sir,

Your most humble and most obedient servant,

GAUTIER."

" I pray you to remember me kindly to Mrs. Hickey. I most heartily wish you both an happy, good and merry year. We must hope that our bad circumstances will be finished with the end of the present."

I found the game of tric trac, which Captain Paardakoper of the *Held Woltemade* taught me, of use in beguiling time at Trincomalay. Almost all Frenchmen play it. I usually spent two or three hours every day playing with Mr. L'Anglade, Captain Mevillard, Mr. Bedell (both belonging to the *Vengeur*) and other officers, both naval and military.

Captain Cuverville brought with him from Acheen two beautiful little horses which were intended for Admiral Suffren. They had been broke in for the saddle, gentle as lambs, with paces so easy one might almost sleep on their backs when going at the rate of eight or nine miles an hour. Their pace was a short quick step called ambling, practised in general in America and the West Indies. Captain Cuverville sent these delightful animals to Mr. Chevillard's, requesting that Mrs. Hickey and I would use them until Mr. Suffren's arrival, which we were glad to do. Nothing contributed so much to the complete re-establishment of her health and spirits as our daily rides about a country full as luxuriant and romantic as any in Jamaica. The French gentlemen were in raptures at the graceful style in which my dearest girl managed her nag, collecting together in a crowd to see us set out on a morning. I certainly never knew a female to surpass her in horsemanship.

Captain Cuverville made frequent parties for us to a distance of twenty miles and upwards. The harbour of

Trincomalay abounds with creeks that run in every direction inland to a distance in many parts of more than an hundred miles, the shores on both sides, though in the state nature formed them, bearing the appearance of the most improved and highly cultivated land.  Captain Cuverville on the evening preceding any of these intended excursions always dispatched some of his sailors and servants in one of the ship's boats with a petty officer to explore the neighbourhood we were to visit, and when they reached any particularly pretty spot they were directed to land there and fix the tents they carried with them, being three in number—one for the party to assemble and eat in, another for the exclusive use of Mrs. Hickey and me, the third for the rest of the gentlemen to sleep in.  These previous matters being arranged, plenty of cold provisions and liquors being also sent off, we then proceeded in the ten-oared pinnace, a pair of very good French horns entertaining us with their music from her bow, the company being sheltered from the piercing rays of the sun by a stout awning.  The woods in Ceylon are full of excellent game, abounding with the cock of the wood or jungle fowl, than which there is not a more delicious bird in the world. We also caught plenty of admirable fish of various kinds.

We usually remained upon these truly pleasant parties three days, spending the mornings in strolling through the thick groves, sometimes embarking in the boat and rowing a few miles up the creeks, whilst some of the gentlemen pursued the sports of hunting, shooting, or fishing, constantly bringing abundant proofs of their success and industry.  About one o'clock we assembled at dinner, our table being supplied with fish, a variety of game, and wild hog.  Thus we lived capitally well.  In the evening we repeated our walks or rowed about until dusk, when we returned to the tents, drank coffee, then engaged at cards, tric trac and music as different fancies led ; at nine we supped upon cold things, after which singing filled up the time until the hour of retiring.

Everybody was delighted with Mrs. Hickey's vocal talents, the most admired pieces being " No, t'was neither shape nor feature," "Kate of Aberdeen," "Auld Robin Gray," "Tally Ho !" and many other songs from English operas, all which she executed with great taste in a sweet and plaintive voice, which was materially assisted by flute accompaniments, Messieurs L'Anglade and Bedell performing inimitably well on that instrument. The whole party were so particularly pleased with the then favourite hunting song of "Tally Ho !" that various attempts were made to translate it into French, but all endeavours failed from the utter impracticability of doing justice to this line, "The patriot is thrown in pursuit of his game," the last word presenting an insuperable difficulty, it not being found possible to give the full force of it and at the same time keep the measure of the music, the great object they had in view.

Mr. and Mrs. Vansenden, who resided in the Fort of Trincomalay, distant from the harbour about half a mile, frequently invited us to their house, where we always met cheerful, pleasant parties. With so many persons exerting themselves to amuse their English visitors time passed merrily away.

# CHAPTER IV

## ADMIRAL SUFFREN

ON the 1st of January, 1783, a large Dutch ship arrived
from Malacca with a cargo of rice. On the 14th the
*Consolante* sailed for Point de Galle in order to bring back a
similar cargo with the addition of some flour. She returned
on the 17th of February accompanied by the *Apollo* frigate
of thirty-six guns from Europe, which had brought out a
large quantity of marine stores for Suffren's fleet, also the
*Naiade* frigate of twenty-six guns, likewise from France with
dispatches for the French admiral. On the 18th the *Fortitude*, an English East Indiaman which had been captured
in the Bay of Bengal by one of the French cruisers, came in,
and the same evening arrived a large grab called the *Blake*,
commanded by Captain Light, who afterwards became
Governor of Prince of Wales's Island, or Pulo Penang. The
*Blake* had been taken by an enemy's cruiser off the coast
of Coromandel.

In the morning of the 20th a signal was hoisted at
Osnaburgh for an approaching fleet, and at eleven Admiral
Suffren with his squadron entered the harbour, exhibiting
a very grand spectacle. It consisted of the *Heros*, of seventy-
four guns, on board of which his flag, as commander-in-
chief, was flying ; the *Hannibal*, a seventy-four, bearing the
the distinguishing flag of the Count de Bruyere, as second
in command ; the *Illustre*, seventy-four, with the broad
pennant of the Count Adhemar ; the *Ajax*, sixty-four ;
*Artisien*, sixty-four ; *Sphynx*, sixty-four ; *Flamand*, sixty-
four ; *Severe*, sixty-four ; the *Le Fin* frigate, thirty-two
guns ; the *Blandford*, an English East Indiaman (a prize)

with two English brigs and two schooners, all captured at different times.

Immediately after the fleet came to an anchor I went off in Mr. Chevillard's boat to the *Heros* in order to pay my compliments to Mr. Suffren. Upon getting on board I was shewn into an apartment similar to what in our East Indiamen is called the cuddy, directly before the round house, where were . already assembled several commanders and officers of the fleet waiting for audience upon matters of duty. Upon my entering the cabin an attendant asked my name, which given he instantly went in to announce to the Admiral. Five minutes after I was admitted to the after cabin, where Mr. Suffren was sitting at a table having a number of papers upon it which he appeared to be inspecting; his secretary, Mr. Launay, and other persons were writing at the same table. He received me with the most engaging attention and politeness, and, pointing to a chair, desired I should be seated until he finished some matters of business that required dispatch. I apologized for my unseasonable intrusion, observing that as I broke in upon him I would take some other opportunity of paying my respects when he might be less occupied. With the utmost good-humour he said he should be at my service in a quarter of an hour, and requested I would sit till then. Of course, I did so, and this afforded me an opportunity of observing his extraordinary dress and figure. In appearance he looked much more like a little fat, vulgar English butcher than a Frenchman of consequence ; in height he was about five feet five inches, very corpulent, scarce any hair upon the crown of his head, the sides and back tolerably thick. Although quite grey he wore neither powder nor pomatum, nor any curl, having a short cue of three or four inches tied with a piece of old spun-yarn. He was in slippers, or, rather, a pair of old shoes, the straps being cut off, blue cloth breeches unbuttoned at the knees, cotton or thread stockings (none of the cleanest) hanging about his legs, no waistcoat or cravat, a coarse linen shirt entirely wet with perspiration, open at the neck, the sleeves being rolled up above his elbows as if just going to wash his hands and arms ; indeed I concluded in my own mind that he had been broken in upon and interrupted whilst at his toilette, but afterwards ascertained that he always appeared as above described during the morning.

Having quickly dispatched the business he was engaged in, he dismissed the gentlemen that had been employed upon it, when, drawing his chair close to mine, he apologized for having detained me so long. He then made a number of enquiries relative to my situation in life, the circumstances of my voyage from Europe, and so forth, observing he believed the *Raynha de Portugal* must certainly be considered as an undoubted seizable ship—nay, from Colonel Des Roys' statement respecting her, which was one of the papers he had under consideration when I entered, he conceived he must make a prize of her. I thereupon mentioned the manner in which myself and the other English passengers had procured accommodation on board the ship at Lisbon, and that we had so done under the perfect conviction that she was to all intents and purposes a Portuguese. To this he replied that let the determination be what it might respecting the ship and cargo, which he again said probably would be a condemnation of both, it should not affect the British subjects on board her, for although he might, and perhaps ought, in strict justice in such case to consider and treat us as prisoners of war, he would not treat us as such ; on the contrary, he would give permission for us to proceed to the places of our respective destinations by the earliest opportunity that offered. He condescended also to express great concern at the situation Mrs. Hickey had been reduced to during the monsoon gale, and how much his inclination led him to alleviate our sufferings by every means within his power.

During my interview with Mr. Suffren several letters and messages were delivered to him ; fearful therefore of trespassing, I rose two or three times to depart, but he each time made me resume my seat, saying he had yet many things to enquire about. Our conversation then continued for upwards of an hour, when the Count de Bruyere being announced, the Admiral observed he must unwillingly break off our conference for the present, as the Count came to speak upon official business. He requested I would dine with him the following day, and come early, as soon after twelve as I pleased, and he would have some further conversation. He then wished me good morning, and I left the cabin. In passing through the cuddy I saw, amongst a number of others, Mr. Bateman, waiting in the hope of an introduction, but which I heard he did not, to his extreme anger and mortification, effect until two days after.

At the commencement of my interview with Mr. Suffren I spoke English, having been informed he understood and spoke it a little. He was, however, often at a loss for words to express what he wished to say, at which he seemed rather impatient, saying in French, " Surely you understand something of French which is in such general use in England." I answered that I understood it tolerably, but spoke it very badly. He replied he was certain we should do better with what I called my bad French than with the abominable, indeed unintelligible, English of his. From that time we always conversed in his language, and he, like a true Frenchman, was pleased to pay me many compliments. His behaviour towards me was at all times exceedingly affable and pleasing.

In the afternoon Mr. Barretto called to shew me a letter he had written and intended sending to Mr. Suffren, wherein, after giving a circumstantial account of himself, of his ship, and the cargo on board, he begged to be honoured with a personal interview, when he had no doubt he should be able to satisfy his Excellency that no possible suspicion as to the neutrality of the vessel could remain upon his mind. This address, which struck me as being admirably well written, being sent to the Admiral, an answer was immediately returned through the secretary naming an early hour the next morning but one at which the Admiral would receive him on board the *Heros*.

When I went on shore from my first visit to Mr. Suffren

I found several boats laying opposite Mr. Chevillard's house, all having poultry in them which had been sent from the *Heros* and other ships as more likely to thrive upon land than stuffed up thickly in coops on board. The whole of them had been laid in at Acheen, where fowls are uncommonly large and fine, the Malays being famous breeders. They were together in bundles of about a dozen, which being carried within the enclosure of Mr. Chevillard's premises, the strings with which each of their legs were tied were cut and the bird set at liberty. The first use made of this was a *general engagement*, each fowl attacking his nearest neighbour with the utmost fury, fighting most desperately, sometimes changing antagonists, and continuing the battle until so exhausted that neither of the combatants had strength left to peck at each other, many of them actually falling down as if dying. It was a most ridiculous sight to see about a thousand pair of fowls thus hostilely conducting themselves towards each other. The violence of the conflict was not entirely at an end for two days ; on the third, however, profound peace prevailed, as if by general consent they became reconciled, eating their rice and picking up the small gravel together in perfect amity.

The 21st while sitting at breakfast Mr. Launay called to say Mr. Suffren requested I would be on board by half-past eleven if not inconvenient, which I promised to attend to.

Mr. Chevillard's house was now a constant scene of bustle and confusion, being crowded from morning to night with the officers and seamen on matters of business, a change far from agreeable to Mrs. Hickey and myself, both preferring the tranquillity and quiet we had thentofore enjoyed, with the society of half a dozen very worthy men. I had reason to think many of the persons made a pretence for coming, hoping to get a sight of the beautiful and accomplished Englishwoman, for under such description she had been represented. She could not stir from home without being overwhelmed with fulsome compliments.

At eleven I went off to the *Heros*, and was directly shewn

into the Admiral's apartment, where I found him exactly in the same deshabille as on the preceding day. The conversation began by his telling me the *Raynha de Portugal* would be detained as a prize. He said he had fully investigated her case, in which he found so many strange and suspicious circumstances that he could not without a dereliction of his duty do otherwise than arrest her. I observed to the Admiral that Mr. Barretto had requested me to accompany him on the morrow at the time he was to be honoured with an audience respecting the rights he claimed as being neutral property, but that I had not accepted the call from an apprehension that he (Mr. Suffren) might deem it intrusive on my part, whereupon the Admiral with great vivacity answered, " Intrusive ! by no means, Mr. Hickey ! On the contrary, I am happy to hear that you are to be present, and I readily add my entreaties to those of Mr. Barretto that you will be so."

Mr. Suffren then asked what was my opinion respecting his naval opponent, Sir Edward Hughes. " For," he said, " I have been very much astonished, Mr. Hickey, to hear several of your countrymen speak in cool, if not disrespectful, terms of that commander, whom I have always considered and found to be a brave, skilful, and in every respect a very able officer. It has been my fate to be opposed to him in three different hard-contested battles, in every one of which Sir Edward Hughes, in my humble opinion, gave positive proofs that he possessed consummate skill and abilities, equal to any man's I have ever had to deal with in my profession. His manners and general conduct, too, has uniformly been that of a brave and gallant officer, blended with the mild and benevolent disposition of a truly philanthropic citizen of the world."

Again the Admiral asked what were my sentiments respecting the English admiral. I replied that I was by no means competent to give an opinion, being altogether unacquainted with his merits or demerits, but judging by the reports of the public prints his character with the people was that of being a diligent, zealous and gallant officer.

"And such a character he surely is deserving of," said Mr. Suffren, "a braver man does not live. I, however, cannot but feel surprized that such a man as Sir Edward Hughes can submit to being controlled by a person every way so vastly inferior to him as is the Governor of Madras, Lord Macartney. You, Mr. Hickey, I presume may have heard how much I have been blamed, nay stigmatized as deficient in humanity, for sending certain English prisoners to an ally of ours upon the coast of Coromandel. Now, sir, I should be glad to have your unbiassed sentiments upon the whole of this case. It stands thus :

"I left Europe with a strong and powerful squadron under my exclusive and sole orders, the objects of this expedition I was going upon being twofold, first, to prevent the British from getting possession of the Cape of Good Hope, and in the event of succeeding in that then to proceed with all dispatch to the coast of Coromandel, there to land a body of men to aid the exertions of our zealous Asiatic ally, Hyder Ali. Having been hurried away from France without near sufficient water for my people, it became necessary to stop for a supply, for which purpose I intended to put into one of the Canary or Cape de Verd Islands. Unfortunately for me I decided upon Port Praya Bay as being the best at which to obtain a speedy supply of that article. Upon running for the harbour I was astonished and vexed to perceive a British fleet riding at anchor ; vexed because I felt the probability that thus unexpectedly falling in with the enemy might seriously interfere with, if not totally derange, all my plans. My surprize was not a little increased when I saw a British commodore's distinguishing flag flying at the masthead of the innermost ship, with a number of pennants around him, a forest of masts of merchantmen laying unprotected and exposed towards the mouth of the harbour.

"Such a spectacle (as novel as unaccountable) struck me forcibly. I at once knew it must be the squadron of Commodore Johnston who I was going out to counteract the measures of, but how to account for a seaman's taking such

a berth as Mr. Johnston had, leaving his convoy liable to
be partially cut off or destroyed, in any other manner than
from a wish to take the utmost care of himself, I knew not.
I therefore resolved, notwithstanding a great superiority of
the British ships, immediately to bring them to action.   I
for that purpose made the *Hannibal's* signal to lead in, run
close alongside the commodore and engage.   This order the
Count De Bruyere executed in a style that covered him
with glory.   I seconded him by attacking two of the enemy's
*line of battle* ships.

" Had all my captains done their duty with the same
ardour the *Hannibal* and *Heros* did it would have proved a
woeful day for England.   Suffice it to say very different was
the case.   Three of the commanders for ever disgraced themselves, involving therein the noble families to which they
were allied.   These poltroons hung back and never brought
their ships within gun shot of the enemy.   The consequence
was after a conflict unparalleled in history, in which the
*Hannibal* and the *Heros* sustained a galling fire from the
whole of the British line for two hours, both were so crippled,
especially the *Hannibal*, which was reduced to an ungovern-
able hulk, having lost all her masts, that I was under the
afflicting necessity of ordering my ships off, not, however,
until we had treated the English commodore and his
squadron so roughly that he permitted me, damaged as I
was, to tow the shattered *Hannibal* from the midst of
them.

" Having got clear out of the harbour I resolved to proceed
without loss of time to the Cape, to which place I was aware
the British squadron were bound.   Willing for form's sake
to have the sanction of those who served under me, I forthwith summoned all commanders to attend a council of war
on board the *Heros*, when, communicating my future intentions, the Counts De Bruyere and Adhemar alone agreed to
the propriety of such intentions, the rest pronouncing my
object impracticable and unjustifiably wild and chimerical.
Two of the dastardly captains in particular said they could
not proceed, not having water for more than twenty days,

besides which the state of the *Hannibal* made it impossible to go on unless I proposed sacrificing that ship altogether. I replied that I had no such intention, so far from it I looked with confidence to the future services and assistance of the *Hannibal*, her gallant captain and crew to aid me in effecting the important plans I had in view. I further declared that the *Hannibal* must and should be new rigged at sea, and as to water, those ships that had the smallest quantity should receive a proportion from others that had more, and an equal partition take place. If the entire quantity in the fleet would not afford a quart per day for each man they must content themselves with a pint, nay, with half a pint, for to the Cape I certainly would go with the utmost dispatch.

"Those who had proved themselves poltroons in the battle were the most violent opponents of my wishes, but I regarded them not. The *Illustre* took the *Hannibal* in tow; every carpenter of the fleet was employed making lower masts, and such was their zeal and industry, as well as that of every seaman, that in eight days, although in boisterous weather, upon a turbulent ocean, she was as completely new masted and rigged as if in Brest or any other harbour. I thus accomplished my purpose, reached the Cape in safety, and thereby defeated the object of Mr. Johnston and his large force, compelling him to be content with capturing or destroying a few empty vessels he found at anchor in Saldanha Bay.

"I then proceeded to India, where I had the mortification to find that Pondicherry, our chief settlement upon the coast of Coromandel, was in the hands of the enemy; Trincomalay, where we are now conversing, the same, so that I had no port into which I could put for repairs, for provisions, or upon any account whatever nearer than Mauritias. Sir Edward Hughes, with his fleet of nine line of battle ships, all in the completest state and fully manned, lay off Madras; I had eleven, several of them exceedingly leaky and in want of stores, and so weak from the sad number of hands we lost at Port Praya I could scarcely manœuvre my ships. I

nevertheless determined to steer for and engage Sir Edward.
I did so, and although no vessel was taken on either side I
reduced the British squadron to such distress as to be incapable of committing further hostilities for some time.
Had not three of my captains betrayed their base cowardice
I should have obtained a decisive victory. I treated those
villains, those traitors to their sovereign and their country,
as they deserved by dispatching them with ignominy and
disgrace to France !

"After running over to Sumatra for a few days, refitting,
and watering there, I again went to sea, scouring the Bay
of Bengal and Indian Seas in every direction, and taking so
many prizes that my fleet for many weeks actually subsisted upon the provisions obtained from them. A number
of prisoners consequently were on board my ships, who
from the peculiarity of my situation became a serious evil,
as I was at a loss how to feed them. As I knew the English
had a number of French prisoners, I addressed a letter to
Sir Edward Hughes proposing an immediate exchange.
An answer was given in the politest and most benevolent
terms, highly respectful and pleasing to myself as an individual. Sir Edward, however, avowed his inability to accede
to my well-intended proposal, much as he wished for
humanity's sake that it should be carried into effect, but
that the exchange of prisoners rested exclusively with Lord
Macartney, the Governor of Madras, to whom he therefore
begged leave to refer me.

"Upon receipt of this information I, without an hour's
delay, addressed Lord Macartney upon the subject. This
arrogant lord deigned not to give any sort of answer. My
prisoners increasing by further captures, I again wrote to
his lordship, and again was insulted by his insolent and
rude silence. Distressed beyond measure, I addressed the
British admiral, from whom I directly received an answer
that did honour to his feelings as a man, but still lamenting
his want of power to promote my humane object. By this
time the evil was become so great that I once more in the
most forcible language depicted to Sir Edward Hughes the

forlorn state I was reduced to, and that if a cartel was not forthwith established I should be under the disagreeable necessity of delivering up the prisoners to Tippoo Sultaun, the only Asiatic prince in alliance with my country. Having been twice treated with contumely by Lord Macartney I particularly desired no further reference might be made to him whom I considered deficient in common good manners, and who had behaved towards me with a rudeness and impertinence unprecedented between gentlemen. The British admiral for the third time lamented his want of power to treat for an exchange in most pathetic terms, entreating that I would not adopt the measure I threatened of sending my prisoners to Tippoo, as he feared such a step would be worse than condemning the unfortunate men to death. To this I replied that I had no alternative, that I was sincerely desirous to avoid doing what he so feelingly deprecated, and would therefore (seriously inconvenient and distressing as it was) wait three days more for a definitive and, I trusted, favourable answer ere I dispatched the poor people, whose fate I deplored as much as he could, and if ultimately driven to the necessity of delivering them over to Tippoo Sultaun would use every precaution in my power to avert the melancholy event he seemed to apprehend by securing for them humane and liberal treatment.

" I was given to understand that the Admiral submitted my various representations to Lord Macartney without any effect, and thus I was compelled to send several hundred English seamen and soldiers to Tippoo Sultaun, but previous to so doing I exacted from that prince's agent the most sacred and positive assurances that they should be humanely treated and exchanged at the earliest opportunity.

" For this, on my part, unavoidable measure I have been stigmatized, abused in the grossest terms, as void of humanity or feeling, as a savage wretch that ought to be scouted from all society. My character thus attempted to be blasted with every opprobrious epithet attached to my name, and yet with how little justice was all this done, for let me ask you, Mr. Hickey, as a candid, unprejudiced

person, what could I do ? I have already told you how
peculiarly I was situated ; without a single port to receive
and assist me on either side of India ; without any other
native friendly prince than Tippoo Sultaun ; in actual
distress for want of provisions, fresh or salt ; with between
four and five hundred prisoners distributed through my
fleet, and increasing my difficulties by what they necessarily
consumed. I exerted my strenuous endeavours without
intermission to effect an exchange, and on my part would
have done it upon any terms, however unfavourable to the
nation I had the honour to represent, but all these endeavours failed ; I could no longer keep the prisoners on
board my ships ; I could not send them to the Mauritias,
having neither transports nor vessels fit to convey them,
and indeed if I had I was conscious it would only have been
throwing the weight off my own shoulders to place it upon
the Governor and inhabitants of Mauritias, for both at that
island and Bourbon the most dreadful scarcity prevailed, the
people were almost starved. It would have been unreasonable in the extreme to suppose that I was to set at liberty
near five hundred, the greater part able seamen ; common
justice to my sovereign forbid such a measure. What then
remained for me but to do as I did, previously taking every
precaution that prudence and foresight could suggest to
secure to the said prisoners humane and proper treatment.
If Tippoo Sultaun, or those serving under him, broke their
faith in this particular, why am I to be so blamed ; why is
the whole odium to be thrown upon me ? I cannot, I declare on my honour, I cannot see the least show of justice
in such conduct.''

In this manner did Mr. Suffren express himself to me,
nor could I do otherwise than give him credit for the force of
his argument, and although the barbarity with which the
unfortunate people were treated, many of whom were
actually murdered, must ever be lamented, I am free to say
I cannot see the justice of attempting to fix the odium entirely and exclusively upon Admiral Suffren. Upon this
subject he always spoke with great warmth, and I could

plainly perceive it preyed upon his mind, yet he invariably insisted the English did not treat him with their natural liberality upon the occasion.

He had but just concluded the above narrative when dinner was announced, whereupon he retired to his state-room, from whence he in five minutes returned dressed in a blue jacket of thin coast cloth, his shirt collar buttoned, with a black stock on. He had also pulled up his stockings, buttoned his breeches knees, and put on shoes instead of slippers. He then conducted me down his private staircase into the cabin below, where about forty gentlemen were assembled, among whom were the Counts De Bruyere and Adhemar. Mr. Suffren seated me on his right hand, a place I made an attempt to give up to the Count De Bruyere, who positively refused, and Mr. Suffren said, " Come, come ! I must have you next me upon one side or the other."

The table was tolerably supplied, and we had as fine bread as ever I saw on shore, the wines light but well flavoured, a very coarse tablecloth, not over clean, the knives, forks and etceteras rough in the extreme. The Admiral eat voraciously, more than once remarking to me that the heat of the climate did not take away his appetite, " though," added he, " I have often with a very keen one been reduced to a musty biscuit, full of vermin, with a small bit of stinking salt pork, as my only sustenance during the twenty-four hours. However, sir, I make it a rule always to conform to the circumstances of the day be they as they may, good or bad ; a military man is ever liable to hard rubs and ought to be prepared to meet them with fortitude and resignation."

Just after we sat down to dinner the arrival of the little *Hannibal* was announced. This was an English fifty gun ship taken by Mr. Suffren on his way to India. On board this ship at the time of her being captured was my London friend, Major George Russell, who left England with Robert Pott and Emily, but whilst laying at St. Helena the *Hannibal* touched there, and Major Russell being intimate with her commander he offered to take him on to Madras, by which he would in all probability save at least a month. The Major therefore removed to the *Hannibal*, which off the Cape unluckily fell in with Suffren's squadron in the night and was taken. Being a good sailer, Mr. Suffren in a few days dispatched her as an avant courier to announce his approach at Mauritias. While upon the voyage she fell in with a Danish Indiaman bound to Tranquebar, and Major Russell obtaining the French captain's leave, after giving his parole not to serve until exchanged, went on board the Dane, otherwise we should have met at Trincomalay.

With the little *Hannibal* there also came in the *Coventry* English frigate, of thirty-two guns, which had been captured some time before by a French seventy-four. Captain Wolseley, who commanded her at the time, had been sent to Mauritias, but left that island in the little *Hannibal*. He immediately came on board the *Heros* and was very politely received by Mr. Suffren.

After dinner coffee was served, and then the Chasse Café, or liqueurs, when the party broke up. As I was passing through the steerage, along the main deck, I beheld such a scene of filth and dirt as I could not have believed had I not seen ; it had more the appearance of an abominable pig-sty than the inside of a ship of the line bearing an admiral's flag, and this was very much the case with all the fleet except two, the *Vengeur* and *Flamand*, both of which were as neat and clean as any British ship of war.

After stopping a few minutes to speak to one of the officers I went up to the quarter-deck where the Admiral was. He told me he was going on shore to take his evening's walk, which he never failed doing when in port. I was rather surprised at not seeing any preparation making, and still more at an uncouth figure, covered with pitch and tar, coming up to him and without the least ceremony saying, "The boat is ready." This person I found was the boatswain. The Admiral then wished me a good evening, saying, "I should have offered you a passage on shore in my boat, small as it is, but that I see Chevillard's smart pinnace coming for you." Although very corpulent and heavy, he went down the ship's side by a single common rope as quick and light as any midshipman could have done, without a man at the side, and seating himself in the stern sheets of the jolly-boat took the helm, pushed off, and four young lads rowed him ashore. I could not help expressing my astonishment at the scene, whereupon I was informed the General never left the ship in any other manner, unless upon occasions of state or ceremony, when he reluctantly yielded to custom. The boatswain was his factotum, nor did he ever apply to any other person for anything he wanted himself.

With all his exterior roughness, the General possessed the insinuating and elegant address of a French man of fashion, and as a proof of attention to the fair sex he had, without saying a word to me, ordered into his jolly-boat some papers of chocolate, liqueurs, China sweetmeats and Acheen fruits, especially the delicious mangosteen, of which, though extremely difficult to keep beyond a few days, he had contrived to preserve some dozens in high preservation. These little articles of real luxury in our situation he in person presented to Mrs. Hickey, paying her many handsome compliments at the same time. He had but just left Mr. Chevillard's house when I reached it.

In the evening a small country boat came in from Anjingo, bringing an account of Lord Rodney's victory over the French fleet in the West Indies on the preceding 12th of April, when the French commander-in-chief, the Count De Grasse, was taken. This was instantly and loudly pronounced to be a gross falsehood, a mere fabricated story, it being utterly impossible that a French admiral should ever strike his flag to an enemy. It was preposterous, it was absurd to send forth so ridiculous a lie! Yet it proved very true.

# CHAPTER V

## RELEASED

ON the 22nd Captain Wolseley called upon us, and as he had heard of our disastrous voyage from Europe, and the serious losses we sustained from the hurricane, he brought with him two pieces of very fine coast longcloth, a quantity of muslins and other articles for Mrs. Hickey, besides some pieces of gingham and nankeen for my use.

The same morning every captain in the fleet visited us, when we gained another most estimable friend in the Chevalier De Salvert, then captain of the *Flamand*, who from that day until the hour that we parted (to meet, alas! no more) treated Mrs. Hickey and myself with an affectionate kindness and an attention that I never can forget. We usually dined twice a week on board the *Flamand*. Had we complied with Monsieur De Salvert's urgent request we should never have been out of her. He made pleasant parties for us up the various creeks, had excellent music, and, whenever the weather permitted, dancing. This, however, was not often the case, as notwithstanding it was called the coolest season of the year the heat was in general so intense and oppressive there was no moving in the day-time. On board this ship there was one of the most extra-ordinary birds I ever saw. It was a minor, from the Island of Sumatra, which sung a number of French and Malay songs, repeated verses, and was an inimitable mimic. It likewise went regularly through the whole manœuvres of putting the ship about, making such a noise at " Main-sail haul " as would have led one to suppose twenty persons were " singing out." Mrs. Hickey was so delighted with this bird we could not get her from its cage.

The following morning just after rising, and whilst dressing, I heard someone singing "Connoissez vous Admiral Anson, ce General de grand renom," etc., a satire, or burlesque, upon Lord Anson's famous voyage round the world, abounding with wit. Going out of my bed-chamber, I was surprised to find the performer was no other than the minor, which Captain De Salvert had sent with a most kind letter as a present to my dearest Charlotte. I need scarcely add that this charming bird became an amazing pet.

I was one day conversing with the Chevalier De Salvert respecting the rare abilities of Admiral Suffren. He spoke of him with enthusiasm in his profession as a consummate hero who reflected the highest honour upon the country he belonged to. He added, however, that notwithstanding all his merit he would fall a sacrifice to the powerful influence of several noble families whose characters he had indirectly sullied by degrading three of his captains (to whom they were nearly related), turning them out of the ships they had commanded, and sending them home to France stigmatized as cowards. He therefore apprehended that the services the Admiral had done his country would be lost in the improper weight of those noblemen, and that instead of being rewarded he would be disgraced. He further told me that one of the three poltroons, who had behaved in the most dastardly manner so that his own officers and crew cried out shame, was nearly connected with one of the dearest friends Mr. Suffren had in the world, which induced him to wish to let the culprit off easy. With this object in view he sent for the captain, lamented to hear that his health was become so impaired by the climate as to render a change of air necessary, that as such was the case he should give him the command of a small vessel he was about to send to France with dispatches, and that he must sail in three days. The stupid blockhead, not understanding the meaning of such unexpected lenity, thought he might presume upon it, and immediately answered that although he had lately been somewhat indisposed yet his complaint was not of so serious a nature as to make it necessary for him to relinquish the command of his ship, and that he felt himself quite competent to do the duties of it. The Admiral, astonished at his effrontery, coolly replied, "You are grossly mistaken, you are every way unfit to retain the command you have held, and have a more fatal complaint than you seem disposed to admit, though you must be conscious of it. You are a rank and infamous coward, so away, sir, join your dastardly colleagues and meet the fate that awaits you in France." The three commanders were sent off together.

I was happy to hear about two years afterwards that the Chevalier De Salvert's fears were not realized. The merits of Admiral Suffren were too conspicuous and too well known to be borne down by any weight of influence or power. Upon his return to France he was received at Court, and everywhere else, with the highest respect and unbounded expressions of gratitude, his sovereign directly creating him a marechal of France.

The universal attention and respect with which I and my dear Charlotte were treated raised the envy and spleen of Mr. Bateman to so great a degree that he began to slander us both, circulating some anecdotes as having occurred at Lisbon which he imagined would lower us in the opinions of the French gentlemen. This ill-temper was further increased at finding a quite contrary effect to what he intended; his illiberality and the motive was seen through and only added to his own disgrace. His behaviour, however, being communicated to me, I gave him my opinion upon such base conduct in very pointed terms.

At noon Mr. Barretto called and we embarked together for the *Heros*. Upon getting on board we were immediately conducted into the Admiral's apartment. Mr. Barretto, after producing the only two documents saved from the general havoc made by the storm, related every particular relative to his ship that had occurred from the time of his arrival at Lisbon until his departure from thence and putting into Trincomalay in the utmost distress. He concluded his narrative with an earnest desire that Mr. Suffren would issue an order for the ship's release that he (Barretto) might get her refitted for sea and conclude a voyage that had already proved so unfortunate.

Mr. Suffren heard him with the most patient attention, nor once interrupted him, but when his story was finished he thus addressed him :

" Mr. Barretto, I have duly weighed and considered every circumstance you have mentioned with the strongest inclination to put a favourable construction upon your case and comply with your desire, were it possible, but the facts are so clear, the proofs so strong and damning that I cannot do otherwise than retain the ship, and, as far as I am empowered, condemn her as a legal prize, subject, of course, to the further and future consideration of the High Court of Admiralty at Paris."

Mr. Barretto, upon hearing this unexpected determination as to his property, said :

" May I, sir, request to know what are those facts and proofs, as you are pleased to call them, and which you consider so clear and damning ? "

" Most freely," replied Mr. Suffren, " and I will unequivocally state them.  Your ship is of British construction, built in a British port, and sold, as alleged, to a subject of a neutral power, but after the declaration of war between France and Great Britain, fitted out at Bombay, from whence she sailed for Lisbon, where you put on board a cargo, not of Portuguese merchandize but consisting entirely of staple articles of England, such as lead, iron, copper, canvas and other marine stores ;  yourself born and bred under the British flag at Bombay and so conscious of your being a subject of that nation that though calling yourself a Portuguese, you deemed it requisite to obtain a naturalization at Lisbon.  With your English cargo you depart from Lisbon for Madras, another English settlement."

Mr. Barretto here interrupted the Admiral, saying :

" You are mistaken, sir, in some of your assumed facts. There are no other marine or naval stores on board ;  the cargo as specified by you undoubtedly was manufactured in England, but I purchased the whole in the city of Lisbon from Portuguese merchants and out of their warehouses, as I surely had a right to do. Equally incorrect are you in asserting that I was bound to an English settlement. I was not, sir. Goa was the place of my destination, as my papers should distinctly have shewn but for an act of providence, and their destruction deprives me of my written evidence."

Mr. Barretto here ceasing to speak, the Admiral resumed :

" This act of divine providence I sincerely lament, Mr. Barretto, and have no doubt that misfortune alone deprived you of the usual papers, but there is yet more ; you have English passengers on board, and, with one exception, no other. I must repeat, too, you were bound to Madras, otherwise (unless going to Bengal) what business could you have off Hog Island upon the coast of Sumatra, that of Malabar being, as you pretend, your destination ? "

Mr. Barretto again interrupted Mr. Suffren to declare upon his honour that, however strange it might appear, such was the truth, and he could only lament the superlative ignorance of his navigator.

Mr. Suffren replied, with more warmth of manner than he had yet shewn : " Fye, sir, fye, I blush to hear you ! Can you for a moment suppose it possible that there is a person to be found who knows anything of seamanship that can or will believe so wild a circumstance could occur as that of a ship under the management and direction of Europeans, bound to Goa, upon the coast of Malabar, making the land off Sumatra ? Indeed, indeed, Mr. Barretto, it is too absurd, the deception is too palpable."

Mr. Barretto renewed his protestations that such was the fact, however incredible, but Mr. Suffren continued :

" Were further proofs required I have them within my power, Mr. Barretto, from the unbiassed mouth of one of your own officers, who has voluntarily assured me that both ship and cargo are exclusively and entirely English property."

This the Admiral had learnt from the cowardly scoundrel of a second mate, who, in consequence of Mr. Barretto's upbraiding him for abandoning his post and his duty in the hour of danger, declaring he would publish his base conduct in Portugal, had adopted that mode of revenge.

Mr. Suffren ended by expressing his deep concern that so heavy a loss was likely to fall upon him (Barretto) individually, and was proceeding in a strain of commiseration when Mr. Barretto very abruptly stopped him, saying :

" Don't, Mr. Suffren, give yourself the trouble of bestowing your pity upon me, as useless as it is void of all sincerity, nor need you take so roundabout a way to disguise the truth or in a fruitless attempt to gloss over your tyrannical and unjust treatment of me. I can, without hesitation, account for the motive that influences you to commit what I can consider in no other light than a direct and absolute robbery, and a positive breach and infringement of the law of nations. Thus, sir, stands the fact. You see my ship, torn to pieces as she is, still a noble vessel, capable of being easily converted into a powerful vessel of war ; you know that she has an immensely valuable cargo on board, which you are desirous of laying hands upon, right or wrong. In short, you want both ship and cargo, and having no means of purchasing or paying for either the one or the other, avail yourself of the strong arm of power cruelly and unjustly to deprive me of my property."

This speech, delivered with the utmost gravity and composure, I conceived would have highly irritated and offended the gallant Admiral, instead of which he betrayed not the slightest symptom of anger, but with a smile upon his countenance mildly replied :

" From my soul I wish, Mr. Barretto, I wish that you may be able to establish what you say, because in that case you would obtain ample restitution from my Court."

Here the conference broke up ; we got into our boat to return on shore, and while on our way had the mortification to see the Portuguese flag, which had till then been flying, hauled down and a French one hoisted in its stead.

The following morning Mr. Barretto called to request that I would draw up a statement of all the facts within my knowledge relative to his late unfortunate ship, and verify the same by affidavit. This I accordingly did, particularly setting forth the manner in which as an utter stranger I had applied for and obtained a passage for myself and family on board the *Raynha de Portugal*. To conclude this part of the history at once : Mr. Barretto having got his liberty, repaired first to Bombay and afterwards to Bengal to procure certain vouchers he was advised to furnish himself with, which having got he embarked for Lisbon, where he applied for and obtained duplicates of his late ship's papers, together with a written instrument under the hand and seal of the Marquis De Pombal, certifying in the most decided language and terms that the ship *Raynha de Portugal* was *bona fide* Portuguese, and that the cargo on board of her had been purchased from Portuguese merchants at Lisbon. Armed with these important documents in support of his claims, Mr. Barretto proceeded from Lisbon to Paris, where upon his arrival he commenced a suit in the Admiralty Court against Mr. Suffren and the other captors of his ship and cargo. After a long investigation of the case the Court decided against Mr. Barretto, condemning both his ship and cargo.

Thus grievously disappointed by this strange decision at Paris, Mr. Barretto's next step was an application to certain underwriters in London to pay policies executed by them to an amount of eighty thousand pounds. This demand they refused to comply with, alleging that the property was not such as was stated in the proposals for the insurance. Mr. Barretto therefore repaired in person to the British capital, where he caused an action to be commenced upon the policy. This came on to be tried at Guildhall before Lord Loughborough, Chief Justice of the Common Pleas, who, upon the plaintiff's counsel stating the case, asked whether there had been any formal adjudication respecting the ship and cargo in the Admiralty Court in France, to which he was answered by the counsel for the underwriters that there had been a formal and regular decision against the present plaintiff, an authenticated copy of which judgment he then held in his hand and was prepared to prove. This being accordingly done, Lord Loughborough observed there was an end of the case, the judgment of the court of Paris being decisive ; that much as the plaintiff was likely to suffer individually, and greatly as he felt for him, it was unavoidable and out of his power to relieve him, but the decision of a foreign court could not be overset or the merits of the case again be opened. Thus was Mr. Barretto foiled in every way and left to sustain the immense loss of two hundred and fifty thousand pounds, which was the value of the ship and cargo.

Whether or not he was the sole owner I cannot decide, but if he was he lived long enough to get over that enormous loss and to acquire another large fortune, as he died several years afterwards possessed of considerable wealth.    I always thought, and do still think, there must have been some palpable neglect or mismanagement on the part of those employed professionally for Mr. Barretto at Paris, for had all the circumstances of the case been clearly before the judges it is impossible such a decision could have been given.

The unfortunate Frenchman of whom I have already spoken who received the injury upon his shin in helping to throw the guns overboard during the hurricane continued his own remedy or mode of treating the wound for some time after we got into Trincomalay, daily applying brandy, vinegar and brown paper.    At the time of Mr. Suffren's arrival the sore had put on a very serious appearance, and the flesh around it became greatly inflamed, attended with much pain.    As I saw the injured man almost daily, and found it likely serious consequences might arise from further neglect, I strongly urged him to apply to Mr. De Boissieres, the surgeon-major, which he most obstinately refused to do.

Towards the end of the month of January Mr. Brown, my shipmate, told me he had just seen the Frenchman's leg and had no doubt a mortification would soon take place. I thereupon immediately went to Mr. De Boissieres' quarters and mentioned the circumstance to him, who instantly went to the Frenchman's room.    He very unwillingly showed the wound, and upon examining it Mr. De Boissieres at once pronounced it to be a fatal case ; that nothing could preserve the man's life but amputation of the limb, and that without further loss of time, there being certain symptoms of gangrene. He, however, dressed the sore, saying he would call again with other surgeons. He accordingly did so in the evening with two of the medical gentlemen, who upon taking off the bandage declared a mortification had already commenced, and they prepared their instruments to perform amputation. The poor man, upon being told this, at once, and in the most decided manner, refused to submit to the operation. Being informed death must ensue, he with the utmost composure said, " Be it so. Since I was fifteen years of age I have been a soldier of fortune, a wanderer over every quarter of the globe, enduring every degree of hardship and bodily suffering that ever man encountered. Such must still be my fate ; what then should I do deprived of a limb ? Far better for me to leave the world than live so mutilated and rendered incapable of following my profession." This absurd reasoning Mr. De Boissieres met and answered with great good sense and judgment, but all in vain ; the self-devoted victim resolutely adhered to his determination. The surgeons, with the most assiduous attention, continued to exert their skill to save life and limb, but without success. In two days the wretched man expired.

I have already mentioned the high estimation Mrs. Hickey was held in by the gentlemen of both army and navy, especially by the latter, she and I greatly preferring them to the military as assimilating more with our dispositions and possessing a degree of plain, straightforward integrity more congenial to us than the perpetual ribaldry and offensive gasconade so prevalent in the French military officers. It may easily be imagined that amongst so numerous a body we found several disagreeable coxcombs. Some of these soon began to address anonymous love-letters to my Charlotte, which I would have let pass with the silent contempt they deserved had I not perceived they annoyed her so much as to affect her health, and she daily urged me to prevail upon the Admiral to let us depart. I therefore addressed the following letter to Mr. Suffren :

"SIR,

Although I am exceedingly unwilling to trespass upon your time, which I am aware must be fully occupied in matters of importance, yet the happiness of a most deserving wife leads me, sir, to entreat your attention for a moment. Our situation here, from various causes, has become extremely irksome and unpleasant, added to which the precarious state of Mrs. Hickey's health makes us both anxious to reach our destination. Upon her account solely I went to Lisbon to procure a passage from thence to India in a Portuguese ship. After waiting in that capital five tedious months we unfortunately embarked on board the *Raynha De Portugal*. A wretched and most disastrous voyage terminated by putting into this place, where we have now been upwards of three months. Mr. Chevillard, our host, has uniformly treated us with a degree of politeness and hospitality I fear rarely equalled, certainly impossible to be surpassed. The nature of the post he fills has, since the arrival of your fleet, kept him employed abroad almost the entire day, and to a gentleman of your experience and knowledge of the world it is scarcely necessary to observe that during the absence of the Master a house is by no means the same or so well regulated as when he is present. Mrs. Hickey flattered herself, sir, that upon your Excellency's arrival we should almost immediately have been sent to the coast of Coromandel. Every day drags heavily on, and the continued detention preys upon her spirits, her health being affected by the uncertainty as to when any opportunity may occur for our departure. Will you then, sir, with your usual humane attention, and for her gratification, inform me when you imagine it likely that an opportunity will present itself for our getting away, as it will be some alleviation to her misery to have a period ascertained for the termination of our distresses. Once more entreating your pardon for the liberty I have taken,

I have the honour to remain,

Your Excellency's most obedient and most humble servant,

W. HICKEY."

To this letter I received a very handsome and condescending answer from Mr. De Launay, the Admiral's secretary, written by the Admiral's special direction, in which he assured me the earliest opportunity that offered should be embraced, the Admiral very sensibly feeling for the disagreeable situation Mrs. Hickey must necessarily be in, and which he was earnestly desirous to put an end to by enabling us to proceed to a British settlement.

Every evening when at home Messieurs Gautier, Cuverville, De Salvert, L'Anglade and our worthy host, Chevillard, afforded us a great fund of entertainment by their excellent singing. Captain Gautier, who had considerable musical talents, wrote a song, which he also set to music, in compliment to Mrs. Hickey.

On the 23rd of February the *St. Michael*, a sixty-four, returned from a cruise in the China seas. On the same day the *Consolante* sailed again for Point de Galle and Columbo.

The 1st of March a small vessel came in from Mauritias announcing that General De Bussy was at that settlement and was to leave it for India the day after she left. The 2nd I dined with Admiral Suffren on board the *Heros*. He was, as I had always found him, extremely affable and attentive, assuring me I should have a passage in the first ship of any kind that sailed for the coast.

The 3rd Mrs. Hickey and I went early in the morning with Captains Cuverville and De Salvert upon a water party for a couple of days, returning on the 6th from a very pleasant excursion, when I had the mortification to find that the *Chaser*, a small ship of sixteen guns, had suddenly been dispatched by the Admiral for Tranquebar, and that a letter had been addressed to me by her Captain Joyeuze telling me that Mr. Suffren had just ordered him out of his own ship, the *Bellona*, a forty-gun frigate, to go upon a secret service in the little *Chaser*, and had further directed him to accommodate Mrs. Hickey and me with a passage to Tranquebar, but that we must be on board within an hour from that time, when he would with the utmost pleasure resign the cabin for our use and endeavour to render the short voyage as comfortable as possible in every respect. The opportunity thus lost was a grievous disappointment to us at the time, though perhaps it was lucky that we missed it, for the *Chaser* fell in with an English frigate that captured her after killing two-thirds of her crew.

On the 8th the *Cleopatra* of forty-four guns came in, having left General De Bussy the preceding day. The morning of the 9th a fleet appeared in the offing, and at one in the afternoon the *Fendant*, of seventy-four guns, bearing General De Bussy's flag at the main top-gallant masthead ; the *Hardi*, also a seventy-four ; and the *Argonaut*, of sixty-four, with thirty-eight transports, having the German regiment of the Prince Le Marque and other Europeans to the amount of two thousand five hundred on board and three hundred Caffrees came to an anchor in the harbour. I directly went off to the *Heros* for the purpose of requesting the Admiral (who had desired I never would scruple applying to him in person when I saw occasion) to bear me and my misfortunes in recollection and to mention the situation I was in to General De Bussy. I found Mr. Suffren oppressed by heat, sweltering under a heavy laced uniform suit of clothes which, however, in no way affected his temper or his customary manner. He in his usual polite terms assured me he should take the earliest occasion of mentioning my peculiarly hard case to the Count De Bussy, upon whom the chief command of both navy and army devolved. He then good humouredly began to talk of himself, facetiously observing that he felt like a hog in armour, for so long a period had elapsed since he had been obliged to dress otherways than in the lightest and thinnest clothing that he was really uncomfortable, but etiquette required his waiting upon the Commander-in-Chief properly equipped, even at the expence of his feelings.

At five o'clock the same afternoon Mr. Chevillard received a note from Mr. Launay wherein, after speaking of some official business, he added that should Mr. Hickey be disengaged the Admiral wished to see him. I therefore went off directly, when he told me several ships would be dispatched to Cuddalore in a few days and I had better apply to Monsieur Le Comte De Bussy for permission to embark on one of them. I accordingly on the following morning, being the 10th of the month, proceeded to the *Fendant*, where after waiting about half an hour I was introduced to the Comte, who upon being told the object of my visit, expressed his concern that I should have had the trouble of coming on board, especially as what I required rested entirely with Mr. De Suffren, that general having the entire and sole management of everything relative to the marine.

From the *Fendant* I went to the *Heros*. I found the Admiral reading some papers he had just received from Monsieur De Bussy with which he appeared highly pleased. He put one of them into my hand, desiring me to peruse it. I found it to be a letter from Mr. De Bussy written in very complimentary terms. After bestowing great panegyrics upon Mr. Suffren's conduct in the command of the fleet he entreated that he would continue to exercise his own superior judgment in all matters respecting the ships without any reference to him, as nothing should induce him ever to interfere in any maritime points. The Admiral then told me he thought the transports might be watered in a couple of days, after which they with a part of his squadron would sail for the coast, and sending for Mr. Launay he directed him to take particular care that Mrs. Hickey and I were accommodated in the best way circumstances would admit of.

In the afternoon Captain Cuverville brought the Prince Le Marque and two other officers of the Prince's regiment to Mr. Chevillard's house, where Mrs. Hickey and myself were introduced to them. The Prince was in every respect a perfect man of fashion and remarkably well-looking. He expressed himself very feelingly upon the extraordinary hardships Mrs. Hickey had undergone, declaring too that a strong dislike would operate in future against every Frenchman bearing the name of Des Roys for the worse than want of gallantry that person had betrayed, by his tyranny and absolute inhumanity in detaining her a close prisoner on board the Indiaman after being made acquainted with the distresses she had undergone during the voyage.

The 11th I dined by invitation on board the *Heros*, where the Admiral gave an entertainment to Mr. De Bussy and his suite. Upon my entering the cabin he very civilly enquired after Mrs. Hickey's health, congratulating us both upon the prospect there was of our being at last released from all our difficulties. He observed that a circumstance had occurred that morning which made it impossible for him to tell me the precise day the detachment would depart, but as it would probably take place very suddenly it would be prudent to hold ourselves in constant readiness. I assured him we were, and should continue prepared to embark at the moment we should be summoned.

The 12th I went round to the various gentlemen from whom we had received the utmost kindness and attention to express my own and Mrs. Hickey's grateful sense of their goodness, for which we returned our heartfelt thanks, and took our leave of most of them for ever. Mr. Suffren's first lieutenant, a fine gruff old fellow, who had shewn uncommon attachment to and regard for us, was particularly affected at our parting interview, observing that in all human probability we never might meet again, " Unless," said he, " the next conflict between the hostile fleets should terminate unfavourably for France," of which he entertained serious apprehensions from the disadvantage they laboured under of their ships, except the four recently arrived from Europe with General De Bussy, being all extremely foul, besides being greatly out of repair, several so leaky it was with difficulty they were kept afloat ; that, of course, they were unfit to contend against an active enemy whose ships were all in prime condition. He observed that the *Vengeur* especially was in a sad state, that they had made an attempt to heave her down at Trincomalay, but found her timbers so decayed and her whole frame so loosened she would not bear the strain, and they were obliged to relinquish it.

In the evening many of the captains, with the Prince

Le Marque and his staff, assembled at Mr. Chevillard's, where many unsuccessful efforts to be merry were made, and without actually knowing why the party sunk into silence and dejection. Mrs. Hickey and myself were sincerely affected at the thoughts of parting with several friends who had treated us with unexampled liberality, and those of that description who were present seemed equally to lament the thoughts of a separation from us.

We were at length relieved from this state of melancholy by the entrance of Captain Duchillon of the *Sphynx*, a lively, facetious man whose common boast used to be that he knew not what sorrow was and that he never allowed the caprices and changes of that fickle dame, Madam Fortune, to lower his spirits or cause him one moment's uneasiness. Observing the company were not so cheerful as he expected, and guessing at the cause, he good humouredly said, " I think it is highly probable we shall speedily meet again with these our agreeable and deservedly esteemed English friends, as Madras you know, comrades, must soon be in our possession, I trust previous to their having quitted it, but should that not be the case it cannot be long ere we renew the intimacy with them in Bengal, where (addressing himself to me) your old friend, Monsieur Suffren, with Monsieur De Bussy and a few thousand followers meditate paying their respects." This facetious gasconade created a general laugh, and though said in joke I really from all I had heard and seen feared there was too much foundation for it.

After supper, upon the party's separating, Captain Duchillon saluted Mrs. Hickey and with unaffected warmth wished her health and happiness, then shaking me cordially by the hand he said, " Adieu, my respected although lately acquired friend, and let me as you will in a few days see Lord Macartney request you to tell him that his old acquaintance Duchillon desired his best remembrances to him, and that as he has always had the honour of conveying him from his Government of Grenada in the West, so he hopes very shortly to convey him to France from his Government in the East." I promised the rattling captain that I would take the earliest opportunity of delivering his civil message to his lordship.

Just at the moment we were parting three guns were fired from the Admiral's ship, and soon after four more, which I was informed were signals for certain ships to unmoor, a few minutes after which I received a letter from Mr. Launay desiring me instantly to go on board the *Blake*, the commander of which had instructions to receive me and Mrs. Hickey. At eleven at night we accordingly left Mr. Chevillard's house, that gentleman being so occupied in dispatching the squadron that I had no opportunity of thanking him in person for the extraordinary generosity and kindness with which he had entertained us. I was therefore reduced to the necessity of doing so by letter. Captain Wolseley insisted upon attending us to the *Blake*, where he assisted in arranging everything for us in our cabin. Our baggage did not give us much trouble, as we had only a few changes of linen, for which, as already observed, we were indebted to our disinterested friends' generosity at Trincomalay. At one in the morning Captain Wolseley took his leave and I have never since had the happiness to see him, but I lately had the satisfaction to hear he is still living and attained the rank of an admiral. At parting he told me Mr. Bateman had applied both to Mr. De Bussy and Mr. Suffren for a passage in one of the men-of-war to the coast of Coromandel and received a positive refusal.

# CHAPTER VI

## FROM TRINCOMALAY TO MADRAS

EARLY in the morning of the 13th of March, 1783, we got under way, as did the *Heros*, bearing the Admiral's flag, the *Fendant* with General De Bussy's, the *St. Michael, Artisien, Sphynx, Petite Hannibal, Cleopatra, Fortune, Bellona, Coventry, Naiade*, and fourteen transports containing the whole of the European troops and stores. Having got out of the harbour, whilst working down the bay, a transport being upon a different tack ran foul of us with a dreadful crash, carrying away our bolt-sprit and damaging the head. Indeed, I thought from the shock we must both have gone to the bottom. We remained entangled upwards of an hour, when the transport's fore-mast went over the side, whereupon we got clear, but the transport was so much injured she was obliged to return to the harbour. When the accident happened the Admiral sent the *Naiade* to our assistance, and the boats of the fleet to remove the soldiers from the transport to the different men-of-war. By the great exertions of the frigate's seamen we had by evening got a new bolt-sprit rigged and our damages repaired so as to be able to proceed.

As Cuddalore was only a short distance from Ceylon, and nearly in the same meridian, I was surprized to find the fleet steering east-north-east. I afterwards learnt the reason of this was an apprehension of falling in with the British under Sir Edward Hughes, then supposed to be on their way from Bombay to Madras. Had the English admiral been lucky enough to have met the enemy the whole squadron, with more than two thousand of the military, must inevitably have been captured. After standing off the greater part of the night they altered their course to north.  Early in the morning of the 15th the fleet came to an anchor in Cuddalore roads, where the weather being moderate and little surf, before three in the afternoon the whole of the troops were landed.

Mr. Boissieres having given me a letter of introduction to the French surgeon-major, I went on shore in search of him, where I was told he resided about two miles from the fort inland.  I therefore walked out to his house through a burning sun, and on the way passed the skirts of a camp of Tippoo's, where a number of ferocious-looking fellows eyed me in such a manner as to create considerable alarm in my mind.  I, however, reached my destination in safety, where Mr. Panchemin received me very politely.  After making me drink a large glass of negus, which I stood in need of, being greatly fatigued and exhausted, he procured a native carriage drawn by a pair of bullocks in which he accompanied me back to Cuddalore for the purpose of taking Mrs. Hickey to his house.  He insisted upon going on board the *Blake* with me, which he did, conveyed Mrs. Hickey on shore, and in the cool of the evening all three went out to his pleasant mansion, where a plentiful repast of well-dressed curry and pilau awaited us, to which we did ample justice.  Our host shewed us into a spacious bed-chamber, but without window-frames, all the woodwork having been torn out by Tippoo's people to light their fires and cook their victuals.

The following morning upon conversing with Mr. Pan-chemin respecting the means of getting on to Madras, I had the mortification to hear it was impracticable for a European, particularly a female, to travel by land, the entire country being covered with Banditti, called Looties, who lived by plunder, sparing neither age nor sex, friend or foe, and who would certainly after robbing put us to death, as they did to all those who were unlucky enough to meet them.  Equally difficult was it to proceed by sea, not one of the French fleet intending to go further to the northward than Cuddalore, from whence they were all to return to Trin-comalay.  Thus circumstanced I thought we should be under the disagreeable necessity of going back to our former station.

On the 16th I went to the fort of Cuddalore to pay my compliments to General De Bussy, but he was so deeply engaged in business I could not see him. He, however, sent an aide-de-camp to apologize for not admitting me and to request I would dine with him. I accordingly went and was not a little surprized to meet there my shipmate, Mr. Bateman, of whom I took not the least notice. Upon enquiry I found that Colonel Des Roys had interested himself on Mr. Bateman's behalf, and by a personal application to Mr. Suffren had obtained permission for him to leave Trincomalay upon any vessel in which he could get a passage, and he had prevailed upon the commander of the *Artisien* to receive him on board, an act of kindness that availed nothing, for not being able to proceed to the coast he was compelled to return with Mr. Suffren's squadron to Trincomalay.

During my stay at Cuddalore the gloomy accounts given me at Trincomalay relative to the forlorn state of Fort St. George was corroborated. The non-appearance of the British fleet was considered as a convincing proof not only of their incapacity to cope with the French fleet, but of their being unable to keep the sea, otherwise they must have been at their station off Madras two months before. In short, from all I heard and all I saw I thought the influence and power of my countrymen was completely at an end in Asia.

The 18th the *Coventry* brought into the roads a large ship under Prussian colours, which upon coming to an anchor was observed to lay with a great heel. The *Coventry* had detained her upon finding from her journal or log book that she had been at Tranquebar, from which place she had taken several English officers on board and was proceeding with them to Madras. General De Bussy and Admiral Suffren conferred together respecting this vessel, after which the Admiral sent for me to tell me the Prussian was for Europe, and in his opinion under very suspicious circumstances, so much so that were he to be governed by his own opinion and sentiments he certainly would have kept her at least until he had an opportunity of further investigation into her legality, but that General De Bussy, always disposed to more lenient measures than he was, and wishing to act with moderation, did not consider himself justified in detaining her, as eventually she might be pronounced neutral property, and he could not deem her having a few English passengers a cause for seizing her. Mr. Suffren then continued, "I am glad on your account, Mr. Hickey, that this has happened as it will afford an opportunity for you to get to one of your settlements. Go therefore immediately on board and arrange matters for your departure, as I shall release her directly."

The boat I had gone off in leaking dreadfully, the men in her refused to take me to the Prussian, saying she lay so far out where there was so much sea running they should not be able to keep her afloat. I was consequently obliged to return on shore in search of another, which having procured I put off and had nearly passed the surf when three seamen hailed, entreating with great earnestness that I would give them a cast to the *Heros*, being already beyond their time of absence and no other boat to be got. I felt myself under too many obligations to several of their countrymen not to comply with their request. I therefore instantly repassed the surf and took them in. They were all stout, well-looking fellows, and expressed their thanks in very complimentary terms. Whilst in the boat I asked them some questions about the different sea fights between their fleet and ours, and what they thought of their Admiral, Monsieur Suffren, whereupon they all spoke together with great volubility, giving such a panegyrical character of Mr. Suffren as must have highly gratified his vanity had he heard it. They spoke of the different engagements as having all been hardly fought for by both parties, and that the two fleets had sustained a dreadful loss of men. "As you will admit," said they, "when told that since the *Heros'* arrival, in the India seas her entire crew have been thrice replaced the whole having been so many times destroyed. One of the men then concluded the account by again declaring the General was the greatest hero upon earth, and ended with " *Oui, ma foi, C'est une bougre determinée.*"

Having put these jolly tars on board their ship I proceeded to the Prussian which lay full two miles on the outside of all the ships except the *Coventry.* I found her upon a deep heel, but the contrary way to what I had observed in the morning, from which I supposed it was done purposely to scrape off the barnacles and clean her sides. I subsequently found that was not the case, and that this extraordinary inclining one way or the other arose from the peculiar construction of her bottom. She had been built by an enthusiastic schemer, who took it into his head that he could build a vessel of such a form as to outstrip every other, besides carrying more cargo than ships of the same burthen usually did, and this strange machine was the production. She sailed remarkably well, but never was upright, and when it blew fresh lay along so that everyone expected her every moment to upset altogether. Upon first putting to sea the commander and officers were so alarmed at the novelty of her movements that they put into Portsmouth to endeavour to get the evil corrected. The ship was docked, when the builders saw the nature of the ship's frame must occasion her to lay along with little weight or pressure from wind, but they did not conceive that any particular mischief or danger would arise from the ship's being so easily affected. They also gave it as their opinion that although the fault could not be entirely cured it might be materially lessened by fastening two timbers to either side of her keel. This was done and fully answered what was expected from it, but did not prevent her having the deep heel one way or other. The anxiety of the captain from having so strange a ship deprived him of his senses, so that for some months previous to their coming into Cuddalore, as above related, he had been confined to his cabin raving mad, the chief officer assuming the command.

Upon my getting on board a ferocious looking man, with

uncommon rough and hard features, rendered still more
uncouth by a large scar across his face, in a fierce and angry
voice and manner accosted me with, " Well, who are you,
and what have you to say ?  Are we to be still detained ? "
I replied that Admiral Suffren had sent me to take a passage
for myself and wife on that ship to Madras, or any English
settlement.  " Your wife," retorted the savage-looking man,
" no, no, friend, that will never do, by God !  No woman
can come here, I'll be damned if she can."  I thereupon
observed that the lady in question would submit to any
inconveniences, having been inured to uncommon hardships
and sufferings for several months, and that it was an object
of the utmost importance to us to get away from the French.
" I don't doubt it, by God," he answered.  " I believe
everybody must be anxious to get out of their clutches, but
I'll be damned if you can get in here."  I then observed
that I would willingly pay any sum he demanded for my
passage in his ship.  " My ship ! " said he.  " You are
damnably mistaken in supposing I have anything to do
with the infernal tub further than having the misfortune
to be a passenger.  No, no !  bad enough without that by
God ! "  I then requested to speak to the captain.  " You
won't gain much by that," said he, " for he is stark, staring
mad, so is his ship, and damn me !  but I believe so are we
all, and you as well as any of us or you would never talk of
bringing a female into such a ship as this."  Again I stated
my peculiar situation ; it was all in vain.

Finding I could make no impression upon this man, who
was the only spokesman, I addressed another gentleman
who stood upon deck, who shrugged his shoulders but made
no answer.  I was therefore compelled to leave the ship and
make for the shore.  On my way it struck me that I might
as well let Mr. Suffren know what had occurred, for which
purpose I stopped alongside the *Heros*, and although then
quite dark I went on board, and, as usual, was directly
shewn into the Admiral's cabin.  After apologizing for my
unseasonable intrusion, I mentioned the ill success of my
application for a passage and the positive refusal I had re-

ceived, whereupon Mr. Suffren said, "I am sorry, Mr. Hickey, you have had so much trouble in vain. I must then try what I can do, and hope I shall have better success." He then rang his bell. An attendant appearing, he ordered him to send the officer upon duty. The lieutenant forthwith coming, he directed him instantly to dispatch a boat to the *Coventry* frigate that lay close to the Prussian with orders that the latter should not upon any account be permitted to stir until Mr. and Mrs. Hickey, their servant and baggage were received and accommodated to their satisfaction on board. Having sent this concise but peremptory mandate, he laughingly said to me, "I fancy, sir, that will do our business and we shall get our object from Master Prussian, so good night. Let me hear to-morrow what has been done."

Before I was off my bed the following morning I received a letter signed "I. Nixon, Lieut.-Col. E.I. Company's Infantry," saying that as I was the sole cause of their ship's detention he, on behalf of himself and others, earnestly requested that myself and family would have the goodness to embark as soon as possible, the whole cabin being entirely at my disposal. To this pleasing information I returned an answer that the moment a boat could be obtained we would go off. At eight o'clock we accordingly did so, my poor Charlotte being much frightened at the surf, which was high, though we passed safely through it.

Mr. Suffren having desired I would let him know the result of his interference with the Prussian, I stopped at the *Heros* not only for that purpose but to offer my grateful thanks to the Admiral for the many favours conferred upon me. He expressed his satisfaction at my having succeeded, asking when I proposed embarking. I replied that I was then on my way, Mrs. Hickey being in a boat alongside. "Is she so?" said the Admiral. "I now heartily lament my ship has not been accustomed to receive the honour of visits from the fair sex, and therefore we are without the means of getting Mrs. Hickey on board, which I should have been happy to have done. But this being the case I must

go to her to offer my compliments and make my adieus."
As he was in his usual undress, he hastily called his servant,
with whom he retired for a few minutes to his private apartment, from which he returned with a uniform coat on and
fully equipped. Notwithstanding the ship had considerable
motion, rolling rather deep, he stepped nimbly down her side
wished Mrs. Hickey joy at the near approach of an end to
her most unfortunate voyage, and was altogether exceedingly
gracious and kind. He with much gaiety of manner observed
that as the present visit must necessarily be his last, he
should for his own sake make it as long as possible. I, however, soon discovered there was a liberal reason for his
saying this, for he had directed his steward to pack up a
variety of things which in about half an hour were put
into our boat, when, taking Mrs. Hickey by the hand, he
requested she would do him the honour to accept a few
articles of refreshment for the short voyage she still had to
perform, and some other trifles which he offered in token
of his respect and regard for his amiable prisoner. Then
gallantly kissing the hand he held, he condescendingly shook
me by the hand, and wishing us both a happy meeting with
our connections and friends, jumped up the side of his
ship with the same agility he had descended, and we
pushed off.

In a few seconds, to my infinite surprize, I saw the *Heros*
manned, her crew giving us three hearty cheers (no doubt
by the Admiral's desire), which we returned. This handsome
compliment was also paid us by two other ships as we passed
close to them, the *Sphynx* and *Cleopatra* frigate. At ten in
the morning we reached the Prussian, where we were received by the same rough personage I had encountered the
preceding day, whom I found to be the Colonel Nixon that
had written to me. Coming up to me, he offered his hand,
saying, " I take it for granted you are very angry with me
for the reception I gave you yesterday, but I was damnably
out of humour and really thought this truly extraordinary
vessel was not a proper conveyance for a female. Such as
it is, however, we must do our best for this good lady who

bears her own recommendation upon her intelligent countenance, and whose pardon I beg for my abrupt speeches of
yesterday. Had she been present they could not have been
made, for those mild and benign features would effectually
have softened and silenced me." After this gallant address
he took her by the hand and led her into the round house,
saying, "This, madam, is your room. The only condition
we are compelled to make is that you will allow the party
to mess in it, there being no other cabin large enough to
contain us, and I assure you eating is no small consideration
here, occurring regularly five times every day." He next
politely thanked me for the quickness with which I had come
off to the ship.

Two gentlemen just entering the cabin, the Colonel begged
leave to introduce two Portuguese shipmates, "Though
perhaps," observed he, " as no further necessity remains
for disguise it may be as well to announce them under their
proper titles. This therefore is Captain Hallam of His
Majesty's 102nd Regiment of foot, and this Major Alcock of
the Company's service. We three left the Southern Army
together, embarking at Tranquebar for Madras. Upon being
seized by the *Coventry* and forcibly taken into Cuddalore we
were apprehensive from the general character of Suffren
that he would, at any rate, lay hands upon us, even if he
allowed the ship to escape his clutches. I am too well and
too generally known to attempt any deception, but my
friends here, not being in a similar predicament, resolved to
assume the situation of Portuguese merchants, under which
description they hoped to escape imprisonment.

From these officers I had the supreme felicity to learn
that our prospects were not quite so forlorn as they had
been represented by the French, that although it was too
true the whole of our possessions upon the coast of Coromandel, but more especially Madras and its neighbourhood,
were suffering under the dreadful calamity of famine, yet
the fortress itself was in the highest order, well garrisoned
and fully prepared to resist any attack the enemy might
think proper to make ; that the Bengal treasury was very

rich, the country in the most flourishing condition, and a powerful reinforcement of men and stores of every description at that time on its way from thence to Madras, under the command of the very popular and distinguished officer, General Sir Eyre Coote. I was further informed that all the three engagements recently fought at sea had ended decidedly in favour of the British, notwithstanding the French had given so totally different an account of the issue of the battles, and had actually shewn me drawings of the relative state of the two fleets, whereby it was made evident that the English had much the worst of it, and only saved from utter destruction by a disgraceful flight. This was indeed a most gratifying history to me who had conceived we were undone.

I found what Colonel Nixon had premised respecting the frequency of the meals on board the Prussian strictly true; it was a perpetual scene of eating and drinking. The Colonel seemed to have the chief command; indeed he early told me such was the fact, the company's agent at Tranquebar having freighted the vessel for Madras and named him the chief director.

In the evening, Mrs. Hickey and myself only being in the cabin, I proposed examining Mr. Suffren's presents. We accordingly opened the parcels which we found to contain some papers of chocolate, a variety of preserves, confectionary, fruits, savoy cakes, liqueurs, etc., a pair of beautiful shawls, six pieces of very fine worked muslin, four pieces of Vizagapatam long cloth, four rich kincobs and six pieces of handkerchiefs. It was a magnificent present. Between the shawls was a note by Mr. Launay, written, as he stated, by Mr. Suffren's desire, requesting Mrs. Hickey's acceptance of the articles that accompanied, and to do away with any scruples she might feel. He was further directed to inform her that the whole was originally English property, having with large quantities of the same things fallen into the General's hands from a prize he had taken in the Bay of Bengal. Mr. Launay in a postscript added that he deemed it a necessary precaution to obtain Mr. Suffren's pass for us in ease we should on our progress to Bengal fall in with any French cruisers. This document I have preserved as a memorial of uncommon attention in so elevated a character as Mr. Suffren undoubtedly was, to two insignificant and unknown foreigners. The pass is in these words :

"PIERRE ANDRÈ DE SUFFREN, CHEVÁLIER GRAND CROIX DE L'ORDRE DE ST. JEAN DE JERUSALEM, CHEF D'ESCARDRE COMMANDANT LES FORCES NAVALES DE FRANCE DANS LES MERS DE L'INDE. Ayant permis a monsieur et madame Hiquet anglois de nation de passer dans les possessions angloises. Deffendons a tout Commandants des Batiments du Roy ou autres de Les arretter, et ordonnons de le laisser passer librement et sans retard quelconque.

A Bord du Heros le 22nd mars 1783.

LE CHR. DE SUFFREN."

For what reason it was post-dated I do not know, but it was so several days.

Colonel Nixon who under an affected misanthropy and general roughness possessed as much sensibility, and as great a degree of benevolence towards the whole human race, with as warm a heart as any person living, behaved to Mrs. Hickey and me with the most engaging attention. He listened to the melancholy tale of her sufferings with sympathetic compassion and feeling. Before we had been twelve hours in his company he gave me a pressing invitation to accept apartments in his house at Madras, assuring me his wife, with three fine girls, his daughters, would be happy to receive Mrs. Hickey and console her for her late misfortunes by shewing her every kindness in their power. He told me he had been absent from his family upwards of a twelvemonth, serving with the army first against Hyder Ali and since his death against an equal tyrant, his son, Tippoo Sultaun, as he was pleased to style himself ; that he had left the Southern Army only fourteen days before in company with Major Alcock and Captain Hallam. This unexpected civil invitation I thankfully declined, telling the Colonel that I had several old friends at Madras who would expect to receive me during my short sojourn in that place, amongst whom were Mr. Hall Plumer, Mr. Josias Du Prè Porcher, and Mr. Stephen Popham, and that I presumed the first gentleman would insist upon once more being my host. Colonel Nixon observed that he believed Mr. Plumer had left India and returned to Europe the last season ; Messieurs Porcher and Popham were, he knew, both at Madras.

The Colonel was so determined a *John Bull* that he could not bear to hear a Frenchman well spoken of, nor seemed to consider the people of that nation one remove from brutes. As he asked me many questions relative to the treatment I had met with while at Trincomalay, common justice, independent of my own inclination, made me a panegyrist, at which he was greatly surprized, declaring he did not conceive there was a Frenchman in existence possessed of generosity or even common humanity, but he readily admitted he was glad to find himself mistaken. He desired I would give him the names of those persons from whom I had received particular acts of liberality and kindness, that if the chance of war should ever put any of them within his power he might avail himself of the opportunity in some measure to repay the friendly acts shewn to an Englishman. With infinite pleasure I complied, and made out the following list, from every individual of which I had received innumerable instances of liberality. At the head I placed my constant and zealous friend, Captain Gautier, then my generous landlord Mr. Chevillard De Montesson, Admiral Suffren, the Counts De Bruyere and Adhemar, Le Chevalier De Salvert ; captains in the navy, Cuverville, Joyeuze, Duchillon, Trommelin and Mallè, Lieutenant L'Anglade of the same regiment as Gautier, lieutenants in the navy, Beddel, Touris, Mevillard and Ritchirie (the last named has since figured as one of the tyrant Bonaparte's admirals), Messieurs Boissieres, Panchemin, De Grange, the Commissary General, and De Launay, the Admiral's secretary. It would have been an unpardonable mark of ingratitude had I omitted to put down the names of Mr. and Mrs. Vansenden, the Dutch chief and his lady, from whom we received a thousand instances of generous hospitality. This list I delivered to Colonel Nixon, remarking when I did so that I might have materially increased it by adding the names of every naval and military man with whom I was acquainted at Trincoma-lay, with the single exception of Colonel Des Roys.

# CHAPTER VII

## LIFE IN MADRAS

ON the 21st of March, at about ten o'clock in the morning, we came to an anchor in Madras Roads, when Colonel Nixon, Major Alcock and Captain Hallam immediately went on shore. In little more than two hours Colonel Nixon returned in the accommodation or Government boat, renewing in Mrs. Nixon's name the most pressing solicitation that we would take up our abode at her house. "However," added the Colonel, "it is but fair in me to tell you that you are not likely to be in want should you still decline my wife's invitation, as I think I left half a dozen different persons waiting upon the beach for your landing ready to seize upon you, so that in the amicable contest I fear we shall stand no chance. Come along, therefore, and we must endeavour to divide you among us as well as we can, but Popham protests you must and shall be his exclusive guests."

My dear girl, who at no period of her life bestowed much time at her toilet, was soon ready, when the worthy Colonel superintended the getting her into the boat and escorted us on shore. The surf was high, but we got safely through it. On the beach stood Mr. Popham and Mr. Porcher. The latter after congratulating us upon our arrival said he was obliged reluctantly to yield us up to Mr. Popham, who claimed a prior right to him. Popham told me everything was ready for our reception at his house in the Black town, and stepping into his chariot we were driven to it, Porcher having accepted his invitation to dinner.

This Mr. Popham is the person I have before mentioned as coming to India with Sir John Day. Mr. Popham was always an extraordinary being. Blest with superior talents, improved by a classical education, he fell a martyr to a speculative disposition and a strong inclination for gambling, the latter foible having so deeply involved him he could not remain in his native country. At the time I arrived at Madras he, by his abilities, had raised himself to the top of his profession, and had for many months been Attorney to the Company, which honourable and lucrative situation added to his private practice must very speedily have secured to him a handsome independent fortune had he stuck to the law alone, instead of which he had twenty wild schemes on foot at one and the same time, which prevented his attending to his business in court, so that every person who employed him had too much reason to complain of his shameful negligence. He had recently built an immense mansion for his own residence, one half of which only was finished when we went to it, the workmen being engaged in the other part. He was likewise building a street in the same neighbourhood consisting of about sixty houses, besides which he had just purchased the hull of the *Hertford* East Indiaman, which ship had been wrecked in a monsoon gale a few days after the fatal one we encountered in the month of November, and was by the extraordinary agitation of the sea washed so far up on the beach as, when the storm subsided, to be left high and dry. This odd purchase he made with a view to converting part of the timber and the whole of the ironwork to his buildings, for which purpose he had about forty persons employed in breaking her up, the labour thereof amounting to so much as to render the materials produced of considerably more cost than he could have purchased them for entirely new.

Mr. Popham, having shewn Mrs. Hickey to a suite of rooms delightfully situated up two pair of stairs, commanding a very extensive and beautiful prospect in every direction, proposed introducing me to the Governor, Lord Macartney, a compliment he thought I ought to pay without delay. We accordingly immediately went to the Government house in the Fort. Lord Macartney gave me a most gracious reception, after the customary salutations, telling me that my father was an old friend of his, which I well knew, having often seen his lordship, when Sir George Macartney, in St. Albans Street. I likewise recollected frequently to have heard my father say that when Sir George was first appointed Ambassador of Russia he was prevented from setting off for St. Petersburgh by a want of money to discharge some pressing creditors, and that he (my father) had lent him five hundred pounds to enable him to discharge them, and that after several of his own connections had positively refused to assist him. My father had been a fellow Collegian with him in the University of Dublin.

His lordship made many enquiries respecting the state of the French fleet, all of which I answered to the best of my knowledge. After having so done I, without in the least softening the matter, told him what Mr. Suffren had repeatedly said about him, at which he appeared greatly hurt, declaring the French commander most unjust in charging him with want of delicacy or politeness, for that he had invariably answered the applications relative to an exchange of prisoners, although from some peculiar circumstances he had it not in his power to establish a cartel. I also delivered Captain Duchillon's message in the very words he spoke, at which his lordship laughed heartily, observing that were it his fate again to be in the situation he was when at Grenada there was not an officer in the navy of France whom he would prefer sailing with to Captain Duchillon, whom he knew by experience to be an honourable and kind-hearted man, to whom he felt himself under high obligation for the greatest attention and civility whilst on board his ship on the passage from the West Indies.

After a conversation of nearly two hours, Lord Macartney remarked that it was then the hour of dinner ; he therefore hoped Mr. Popham and I would do him the favour to stay, which, of course, we did, Popham sending home to Mrs. Hickey to apologize for his absence the first day of her being his guest.

We sat down to what seemed to me very indifferent fare

for a Governor's table. Indeed, his lordship, at the beginning of the meal, said the melancholy effects of the dreadful famine with which they had been afflicted, though lessened, had by no means ceased ; that provisions were still scarce from the distress of the country people who used to bring poultry and other articles to market, and that in such a time of dearth he thought it right to be as frugal as possible.

As it happened to be one of the public days we found a large party assembled. Amongst the company present was my old friend Colonel Pearse, of the Bengal Artillery, then commanding a detachment of several thousand men recently arrived from Calcutta, and preparing to take the field by joining the Southern Army assembling to attack Cuddalore. Another of his lordship's guests was Sir John Burgoyne, Colonel of a noble regiment of light dragoons in His Majesty's service, also Colonel Floyd and some other officers of the same regiment. We had, too, Sir Erasmas Gower, of the *Medea* frigate, my friend Mr. Porcher, etc.

The whole party were much disconcerted at hearing of the important reinforcements, both naval and military, that had joined Mr. De Suffren from Europe, under the Count De Bussy, of which no information had reached Madras until I gave it, all communication to the southward being cut off by Tippoo's troops being in complete possession of the country between Cape Comorin and Fort St. George. This information became of more consequence from the unaccountable absence of Sir Edward Hughes's fleet, also from the hourly expectation of the arrival of a number of Indiamen from Europe, and two large country ships with military stores, men and money from Calcutta, Sir Eyre Coote, commander-in-chief, being on board one of them, so that there was but too much probability of these two ships and the East Indiamen being intercepted and cut off by the French.

The 22nd in the morning, upon Mrs. Hickey and my descending to the breakfast-room on the middle floor, we there saw a gentleman sitting at the window, having much more the appearance of a corpse than a living creature. I never beheld a person looking so ill, an absolute skeleton. Upon our entering the room he made an effort to rise, but tottered from extreme weakness, on perceiving which my darling girl was greatly distressed, kindly entreating he would keep his seat, and expressing her concern at seeing him so much indisposed. In a languid and feeble voice he returned thanks, saying he was materially better than he had been. Mr. Popham coming in, introduced us to the invalid as Captain Isaac Humphreys, private secretary and aide-de-camp to Colonel Pearse. He had been long confined from a jungle fever (something like our ague) with which he had been attacked whilst in a forest on the march from Bengal, and which had brought him to the brink of the grave. I afterwards became very intimate with this gentleman.

Breakfast being over, I went to call upon several of my former acquaintances, particularly Major Cotgrove, Mr. Perryn, Porcher, Torin, Sullivan, the Advocate-General, Dr. Lucas, and Captain Sydenham, the Fort Major. I likewise left my name at Sir John Burgoyne's.

Upon returning home I found the famous Mr. Paul Benfield sitting with Popham and Mrs. Hickey. He had left England many months subsequent to me, having been only eighty-one days from London to Madras overland. He had done me the honour to visit me several times in St. Albans Street, he having quitted India soon after I did, and getting home long before me. I had also been invited to, and was present at, some grand entertainments he gave at his magnificent house in Portland Place, our intercourse continuing until he one morning upon calling at my father's found Mr. Edmund Burke there, who had then recently attacked him in Parliament as a notorious defaulter, who had embezzled large sums of his employer's money which came to his hands from official situations he filled, had basely and iniquitously robbed and plundered the Nabob of Arcot, and was in many respects the greatest delinquent that ever had left India. Benfield appeared extremely awkward and embarrassed, spoke not a word from the time of his entrance, and in a few minutes made his retreat ; from this time he never more called, and if I accidentally met him in public he always looked another way to avoid the necessity of a salutation, concluding, as I presume, that a member of a family upon the intimate terms he observed mine were with a person who had avowed himself so hostile towards him as Mr. Burke was not a fit acquaintance for him.  I was therefore a good deal surprized at receiving so early a visit from him at Madras.  He made a number of civil speeches, invited us in pressing terms to his house on Choultry Plain, offered us the use of his various equipages, and having learnt that Mrs. Hickey was fond of the exercise of riding on horseback, said he would send an Arab she would admire that would carry her delightfully, being as docile an animal as any in Europe.  He accordingly did send a most beautiful creature, also another for me.  A European servant attended with them, who said his master had directed him to wait upon me every evening to receive my orders for the following day.

Mrs. Hickey had this day a number of female visitors, amongst the first of whom was Mrs. Nixon, with two of her daughters, Lady Gordon, Mrs. Barclay, Mrs. Floyd, Mrs. Taner, Mrs. Latham, the lovely Widow Maclellan, the Belle Johnston, etc.  The return of these and many other visits, with the numerous parties made for our entertainment, occupied several days.

The 24th the *Medea* sailed on a look-out cruise.  That day we spent very agreeably with Colonel Nixon's family, whom we found truly amiable.  In the evening the Colonel said he must be absent for a few minutes in order to pay his respects to the Governor.  He accordingly walked across the parade.  After a very short absence he returned.  Upon entering the room where a large party were then assembled he bellowed out for the servants to attend, upon whose appearance he ordered them instantly to blow out all the candles except one.  During this whimsical operation Mrs. Nixon looked on with the utmost composure, without interfering, but as soon as the candles were extinguished, addressing her husband, she mildly said " Pray, my dear, what is the meaning of this odd freak ? " To which he replied : "I have just been to the Government House, where there was not a single taper burning, and that being the case, by God! madam, you ought to consider yourself damned well off in having a pair of candles." " Oh! if that be all, my dear," said Mrs. Nixon, "let the candles be lighted again," which was instantly done. The Colonel then gave us the following ludicrous account of the visit he had just been upon.

"I went up the great staircase without seeing a single domestic or any person whatsoever ; the hall was in the same deserted state, without light. I therefore gave one of my most powerful holloas ! (and he almost deafened us with the imitation). ' Is there a living soul in the place or not ? ' Whereupon a mean-looking little rascal, who I verily believe had been purloining the bread and butter, popped his head out of a door that looked like a pantry, with a cocoanut shell about one-fourth part full of oil and a single wick. Upon the little fellow's nearer approach I discovered him that contemptible wretch Green, a sort of understrapping *sub sub* secretary of the Governor's. I enquired whether Lord Macartney was at home, adding that the question was superfluous from the state of the mansion. The despicable little animal answered that his lordship was out taking his evening's airing in a carriage, but he expected his lordship home every moment. ' The devil you do ! ' said I, ' and give me leave to ask,' ' Is this the way the house is darkened to receive him ? ' ' Candles will be lighted when his lordship comes in,' said the little *maître d'hôtel*. ' Oh, ho ! will they so,' says I, ' then damn my blood but this is a good lesson for me who left about thirty wax candles blazing in my hall. They shall be extinguished directly, and for once I'll live like a lord ! So good night, my little soup maigre, water-gruel visage. Tell your master —Oh, zounds ! I beg your pardon, Mr. Sec., the Governor I ought to have said—that I, Colonel Nixon, have been here to pay my respects,' and having had sufficient of the little *sub sub* I walked away."

Before seven o'clock the following morning Colonel Nixon called upon me at Mr. Popham's and expressed both surprize and pleasure at finding me up so early. "I am glad to see this," said he; "it augurs well, looks like a man of business, and therefore I'll be your first client." He then pulled from his pocket a bundle of papers which he desired me to read over attentively, and when I had so done to read a sketch of a memorial he intended to present to the Governor and Council, demanding redress of some great grievances he had suffered by two supercessions that had recently occurred whereby he was deprived of the rank of full colonel, which he was strictly entitled to, not only from his length of service but from actual seniority, and he desired me to make such alterations in the memorial as I deemed prudent. Having complied with his wish, and new modelled the document without taking away any of its energy, I returned the same to him, with which he appeared perfectly satisfied, presenting me with one hundred and fifty pagodas for the trouble I had taken. This was nearly sixty pounds sterling. He also hoped his commencement would prove fortunate, and that I should meet with the success he was sure I deserved.

This day a signal was made from the flag-staff that a strange sail was standing for the Roads from the southward. At first it was hoped she would prove one of the fleet of India-men from Europe or, what was of equal consequence, one of Admiral Sir Edward Hughes's squadron from Bombay. Everybody with the most eager solicitude ran out of the fort to the Master Attendant's apartment upon the beach to mark the approach of the vessel, who continued standing in with her top-sails lowered down upon the caps, and without shewing any colours until within a quarter of a mile of the surf, when she hoisted a French Jack and commenced a brisk fire upon a large Dutch prize and two country ships, although all three were as close in as they could possibly lay. The prize-master on board the Dutchman, by this time having recognized the stranger to be the *Coventry*, which had been taken by Suffren, and that she was preparing to board him, instantly cut his cables and let his ship drift through the outer surf and take the ground, in preference to allowing her to fall into the hands of the enemy. To the inexpressible astonishment of many hundred spectators assembled on the ramparts and the beach not a shot was fired from the fort, notwithstanding with unparalleled effrontery the enemy stood so near in that she undoubtedly might have been sunk by the battery of the sea line which bore full upon her, she having the impudence to heave to and lay in that state for above half an hour. Having thus driven our three ships on shore, she leisurely made sail to the north-east. After she had got an offing of about two miles the fort began to pepper away at an immense rate both shot and shells without the least effect. Upon enquiring into the cause of this strange conduct we were informed that the keys of the store-rooms under the works, in which the ammunition was kept, had been mislaid and could nowhere be found for more than an hour. An unpardonable neglect somewhere, and hardly to be credited that such a disgraceful event could have occurred in a British fortress, and that too during the midst of an active and severe war. Yet so it undoubtedly was. The civilians of Madras were exceedingly smart in their animadversions upon this occasion.

In the evening the *Medea*, who had been looking out for the two valuable ships from Bengal without success, returned to the Roads, Captain Gower, his officers and crew being very indignant upon receiving information of the circumstance respecting the *Coventry* and the insult thus offered by an enemy's frigate to the British flag. During the short time the *Medea* was at sea Captain Gower had been violently attacked with the gout and was brought on shore upon a mattress, totally incapable of moving hand or foot.

The following day (the 26th) a signal was made in the morning for seven ships coming in from the south-south-east. These it was hoped would prove the expected Indiamen from Europe or, if not them, a part of Sir Edward Hughes's fleet, but as the strangers advanced it was ascertained that some of them were line of battle ships and foreign. The usual private signal being made from the fort was not answered, nor did they shew any colours.

Captain Gower, notwithstanding the dreadful pain he laboured under, was brought down to the water-side to be conveyed on board his ship. Lord Macartney upon seeing this went up to the palankeen he was in, and said, "Captain Gower, as you are so extremely ill surely you had better not think of embarking, but remain quietly on shore. There can be no risk of the *Medea*, which can be protected by the fort." "I thank your lordship," replied Captain Gower, "for your attention to me,.but on board my ship I must and will go, it being my proper station sick or well, nor do I choose to rely upon the protection of a fort that suffers an enemy to insult it for two hours together without firing a shot!" He accordingly was put into a boat and carried to his ship.

The *Medea* then made the private navy signal, of which no notice was taken by the strangers. By this time they were within two miles, when I recognized the leading ship to be the *Cleopatra*, closely followed by the *Fendant*, of seventy-four guns, both those vessels sailing uncommonly well. We afterwards learnt that the others were the *St. Michael, Artisien, Sphynx, Little Hannibal* and *Bellona* frigate.

Captain Gower, well acquainted with what the *Medea* could do, and who had upon many occasions run round Mr. Suffren's fleet, was greatly surprized at perceiving two ships with which he was wholly unacquainted, and that seemed to sail in a very superior style to any of his old friends. Considerably alarmed at their rapid approach he deemed it high time to get under way. He therefore slipped his cables (the *Cleopatra* and *Fendant* being within little more than a mile) and in about four minutes there appeared one entire crowd of sail, standing directly away before the wind to the northward. It was a most interesting scene ; all eyes anxiously followed them. While in sight the two Frenchmen seemed to gain upon the *Medea* so fast that she was given up for lost ; the rest of the French squadron jogged on gently under their top-sails.

On the 27th we had the pleasure to hear that the seven French ships were seen in the offing, standing to the south-ward, from which it was concluded the *Medea* had escaped, as if not she would have been with them. In the afternoon we had the further gratification to see that frigate once more at an anchor in Madras Roads. Captain Gower admitted there was not a doubt but he should have been taken had the enemy chosen to continue the pursuit a couple of hours longer than they did, instead of doing which when abreast of Sadrass they hauled their wind and stood to the eastward, from which he supposed they had a greater object in view than that of capturing his frigate, and did not deem it prudent to run further to the northward, the current then setting strong in that direction. He was right in his conjecture.

The 28th the same seven ships again passed through the Roads, at the distance of six miles from the shore, standing under very easy sail to the northward. Great apprehensions were therefore entertained for the safety of the two rich vessels from Bengal, as well as for the outward bound India fleet.

On the 31st two large ships were seen in the south, which as soon as their signals were visible proved to be the *Resolution* and *Royal Charlotte* from Bengal, Sir Eyre Coote's distinguishing flag, as commander-in-chief, flying at the top-gallant masthead of the former. Everybody was delighted at this sight, not only on account of the advantages likely to arise from his taking the field in person, but from his being revered by the whole army, both European and native, who had the greatest confidence in his skill and abilities as a general officer, besides which the supply he brought with him of men, money and military stores, all which were greatly wanted, was of the highest importance.

The first boat that came from the *Resolution* threw a damp upon the general joy that had prevailed on these two ships safe arrival by bringing the sad tidings that Sir Eyre

Coote was dying, if not already dead.  The principal medical gentlemen of the settlement were forthwith sent off to the *Resolution* to give their aid to the lamented officer.

In the evening Sir Eyre Coote was brought on shore in a state of determined apoplexy, in which unhappy state he remained, quite insensible, until the following morning when he expired.  We then learnt these particulars from Captain Mercer of the *Resolution*, who was universally considered to be as able a seaman and skilful a navigator as ever stepped a quarter-deck.

This captain, being sensible of the danger that existed of his falling in with some of the enemy's cruisers, kept as far out at sea as he dared venture to do without risking the being driven off the coast altogether by the current.  His intention was thus to keep out at sea until in the latitude of Madras, then immediately to haul in for the land.  In the morning of the 28th (March) he discovered two sail in the north-east quarter, courses down, in consequence of which he hauled more off the land.  He, however, soon had the mortification to find the two strange sail had seen him and his consort, and were in full chase.  By noon they had gained considerably ; soon after that hour five more ships of force were seen in different directions, completely surrounding them.  Being senior officer, he spoke his consort, giving him instructions how to act during the night.

From the moment the strange ships hove in sight Sir Eyre Coote shewed so extraordinary a degree of anxiety and uneasiness of mind as to make Captain Mercer quite apprehensive it might affect his health.  By evening of the day they saw them the enemy were within two miles of the English ships, but in the course of the night Captain Mercer manœuvred with such skill and so successfully that at daybreak of the 29th they had increased the distance to nearly nine miles, the French then standing the contrary .way to the *Resolution* and *Royal Charlotte*.  They renewed the chase for the whole of the day, and by evening the *Cleopatra* was so near as to commence a fire upon the *Royal Charlotte* from her bow guns, none of which took effect.  '

As soon as it was quite dark the two ships stood due east for one hour, then suddenly took in every sail, thus remaining stationary and the enemy losing sight of them. In the morning of the 30th they had the pleasure to find this scheme had completely answered, there being only one sail just discernible from the masthead, bearing west. By reckoning they were now in the latitude of Madras; Captain Mercer therefore determined to let the ships continue without canvas, hoping so small an object as the bare masts might escape observation. Unfortunately that was not the case, as two hours afterwards three of the French ships were seen standing for them. Sir Eyre Coote, who had never quitted the deck, and had little or no sleep for two nights, suddenly fell from the chair in which he was sitting in a fit. In an hour he so far recovered as to enquire, with much agitation, whether the enemy gained upon them, and whether Captain Mercer thought there was a chance of escaping. Captain Mercer, observing him to be in so desponding a state, assured him he had not a doubt but that they should reach Madras in safety, although, in fact, he had scarce a hope left of so doing. He then used all his influence to prevail upon the General to take some refreshment and lay down for a few hours to recruit nature. He thereupon consented to drink some mulled madeira wine, but said attempting to sleep would be fruitless.

The enemy gained considerably, but towards evening were still at a distance of four miles. Captain Mercer told Sir Eyre that just before dark he would stand to the northward, which he trusted would induce the French to imagine he meant to push for Bengal again, and that they would follow in that direction. He then hailed the *Royal Charlotte*, directing her commander to keep as close as possible upon his quarter and when quite dark to hand all his upper sails and haul in direct for the land. The night favoured them, being extremely squally with hard rain. Sir Eyre Coote's agitation, if possible, increased; he every minute enquired if the ships were seen. About midnight the man stationed at the bolt-sprit end to look out suddenly called out that a large ship was running on board of them, whereupon Sir Eyre instantly fell into a fit of apoplexy, from which he never recovered. This alarm arose from the *Royal Charlotte* having her tiller rope broke in a severe gust of wind, upon which she flew short round and very nearly fell aboard the *Resolution*.

In the afternoon of the day on which the General died his funeral took place with great solemnity. The church, from a want of room in the fort, had, during the famine, been entirely filled with bags of rice. It therefore became necessary to clear the principal aisle, at the end of which near the pulpit the grave was dug. The corpse was carried from the Admiralty House by eight European sergeants, the pall being borne by Lord Macartney and five of the principal gentlemen of the settlement. The funeral party was commanded by Sir John Burgoyne, and consisted of his regiment of Light Dragoons, part of the 101st regiment of Foot, a complete regiment of Hanoverians, with two battalions of Sepoys. These Corps formed a street through which the procession passed, preceded by the Hanoverian band playing the Dead March in Saul, the whole having a very grand though melancholy effect. The church being situated in a narrow and confined part of the fort did not admit of the three volleys being fired ; the Dragoons which were appointed to fire them therefore upon the body entering the church marched off to the parade for the purpose, and did so to quick time, the fifes playing "Nancy Dawson," an awkward change from the solemn ceremony and certainly ill-judged, notwithstanding in a military sense it might be strictly correct.

Sir Eyre Coote's corpse was the only one I ever heard of that went through two formal burials. Lady Coote, who was in England at the time of the General's death, being desirous that her husband's remains should be deposited in the family vault with his ancestors, sent orders to that purpose to India, in consequence whereof the body was taken out of the grave at Madras, put on board ship, and conveyed to England, where it was once more interred in the presence of a number of relations and friends of the deceased.

# CHAPTER VIII

## ADMIRAL SIR EDWARD HUGHES AND THE RIVAL FLEETS

ON the 2nd of April Mrs. Hickey and I went to pass the day at Mrs. Barclay's garden-house a few miles from Madras, where both she and Mr. Barclay, her husband, gave us a most pressing invitation to fix our abode altogether, which I promised to do in a week or ten days, as it would take that time to prepare a sufficient stock of apparel for Mrs. Hickey and myself. In going to their house a truly melancholy spectacle met our sight, at which my dearest Charlotte was beyond measure affected, the whole road being strewed on both sides with the skulls and bones of the innumerable poor creatures who had there laid themselves down and miserably perished from want of food, being on their way from different parts of the country to Madras, in the hope of obtaining relief there, a relief it was not, alas! in the power of the British inhabitants to afford from the thousands and tens of thousands that daily flocked towards the Presidency.

While sitting after dinner at Mr. Barclay's we heard a salute from the fort, and soon after received the agreeable intelligence that Sir Edward Hughes with his fleet was arrived from Bombay. In the evening Mr. Popham came out to say he had visited the Admiral, who, having heard there was a gentleman at Madras that had very recently been a prisoner at Trincomalay, was desirous of having some conversation with him ; that he (Mr. Popham) had therefore promised I would accompany him to breakfast on board the following morning. He and I accordingly went off before seven o'clock of the 3rd in the Government boat. Having passed the surf, the Admiral's barge, which was waiting there for the purpose, received and rowed us in capital style to the *Superb*, the flag-ship. Upon getting up her side we were received by two officers, who conducted us aft. In passing the quarter-deck I there saw a gentleman in a lieutenant's uniform whose face was perfectly familiar to me. I had, however, then no opportunity of asking about him.

Sir Edward Hughes received us with the utmost politeness. After asking me a number of questions respecting Admiral Suffren and his fleet, all which I answered very fully and particularly, I mentioned the handsome terms in which the French commander always spoke of him, at which he appeared highly gratified, returning the compliment by pronouncing an encomium and panegyric upon Mr. Suffren's qualities and talents as a seaman, saying, " Mr. Suffren, sir, is as gallant a man as ever lived, of which I have in many instances been an eye-witness. In the last action, after fighting his ship in a manner bordering upon desperation and performing wonders, the superior fire of the *Superb* and *Sultan* completely silenced that of the *Heros*. Those two British ships continued pouring broadsides into her without her being able to return a single gun. My ship being within pistol shot, I could distinctly see all that occurred. Her upper deck was more than once completely cleared, scarce a man remaining upon it except Mr. Suffren himself, who ran up and down the quarter-deck like a lunatic, crying out most earnestly for some fortunate shot to take him off. I have never thought of the scene but with astonishment, and how the *Heros* sustained such a tremendously galling fire is still incomprehensible to me. A very few minutes must, however, have decided her fate by inevitably sending her to the bottom, when an accidental explosion took place on board the *Superb*, blowing up the entire forecastle, whereby thirty of my brave fellows were destroyed and the rest of my crew thrown into confusion, not only from the lamentable circumstance itself but from the fire's communicating to the middle part of the ship, which was soon in a blaze. The extraordinary exertions of my officers, ably supported and aided by the ship's crew, at last extinguished the flames and saved us from destruction. In the midst of this truly awful and terrific misfortune the *Hannibal*, having silenced her former adversary, came down in the most resolute and determined manner, running in between the *Sultan* and *Heros*, whereby he clearly preserved his Admiral's ship. The conflict ended only with the daylight, both squadrons being at that time so shattered the battle could not have continued much longer, the ammunition of both being nearly expended. The two fleets then, as if by agreement, let go their anchors higgledy-piggledy, a Frenchman and an Englishman close together, and thus they remained not only the whole of that night but all the next day, mutually repairing their damage, in the evening getting up their anchors and separating like tired, worn-out bulldogs after a desperate struggle, neither party shewing the least inclination to renew the contest. The fact is, it was a drawn battle ; neither did nor would have been justified in calling themselves victors. The slaughter in both fleets was dreadful, and our rigging almost totally destroyed."

Sir Edward requesting I would give him a list of the enemy's fleet, with my observations upon the condition of each ship, I sat down in his cabin and there made out the following :

*Heros :* 74. The Admiral's ship. The hull in a tolerable state, but the whole of the rigging greatly worn and no new on board to replace it.

*Hannibal :* 74. Count De Bruyere, second in command. Hull tolerable, rigging very indifferent, and the mainmast badly sprung.

*Illustre :* 74. Count Adhemar, third in command. The ship very leaky, the rigging as bad as either of the last-named ships, and in want of a set of top-sails.

*Fendant :* 74. The Count De Bussy came from France in this ship a few weeks back. Every article on board, as well as the ship itself, in the best condition and greatest order. The *Fendant* is by far the best sailer of the fleet.

*Hardi* : 74. Another of De Bussy's squadron. In perfect order in every respect.

*Vengeur* : 64. So extremely leaky and generally out of repair that it was with difficulty she was kept above water.

*Argonaut* : 64. Leaky, rigging all to pieces.

*Ajax* : 64. In tolerable condition, having recently been refitted and new rigged at the Isle of France.

*Artisien* : 64. Her upper works very open, rigging indifferent.

*Sphynx* : 64. Hull in tolerable condition, rigging the same, but short of sails.

*Flamand* : 64. Tolerable state in every respect.

*St. Michael* : 64. One of De Bussy's squadron. Leaky, amply stored.

*Le Severe* : 64. In a good state as to hull, rigging very indifferent.

*Brilliant* : 64. Much in want of repair and stores.

*Petit Hannibal* : 50. In good order in every respect.

*Cleopatra* : 44. A very fine frigate, one of De Bussy's squadron, and in the best possible state.

*Consolante* : 44. Lately refitted at the Isle of France.

*Pourvoyeuse* : 44. Almost tumbling to pieces, and in want of every kind of stores.

*Apollo* : 36. Recently from France. In good condition.

*Le Fin* : 32. The same.

*Coventry* : 32. An English prize. Out of repair, both hull and rigging.

*Bellona* : 32. Very leaky, rigging good.

*Naiade* : 26. In good condition in every respect.

*Fortune* : 20. The same, being recently from Europe.

After I delivered the above to Sir Edward he sent for the second lieutenant, whom he requested to shew to me every part of the ship. I was equally surprised and pleased at the contrast between the main deck of the *Superb* and that of the *Heros*, the former being delightfully neat and clean throughout, the latter disgusting to behold from filth and dirt. Whilst between decks I observed the same gentleman pass I had seen upon the quarter-deck on coming on board, who immediately came up and, addressing me by name, hoped I was well and had left all my family so. Still at a loss who this was, I was obliged to acknowledge that fact, when he told me his name was Norris, and I then recognized an old London acquaintance whom I used frequently to meet in parties at Mrs. Broadhead's and at my sister's. He at that time commanded a troop in a regiment of Light Dragoons, had an excellent house and establishment, kept his carriage, and was in possession of an estate of two thousand pounds per annum, the whole of which he ran through. When nearly at the end of his career a daughter of the wealthy Mr. Andrew Moffatt danced with him at an assembly, became desperately enamoured, and in ten days afterwards went off with him to Gretna Green, where the useful Cyclops joined them together in holy matrimony. The young lady being a favourite child, it was generally supposed her father would easily be reconciled to the match and would give her at least thirty thousand pounds, but, on the contrary, the old man proved so obdurate he never would see either of them or advance a single guinea. Various attempts were made to soften him, but all in vain ; he was inexorable. Thus the distresses and embarrassments of Captain Norris were increased by being burthened with an extravagant wife whom he had married solely from an interested motive, in the hope of clearing himself from all difficulties by means of her fortune. Disappointed in this object, the wife became his abhorrence, for the expected cash failing, she had not qualifications to fix the affections of a gay, volatile young man. The newly made husband, indifferent even to appearances, forthwith abandoned her to her fate, which she, being viciously disposed, soon rejoiced at and became an absolute profligate. He, who had in early youth been a midshipman in the navy, availed himself of an intimate friend's going into the Mediterranean in the command of a frigate, to accompany him, resuming his old profession. This friend promoted him to the rank of lieutenant, in which situation he acquired a considerable sum of prize money, liquidated his debts, sold his troop of Dragoons, and finally accepted the situation of third lieutenant on board the *Superb* upon Sir Edward Hughes being appointed to the India station. At the time I fell in with him, as above mentioned, he was second lieutenant.

After talking of several old friends, I happened to mention the Forrest and Byng families, when he told me Colonel Byng's eldest son, George, was a midshipman of the *Superb*, a fine pickle fellow. I therefore begged to see him, but Mr. Norris told me he was absent upon duty on board the *Sultan*, that he would mention my arrival to him, and was sure he would soon find me out.

Having seen every part of the ship, I returned to the Admiral's apartment, when I expressed the great satisfaction it afforded me to see the *Superb* in such perfect good condition. Sir Edward replied, " She undoubtedly is in excellent condition, and I have the satisfaction to assure you, Mr. Hickey, that every ship in my fleet is equally so. Their present state is very different indeed to what it was four months ago, when the whole of them were sadly shattered from the different conflicts we had with your friend, Admiral Suffren. The cabin you are now sitting in was then an absolute cullender, being perforated in every direction by cannon-balls. In the very spot where you are standing my secretary, Mr. Cuthbert, was sitting at a table writing my minutes during the last battle. Fortunately I, having occasion to speak to him, called him out to the quarter-deck. Almost in the instant he rose to come to me a six-and-thirty pounder struck both the table and the chair in which he had been seated, shivering them to pieces. The shot then lodged in one of the knees on the opposite side. This was a narrow escape."

Mr. Popham, looking at his watch, observed he must go on shore, and asked if I were ready, whereupon Sir Edward Hughes directly said to me: "No, no, sir, that cannot be.

I insist upon your spending the day with me. You will find some pleasant men who are to dine here ; in the meantime I will endeavour to amuse you as well as I can." Then, turning to Mr. Popham, he continued, "Probably, Mr. Popham, your professional avocations may render it necessary for you to go on shore for a few hours. If so, you shall have a boat to take you to the edge of the surf and bring you back a little before two o'clock, at which time dinner will be on the table."

This matter being so arranged, Mr. Popham departed, and the Admiral, seating himself by me, resumed the conversation upon the different actions with the French, when he told me he, as well as Mr. Suffren, had suffered from the misconduct of two of his captains who had certainly not acted like the rest, although Sir Richard King, the next in command to himself, was not of the same opinion, upon which subject some high words had passed between him and Sir Richard which had occasioned a coolness, and they had not since had any intercourse or communication together except upon points of duty. "However, I am glad to say we now understand each other, the coolness has subsided, and this day we are to meet once more as friends. It is to be a reconciliation dinner."

A servant entered to say the Captain requested to speak to the Admiral, when I offered to leave the apartment, but was prevented by Sir Edward, who bid the servant say, with his compliments, he was ready to receive the Captain. In a few minutes afterwards I had the pleasure to see my old acquaintance, Captain Newcome, whom I had left in the year 1779 a lieutenant of the *Rippon*, Sir Edward Vernon's flag-ship, and who now was Sir Edward Hughes's captain. He was rejoiced at the meeting, and the Admiral appeared pleased at our knowing each other. The business he came upon being concluded, and the Captain about to leave the apartment, Sir Edward good-humouredly said, "Having already engrossed so much of your time, Mr. Hickey, and as it will not be fair in me to monopolize you, I must, though I acknowledge unwillingly, resign you a little to others, so if you please accompany Captain New-come to his cabin. We shall meet again before two o'clock."

I accordingly went out with Captain Newcome, and spent a couple of hours very agreeably talking over former occur-rences. I found he was the third commander the *Superb* had had within the short space of eight months, Captain Maclellan and another whose name I do not recollect having been killed in action. Captain Newcome spoke in the highest terms of Sir Edward Hughes's gallantry, saying he always exposed himself to the hottest of the enemy's fire, and had several hairbreadth escapes, especially in the last battle off Battecola, on the island of Ceylon, where in the severest part of it, oppressed by heat and fatigue, he called for a glass of water, which his steward, an old and faithful servant who had been with him from infancy, had just brought and was holding to him when a cannon-ball literally cut the servant in two, the mutilated body falling at the Admiral's feet and the blood flying all over him. A severe trial for any man's fortitude.

In the course of our conversation Captain Newcome told me there was another old acquaintance of mine in the fleet, Captain Mitchell, whom I had left a midshipman of the *Rippon*, but who now commanded the *Sultan*, a seventy-four, and who would sail that evening commodore of five ships of the line in search of the French squadron that had lately been seen cruising on the coast, to expedite the sailing of which five ships all the boats of the fleet were employed supplying them with water and provisions.

Captain Newcome proposing that we should take a walk, we went upon deck, where I observed a dapper little fellow whom I conceived to be a midshipman exceedingly busy giving orders respecting a variety of signals that were then flying. From an extraordinary likeness to John Buller of Bengal, I imagined he must be of the same family, and asked the Captain whether that midshipman, in the plain blue coat, was not a Buller. "The person you point to," said Captain Newcome, "certainly is a Buller, though you are a little mistaken as to his rank, for instead of being a midshipman he is the *first lieutenant* of this ship and will to-morrow be a post-captain, the Admiral having made him into the *Chaser*, a prize taken from the French."

At two o'clock Sir Richard King, Captain Mitchell and all the other captains of the fleet were assembled on board the *Superb*, soon after which we sat down to a dinner so magnificent, and so capitally dressed, that it would not have discredited the cooks of the London, or any other equally celebrated tavern. Captain Mitchell who sat next to me at table asked me what I thought of Sir Edward's fare, to which I answered I never had seen so splendid an entertainment, and had no idea such a one could have been produced on board a ship. "Oh," says my neighbour, "our gallant Admiral likes good living, and always takes care to provide himself with a professed cook. Indeed, he usually has both a French and an English cook. His present chief performer is of the former country, his English cook being killed in the last action, but notwithstanding this loss you will presently see one of John Bull's favourite dishes in all its glory," and sure enough after two courses of all sorts of finery there were served up most admirable beefsteaks, smoking hot, and which to the eye and to the palate could not have been surpassed at Dolly's. A succession of these followed each other for half an hour, and I afterwards discovered that Sir Edward Hughes's nickname in the fleet was "Hot-and-hot," he being remarkably fond of, and always doing complete justice to, this truly English dish.

After a liberal allowance of the best French wines and madeira, and drinking nine public toasts, coffee was served. At dusk the party broke up, the different commanders repairing to their respective ships, Mr. Popham (who had returned on board a few minutes after we sat down to dinner) and I going on shore wonderfully pleased with the day's entertainment. Just as we landed, the five ships, the *Sultan* bearing a commodore's pennant, got under way, standing to the northward to look after the enemy.

On the 4th a large fleet made its appearance, whereupon the remaining British ships prepared for action. It, however, proved to be the expected Indiamen from Europe, under convoy of the *Bristol*, of fifty guns, commanded by Captain Burney. Upon coming to an anchor we heard that they had not seen anything of the French, nor been at all aware of their imminent danger. In fact, Madam Fortune seemed to have distributed her favours with an even hand to both nations, for we soon afterwards understood that Admiral Suffren, returning from his expedition to Cuddalore, having with him all the empty transports, and the *Blake*, in which we were conveyed from Trincomalay, was one dark night so close to Sir Edward Hughes's fleet that one of the latter's frigates captured the *Blake*, and had the British Admiral known the situation the respective parties were in the French commander-in-chief, with three line of battle ships and a number of transports, must have fallen into his hands. The captain of the *Blake*, being a shrewd fellow, when taken and being asked about the French fleet, without hesitation said they were all in the harbour of Trincomalay refitting and taking in water, though he felt he was telling the falsehood at the risk of being detected every moment. The deception, however, succeeded, the fleets, happily for Mr. Suffren, passed each other unseen; but to balance this piece of ill-luck was the safe arrival of the valuable Indiamen, which had been in the threefold peril of meeting with Mr. De Bussy's squadron, also Mr. Suffren's on his return from Cuddalore to Trincomalay, and the five ships he had dispatched for the express purpose of intercepting them.

It was a curious circumstance to which the *Bristol* and her convoy owed their safety. Captain Burney, when about an hundred leagues to the southward of Ceylon, informed the senior captain of the company's ships that it was his intention to make the southern point of that island, and run up along shore to the coast of Coromandel, to which proceeding the Indiaman's commodore objected as being replete with danger, "For," said he, "the French well know that such is the usual custom of the English ships from Europe; they will consequently look out in that direction." Instead, therefore, of making Ceylon at all he recommended passing it at least fifteen leagues to the eastward, running in that direction until nearly in the latitude of Madras and then at once hauling in for the land, and all the commanders of the India ships concurred in the propriety of so doing. Captain Burney therefore, with a diffidence and modesty that did him honour, gave up his plan and adopted that of a number of gentlemen to whom he gave credit for superior local knowledge, and he had the gratification to find that by so doing the whole of the valuable fleet were saved from falling into the hands of the enemy, as must inevitably have been the case had he pursued his intention, for Mr. Suffren after his return from Cuddalore continued cruising between the southernmost point of Ceylon and northern extremity of that island.

The same afternoon that the India fleet thus arrived the *Sceptre*, Captain Alms, came into the Roads, bringing with him the *Naiade* French frigate, then under the temporary command of Monsieur Joyeuze. The *Sceptre*, being some miles to the eastward of the fleet coming round from Bombay, discovered from her masthead a strange sail which evidently endeavoured to avoid him. He therefore communicated this to the Admiral by signal, asking permission to chase, which was granted, but with an order not to lose sight of his own fleet. Captain Alms, however, finding he gained upon the ship he was in pursuit of, ventured to trespass upon the order he had received by continuing the chase. In six-and-thirty hours he came up with and captured her. Sir Edward Hughes was, notwithstanding Captain Alms had effected his object, very angry, at first threatening a court martial, but Captain Alms being a favourite, and a man of consummate skill and abilities in his profession, the infringement of strict discipline was overlooked.

—

# CHAPTER IX

## LIFE IN MADRAS (*continued*)

ON the 5th I had the pleasure to meet my *ci-devant* Trincomalay acquaintance, Captain Joyeuze, at Lord Macartney's. He appeared dejected and low-spirited at the "Fortune de Guerre," observing to me that through life he had been an unlucky dog whom the fickle dame was perpetually at war with and pelting him in every direction. Soon after his arrival at Madras he informed me that Lord Macartney had just agreed to an exchange of prisoners, and a cartel would in a few days depart for Trincomalay, by which opportunity I might forward anything I pleased to that place. I thereupon directed my Dubash to procure for me a variety of different articles as presents for Mrs. Vansenden, Captain Gautier, Mr. Chevillard, the Chevalier De Salvert and others.

While sitting in Mr. Popham's hall with Mrs. Hickey and the invalid Captain Humphreys, a servant came into the room to tell me a boy who looked like a sailor was below stairs and wished to see me. Conceiving it to be some beggar, I desired the man to go and ask him what his business was and his name. The man replied he had already done that, but the boy would not tell what he was nor his name, merely saying I knew him perfectly well. I then desired he might be shewn up. The servant again returned, saying the boy declined coming and was desirous of speaking to me below. I therefore went down, when I saw a plain-looking lad, apparently about fourteen years of age, with whose face and person I was totally unacquainted. He looked excessively shabby and dirty, being in an old blue jacket, very coarse trousers, without stockings, and instead of shoes a nearly worn out pair of slippers. I immediately asked him who he was, to which he answered, "George Byng." Greatly surprized at his uncouth appearance, I took him into Mr. Popham's office, where, enquiring the reason of his being in such miserable trim and without shoes, he, with a piteous countenance, said he could not get clothes for want of money, the Admiral, into whose charge he had been given by his father and mother, positively refusing to supply him with cash, at a time, too, when he had not a pair of shoes to put on.

Somewhat incredulous upon hearing so improbable a story, I observed, if such was the case, I was afraid there must be some powerful motive to induce Sir Edward Hughes to refuse all assistance, to which the youth answered he knew of none except that the Admiral complained of his extravagance at Bombay. "And was that complaint well founded?" I asked. "Oh dear, no," said he quickly. "I got nothing there but what I was absolutely in want of, and could not do without, as everybody in the ship knows." "Well, my dear George," said I, "although your present call upon me comes at rather an unlucky time from Mrs. Hickey and my having lost everything we brought out from Europe, and having been obliged to reclothe ourselves at a great expence, to do which I was under the necessity of borrowing money at an interest of twelve per cent per annum, nevertheless I must contrive to relieve you from your difficulties, so sit down at this table and calculate what the things you are in want of will cost, and I will furnish you with the amount." Then placing pen, ink and paper I left him, saying I would return in a quarter of an hour, at the end of which time I did so, and he told me he could make shift with fifty pagodas! I accordingly gave him that sum, after which I took him upstairs and introduced him to Mrs. Hickey, who filled his belly with an excellent breakfast. He then marched off in high spirits. His back was scarcely turned when Mr. Norris called to pay us a visit.

After paying his compliments to Mrs. Hickey and chatting with her for some time Mr. Norris observed to me that he had just met my young pickle friend, George Byng, in a most extraordinary cöndition, nor could he make him explain the reason. He (Norris) then told him it was lucky for him that a friend met him in such a masquerade dress who would not peach, for were the Admiral to hear of it he would be in a pretty scrape. I thereupon smoked my young gentleman and could not suppress a smile, which Mr. Norris observing, exclaimed, "Why, surely the young rascal has not been here? Saucy as he is, I scarcely think he has impudence enough to appear before Mrs. Hickey and you in such a trim as I saw him, and without shoes!" "Why, what could the poor boy do?" said I. "He has no shoes nor the means of purchasing any, as I understand." "Oh, the little villain! I see the trick he has been playing. There is not a midshipman in the *Superb*, I believe I might safely say in the whole fleet, that is so abundantly stocked with clothes of every kind as he is. As to money, perhaps he may be short, for he was so profuse while living on shore at Bombay that the Admiral was exceedingly angry, and has since supplied him very sparingly. I hope the rogue has not hummed you out of any cash." I answered, "Not much —a trifle." "Upon my word," said Norris, "this is too bad, I certainly shall acquaint the Admiral of his conduct." I entreated that he would not, but really believe I should not have succeeded. Upon Mrs. Hickey's joining in the request, however, he promised to keep the secret and not betray him. From that day I never set eyes upon George Byng until about four years ago, when I found him in the command of a line of battleship, the *Belliqueux*.

On the morning of the 6th Mr. Popham and I went to the Government House to breakfast with Lord Macartney, where I was introduced to his chief and confidential secretary, Sir George Staunton, who told me he was well known to all my family and made many kind enquiries after my father and eldest sister, as likewise did another gentleman present, who was a stranger to me. I found this was Mr. Lascelles, who held a lucrative situation under the Governor and was in his suite. There was at breakfast the same morning several of the commanders of His Majesty's ships and some captains of East Indiamen, among the latter Captain Rattray of the *Duke of Athol*.

The breakfast being finished, the company were talking of the dreadful consequences of the late famine when a report of a gun, as it was supposed to be, drew the general attention, Lord Macartney saying it appeared to him more like an explosion than a gun. The whole party rose, and going to the windows that looked towards the sea saw a prodigious column of smoke ascending from the midst of the fleet. Sir Richard Bickerton, who was present, expressed his fears that it was a ship blown up, whereupon Captain Rattray exclaimed, "Not a doubt but it is, and equally certain that it is my ship." This proved too true ; it was the *Duke of Athol!* She had by some accident taken fire, the first intimation of which was the flames bursting from between decks. Signals of distress being made in consequence, a boat full of men with an officer was instantly dispatched from every ship to her assistance. As she lay in the centre of the fleet the boats reached her in a few minutes, one of the earliest on board being the *Superb's*, with her first lieutenant in it, a very active and zealous old officer. This most unfortunate man lost his life in the *Duke of Athol* whilst exerting himself in endeavours to extinguish the flames, he and three other lieutenants belonging to different ships being blown up.

The explosion taking place within twenty minutes after the fire was first discovered occasioned dreadful havoc, almost all the boats that went to her assistance having reached her. For several days after the accident bodies were constantly driven on shore, sadly disfigured and mutilated ; spectacles shocking to behold. They were all decently interred. It never was ascertained from what cause the fatal accident arose, though rumoured that it originated in the carelessness of the steward who, whilst in the lazaretto drawing off spirits from a cask, suffered his candle to communicate thereto, but this was only conjecture from the rapidity and violence of the flames and her blowing up in so short a time after the fire broke out.

The 8th and 9th were spent at Mr. and Mrs. Barclay's, when they made us promise to go and reside with them entirely the following week.

About the middle of the month I received a letter from Captain Joyeuze, who although he wrote and spoke English exceedingly well, was always backward in doing either ; he therefore addressed me in his own language and, according to my translation, to the following effect :

" Sir,
        The clerk and surgeon of my late ship leaving this place to-day for Cuddalore, will with pleasure take charge of the parcel you sent me for the purpose of forwarding. I could not find out the house in the country at which you reside, and it was only just now that your Dubash announced to me that Mrs. Hickey is at Mrs. Barclay's, in the neighbourhood of whose mansion I spend most of my time, I mean at General Burgoyne's, who has shown me the greatest kindness. I hope, sir, to have the gratification of seeing you at home this evening, for I will not let another day pass away without paying my respects to our fair and amiable prisoner, and assuring her and yourself of the sentiments of esteem with which I have the honour to be, Sir,

        Your most devoted and humble servant,
                                DE JOYEUZE."

We were so hospitably received by the inhabitants of Madras, and so many entertainments were made for us, that Mrs. Hickey could not accomplish her visit to Mrs. Barclay until the 30th, on which day we went out to her country house to stay, but I daily went to town, not only to call upon my numerous friends, but to make enquiries relative to the means of getting on to my ultimate destination, Calcutta, with which same object I occasionally visited my naval acquaintances, not omitting the Admiral, who was always attentive and polite, assuring me he was not unmindful of me, and that if he should have occasion to send any ship to Bengal I certainly should have a passage.

Whilst residing with Mr. and Mrs. Barclay I had the pleasure to hear from my respected and highly valued friends, Captain Gautier and the Chevalier De Salvert. Captain Gautier's letter was as follows, and in English :

> "TRINCOMALAY,
>
> 21st April, 1783.

"MY DEAREST SIR,

Your kind letter dated from Cudalour I received in due time. It gave me a great deal of satisfaction in informing me of your both good health and happy arrival in India without further misfortune. I do assure you that in every time I will receive your letters with the greatest pleasure. I would have wrote to you by Mr. Kemp's way had I not thought that Mr. Barretto's departure would allow me very nearly that first opportunity. You will find enclosed here your draft for the little sum which I have lent you at Trincomalay. As you know very perfectly my way of thinking upon the matter, I hope that you will act according to it, and that were you not in a position fit for sending me the goods which I desire, you will write me it without the least hesitation. I think that I have some right to inspire you with an unreserved trust in pecuniary affairs.

As Mr. Barretto tells me that he certainly will come again here, I lay hold of this opportunity, which I find very sure, to receive from you (if possible) three shawl handkerchiefs, from sixty to eighty rupees each ; three dozen of tolerably fine and trimmed shirts for my own use ; three or four pieces of linen cloth fit for making breeches and vests, and four pieces of fine bordered handkerchiefs. The last article and the shawls are to be carried along with me into France to make gifts of to some considerable ladies, but I pray you to expend for these things but a sum like that which you have received from me, and to diminish the quantity according to the means. I do repeat and assure you, dear sir, with the sincerity of my heart that you can use in this circumstance as freely as if you had not received this letter, because you know well that I have not obliged you to be inconvenient to you in any case whatever.

I am very glad for your happiness about your sudden departure for Bengal in a Prussian ship. I am glad likewise that your trinkets have been delivered up to you. You will find here the addition of the sum that I have paid to the watchmaker. He has assured me that you had promised him ten dollars for the reparation. I hope that you are both now well settled in Bengal. I desire my best compliments and respects to the cheerful and amiable Mrs. Hickey. Messieurs De Salvert, Cuverville, Mevillard, Ritcherie, Beddel, etc., pray me to remember them to her. All they, with Mr. Adhemar, Langlade, Mallè, and I, are very thankful for her kind remembrance. I particularly congratulate myself to have made an acquaintance with you both. Here are enclosed the patterns which I forgot to send to Mrs. Hickey. With the sentiments of a true friendship,

I remain, dear sir,<br>Your most humble and obedient servant,<br>GAUTIER."

"Did not Barretto come here again I think that you can send me the goods which I ask to you by the way of Tranquebar.

I pray you, Dear Sir, to present my complimens to all French officers prisoners in Bengal whom I am acquainted with, and I believe that every one is in the case. We every day expect the news of peace, or, at least, an exchange between prisoners. I wish the last article for the good of humanity."

Mr. De Salvert's letter was addressed to Mrs. Hickey. This gentleman, shortly after we became intimate, was in the habit of calling my Charlotte his *chère sœur*. His letter, also in English, was as follows :

" On board the *Flamand*,<br>TRINCOMALAY,<br>9th April, 1783.

" DEAR MADAM,
    Captain Gautier shew me the polite letter he received some days ago from Mr. Hickey, and it was with the utmost pleasure I saw my name reminded in a very kind manner. I will never forget the pleasant hours I spent in your company, but, my dear madam, how short have been that happy moments, and how slowly passes now the tedious glass of a tiresome life. Since you left Oostenburgh I went but once to Mr. Chevillard's house, and I found it so unlike, so empty, it appeared to me no more as a Temple favoured with the presence of the Goddess we revered in it. Your behaviour when at Trinquemalay was so prudent, your mien so obliging, your conversation so polite,

that you left behind you the regrets in every heart, and esteem in every feeling breast.

The Captain Wolseley is gone to Mauritias some days ago, and begged of me to be remembered to you. All the officers on board the *Flamand* request of me the same favour. Their Captain was extremely sorry that he had in his power so few means to be serviceable both to you and your amiable consort.

I hope that my beloved sister, though hurried from pleasures to pleasures, surrounded with all the enjoyments of life, and of the gifts of nature, will cast behind her some kind remembrance on the most loving and affectionate brother. I can receive by the way of Tranquebar, and under the cover of Monsieur Guignace, the letters I hope you will favour me with. My best compliments to Mr. Hickey. He must be very pleased to be at the end of his tedious voyage. My wishes to Heaven for success, health, and happiness in all the circumstances of your connubial life. I have the honour to be for ever, my dear madam,

Your most obedient servant and good brother,

CHR. DE SALVERT."

In a conversation I had with Captain Joyeuze he told me that the *Fendant* and *Cleopatra* could undoubtedly have captured the *Medea* had they continued the pursuit of her three hours longer, but which the senior officer did not think himself justified in doing, Admiral Suffren's orders being peremptory that they should not upon any pretence whatever stand more than fifteen leagues to the northward of Madras, then stretch over to the eastward twelve leagues, and again to the southward, to the latitude of fourteen degrees and a half, and thus to continue during the cruise, or until they accomplished their object, the principal one being to intercept two rich ships from Bengal with money and stores, of the departure of which two ships from Calcutta they had correct information. They were further directed to spread the squadron so as to extend over a space of ten leagues. Another of the French commander's views was to take the chance of falling in with the outward English East Indiamen, a fleet of which we also knew were daily expected in the Eastern seas. Certainly therefore the escape of the whole was particularly lucky.

At Madras I heard much of my friend Bob Pott, who, with his lovely favourite, Emily, had made a considerable stay there. The men universally declared they had never beheld so beautiful a creature as Emily, and even the women admitted her extraordinary beauty of face and person. I also learnt that she died immediately upon her arrival in Bengal.

Upon examining the wreck of the contents of the escritoire I had with me on board the *Raynha de Portugal* I found a letter which the salt water had not entirely effaced the direction of, and it brought to my recollection the manner in which it came into my possession. Shortly previous to my leaving London I called upon my old Westminster acquaintance, Dicky Roberts, the boat builder at Lambeth, who, understanding I meant shortly to return to India, requested I would endeavour to procure for him payment of a debt of many years' standing from Mr. Stephen Popham for boats built by his order, and forwarded to him at his estate in Ireland, where he had put them on a large canal in his park. Popham was educated at Westminster School, like the rest of the boys hiring boats from Roberts to row and sail about the Thames during the hours of play. Upon reaching manhood and getting into possession of his estate he, like many other old Westminsters, employed Roberts to build the boats in question, which being done Roberts shipped them for the sister kingdom, paying freight and all expences. Mr. Popham wrote to express his approbation, saying they were exactly what he wanted, but there he stopped, never paying a single guinea or answering any of the various applications made by Roberts during a period of fifteen years. The amount was forty-six pounds. To demand payment of this sum with interest was the purport of Roberts' letter conveyed by my hand. Upon my delivering the same to Mr. Popham, he perused it with the utmost indifference, remarking when he had done what an unlucky fellow he was that this letter should be one of the very few preserved from the destructive fury of the elements. Offended at the cool levity of his manner, I resentfully and in some degree contemptuously observed that I should have thought it would, as it undoubtedly ought, have rather been a matter of joy than of concern to him to be reminded of a debt of so long standing, contracted too, as that had been, and thereby putting it in his power to do justice to an honest, industrious and hard-working man. To which observation of mine, although he appeared nettled by it, he with affected unconcern said, " Oh certainly, my dear Hickey, I cannot but be pleased with so agreeable a communication, but I really think, indeed, I am quite sure, that I paid the extravagant demand for these boats at the time of their delivery. I will, however, look over my accounts, and if I find I am mistaken, and that it is still due, I will immediately remit the amount to master Dicky." Notwithstanding the above pretence the unprincipled man knew perfectly well he never had paid a sixpence, nor had he the least intention ever to pay. He died, as he lived, poor Roberts's debtor.

Early in the month of May the Bengal detachment, and some additional regiments from the coast, prepared to march from Madras to join the army destined to make an attack upon Cuddalore, which in due time they did, and had a deal of exceedingly hard fighting. In one of the assaults upon the outworks His Majesty's 101st Regiment of infantry were so dreadfully cut up that the few survivors gave way and ran for it, from which circumstance they were by some ill-naturedly stigmatised with the title of the " Hundred and worst," meaning a miserable pun upon " first." I say ill-naturedly, because unprejudiced men pronounced the odium unmerited. In the above regiment one of the very few officers that escaped unhurt was Mr. Thomas, grandson to an intimate friend of my father's, a respectable clergyman in Ireland, whom I used, when a boy, to endeavour to rouse from a lethargic stupor by pulling his wig off and playing other monkey tricks. In the above-mentioned attack upon the fortress of Cuddalore the Bengal Sepoys by their gallant conduct acquired immortal honour.

# CHAPTER X

## FROM MADRAS TO CALCUTTA

ON the 20th I received a very polite note from Mr. Robson, purser of the *Superb*, to say the Admiral had directed him to inform me that the *Tortoise* store ship would be dispatched for Bengal, and that he had requested Captain Serocold, who commanded her, to give Mrs. Hickey and me a passage. I thereupon immediately went to town, where I had only been a few minutes when Mr. Robson brought Captain Serocold, who in the kindest manner expressed the pleasure it would afford him to comply with the Admiral's wishes ; that the *Tortoise's* great cabin, with everything on board, would be heartily at my service, and he should feel proud of the honour of Mrs. Hickey's company. He told me he expected to sail in five days, and should only have one other passenger, Mr. Henry Thomas Colebrooke, third son of Sir George Colebrooke, and who was just appointed to the Company's civil service.

The 21st we spent at Mr. Porcher's, where we had a pleasant day and merry dance at night. The following day we were at Mr. Paul Benfield's, where everything appeared in the first style of magnificence. The 23rd we had a cheerful party at Colonel Nixon's, and were most kindly received. He told me, with great glee, that his memorial had succeeded, Government having admitted his claim by giving him the rank and allowances of full colonel from the period at which he stated it to be his right.

This gentleman subsequently became a major-general. Having accumulated a noble fortune, and seen all his daughters advantageously married, he about the year 1804 or 1805 embarked for England on board the *Prince of Wales*, Captain Price, taking with him two of his daughters with their respective children. The fleet in which this ship was, sailing without convoy, Captain Price as the senior captain acted as commodore and directed their proceedings. Off the Cape of Good Hope they encountered a severe gale of adverse wind, and were consequently obliged to lay to. During the height of the storm, in the middle of a dreadfully dark night, the chief officer of one of the ships, upon being relieved by the second, pointed out to him the Commodore's light, observing at the same time the gale was, he thought, rather increased than abated since his watch commenced, and as there was a tremendous sea running he had better try to get a little further from the *Prince of Wales*, she being close upon their starboard quarter. The second mate said he would set the fore-staysail for a few minutes in order to increase the distance, but before the people could execute the order a prodigious sea broke on board, carrying a boat and some of the spars overboard. This mishap engaged the attention of all hands for near half an hour. Upon the confusion subsiding the second mate again looked out for the Commodore's light, and not being able to find it he desired the other officers and the watch upon deck to try to discover it, pointing out the direction in which it ought to be. All eyes were employed, but in vain. She never more was seen, nor the least trace of her. This was the more extraordinary from her being in the middle of a large fleet, and very near several of the ships, yet not a remnant of her ever appeared. The general opinion was that she must have been suddenly overwhelmed by the sea and instantly gone to the bottom. Captain Price had the reputation of being a perfect seaman.

The 24th I dined at Lord Macartney's, previously leaving Mrs. Hickey at Lady Gordon's with a gay party. Having received notice from Captain Serocold that he should depart the next day but one, the 25th was therefore fully occupied by taking leave of our numerous friends. Upon my return home I found the following letter from Mr. Benfield :

"MADRAS,
25th May, 1783.

"DEAR SIR,

Will you allow me to request your care of the accompanying letters. I beg to offer my best respects to Mrs. Hickey. I
sincerely wish you both a pleasant voyage, and that you will
meet with no more untoward accidents, of which you have
already had more than your share. It will be very flattering to
me if you will let me hear of your arrival.

Believe me, dear sir,

Very affectionately yours,

PAUL BENFIELD."

On the 26th directly after breakfast we were accompanied
down to the beach by Mrs. Barclay, Lady Gordon, Mrs.
Latham, Mrs. Garrow, and other female friends, and quite
a host of gentlemen, who all remained at the seaside until
they saw us over the surfs, when they finally saluted by
waving handkerchiefs and hats to us, and departed. Upon
getting alongside the *Tortoise* we were politely received by
Captain Serocold, who conducted us into a neat and commodious cabin. We found the people heaving up the anchor,
and in an hour after we were on board the ship was under
way.

Captain Serocold was a most pleasing young man, a
lieutenant in the navy, and a prime favourite with Sir
Edward Hughes, who in less than a twelvemonth after the
time I am now speaking of promoted him to the rank of
post-captain, in which station he was employed in a line of
battle ship, on board of which he was killed gallantly fighting
her against two French ships of superior force in the Mediterranean. By his death the navy and the British nation lost
an officer who was an equal honour and ornament to
both.

Our fellow-passenger, Mr. Colebrooke, was a sensible and
well-informed young man. He is now a member of the
Supreme Council in Bengal, which elevated situation he
gained entirely from his abilities, indefatigable attention to

business, and superior acquirements in Oriental literature. Upon Sir John Anstruther's leaving India he was chosen to succeed him as President of the Asiatic Society.

The *Tortoise* had come out from England under Mr. Serocold's command with a cargo of naval stores for the use of the fleet. The Admiral's sole object in sending her to Calcutta was to procure men, of which most of his ships were sadly in want, some of them being one hundred and fifty short of their complement. It may therefore be imagined we were not overstocked on board the *Tortoise*, which was a vessel of three hundred and fifty tons. Our whole crew consisted of twelve men and two officers, not being a third of what she ought to have had, but being at a season when the south-west monsoon was completely set in, and generally blows fresh, it was supposed we should reach Calcutta within a week. The Admiral had taken the precaution of writing to the Government of Bengal by the *Dauk*, or Post, to say one of his ships would be there by the 1st of June, and therefore desiring a pilot might be in Balasore Roads ready to take charge. The reason of doing this was that upon the change of the moon there is often exceeding bad weather in those seas, and the pilots knowing that to be the case are not apt to expose themselves to it, but skulk into creeks and narrow rivers for shelter.

We had a tolerable passage from Madras, arriving in Balasore Roads on the 2nd of June, on which day there was a new moon, and we had the mortification to find there was no pilot. As the weather appeared unsettled and the clouds looked wild, after cruising about almost the whole day, Captain Serocold considered it prudent to come to an anchor, which we accordingly did in twenty fathoms of water. A heavy sea running, and the ship being light, we rolled and tumbled about dreadfully. The *India Directory* (a very valuable and excellent work) advises all commanders of ships who reach the Roads at any time between the new and full moon of June, and do not find a pilot there, by no means to come to an anchor but stand out to sea. Captain Serocold, however, being in hourly expectation of seeing a pilot schooner, deemed it more prudent to remain in the usual track of them.

The 3rd and 4th it blew fresh with a high, short and breaking sea. Every person on board became impatient and uneasy under this unexpected and disagreeable detention in so wild and dangerous a sea. In the evening of the 4th an old Bengallee Serang, who had begged a passage from Madras, said he had often taken his own vessel of about sixty tons over the sands, being well acquainted with the channel from long experience, and that he was ready and willing to go in a boat to see for a pilot. Captain Serocold asked him if he could not conduct the ship in, to which he modestly replied that although he thought he could it might be considered presumptuous in him to attempt it, and the ship being of much consequence even his alarms on that account might lead him into error, and he would not upon any account attempt it short of indispensable necessity. Captain Serocold, after considering what would be best, resolved to dispatch this man in a boat. He accordingly had the longboat rigged, put his boatswain and four of the men into her, desiring them to follow implicitly the directions of the Serang, and dispatched them with the flood tide, the Serang saying he hoped to be back the following morning with a pilot.

The 5th the weather was dark and squally. In the morning a large ship from sea passed us. Captain Serocold made the signal to speak her, which she either did not see or did not understand. After running about four miles further in than we were she came to an anchor. We had fired a gun every half-hour during the nights from the time we had anchored. This night the newly arrived ship did the same.

The 6th and 7th there was a great deal of rain ; at times most severe gusts of wind with dreadful thunder and lightning and a high sea, then suddenly falling quite calm for a few minutes ; a dismally black, threatening sky all round. Captain Serocold became extremely uneasy, not only on account of his ship, but for the safety of the people sent off in the longboat.

The 8th the strange sail was observed to fire several guns in quick succession, and Captain Serocold looking through his glass thought she had a signal of distress flying, though from her distance and the thickness of the weather he was not able to ascertain with certainty whether such was the case, but as she continued firing guns he said he would make an effort to get nearer to her if he could manage to weigh the anchor. Every soul on board, passengers and all, turned to at the capstan and hove with hearty good-will, but in vain. We could not stir the anchor in the least and were obliged to desist.

After dinner, the tide not running so strong, another attempt was made, but equally unsuccessful. Captain Serocold then determined to slip his cable, leaving a buoy over the anchor to point out its situation, which having done we ran within a mile of her, when Captain Serocold observed she must be upon the very edge of a sand over which the sea broke dreadfully, and being directly leeward with a strong gale blowing he was afraid to venture any nearer. He therefore let go the sheet anchor, when we perceived the ship to be an East Indiaman, and in an extremely awkward situation, for had she driven one hundred yards her loss must have been inevitable. She made many signals to us for assistance, which it was out of our power to render, nor could any boat possibly get from her to us, from the set of the tides and point the wind was in.

In this truly unpleasant way we remained until the 10th, when, the wind shifting to the northward during a severe squall, our companion in distress got under way and stood close to us. Captain Serocold then hailed, mentioning the helpless situation we were in with respect to hands, and requesting they would send twenty hands to assist in weighing our anchor, and that we should keep together until we fell in with a pilot. They immediately hoisted out a boat, sending her off with the people required. The third mate who accompanied them told us it was the Company's ship *Chesterfield*, commanded by Captain Bruce Boswell, last from Bombay. He also informed us she was so leaky as to keep two pumps constantly at work night and day, that they had only twenty-five Europeans on board, including officers, all the rest being Lascars, who are miserable wretches at best, and who were nearly worn out with the fatigue of pumping. Captain Boswell therefore hoped we would detain his men as little time as possible. We found the *Chesterfield* upon coming in, not reckoning themselves so far on as they proved to be, had stood too near the tail of a dangerous sand called the Western Brace, and being high water when they brought to, as the tide ebbed they had the disagreeable view of breakers within a quarter of a mile of them, with a fresh wind blowing dead upon them, so that they dared not attempt to move from an apprehension she might strike in getting under way, and had she once touched the ground it would have been all over with them.

The *Chesterfield* people having soon accomplished the business they came upon, returned to their ship, when we both made sail, going in search of the best bower from which we had slipped, but after cruising about three hours without being able to find the buoy, we were under the necessity of giving up the hopes of recovering it. We then stood more to the eastward together, anxiously looking out for a pilot. As we now gave up the longboat's crew for lost, it was some consolation to us to have the *Chesterfield* near. Our situation certainly was very alarming, being in constant dread of bad weather from the season, the critical time of the moon and threatening appearance of the sky all round.

Two more days we had to endure this scene of constant anxiety and suspense, but at daylight in the morning of the 13th had the satisfaction to see a pilot schooner approaching, and as she neared us Captain Serocold afforded us inexpressible pleasure by saying he saw his boatswain and people on board of her. At ten o'clock a pilot came to the *Tortoise* and took charge, one of his mates at the same time going to the *Chesterfield*.

Captain Serocold, although a remarkably mild, good-tempered man, was so offended at the shameful negligence he had experienced that I really thought he would have flogged the pilot, especially when the rascal impudently observed it was unreasonable to expect small vessels could cruise in the Roads during such tempestuous weather. Captain Serocold, however, commanded himself so far as not to strike him, but assured him he would represent the matter to the Admiral, which would cause him to be dismissed the service.

The boatswain said the old Serang had taken the longboat up in a capital style, most correctly telling the depth of water there would be all the way ; that not finding any pilot off Ingelee, nor in the creek, into which they looked, they proceeded up the river, stopping at every place they thought it likely to hear of one, but none were to be met with, and thus they reached Calcutta, where, without losing a moment, they applied to the Master Attendant, who forthwith ordered a vessel to be dispatched. Four-and-twenty hours nevertheless elapsed ere she was ready. Off Fulta, on their way down the river, they ran her upon a dangerous sand called the James and Mary, where she lay aground two entire days and nights in the most imminent risk of oversetting every tide. The springs having commenced, the afternoon of the 11th she fortunately righted and once more got afloat. So careless or so ignorant were the people on board that she again grounded a few miles below Kedgeree, remaining fast for six hours.

Captain Serocold upon hearing so extraordinary an account of the pilot's conduct on his way down, sent for him upon the quarter-deck, and calling for the boatswain he directed that officer to have a rope reeved to the main-yard-arm with a running noose, which being immediately done, he turned to the pilot and said, " You have already, in my opinion, proved yourself a very worthless scoundrel. You see that rope that I just ordered to be rigged out, now by God ! if you run my ship on shore between this and Culpee the instant she takes the ground shall be the last of your life, for I'll certainly hang you at that yardarm ! " The fellow looked very simple, and after a pause said, " I hope, sir, there is no danger of any accidents happening ; I shall take all the care in my power to prevent it."

At noon we got under way to go once more in search of the anchor and cable we had slipped from, and the buoy was soon discovered by the people of the pilot vessel from the Captain's describing the direction of the courses steered, and when the anchor and cable were recovered we directly stood for the mouth of the Hooghley River in company with the *Chesterfield*, the sky continuing very black and lowering. At five in the afternoon it fell quite calm, torrents of rain pouring down upon us, and in the night we had much thunder and lightning. The whole of the 14th it continued calm, which kept us fast at anchor. The 15th we proceeded about twelve miles ; the 16th, 17th and 18th it blew strong from the north-west, we could not therefore stir, all the time pitching, forecastle under ; almost incessant rain. In the afternoon of the 19th the weather cleared up, and the wind veering round to the southward, we got under way ; at sunset saw the land near Ingelee. On the 21st came to an anchor off Culpee (the place I passed a wretched night at on my first arrival at Bengal in the year 1777 with Colonel Watson, chief engineer).

In approaching this dreary spot I observed in the midst of the jungle a beautiful column, apparently of stone. Enquiring what this could be in so desolate and wild a place I was informed the seafaring people had christened it " Pott's folly," though it ultimately proved of public utility, being of considerable advantage to the pilots when bringing ships in from sea, from its being a conspicuous landmark, always visible when no other object was so in blowing weather. I shall say something more of this column presently.

There being no means of getting Mrs. Hickey away, we were under the disagreeable necessity of remaining in the abominable hole three days, at the end of which time, by bribing high, I prevailed upon the mangee of a pinnace I found laying in the creek, waiting the arrival of a gentleman hourly expected from Vizagapatam, to convey us up the river as far as Budge Budge, where my old *Sea Horse* ship-mate, Major Mestayer, commanded, who I knew would give us a hearty welcome, as well as furnish the means of taking us on to Calcutta. We arrived at his quarters, an excellent and spacious house within the fort, on the 26th, where we experienced the most cordial reception.

The following morning he dispatched a servant with a letter from me to Robert Pott (to whom I had also written during my stay at Madras requesting he would take a house, hire a set of servants, etc.) to ascertain whether he had done anything for me. On the 28th, in consequence of my letter, he made his appearance in person, having come down in a beautiful and elegantly appointed boat of his own construction and building.

As I had in my letter from Madras informed him of the companion I had with me, and the footing she was upon, notwithstanding my repeated offers to make her my wife, he was prepared to receive her as an utter stranger, and in spite of his disposition at all times to laugh, and his having been well acquainted with her in England, he conducted himself with the utmost propriety and decorum. He with great ceremony told her he rejoiced much at the introduction, bespeaking infinite pleasure in the acquaintance, adding that he had comfortable apartments, with everything suitable, prepared for us at his country house, to which he was ready immediately to escort us, but Major Mestayer would not hear of our leaving him until the 30th, on which morning soon after breakfast we embarked in the before-mentioned splendid vessel, which in three hours transported us to Pott's residence, a noble mansion situated upon the bank of the river, five miles from Calcutta, the property of Mr. Stephenson, a gentleman at the top of the Civil Service. Here we landed on the said 30th of June, 1783, thus terminating as disastrous a voyage as ever unfortunate people made, of exactly *eighteen* months from the day I left London.

I found Pott's family consisted of himself, his first cousin, George Cruttenden, who came out with him as a cadet, and Mr. Thomas Trant, a cadet for Madras, likewise a shipmate.

Robert Pott

From a painting by George Romney
by permission of the owner The Revᵈ. Alfred Percivall Pott.

This gentleman, who was about thirty years of age, had been brought up in a merchant's comting-house in Ireland, and was conversant in all matters of business and account. During the voyage Pott persuaded him to relinquish the army and to depend upon him for his future success in life. Upon their arrival in Bengal he employed him as a sort of general steward, giving him the entire management and control over all his servants and domestic concerns.

Mr. Trant informed me that Pott had at first suffered severely at the sudden and unexpected loss of his favourite Emily, but that the violence of his grief was not of long duration. At the time of my arrival in Bengal he certainly appeared to be in excellent health and high spirits. From Mr. Trant I also heard the following particulars of her death. Pott and she sailed from Madras in the month of May (1782) on board a ship belonging to, and commanded by, Mr. John Maclary, a very respectable and worthy man, Emily then being in perfect health. She was, however, greatly annoyed by what is called the prickly heat, a sort of rash or eruption upon the skin very prevalent in hot countries, especially in Asia. It is attended with a sharp pricking pain like the point of pins penetrating the body in every part, so that it is difficult to lay down in bed. It is, however, considered a sign of vigorous health. New-comers are more subject to it than old residents, arising, as is supposed, from the superior richness or nicer susceptibility of the blood and general system. Drinking anything cold instantaneously greatly increases it. Emily, impatient under the torture of this teazing complaint, and with an insatiable thirst upon her, had frequent recourse to draughts of extremely cold water (made so by art) mixed with milk. The ship they were on board of was to go quite up to Calcutta. Just as they were off Culpee Emily, in quick succession, drank two large tumblers of the above-mentioned mixture, the last of which was scarcely down her throat when she complained of feeling excessively faint and ill, that her sight was failing as she could not distinguish any object before her. The prickly heat was observed suddenly and entirely to disappear. She fell back upon the couch she was sitting on and in a few minutes was a corpse. So rapid and so unexpected a proof of the uncertainty of life gave a great shock to every person on board, more especially to poor Pott, who was inconsolable and outrageous in his grief. For several hours he would not be persuaded she ceased to exist. He, however, but too soon had unanswerable evidence such was the fact from the body's becoming black and putrid, emitting the most offensive smell. A coffin therefore being prepared, with the utmost dispatch, the corpse was finally enclosed therein, placed in a boat astern of the vessel, with a very long painter or headfast, and thus was towed up to Calcutta, where it was interred in the burial-ground of the town. Pott caused a magnificent mausoleum to be constructed over the grave by Mr. Tiretta, the Italian architect, alias "Nosey Jargon," of whom I have already spoken, at an expence of near three thousand pounds, and not content with paying this compliment to her remains he employed the same Tiretta to build the column I before mentioned, amongst herds of tigers at Culpee, because off that wild, jungly place she breathed her last, which column cost him another thousand pounds.

# CHAPTER XI

## GETTING BACK TO WORK

ON the 1st of July my former Banyan Durgachuru Muckerjee came to pay his respects to me and express his surprize and concern at my returning without being appointed to the Company's civil service, a situation he did not seem disposed to believe so difficult to procure as in fact it was. He had provided a smart palankeen for me, likewise a complete set of bearers to carry it, besides various other necessary servants. The same morning Mr. Stackhouse Tolfrey and several other of my former acquaintances came to visit me. Tolfrey gave me the mortifying intelligence of my name having been struck off the Roll, so that I was no longer an attorney of the Supreme Court. The chief justice, Sir Elijah Impey, upon the arrival of Mr. and Mrs. Pawson in a Portuguese ship, having heard that I was at Lisbon on my way back to India, he forthwith caused written notices to be stuck up at all the customary places in Calcutta requiring all and every attorney who had suffered twelve months to elapse without doing any business in the line of their profession, within *fourteen days* from the date of such notice, to appear in court and there assign their reason for not practising, and in case of any attorneys not complying with that order and accounting satisfactorily for his ceasing to practise, their or his names or name would directly be struck off the Roll.

This extraordinary measure was evidently levelled at me in revenge for my having been instrumental in forwarding the petition to Parliament soliciting for trial by jury in all civil as well as criminal cases, the prayer of which petition had the legislature complied with to the extent demanded would materially have abridged the power and consequently the influence of the judges. That Sir Elijah suffered private pique against me to affect his conduct there could be no doubt, no other attorney being in a similar predicament with myself, that is to say having been a year without practising his profession. At the time the said notices were published I was at Trincomalay, a prisoner with the French, quite ignorant of any such step having been taken. The fourteen days having passed and I not appearing, my name was thereupon erased from the Roll by the Clerk of the Crown under the direction of the judges.

As I considered this step a premeditated piece of malice, and had no doubt of the same sentiment being adhered to, I resolved at least to let the proud Chief Justice know what were my sentiments upon the occasion. I accordingly addressed a letter to him wherein I, in most unqualified language, reprobated such illiberal behaviour as he had betrayed, concluding by expressing the most sovereign contempt for this great luminary of the law. This letter I read to Pott, who said it certainly was ill-calculated to conciliate, but nevertheless he had so high an opinion of the goodness of the Chief Justice's heart and of his (Pott's) influence over him that he would himself undertake the delivery of the hostile letter, adding at the same time that he would *wig* the lawyer for the farce of fourteen days' notice for a man to appear who, for aught he knew to the contrary, might be some thousands of miles distant.

At dinner I found a large party, amongst whom was Ulysses Browne, the *ci-devant* Horse Guards man for whom I had obtained a passage to India in Bob Pott's ship. He was just recovering from a dangerous illness, which had so altered and reduced him that except from the voice I should not have recognised him. During dinner another old friend of mine, Mr. Thomas Evans, who happened to be seated next to Browne, recommended some malt liquor he was drinking as remarkably fine and *small*. The last word catching Pott's ear, he directly said that the smallness would be no recommendation to Browne. Browne, taking up the

remark, agreed that it was not, continuing, " I have sometimes heard the master of the house in which I have been
a guest declare he had the best small beer that ever was
brought to India.  Upon my asking was that really the case,
and being answered, ' Yes, it is really very small,' I decline
tasting it ; on the other hand, when my host has replied to
my question by saying, ' I bought it as small beer but
really think it far otherwise,' I directly call for a tumbler
of it, candidly admitting that I like strong and detest small
beer."  I own I am very much of Browne's way of thinking
as to malt liquor.

The following morning Pott presented me with a letter,
the contents of which very much surprized me.  It was, as
my friend told me when he delivered it, from Sir Elijah
Impey, whom he described as being in a damnable rage
when first perusing mine to him, but that he soon laughed
him into better temper.  It was as follows :

" To Mr. Hickey.

    " SIR,

         The Court some time since, on the petition of the prac-
tising Attornies, stating the decline of the business of the Court,
thought proper to limit their number.  To ascertain the number
proposed and that it might not be prevented from being full
by the names of persons standing on the record who had no
further thoughts of practising, the Court framed the rule under
which, as I suppose, your name was struck out, the Court
esteeming absence for a long time without any cause for it
known to the Court to be evidence of having no further thoughts
of practising.  You will see by this that what has happened to
you could not proceed from any idea of your having given any
cause for dismission, but of your having voluntarily relinquished
your profession.  As that was not your case, and, on the contrary, you have returned with an intention to prosecute it, and
more especially as you could have no knowledge of the rule
until your arrival, I should esteem it severe and I may say
unjust not to restore your name to the Roll.  I will take on
myself to say you will find no difficulty in it, and if you will
call on me I will recommend to you what I think the proper

mode of getting it done, as I wish to give you every assistance in obtaining what I think to be your right.

I am, sir,

Your very humble servant,

E. IMPEY."

In consequence of this advice coming from such high authority, Pott the following morning conveyed me in his carriage to Sir Elijah's at the Court House, where, during my absence in Europe, the Court had been removed to, it being a noble pile of buildings, close to the edge of the river at Chaund paul Ghaut, and in which Sir Elijah, with his family, resided.

Being shewn into the study, the Chief Justice in a few minutes entered. I rose and bowed, to which salutation he made a slight return by a doubtful bend of his head, whereupon my friend Robert, who knew the former habits of intimacy I had been upon with the great man, burst into one of his laughs. The Chief, offended thereat, angrily and haughtily said, " 1 cannot discover any cause for your boisterous and ill-timed mirth, Pott. Give me leave to ask what has occasioned it ? " Pott made no answer, but continuing to laugh violently, Sir Elijah said peevishly, " Unless you can restrain your unseasonable mirth, sir, and conduct yourself more decorously you had better leave the room." Then, turning to me, he said, " I am going into Court directly ; if you think proper, follow me there, sir." Pott, taking up his hat, and still laughing, went to the door, from whence he called out, " Good morning, Sir Elijah. While you are doing my friend Bill Hickey justice I'll go and chat with Lady Impey, whom I hope to find in a somewhat better humour than you are," and he darted away.

I, according to the Chief Justice's advice, followed him into the Court room. The moment he had taken his seat upon the bench he addressed the Bar and officers, saying, " The judges being satisfied with the reasons assigned by Mr. William Hickey, lately an attorney of the Court, for his absence, have consented to comply with his desire of being readmitted. Let the usual oaths therefore be administered, after which, Mr. Clerk of the Crown, restore his name to the Roll of Attornies." This being immediately done, I once more became an Attorney upon Record.

From the Court house I went into Fort William to call upon my friend Colonel Watson, who had during my absence become a benedict, having married a Miss Kearman under somewhat peculiar circumstances. An intimate friend of his, a Major Burn, who was stationed at one of our most distant military posts, had been attached to this young lady previous to leaving Ireland when quite a lad. The partiality continuing and an intercourse being kept up between them by letter, upon his attaining the rank of a Field Officer, having also laid by a considerable sum of money, he proposed marriage if she would come out to India, remitting sufficient to equip her as well as to pay the passage. She lost no time in obeying the summons, taking out with her a younger sister. They embarked on board one of the Company's ships, and in the usual time reached Bengal. Major Burn being engaged in the field upon actual service against the Rohillas, could not leave the army. He therefore requested his sworn and bosom friend, Colonel Watson, to receive the sisters and shew them every civility and attention until the duty he was upon should be finished and he thereby enabled to go down to the Presidency. Colonel Watson accordingly sent a young gentleman of his corps in a large boat down to the ship at Culpee to escort them up, took them into his house, and in about three months became so deeply enamoured of the Major's intended as to render him quite miserable, the lady also returning the Colonel's passion, increased his struggle.

After much consideration Colonel Watson resolved to state what had unluckily happened to Major Burn, which he did with candour, taking upon himself every degree of blame, concluding that notwithstanding the young lady positively declared she never would be united to him (Major Burn), he (Colonel Watson) could not think of marrying her unless he (Major Burn) consented thereto.

III.—L

To this very extraordinary epistle of Colonel Watson's, Major Burn, without a moment's hesitation, replied that Colonel Watson was heartily welcome to the capricious lady, for as the affection and regard she for several years professed could not have been sincere, and she now chose openly to avow it by bestowing her love upon another, he would not for any consideration upon earth unite himself to so errant a jilt ; that as the lady appeared willing to release him from the promise of marriage she had entered into so was he perfectly ready to waive any former pretensions he might have had to her hand, and that he certainly could do so without the least reluctance or feeling a particle of uneasiness. A week after the receipt of this disclaimer Miss Kearman became the wife of Colonel Watson. Her sister some time after married Captain Humfrays of the Bengal Engineers.

Colonel Watson received me with all his former kindness, expressing his sorrow that I had abandoned such excellent business as I was in at the time of my departure for England, especially as it might not be an easy matter to regain it. "However," added he, "we must do all we can, and I trust, Hickey, I shall have it in my power to recommend to you some opulent native clients. As for myself, I must continue with the man I now employ whom I look upon to be as great a thief as ever was unhung, but a devilish shrewd, clever fellow, fit for the practice of the villainous profession he belongs to, and fully competent to encounter all the chicanery and dirty tricks of his scoundrel brother attornies."

The name of the person alluded to was Solomon Hamilton, and I firmly believe a more correct character never was given than Colonel Watson's of this man. He had been bred for, and called to, the Irish Bar, but upon his arrival in Calcutta, which happened while I was in England, finding the line of an attorney better suited to his capacity and his talents he abandoned the gown to adopt the practice of an attorney, in which he soon got immense business, and by his general conduct shewed how well he deserved all that Colonel Watson said of him.

I found all my other *Sea Horse* shipmates alive and well, except two, my first Calcutta chum, poor Cleveland, who had died of a bilious fever about two years after I left India, and the youngest Miss Bertie, who married Mr. North Nailor, the Company's attorney, falling a sacrifice to her sensibility and anxiety on account of her husband. He had unavoidably got into a dispute with the judges of the Supreme Court upon a point contended for between them and the Supreme Government. The Governor-General and Council ordered a measure to be pursued which the Court considered an infringement of its power. The attorney, Mr. Nailor, was necessarily the channel of this measure being executed, whereupon the Chief Justice, with his usual impetuosity and violence, ordered an attachment to issue against Mr. Nailor for a contempt of Court, although this gentleman was an *élève* of his own, and he was aware that he could not do otherwise than obey the orders of his employers. Upon the attachment Mr. Nailor was arrested and confined in the common jail of Calcutta, which so hurt his feelings that, not being in strong health at the time, it seriously affected his health and he became alarmingly ill. This unfortunately coming to the knowledge of Mrs. Nailor, who was pregnant, expecting every day to be delivered, it brought on labour, and in giving birth to her child she died, the infant following her unhappy mother in a few hours. This double misfortune proved fatal to the husband; he gave himself up from the moment he heard of his loss, and in seven days followed his lamented wife and child to the grave.

Sir Elijah Impey's rancour and violence extended to Mr. William Swainston, the Company's servant in charge of the district in which the native who was the subject of the dispute resided. It being his duty, as a public officer, to carry into execution the orders of the Government, he naturally protected the native according to his instructions and would not allow the process of the Court to be executed upon him, for which he likewise was taken up on a writ of attachment and lodged in the same prison with Mr. Nailor, but being a man of stronger nerves than the attorney and the consequences of the confinement not operating upon his mind, he bore it with the utmost philosophy.

The elder Miss Bertie married one of the Mr. Cators, but did not survive her sister more than a twelvemonth.

Mrs. Wheler, wife of the member of Council who went out in the *Duke of Portland* in the year 1777 in the same fleet I was, also departed this life while I was away from Bengal, her widower in a few months after her decease marrying Miss Durnford, a cousin of his first lady's.

I found but little alteration with respect to the members constituting the Supreme Court. The only one that had quitted the Bar was Mr. Charles Newman, the Company's senior counsel. This gentleman, having served his employers for several years with equal zeal and ability, felt so hurt that they should supersede him by sending out an Advocate-General that he immediately resigned his situation, and having acquired a very handsome fortune in his profession embarked for Europe on board the unfortunate *Grosvenor*. This ship left Bengal at a period when lunar observations were little known or practised. By their common reckoning they were within a degree or two of the latitude of Cape Lagullas, though several hundred miles to the eastward of it. They therefore stood on for the land with the utmost confidence, as was thought, too, in perfect security, but in the middle of the night the ship ran on shore upon the continent of Africa, where she was totally lost. At break of day they found themselves within two miles of the shore, the sea breaking so heavily over the wreck that all expected every moment to perish. Nevertheless, by the exertions of the crew, aided by the Caffre inhabitants of that part of the coast, the greater part, with all the passengers except two children and some native female servants, reached the shore in safety. They were, however, instantly made prisoners of and conveyed a great distance inland. During their long and fatiguing march two of the common seamen made their escape, and after undergoing incredible hardships succeeded in reaching the Cape of Good Hope. The fate of the rest of the sufferers has never been ascertained, although several persons were sent in search of them but without success. This unfortunate event occurred in the year 1780 or 1781.

Mr. Chauncy Lawrence, the Company's junior counsel, and brother to Sir Soulden Lawrence, a judge of the Court of Common Pleas, died soon after my return to Bengal.

The remaining gentlemen at the Bar then were Messieurs Thomas Henry Davies, Advocate-General, William Dunkin, James Dunkin, Charles Sealy, Charles Brix, Stephen Casson, Ralph Uvedale and Phinehas Hall. The attornies were nearly the same as when I left Bengal.

On the 7th of July Mr. Ley, second mate of the *Chesterfield* Indiaman, who had been in the same situation on board the *Lord Mulgrave* when Pott was passenger, came to his house, in which from that day he continued a settled inmate, shamefully abandoning his profession when in the prime and vigour of life to become an indolent dependent and toad eater to Pott, in which disgraceful situation he remained for several years, indeed until Pott, from losing his office of Resident at the Nabob's Court at Moorshedabad, could no longer afford to maintain him in sloth and idleness.

On the 8th, being told a gentleman wished to speak to me in private, I went into an ante-chamber, where I found Captain Samuel Cox, who after the usual congratulations upon my being once more an inhabitant of Calcutta, expressed great concern that his first visit should be of so unpleasant a nature, but that attachment of a very long standing made it incumbent on him to accept the disagreeable office. After premising this much, he said he called on the behalf of Mr. Nathaniel Bateman, who so strongly felt the language I had held towards him when personally present, as well as the contemptuous and disrespectful manner in which I had often spoken of him to various French officers, naval and military, whilst we were both residing at Trincomalay, rendered it imperiously necessary for him to demand of me *satisfaction*, his (Captain Cox's) business therefore was to request I would name time, place and weapons for the meeting, unless, as he sincerely hoped might be the case, I made so violent a proceeding unnecessary by apologizing for what had passed. I instantly observed that anything in the way of apology from me was wholly out of the question, as I really and truly thought the illiberal and unhandsome behaviour of Mr. Bateman deserved all I said of him. It was therefore arranged that we should meet the following morning at sunrise, at the back of Belvidere House at Alypore, with pistols, each attended by a friend ; that he (Captain Cox) should accompany Mr. Bateman.

Upon the departure of my unpleasant visitor I informed Pott of all that had occurred, entreating he would go with me, which he instantly consented to, saying, " By God, Bill, you shall shoot the dirty little rascal through the head. I have a delicate pair of Wogdens that will do his business effectually."

This 8th of July was to be an eventful day to me, for whilst sitting after breakfast in Pott's verandah towards the river I received a letter from Mr. John Lewis Auriol, the person who had made a present of little Nabob previous to my embarking for England, in which letter, after complimenting me upon my marriage and safe return to India, he enquired about the boy he *lent me* to act as servant during the voyage, adding that if I had no further occasion for him he should be glad to receive him back, being at that time greatly in want of his services.

As Nabob had clearly been an absolute and unconditional gift of Auriol's, I felt somewhat vexed at so unexpected and unjust a claim. I knew Auriol to be a niggardly, parsimonious fellow in all his pecuniary transactions, but I could not have thought him capable of such deliberate meanness. Nabob had never been the least use to me as a servant ; he had, however, been treated by myself and the whole of my family with the utmost generosity and kindness, which he repaid with the basest ingratitude, yet still I conceived he was personally attached to me, for which reason, although I considered him undeserving further attention, I resolved not to give him up to so different a master as Mr. Auriol would prove, unless he himself voluntarily consented to the change, which I own I thought impossible.

Sending for Nabob into the verandah, I mentioned the purport of the letter I held in my hand, asking if he had any recollection of his former master, Mr. Auriol, to which he answered, " Yes, I remember him very well." My next question was whether during the four years he had lived with me he had not been treated in the most kind and indulgent manner by me and by every one of my family in England. He replied coldly, " Yes." I then said, " Mr. Auriol now desires to have you back, claiming you as his exclusive property. This he undoubtedly has no right to do, nor shall he have you unless you should be desirous of changing masters. Now therefore, what say you ? Will you stay with Mrs. Hickey and me, or do you prefer going to Mr. John Auriol ? " Without a moment's hesitation, and with an exulting smile, he answered he had rather go to Mr. Auriol.

Mr. Pott had before him a folio volume of the *Encyclopædia* into which he had just been looking. So enraged was he at the little wretch's extraordinary ingratitude that uttering a great oath he let fly the immense volume at the young culprit's head, but it luckily missed him. I ordered the unfeeling boy out of sight, telling him he might go to Mr. Auriol's with the servant who had just brought me the letter.

As I was determined the shabby conduct of Auriol should not pass unnoticed, I addressed a letter to him expressive of my astonishment at his demand of the boy, the impropriety of which he must be conscious of. I nevertheless assured him I had no inclination to detain a worthless object ; at the same time I took leave to remind him that worthless and ungrateful as the boy in question certainly was, yet being now a Christian he (Mr. Auriol) could no longer be justified, nor would the law permit him, to treat him as a slave.

I had but just dismissed Mr. Nabob when Durgachuru Muckerjee came in. Immediately producing the bond I had executed to him upon my departure for England, he observed the principal and interest then due upon it amounted to upwards of eight thousand rupees, which sum he should be glad if I would forthwith pay, and also provide myself with another *banyan*, as he did not choose any longer to be in the service of an attorney.  As at no period of my life was I disposed to submit to insolence from any description of person, but more especially from a native of Asia, I told Master Durgachuru he was an impertinent scoundrel, bidding him leave the house as quickly as possible otherwise I should order my servants to kick him out.  He followed my advice without a moment's pause, proceeding from Mr. Pott's to his attorney's, whom he instructed to issue a writ of *capias ad satisfaciendum* against me, in consequence of which I was obliged to borrow the amount and discharge his demand.

Before daybreak of the 9th I gently left Mrs. Hickey in a profound sleep, and dressing myself in the next chamber, Pott, whom I found up and dressed, and I stepped into his post-chaise, driving to the appointed ground at Belvidere, distant about three miles.  Mr. Bateman and Captain Cox arrived almost at the same instant that we did.  The ground being measured (twelve paces) by the seconds, it was, after a short discussion, determined that we should toss up for the first fire.  Mr. Bateman won, discharged his pistol and missed.  I then fired mine, but equally without effect, whereupon Mr. Bateman said it was then the time for him to declare upon his honour as a gentleman he never had used any disrespectful expression either to me or Mrs. Hickey, neither by writing nor parolly, and that I had been entirely misinformed relative thereto, his language of complaint having been confined to the injustice of illiberality with which he and the other two English gentlemen, Messieurs Kemp and Brown, were treated by the French at Trincomalay, and that he had never even introduced my name or made any comparison as to our relative treatment.  Upon this declaration, so seriously made and at so momentous a time, the seconds interfered, a reconciliation instantly took place, when I felt not the least reluctance to apologize for the improper language I had used, and which I was now convinced I had used under a mistaken impression upon my mind. The seconds were much pleased with our respective conduct, Mr. Bateman and I shook hands, and thus we parted perfectly reconciled.

On the 10th I had the honour of visits from two members of the Supreme Council, Mr. Macpherson and Mr. Stables. The former I had seen several times, and had dined with, but Mr. Stables I had not met with, he being upon a visit at the city of Moorshedabad when I arrived and left my card at his house. Mr. Macpherson made a number of civil speeches, hoping he should frequently see me and Mrs. Hickey when we were settled in Calcutta. He also said his esteemed friend Mr. Benfield had mentioned us in the most flattering way in his letters to him.

The 12th my London hairdresser, Freskini, arrived and took up his abode at Pott's as one of my establishment. He came from Europe in one of the China ships to Madras, and from thence in a small country vessel. I agreed to pay him one hundred sicca rupees a month, with board and lodging, besides which I gave him permission to dress as many ladies as he could without interfering with his attendance upon me.

The remainder of the month passed in receiving and paying visits. Every evening Pott drove Mrs. Hickey and me in his phaeton to the racecourse, where it was then the fashion for the carriages to draw up round the stand, the gentlemen and ladies passing half an hour in lively conversation.

# CHAPTER XII

## OLD FRIENDS AND ACQUAINTANCES

AS many of my former native clients had applied to me
on matters of business, I was obliged to go to town daily,
Mr. Tolfrey having very obligingly accommodated me with
an apartment in his house to receive them. He, however,
strongly urged me to fix myself in Calcutta as speedily as
possible, being convinced I was losing a great deal of money
by residing out of town and not being accessible at all times
to the natives who were desirous of consulting me professionally. I therefore began to look about for a suitable
house, in which I was materially assisted by Stackhouse
Tolfrey, by Mr. Hesilrige, and his lady. With the latter pair
we spent much of our time, Mrs. Hesilrige and my Charlotte
becoming greatly attached to each other.

In the middle of August I succeeded in getting a capital
house in a central part of the town and not far distant from
the Court house, which was particularly desirable to me who
was obliged to attend there daily in the execution of my
business as an attorney. It was the property of an old
woman, a Mrs. Brightman, who let it to me at three hundred
sicca rupees a month, I binding myself to pay at that rate
of rent for one year certain.

Towards the end of the same month the *Crocodile* frigate,
or rather, I believe, sloop of war, commanded by Captain
Williamson, who several years afterwards disgraced himself
in the famous action with the Dutch on the Dogger Bank,
he at that time commanding the *Agincourt*, arrived at Calcutta, having on board passengers from Europe, Sir William
and Lady Jones. Sir William was appointed to fill the
vacant seat on the Bench occasioned by the death of Mr.

Justice Le Maitre, which happened so far back as the month of November, 1777. Sir Robert Chambers, being upon an excursion to Benares and the upper provinces, left directions that in case of Sir William Jones's coming during his absence he might have the use of his house until he could meet with one to his liking. He accordingly went into it.

The second morning after Sir William's arrival Sir Elijah Impey sent a written paper in circulation to every gentleman belonging to the Court, inviting them to breakfast at his apartments the following day, and proceed in a body from thence for the purpose of being individually introduced to the new judge previous to his being sworn into office. The advocates, officers and attornies in consequence obeyed the summons, but as I did not choose after Sir Elijah's reception of me, as already stated, to partake of his coffee or tea I joined the cavalcade on their way from the Court house to Sir Robert Chambers's, and in my turn was made known to Sir William Jones, who upon my name being mentioned said he believed we had formerly been schoolfellows at Harrow. I replied it was not me, but two elder brothers of mine who were there in his time.

After this introduction was over my friend Morse carried me to see two sisters of his who had come out to him while I was in England. They both married admirably well soon after their arrival, one to Mr. Middleton, who afterwards rendered himself famous by the evidence he gave before Parliament upon the trial of Mr. Hastings, when his total want of recollection respecting any fact or circumstances which he conceived could tend to the prejudice of his patron was so very marked and determined that he acquired the nickname of " Memory Middleton," and retained the same to the day of his death. The other sister became the wife of Mr. Cator, a man of large independent fortune, who late in life having lost a material proportion thereof in some unsuccessful speculations was induced to return to Bengal in the hopes of once more increasing his substance, and was killed on board the *Kent* Indiaman in an action with a French privateer close to Balasore Roads.

Mr. Morse, through the influence of these brothers-in-law, in the year 1781, obtained the situation of paymaster to a large detachment of troops sent overland from Bengal to the coast of Coromandel, and marched with them, consequently relinquishing his profession of a lawyer by which he had been making a great deal of money, the temptation of a paymastership, which was then considered the most lucrative situation a person could be placed in, inducing him, for a time at least, to abandon the certainty, and that, too, for what ultimately proved a delusion.   During the tedious march he was unfortunate enough to quarrel with the commanding officer, who from that moment not only thwarted him in all the customary modes of making profit of the post he filled, but likewise rendered his situation so extremely disagreeable as at last to force him in disgust to resign the paymastership and return to Bengal, where he resumed the gown and band.   Short, however, as had been his secession, for he was absent no more than seven months, his place at the Bar was already filled up by a gentleman who had been admitted as an advocate near a twelvemonth before without, however, getting into practice until Morse's departure made an opening.   This gentleman was Mr. Thomas Henry Davies, who came to India with Captain Rainier in a man-of-war.   Mr. Davies, though inferior to Morse in point of legal knowledge, had greatly the advantage in every other respect.   He was eloquent, quick, and possessed of splendid natural talents improved by the best education and much reading.   Morse, previous to his whimsical experiment, had been engaged on one side or the other in every cause, but on his resuming his original profession sat whole days in Court unemployed, a circumstance that mortified him excessively, for independent of the pecuniary consideration he had a large share of pride.   He derived some consolation from having secured a promise of the judges to appoint him sheriff the ensuing year, and he told me that if I chose to accept the office I should be his under-sheriff.

Mr. Davies owed his rise principally to his being counsel against a bye-law proposed to be brought forward by

Government, which, had it taken effect, would have been extremely prejudicial to the commercial interests of Bengal. The merchants therefore strongly opposed it, and Mr. Davies handled the subject with such skill and ability that the measure was rejected by the judges, notwithstanding they. had before approved and promised to support it. This triumph wonderfully increased the popularity of Mr. Davies, so much so that every suitor was anxious he should plead for them. He became the Company's Advocate-General, being nominated to that station by the Supreme Government of Calcutta, and so ably did he execute the various duties of the office that the Court of Directors presented him with the sum of thirty thousand sicca rupees over and above his salary and allowances, with a handsome complimentary letter expressive of the high sense they entertained of his zeal on their behalf, shewn in a great variety of instances.

Amongst the numerous visitors I had while I continued at Mr. Pott's gardens was Sir John Day, who overwhelmed me with fulsome and unmeaning professions of regard. He pressed me much to let him enjoy as large a portion of my time as I could spare from the claims of other friends. Although I considered all these as words of course, without meaning or sincerity, still I thought myself bound in common civility to call upon the knight and his lady. I accordingly did so, and was introduced in form to her ladyship, who affected to receive me as a stranger although she knew me just as well as her husband did. Being fully aware of her impertinence, I never took the least notice of her when we met casually, nor paid her the common compliment of touching my hat, neither did I ever enter the knight's house except upon special invitation, but whenever I did accept their summons I constantly went through the same ceremony of introduction, for as she coldly returned my salutation I imagine Sir John thought she did not recognize me ; he therefore, approaching and taking my hand, led me close up to his vain and silly wife, saying, " My dear, Mr. Hickey ; Mr. Hickey, Lady Day," after which she and I never exchanged a word.

We now heard of another battle having been fought between the British and French fleets off Cuddalore, the issue of which, notwithstanding the superior condition of Sir Edward Hughes's ships over those of the enemy, was in no way creditable to the English, the most that we could say being that it was a drawn battle. No ship was taken or destroyed on either side, but the conflict was most sanguinary. I was greatly concerned to hear that in this action my worthy and respected friend the Chevalier De Salvert lost his life, being cut in two by a cannon-ball on the quarter-deck of the *Flamand* whilst gallantly fighting his ship and encouraging her crew to use their utmost exertions to ensure success. I truly grieved at his death, notwithstanding he died fighting against my country, but that was no fault of his, and I firmly believe a better man never lived. Such are the dire and lamentable consequences of war, the best men often being the most unfortunate. This brings to my recollection a couplet I used to admire when a boy :

"God takes the good, too good on earth to stay,
And leaves the bad, too bad to take away."

The French according to their custom claimed a victory in this battle, and probably with more foundation than upon any of the former occasions, for they kept their station at an anchor off Cuddalore, while Sir Edward Hughes and his fleet retired to Fort St. George, there to refit his crippled ships. The reason assigned for our want of success was that all the British ships were far short of their complement of men, some of them being deficient in nearly two hundred. Of that fact I have no doubt, but I also know that the French were equally short of hands, and several of their vessels in a wretched state.

A rumour prevailed in Calcutta that the *Crocodile* had brought out Sir Elijah Impey's recall in order to answer certain charges of having been guilty of several acts incompatible with his public station of Chief Justice of the Supreme Court, which charges it was intended to bring forward as soon as he arrived in England. This rumour proved to be well founded, as Sir Elijah took his passage and embarked in the month of January.

Having furnished my house very handsomely, at an expence of upwards of twelve thousand rupees, including plate, we, on the 1st of September, went into it and commenced regular house-keepers, my Charlotte undertaking to manage the interior business. Upon thus settling in town it became necessary for her to go through a disagreeable and foolish ceremony, in those times always practised by new-comers of the fair sex, and which was called " setting up," that is the mistress of the house being stuck up, full dressed, in a chair at the head of the best room (the apartment brilliantly lighted), having a female friend placed on each side, thus to receive the ladies of the settlement, three gentlemen being selected for the purpose of introducing the respective visitors, male and female, for every lady that called was attended by at least two gentlemen. One of the three gentlemen received the hand of the fair visitor at the door, led her up to the stranger, announcing her name, whereupon curtseys were exchanged, the visitor accepted a proffered seat amidst the numerous circle, where after remaining five, or at most ten, minutes she arose, the salutations were again exchanged and the party retired to make way for the quick successor, this moving scene continuing from seven o'clock in the evening until past eleven. The same occurred the two following evenings, to the dreadful annoyance of the poor woman condemned to go through so tiresome and unpleasant a process. A further inconvenience attended this practice, which was the necessity of returning every one of the visits thus made.

As the society of Calcutta increased in number " setting up " became less frequent, and about the year 1786 ceased altogether, persons from thenceforward selecting their acquaintances according to liking as in Europe.    .

To give an idea of the fatigue attending the above monstrous ceremony I will mention that the names of those ladies I recollect to have come to Mrs. Hickey number nearly one hundred, upon each of whom she was in return obliged to call.

A few days after my coming to reside in Calcutta I received the following letter from Mr. Macpherson :

" DEAR SIR,

I am glad to hear you are come to live in town. I mean soon to pay my respects to you and Mrs. Hickey. For some time past I have been very little at home, and have been obliged to live as retired as possible, and which I must continue to do until my health is re-established.

I am very truly and with great regard,

Your faithful humble servant,

JOHN MACPHERSON."

I was also honoured with an epistle from my former troublesome client and namesake Mr. James Augustus Hicky, dated from his old quarters, the gaol of Calcutta, earnestly beseeching that 1 would have the goodness to call upon him. I complied, and thus put myself into the unpleasant predicament of being compelled to listen to his incoherent rhapsody of violence and scurrilous abuse of all those whom he fancied had offended him. He told me " he was most iniquitously and unjustly confined, that in him I beheld a victim to arbitrary power, illegally exercised, his enemies and persecutors being Warren Hastings, Governor-General, and Elijah Impey, the unworthy Chief Justice of the Supreme Court of Judicature." He further asserted " that as those despots found they could not crush him by open, fair and legal means they without scruple or compunction had recourse to the most diabolical machinations to effect their wicked purpose and complete his ruin, for which end they first tampered with and finally actually *bought* over the High Sheriff of Calcutta to their interests ; that at their instigation and under their instructions that public officer had been base and infamous enough to *pack a jury*, well convinced that without such a step no twelve British inhabitants would be found to perjure themselves to suit the inconvenience or vindictive minds of Hastings and Impey ! ''

The real fact was that this turbulent man having published various paragraphs in his famous newspaper reflecting in the strongest and most abusive language upon both the public and private conduct of the Governor-General, Mr. Hastings, that gentleman at last resolved to make an example of the author of such gross and indecent scandal by prosecuting him on the Crown or Criminal side of the Court for the libels. Three different Bills of Indictment were accordingly presented to the Grand Jury and all returned "True Bills." The first of these coming on for trial before a *petit* jury in Court, two of the jurors being for an acquittal starved out the other ten, who contended the libel had been clearly brought home to the defendant and he must be pronounced guilty. After being closely shut up for thirty hours the majority yielded, consenting to a verdict of *not guilty*, which was returned, whereupon the Chief Justice flew into a prodigious rage, violently declaring he would not suffer such a verdict to be recorded, it being directly and positively in the teeth of the evidence, and he ordered them to retire again and reconsider it, upon which Mr. Thomas Lyon, one of the jurymen, with a becoming spirit observed " he well knew the nature of the oath he had taken, which required him to do justice between the parties, that is between the Sovereign and the prisoner at the Bar ; that he had not hastily, nor without due consideration, formed his opinion, nor should he lightly change it, or be threatened into giving a different one." They, however, obeyed the order of the Court by retiring to their private apartment for a few minutes, when they returned the same verdict, *not guilty*, which the Chief Justice could not help receiving.

This was an amazing triumph for Hicky and his partisans. Sir Elijah Impey, after very indecorously commenting upon the verdict that had just been recorded and reprobating a jury capable of giving such a one, haughtily desired twelve different persons might be called to try the Second Indictment. He was, of course, obeyed, but again there happened to be (as Hicky expressed it) "at least one independent, honourable man of persevering integrity and not to be browbeat." They brought in a similar verdict, *not guilty.* The Third Indictment shared the same fate, and Hicky went off triumphant.

The following Sessions, however, "the scoundrel Chief Justice " (to use Hicky's language) "and his equally abandoned and unprincipled partner in iniquity, Warren Hastings, aided by the villain of a Sheriff, managed matters so as to suit their sinister purposes. A *petit* jury consisting of despicable wretched tools and dependants, at the head of whom appeared the names of John Rider, that arch old fiend Levett, Miller and others of the same stamp, being summoned. Fresh Indictments were preferred, *True Bills* found, and finally, to the eternal shame and disgrace of twelve Englishman, they returned in each of the three cases a verdict of guilty, notwithstanding the evidence given was precisely the same as upon the former occasions," whereupon the Court immediately pronounced judgment, sentencing him to six months' imprisonment from that day upon each Indictment, making altogether a period of eighteen months; to pay a fine to the King of three thousand sicca rupees in each case, being nine thousand in the whole, and to be further imprisoned until those fines were paid.

"Thus," continued Hicky, "am I immured in a loathsome prison for life, for all patriotism and public spirit is fled from this quarter of the globe. A few persons, very few indeed! who had not entirely lost their sensibility or the glorious feelings of Britons, pitying the hardships I had endured and the cruelty of my then situation, made an unsuccessful effort towards my relief by calling a meeting of those European inhabitants who were friends to freedom, where it was intended to propose a subscription for paying the fines, as well as the exorbitant fees of the Clerk of the Crown, and to present me with a sum of money sufficient to maintain me until I could resume my business upon enlargement, but only five gentlemen attending the meeting so summoned (every person being more or less fearful it should be known they were disposed to aid a man whom the Governor-General and Chief Justice had devoted to destruction), the matter dropped, and here, after a confinement of upwards of two years, am I doomed to terminate my miserable existence, gradually sinking with a broken heart to the grave."

Hicky, as I have already remarked, was just such another man as Cressy, blessed by nature with considerable talents, but quite uneducated, violent in temper, especially when opposed or thwarted in any of his wild plans, to the highest degree. While upon his trials he shewed much acuteness of judgment, cross-examining the witnesses for the prosecution in a manner that would not have discredited a lawyer in a first-rate practice. In his challenges of particular jurymen he excited much laughter and mirth from the objections he brought forward to some of their going into the box. One was unfit from being an open and avowed friend and supporter of Mr. Hastings ; another was upon equal good terms with Sir Elijah Impey ; a third he boldly taxed with having been bribed to find a verdict of guilty ; a fourth held a lucrative post under Government, consequently could not act independently. His objection to John Rider was delivered in these words, " I might as well at once plead guilty as have that sycophant upon my jury. He will do just as you (looking up at Sir Elijah Impey) direct him. He is absolutely at your beck and at your disposal. The man has no soul : a corrupt, sordid, contemptible toad eater of the Chief Justice, with whose wife he is tolerably familiar, plain as is his person and deficient as is his understanding. Besides, he is running about the town all day long peeping into every Europe shop in order to buy frippery (meaning millinery) for that said favourite lady." This threw the auditors into a roar of laughter. The grossness and the absurdity of the speech disarmed even the Chief Justice of his wrath, exciting only in him a contemptuous sneer.

Whilst residing at Pott's Gardens I renewed my acquaintance with Mr. Peter Moore and his family, which gentleman is now become a prodigious politician. He still continues to represent the city of Coventry in Parliament, and frequently speaks in the House, always in the opposition. His change from poverty to affluence was uncommonly rapid. At the time of my return to India in 1783 I found him no better situated in point of circumstances than when I left him in 1779. He had a wife, with a host of children, was deeply involved in debt, without a prospect of ever being able to extricate himself, for, having rendered himself obnoxious to Mr. Hastings, he had long been out of employ, for several years receiving nothing more than the three hundred and odd rupees a month allowed to senior servants who held no post or office. From some unknown cause Mr. Hastings suddenly relaxed from his hostile conduct, offering Mr. Moore a lucrative employment, which he, with the utmost contempt, refused to accept, accompanying such refusal with a letter, wherein he wrote that having already waited so unreasonable a time in expectation of being treated with justice, and disappointed in such expectations, he was resolved to wait yet longer in preference to receiving anything in the shape of a favour from the then ruling power, whose reign of tyranny and injustice he had reason to hope was nearly at an end. Strange as it may seem after such arrogant and insulting language, it is nevertheless a certain fact that within two months after thus insolently spurning at Mr. Hastings' offer to serve him, and within three months of that gentleman's quitting the Governor-Generalship, this very Mr. Moore did accept the Residency of Rungpore, to which station he accordingly went, and from whence in somewhat less than eighteen months he returned to Calcutta with so overgrown a fortune as to be enabled to return with all his family to England, get into the House of Commons, and purchase a fine estate in Essex. By what means such wealth was so suddenly acquired he best knows.

Upon my return to Bengal I found my Margate acquaintance, Metcalfe, with the rank of major in the army, and filling the post of military storekeeper, a situation in those days the most lucrative in the Company's service, which he had attained by most perseveringly courting the heads of the Government. Shortly after his last arrival in Calcutta he married Mrs. Smith, widow of Major Smith of the Company's infantry, who was brother to the far-famed General Richard Smith of cheesemongering celebrity, of whom I have already spoken upon meeting him at the Governor of St. Helena's table when on my way home in the beginning of the year 1770. This fair dame (who is now Lady Metcalfe, her husband having purchased the title of baronet) had no one merit to recommend her, at least that I could discover, unless it was a great similarity in figure, in masculine and vulgarity of manners to his *ci-devant* favourite the notorious Mrs. Cuyler. But having expressed these unfavourable sentiments of the lady it is only common candour to admit that everyone did not see with my eyes, for Mr. William Pawson, an old civil servant of the Company's upon the Bengal establishment, was so deeply enamoured with her charms that although she had not a single guinea in the world he proposed marrying and settling a handsome sum upon her, an offer she spurned at with the utmost scorn, notwithstanding which the unhappy lover persevered in his endeavours to make her relent, renewing his attack three different times, all equally unsuccessful. He was as worthy a creature as ever breathed, but clearly not the brightest genius. In proof of which I must state that I was once present with him in a large company where matrimony was the topic under discussion. After much had been said pro and con upon the subject, Mrs. Smith, looking full in Mr. Pawson's face, with a marked and peculiar manner, and in a sharp angry voice, said, "I certainly cannot tell who is destined to be my future husband, but this I can confidently affirm that I never will become the wife of a fool!" Poor Mr. Pawson, who was on the next chair to the one I sat in, thereupon turned to me and with the utmost simplicity, accompanied by a long-drawn sigh, said, "*That's me!*"

One of my earliest clients upon resuming the practice of my profession in Calcutta was this said Major Metcalfe, the subject as follows : His wife's first husband died insolvent, leaving her, as before mentioned, utterly destitute, in which pitiable situation Mr. Bromley, an attorney of great eminence in the Mayor's Court of Madras, and a truly respectable man, out of regard to the memory of her deceased husband as well as to that of her late father, Mr. Debonaire, thentofore a merchant for many years resident at Fort St. George, with both of whom he (Mr. Bromley) had lived in habits of the greatest friendship and intimacy, received her into his own family, where she was treated just as affectionately and kindly as if she had been his child. He not only paid every one of her debts, but supplied her with an ample stock of clothes and necessaries which she was previously extremely bare of, gave her money for her own private disbursements, and likewise paid the undertaker's bill for the charges of burying Major Smith.

After living in this manner for three[1] —— at Mr. Bromley's her health became so indifferent that the medical gentlemen, finding their prescriptions of no avail, advised, as is frequently their plan in similar cases, a change of air, whereupon Mr. Bromley with the same benevolence that had influenced him throughout resolved to send her to Bengal for the advantage of three cool months, which he hoped might completely restore her. He accordingly arranged everything for her, paid her passage on board a large and commodious ship, making the captain engage to convey her quite up to Calcutta, and gave her several letters of recommendation to female friends of his in Bengal, all of whom he earnestly solicited to shew every attention in their power to his poor invalid. In short, he left no effort untried for her benefit, in consequence of which she was not only most hospitably received and treated in Bengal, but soon after being restored to perfect health had the good fortune to gain the affections of Major Metcalfe, who made his offer, was accepted of course, and they married.

Impressed with grateful sentiments to Mr. Bromley, as the founder of her fortune and restorer of her health, she

[1] Word omitted in MS.—ED.

probably felt, and certainly expressed, her sense of the obligations she lay under in the most feeling language in her various letters to that gentleman, always acknowledging how much he had done for her, and that no change of situation should ever make her for a moment lose sight of the infinite obligations he had conferred upon her ; that with respect to the considerable sums of money he had disbursed on her account, should she ever marry a second time her first object should be to reimburse him the amount he had so nobly and so disinterestedly expended upon her, which she ever must consider a debt of her own, a debt, too, of such a nature as imperiously required her earliest attention to the liquidation of. Yet all these proper and grateful effusions were ultimately forgotten or not acted upon.

It so happened that Mr. Bromley from a variety of causes unnecessary here to relate became involved himself in pecuniary embarrassments, when, hearing that his late protégé, the widow Smith, had become the wife of a man possessed of immense wealth, who likewise filled a public station of great emolument, he addressed a letter to the bride wherein he informed her of the sad reverse that had occurred to him, a reverse so melancholy as to render a return of those sums of money he had advanced and paid for her when in distress and indigence an object of the utmost importance, and therefore hoping she would forthwith reimburse him according to promise. To this demand she at first replied evasively ; a regular correspondence on the subject followed, which having continued more than a year and an half, and without a single rupee being returned, he was convinced neither gratitude nor a sentiment of common honesty operated with Mrs. Metcalfe ; he therefore thought it high time to alter his mode of proceeding. He therefore wrote to Major Metcalfe, calling upon him to fulfil the engagements his wife had entered into, admitting, however, that such engagement had been so entered into during the latter part of her widowhood. With the Major he had no better success than with the wife, meeting only with shuffling and evasion. Irritated beyond measure at the woman's base ingratitude and breach of promise so repeatedly given, he resolved to proceed to coercion, for which purpose he caused a Bill in Equity to be filed in the Supreme Court against Major and Mrs. Metcalfe, wherein the whole of the particular facts herein before alluded to were set forth, to which Bill was annexed a schedule containing an account of the different sums of money he had advanced and paid to and for Mrs. Smith, and the amount then due from her. The purport of the different letters of Mrs. Metcalfe when widow Smith to the complainant Bromley wherein she expressed the high sense she entertained of the innumerable favours conferred and her fixed determination to repay the amount advanced whenever the means were within her power, etc., were stated to have been written and sent by her, but that since the receipt of them they had been lost or mislaid, and though searched for very strictly could nowhere be found.

Upon my perusing this said Bill and ascertaining that it was the handiwork of the enterprising and ingenious Mr. Solomon Hamilton, who from his peculiar merits had become the favourite attorney of Colonel Watson, and of whom I have already made honourable mention, it struck me as smelling very much of the lamp, that is to say, as one of the artful devices of a true Newgate solicitor, used as a trap to draw a person, of whose integrity and good faith he probably entertained some doubt, into a scrape by inducing the denial of ever having written or sent such letters as charged by the Bill and stated to be lost, but which letters were at that very time actually in existence to speak for themselves. With this impression upon my mind I therefore, when taking instructions for the lady's answer, and finding she boldly said she never had written any such letters, and the assertion by Bromley that she had, an infamous falsehood, very pointedly and particularly cautioned her respecting so unqualified a denial, observing it was possible the writing of them might have escaped her recollection. To which remark of mine she hastily replied, "No, no! I say, and I insist upon it. I never did write

anything of the kind ; it is an abominable lie to say I
did."

Notwithstanding these confident assertions, repeated
vehemently over and over, I again observed what an
extremely disagreeable situation she would place herself in
should such papers ever appear, a circumstance I could not
help thinking likely to happen from the explicit manner in
which their contents were set forth in the Bill and the artful
way in which the subject was treated.  So satisfied was I
that the pretence of loss of the letters was one of Mr. Solomon
Hamilton's tricks that I could not reconcile to myself the
permitting Mrs. Metcalfe to swear she never had written
such.  I therefore once more strongly urged her to qualify
the denial by adding the words " to the best of my knowledge and belief," but no, she would not listen to anything
I said on that head ; nothing short of a flat and positive
denial would satisfy the unfeeling woman, Major Metcalfe
supporting her and appearing offended at my persevering
in a wish she should be less positive.  He even asked me if
I imagined his wife to be so egregious a blockhead as to be
capable of a forgetfulness beyond probability, he might
safely say beyond all possibility.

I could add no more to what I had before said upon the
subject, but when I submitted the draught of the answer
to Mr. Morse for his perusal and signature as counsel for the
defendants I plainly told him I had not the shadow of a doubt
but that the lady was resolved to commit the grossest perjury, for I firmly believed not only that she had written the
letters as charged in the Bill, but that she had the most
perfect recollection of the fact, and basely and infamously
meant to deny it under the idea that those letters were lost,
as the Bill stated them to be, which had it been the case,
she had probably learnt, her denial would preclude all
further evidence respecting them.

Mr. Morse was shocked at my suspicion, declaring he could
not suppose a woman of Mrs. Metcalfe's rank and station in
life capable of such abandoned and infamous profligacy !
The event nevertheless shewed I was right.  Upon publica-

tion passing and my obtaining a copy of the depositions and exhibits I found every one of the letters alluded to in the complainant's Bill, besides many others, couched in equally forcible language, appeared, all in the lady's own proper handwriting, every one fully proved by competent and irreproachable witnesses.

With such damning documents in evidence the consequence naturally was a decree against the defendants for the full amount claimed by Mr. Bromley, with interest thereon at ten per cent, attended likewise with some very severe comments upon the female defendant's conduct from the Bench and the Bar, which she as well as her husband were out of the way of hearing, for before the trial of the cause they had embarked for Europe, thus avoiding the severe remarks that were made in the public newspapers and the general odium attached to their characters upon so disgraceful an issue of the cause. So much for the gratitude and the honour of the amiable Lady Metcalfe!

# CHAPTER XIII

## CHARLOTTE AND HER FRIENDS

UPON settling in Calcutta I soon got into considerable practice, and I had the gratification to find that I gave general satisfaction to my employers and was sometimes complimented by the adverse party for my candour and liberality. I kept, as I had always done wherever I resided, the first company of the place, upon all occasions treating my inferiors with civility and respectful attention, but ever discouraging any attempts towards familiarity, and thus I retained the good opinion of all ranks.

It being necessary to keep a carriage for Mrs. Hickey, I purchased a neat London-built chariot, for which I paid three thousand sicca rupees, a phaeton for my own use at eighteen hundred, and three excellent draught horses which cost me seventeen hundred and fifty, then considered a very reasonable price. All these heavy purchases, with the addition of wines and other liquors, always the most serious article in India, involved me in debt to an amount of upwards of forty thousand sicca rupees, for the whole of which I was obliged to pay an interest of twelve per cent per annum, a debt so heavy as to prove a load about my neck for full twenty years afterwards.

In the month of September the Honourable Frederick Fitzroy, then a fine boy of thirteen, arrived. He was a younger son of Lord Southampton's, which nobleman having a numerous family, with a moderate fortune to support them, was glad to accept a writership in the East India Company's service on their Bengal establishment for Frederick. As I always admired what I had been myself in my early days, that is a complete pickle, and young Fitzroy being as I conceived exactly of that description, I took notice of him by frequently inviting him to dinner with pleasant parties until from long acquaintance I discovered there was more of sheer vice than boyish mischief in his pranks and his disposition. I therefore dropped him. He was quick and acute enough, but of a depraved mind ; perhaps in common candour I ought to add that I believe he at times partook of an infirmity that prevailed in his mother and her family—insanity. He certainly was more than once deranged.

I remember a circumstance respecting that which created a great laugh. A gentleman recently arrived in Calcutta called at Mr. Macpherson's to visit one of his family named Macaulay. Meeting Fitzroy, to whom he had been introduced the preceding day, he enquired of him whether Mr. Macaulay was at home and which was his room. Fitzroy replied, " Which of them ? " The stranger said he did not know there had been more than one of the name ; that his friend was a Scotchman. " Oh zounds ! " cried Fitzroy, " that's no description here, the house is crowded with them. I am the only *foreigner* of the family. However, let us endeavour to find your friend. Should you know him when you see him ? " " Aye, surely," said the gentleman, " perfectly well." "That's lucky," replied the young pickle, " then I'll tell you what to do. Go out into the street, stand opposite the middle of the front of the house and call out in as loud a voice as you can, ' *Mac !* ' . In an instant you'll see a head pop out, of every window in the house, and you can then fix upon the identical Mac you are in search of ! "

I was scarcely settled in my house in Calcutta ere my dearest Charlotte's health began visibly to decline, although to my daily remarks thereon and entreaties that she would take care of herself and let me consult a physician she invariably desired I would not do so, for that nothing ailed her that could be attended with danger, and she was sure the approaching cool weather would entirely carry off the trifling complaint she had. Whilst at Pott's country house she had been more than once attacked with sudden and violent pains in her breast, upon which occasions I procured the medical assistance of Dr. James Wilson, who resided in the neighbourhood, when he gave me the comfortable intelligence that nothing was to be apprehended, the attacks being altogether nervous, and he agreed with her in thinking the change of weather would entirely restore her. This made me less uneasy than I otherwise should have been. The seeds of a fatal disease were nevertheless then lurking about her, the progress of which was probably hastened by the uninterrupted course of entertainments she was engaged in, and the late hours she necessarily kept in consequence, for all my old acquaintances and many new ones were abundantly civil. Among the former no one surpassed Mr. Stackhouse Tolfrey, from whom I received a small box containing a beautiful pearl necklace, ear-rings and bracelets, accompanied by the following letter :

" My Dear Hickey,

From the unkindness of Mrs. Hickey I am obliged to request the exercise of a husband's authority. Would you believe she could have been so cruel as to treat me as the most entire stranger by refusing a very trifling mark of my esteem. Yet this I assure you she has done, and I must now be indebted to your influence for a favour which I acknowledge I should have been more gratified to have owed to her good opinion. Tell her, my inestimable friend, of the many many, the innumerable obligations I lay under to you, and she surely will not continue to make me unhappy by denying me the pleasure of showing by any little attentions in my power the truly grateful sense I have, and surely ought to have, of the kindnesses conferred, kindnesses so unbounded that I feel conscious I never can sufficiently return them. Mrs. Hickey's unkindness towards me must appear the more extraordinary and the greater when I tell you that the object of her scruples is the trifle that I send herewith, which I beg and hope you will compel her to receive, and, if she does not deem them unworthy, to wear them in remembrance of a truly grateful friend of her husband's.

Yours ever,

St. Tolfrey."

This magnificent present, which the donor made so light of, was of the value of two hundred pounds at least, and it was their costliness that induced my poor darling to refuse accepting them.

The following complimentary letters were from Mr. William Johnson and Mrs. Hesilrige :

" MY DEAR MRS. HICKEY,

I could not write to you before this instant because I wanted first to see Lady D'Oyley, who dines here, and we expected she would sup here also. That, however, is still in suspense, and if she does not my sister is to sup with her. I have asked my sister what I shall say from her, to you, and these are her words, ' I shall be very sorry indeed to have Mrs. Hickey call again without my seeing her, and as there is a probability of my going out this evening and I might thereby be deprived the happiness of meeting her should she call during my absence from home, which would be a great disappointment to me, do therefore, my dear brother, present my kindest respects to her and request the favour of her to spend the evening and sup here on Friday, as I am to pass to-morrow at Champion's Gardens.' I hope, my dear madam, that Hickey's indisposition will not prevent you from complying with her request, and that we shall see him with you. I shall rejoice to hear he is better. You seemed so uneasy about him last night that I was really alarmed, and could I possibly have got out to-day should have called to see him.

Yours very respectfully,

WM. JOHNSON."

" I want much, my dear Mrs. Hickey, to come and sit with you, but the ugly doctor will not let me go out in the sun as I yesterday had some return of fever, and I assure you it increases my uneasiness from knowing I have already been tormented with this fever near five months. I am told great attention and care, aided by the bark, will soon rid me of it entirely. I do assure you nothing but the care I am compelled to take of my poor weak and debilitated frame could prevent me from being constantly your companion during your confinement. It is every way a mortifying circumstance to me not to be able to do so, as I should thereby not only pass my hours happily, but feel a particular gratification in endeavouring by every means in my power to contribute to your ease and comfort.

Believe me,

Most affectionately yours,

E. J. HESILRIGE."

My dearest Charlotte had the further gratification to find that she was not forgotten by the friends she acquired during our stay at Madras, as the following kind letters fully evince. The first was from Mrs. Barclay in these words :

" MADRAS,<br>19th July, 1783.

" MY DEAR FRIEND,

I had the pleasure to receive your letter dated the 29th of June two days ago, and it gave me very sincere satisfaction to hear of your safe arrival at Bengal, where I sincerely hope you and Mr. Hickey enjoy good health and find Calcutta answer your expectations. This is the hearty and cordial wish of your firm friend. I have the inexpressible pleasure to inform you of the long and much wished for peace. Yesterday a man-of-war of sixty-four guns arrived here from Europe, bringing the glad tidings. Likewise, that two Indiamen left Johanna four days before she did, so that we are in hourly expectation of seeing them. There has been sad and melancholy doings at Cuddalore, many lives lost on both sides without any material advantage to the respective powers at variance. Poor Cotgrove, a most worthy body, fell from a mistake of our own people. This naturally dull spot affords nothing new or entertaining to write about. Undoubtedly we are as stupid as we can *wish* or *desire !* The Taner family leave the Presidency in a few days, going to a far-distant province. Mrs. Latham precisely in the same situation that you left her. Her sister, Lady Gordon, poor dear, has been and continues materially indisposed. I shall expect volumes of news from you who reside in the midst of elegant gaiety and festivity. I very seldom see Mr. Popham, *entre nous,* he is a strange oddity. The few merits he has are infinitely outweighed by his *peculiarities.* I must not presume to use a stronger word. Adieu, Mr. Barclay joins me in kind compliments and best wishes to you and Mr. Hickey.

And believe me, my dear Mrs. Hickey,

Your sincere and ever affectionate friend,

Augusta Barclay."

The following was from Mrs. Garrow :

"Madras, 31*st July*, 1783.

"My Dear Mrs. Hickey,

I have received your letter and am very happy to hear of your safe arrival in Bengal after so uncommonly bad and disagreeable a passage as you had, but you was most fortunate in meeting with such a man in the command of the ship as Captain Serocold. I make no doubt but you will like your situation, as I hear the inhabitants of Bengal are much more sociably disposed than we hum-drum Madrassers. To add to your society there are a great many ladies arrived here whose final destination is your quarter. Many of them are single, and some very pretty, really beautiful. I have not yet been to see any of them, being, as you well know, a sad visitor. I hear nothing talked of now but *the fashions !* It is reckoned the height of indelicacy to show the ear or any part of it ; the hair is therefore cut in such a manner as wholly to cover that part of the head, not even the tip must be seen. For my own part I am very well satisfied with the old custom, and too sedate to adopt every absurd and preposterous innovation.

I called lately upon Lady Gordon and delivered your message. I never saw anything like the alteration that has taken place in her appearance. Poor woman, she has been alarmingly ill, and this last attack has increased her eager desire to leave this sultry place and return to Europe. Her sister is considerably better, so much so that she daily goes out in a carriage for air and exercise. Our friend, Mrs. Barclay, told me she had written to you, and she would, I am sure, give you all the news and little occurrences of Fort St. George. Mr. Garrow joins me in best wishes to Mr. Hickey and you.

I remain,

Yours very sincerely,

S. Garrow."

"P.S.—I return you many thanks for your kind offer to assist me with any little articles I may want from Bengal, and for which I certainly will take the liberty of applying to you."

Mr. Josias Du Prè Porcher's letter was in these words :

" MY VERY DEAR MADAM,

If you recollect I often told you that you would forget your promise of writing to me, and I am sorry to àdd I was too true a prophet. In revenge I shall plague you continually with my scrawls, which are always dry and therefore happily adapted to the purpose. Hickey, I hope, is as busy as possible, for I wish both so well in spite of your usage of me that nothing would give me greater pleasure than to hear he is in a fair way of soon completing his business. After all, this is but a poor country, and certainly not an agreable one for a lady. On your return to England you must positively call here, and if at that time I possess a house good enough for your ladyship I shall insist upon you being my guest. Besides a settled determination to tease you, I have an additional motive for writing this, which is to introduce the gentleman who will deliver it to you. I do not hesitate requesting you and Hickey to show him a little civility on my account, the compliance with which will in some measure induce me to forgive you. I think I hear you say that I am grown impertinent and saucy, possibly it is true, but be assured I still possess the greatest esteem for you, and this is the only excuse I can make for my freedom. To return to my young friend who bears this : I have long lived in habits of friendship with his family, for whom I have an high regard. They have a right to expect every attention from me, and I feel pleased at transferring those attentions from them to their son. I have promised him a smile from you, and I trust you will not, indeed it is not in your nature to, disappoint him. He has a brother in Calcutta who he may probably take occasion to introduce to you. I wish . . . but I will ask no more favours at present, one in all reason is sufficient. Pray remember me most kindly to Hickey, and believe me, as I am, with truth, my dear madam,

Your hearty well wisher and most obedient servant,
J. DU PRÈ PORCHER."

FORT ST. GEORGE,
10th August, 1783.

" I had nearly forgot to mention the name of the gentleman who I have thus taken the liberty to introduce to you. It is Fletcher."

III.—N

Then came another from Mrs. Barclay :

" MADRAS,<br>
20<i>th November</i>, 1783.

" MY DEAR MRS. HICKEY,

You judge right in supposing my long silence proceeded from indisposition. I have been exceedingly ill with a severe bilious fever which for some time made me quite indifferent about everything, nor could I bring myself even to set down to write to you, my friend. I hope the truth thus really stated will be a sufficient apology. I can give you very little news from this place. We have a ball monthly, by subscription, which makes us rather less dull than heretofore ; no marriages on foot nor any talked of. I do not recollect whether Miss Maule became Mrs. Wickens before you left us. On his side I believe it was more a match of *interest* than *love*. She appears several years older than her hubby. Rather unfortunate that ! Proposals for a concert are going about ; how long it will last who shall presume to say. Many of the performers, both vocal and instrumental, must necessarily be ladies and gentlemen. It will be an agreable way of passing what otherwise might hastily be pronounced a stupid evening. I am sorry you do not like Bengal, which I plainly perceive is the case. Many thanks for your kind invitation, perhaps when you perform your promise of visiting me at Fort St. George I may return with you to the far-famed Fort William. Your little admirer, Doctor Lucas, is quite happy, for his fair *rib* will shortly be here. I am told that the beauteous widow Maclellan is shortly to become the wife of one of our Coast Gentlemen. I think she has no great reason to be over pleased with the galantry of Bengal.

Your friend, Mr. Popham, is become quite gay, only think of his dancing until morning at the last ball. Nothing like it, you will say. Lady Gordon and her sweet little ones are gone home on a man-of-war. Mrs. Latham is quite recovered and talks of following her sister's example as soon as she is able to procure a passage. Mrs. Johnson is very well, but I apprehend Mr. Johnson, poor fellow, is not long for this world. Mrs. Garrow told me she had written to you some time ago. She is perfectly well. The *Crocodile* from Bengal is just anchored in the roads. Pretty daring of her captain to venture here in the height of the monsoon. Advices have just been received here from Anjingo giving an account of the total loss of the admiral's flagship, the *Superb*, which foundered off the Island of Ceylon. Most fortunately the whole of the ship's crew were saved. By the same route letters are come from England of so late a date as the 4th of June. By these letters a report is mentioned that a Bill was immediately to be introduced into Parliament by the Lord Advocate of Scotland, empowering the Government to undertake the management of the Company's affairs, and which measure it was supposed was not likely to meet with much opposition. The latter our politicians and sage heads in this place seem to doubt the probability of. Indeed, so do I! Adieu, I feel that I have exhausted your patience. This moment Captain Thomas has brought me your kind letter, for which accept my best thanks. It affords me real and sincere satisfaction to hear that your health is compleatly established. That you may long enjoy it is the cordial wish of your sincerely attached friend.

AUGA. BARCLAY."

In the latter end of September Mr. and Mrs. Hesilrige left Calcutta to spend some time with different friends of theirs up the country, particularly Sir John D'Oyly and his lady at Moorshedabad, where the Baronet filled the high and lucrative post of Resident at the Durbar of the Nabob, a situation to the succession of which my friend, Robert Pott, had procured the appointment from the Court of Directors previous to his leaving London, and which he had so obtained upon the personal application of Lord Thurlow, at that time Lord Chancellor.

The departure of Mr. Hesilrige's family from the Residency was a serious loss to my darling Charlotte, who had spent much of her time with Mrs. Hesilrige. A few days previous to that lady's setting out upon the excursion she one morning took Mrs. Hickey a-shopping, going to a number of different ones kept by Bengallees in the China Bazaar, in all of which Mrs. Hesilrige tumbled over the goods without laying out a single rupee, to the extreme annoyance of my dear girl, who never could bear to give trouble without making some sort of compensation, under which impression she took from a shop, wherein her fair companion had been particularly troublesome and bought nothing, a couple of pieces of Europe ribbon though not at all in want of them, of which circumstance she told me the moment she got home, but it escaped my recollection, to which it was brought back in a manner not the most agreeable three days after the purchase, when I received a letter signed " Sol. Hamilton, Attorney at Law," saying if I did not immediately pay thirty-two sicca rupees for two pieces of ribbon, due to Gopee Day, together with five sicca rupees, the costs of that application, an action would forthwith be commenced against me in the Supreme Court for the recovery thereof.

Indignant at such a demand for so paltry a sum I wrote an answer to the blackguard attorney in a style that galled him to the quick, accompanying my letter with the amount required. I also shewed this elegant epistle to the judges, to every officer of the Court, and to the most respectable gentlemen of the settlement, who one and all expressed their disapprobation. The mean wretch made the most abject apologies, protesting it was inadvertence, entirely the fault of his clerk, who brought the letter to him to sign with a variety of other papers, to all of which he put his name without looking at them. In reply I merely observed that it was disgraceful in him as a professional man to acknowledge he ever fixed his name to a paper he had not first read. From that day I always avoided having any intercourse with Colonel Watson's " shrewd attorney," Solomon Hamilton.

Early in the month of November the subscription Assemblies for the season commenced. Beaux without number proffered their services to escort Mrs. Hickey, whom I endeavoured to dissuade from going from her indifferent state of health, but my entreaties and arguments were all thrown away. Nothing short of a positive command would I saw be observed, and so strong a measure I did not like to use. She assured me she felt considerably better and stronger than she had been, and was quite sure it would do her no harm. All the ladies of her acquaintance encouraged her to be at least present, even if she had fortitude enough to resist dancing, an amusement she was remarkably fond of and which she excelled in. Indeed they could not see any serious objection to her partaking of a couple of dances, but that I did take upon me peremptorily to forbid.

Before the month of November was over Mrs. Hickey's health became evidently worse, although she would not confine herself to the house nor admit that she was so ill as to require either particular care or the advice of physicians, but I, who anxiously watching, perceived an almost daily increased weakness and languor, insisted upon her receiving Doctor James Stark, then the favourite practitioner of Calcutta, and I accordingly summoned him. After asking her a variety of questions he wrote a prescription, recommending her continuing quiet at home and not to have any large parties for some days at least. All which conditions she reluctantly yielded to. During her confinement, as my business necessarily occupied much of my time, I was glad to find our friends exceedingly attentive, several ladies coming to sit with her a great part of the day. Bob Pott often called, contributing much to raise and keep up her spirits by his extraordinary cheerfulness and vivacity. Very early in December we were deprived of his agreeable society by his being appointed Chief of the District of Burdwan, a place about sixty-five miles distant from Calcutta, then considered one of the most lucrative situations in the Civil Service, but which Robert notwithstanding affected to dislike and to be offended with Mr. Hastings for giving him so insignificant and *paltry* an office, he loudly declaring the Governor-General ought to have turned out Sir John D'Oyly from the Residency at the Nabob's Durbar at Moorshedabad and put him into it, he having been nominated thereto by the Court of Directors, a presumption and expectation of Pott's that certainly was unreasonable in the extreme.

My poor Charlotte's hours of pain and lassitude were further beguiled by the good-humoured letters of Mr. Hesilrige, who, whilst on his excursion up the country, addressed the following to her :

"It is with much pleasure, my dearest madam, that I avail myself of the indulgence you granted me of writing to you. I cannot recollect an instance of my commencing a correspondence with so much satisfaction as I do the present. I promise myself every advantage from it, whilst I cannot but regret that the liberality of nature has not put it in my power to make you an adequate return. In the epistolary style your sex certainly possess every advantage over us. You have a delicacy in the manner of expressing your sentiments to which we have never attained, whilst the beauty, ease, and elegance for which you are so much admired shine conspicuous throughout your writings. This being the case in general, what may I not expect from you who so much excel in every polite accomplishment, and was it not for the prospect of being upon the most friendly footing with you as a neighbour upon my return to Calcutta, I should exceedingly regret that my absence from thence promises to be of so short a duration. Was it not that I am upon the point of re-visiting a very valuable wife I confess I should be somewhat melancholy in my solitary Budgerow. Indeed, I sometimes suspect that I actually am so, for my companions, who are of the canine race, look up in my face with dejected countenances, and absolutely appear low-spirited. Now, as I believe I do not in general deserve to be dignified with the Spanish Don's title of 'Knight of the sorrowful countenance,' I know not how to account for this unless it is that these sagacious animals perceive that I am less cheerful than usual. But now, my sweet little woman (There's for you !), can I be otherwise after quitting so lively and so inspiring a society as that to which I devoted almost my whole time in Calcutta. Hickey may say, if he pleases, that I am making downright love, and in due form ! I care not a button what he says, but this I will say that I never was happier than when in Mrs. Hickey's company ; that I admire and esteem her, and set the greatest value upon her friendship. You see that I have been only three days from Calcutta, and that I am already advanced on my way to Rangamatty as far as Nuddea.

I should have written to you before had there been a post office upon the way into which I could have put a letter. It would have been an interesting amusement to me to have done so, for absent as I am from my friends I assure you time often hangs heavy upon my hands. I rise early in the morning and amuse myself until towards eight o'clock (when the day begins to be oppressively hot) with my gun. I then breakfast and kill the middle hours as well as I can with books or my pen, writing letters to relations in Europe who care quite as little for me as I do for them. I dine at two, and as I do not profess to sleep in the afternoon, only *nap it* from half-past three to five, about which time I go on shore to walk on the banks of the river until dusk. I next drink tea, and smoke my hookah until eight, when I sup and retire to bed about the time that I conceive Bradford is entering your hall with his usual smiling countenance, or the gentle Stackhouse looking *languishingly* upon a certain lady who shall be nameless.

I think you would have been pleased could you have made the little excursion that we once talked of. The weather has been delightfully pleasant, and although at this season of the year the face of the country is not altogether so beautiful as during the rains, still you would have been much pleased with the infinite variety of scenes the river affords. In point of mere prospect Bengal has little to boast. It admits of no other diversity than what a different disposition of ·wood and water can be supposed to give to a flat country, but it is so highly cultivated and so very populous that it at once conveys to you the pleasing idea of peace, plenty, and content. The party should have been composed of none but your particular friends, and every one would, I am certain, have exerted themselves to amuse you. I hope, however, for Mr. Hickey's sake that things are better as they are, for I take so warm a part in his welfare that I would at all times give up every consideration of self for his advantage.

I much regret that I forgot to ask you for the book you promised to lend me. Having with me only *Priestly* on matter and spirit, the gentleman is endeavouring to persuade me that I have no soul, and that we have all laboured under a mistake in supposing that we had anything immortal about us. If Tolfrey never puns, pray ask him for his opinion upon this subject. It will afford him a fine opportunity of entering into a most learned dissertation, such a one as I conceive must be equally edifying and entertaining. Besides, it may give him occasion to make a digression (which he likes to do) to the Beauties of Sentiment ! The Charms of Society ! The Harmony of Souls ! and he may conclude by labouring to convince you that there is such a thing as platonic affection ! These are matters I never attempt to discuss myself, conscious of my inability for so doing ; I therefore leave those knotty points to men of superior talents or understanding. Sufficient is it for me that I have started a topic. By this time I may fairly presume you think that I have written quite enough for one letter. Indeed, I cannot entertain a doubt upon that head. I hope, however, that as Lady D'Oyly did by my singing you will not lay an injunction upon me ' *not to favour you with any more of it !* ' for although I am ready to admit that I write the greatest nonsense in the world, and that my letters are in general hardly legible, nevertheless I am fond of writing to those I feel a regard for. Permit me, my dear madam, to remind you of your promise and beg the favour of you to direct to me at Sir John D'Oyly's, Afzoulbang. My best respects attend Mr. Hickey, and I have the pleasure to subscribe myself with every sentiment of esteem, my dear madam,

Your very obedient and devoted humble servant,

ARTHUR HESILRIGE."

" MY DEAR MADAM,

I have been not a little flattered by the receipt of your letter, and notwithstanding your threats, of which the parties are apprized, I beg leave to renew to you my assurances of the sincerest attachment and regard. Permit me also to tell you that I am not a little proud of my new correspondent, and am very far from being disappointed in my expectations. Your letter was exactly what I could have wished it, and if I possessed half the vanity which you sometimes laid to my charge I should on my return to the Presidency be insupportable to half your Beaus. However, I will say nothing further upon the subject lest you should again pretend to be angry, for I should, I suppose, be pronounced a most impertinent fellow if I was to tell you that I am convinced the anger was a mere pretence. Not, by the by, that I recollect a syllable in my last letter that could be construed into the most distant degree of flattery. I endeavoured to express my genuine sentiments, nor can I tax my memory with having used a single expression the whole force of which I did not feel at the time. It gives me much pleasure to inform you that upon my arrival here I found my *better half,* as I am convinced you will without much difficulty allow her to be, in good health. The air of Rangamatty has agreed so surprizingly well with her that I think she now enjoys as good a state of health as she has ever done since I had the happiness of knowing her.  She begs me to present her best respects to you, and to assure you that she shall consider herself not a little flattered in possessing your esteem which on her part has already commenced, and that nothing shall be wanting to encrease and cultivate an acquaintance from whence she truly hopes will proceed the strictest intimacy and the sincerest friendship.  We shall certainly leave Belvidere on Tuesday next, but I fear that we shall be some time in getting down to Calcutta as the river is, I understand, very low, having fallen two feet within the last three days.  I do not, however, despair of having the honour of kissing your hand by the Monday or Tuesday following at farthest.  We are both equally anxious to get back, for though no society can be more cheerful than that of Belvidere, and though Sir John and Lady D'Oyly study to make their visitors happy, yet, after all, there is no place like one's own home, and however engaging pleasure and dissipation may be for a time they at last lose their charms, and we all willingly revert to the calm domestic scene which is in no part of the world so conspicuous as in Calcutta.  I have a great inclination to write a lecture upon the sweets of retirement, but as my ink is wretchedly bad and pen still worse, and having no means of rectifying either one or the other, I believe I may as well postpone the attempt until a future day, so for the present, my dear madam, adieu.  My kindest remembrances, if you please, to Mr. Hickey, and pray tell him not to despond.  Surely if he finds reason to be low-spirited I ought to hang, drown, or shoot myself.  We may be poor spite of ourselves, but let us at least be merry. Apropos, I hope you have no more fits, except it be of laughing, and of those long may you live to enjoy very many.

I am, my dearest madam,

Your most devoted and most obedient servant,

A. HESILRIGE."

"  1st November, 1783.

"MY DEAR MADAM,

As is usually the case when there is a large party we have experienced innumerable stoppages and vexatious delays, nor did we get fairly clear of Moorshedabad until Thursday last. We are now parading down the stream of the Cossimbuzar River with seventeen pinnaces and Budgerows, besides an immense train of boats of all descriptions, consequently our progress is slow, nor will it be possible for us to reach Calcutta so early as I expected by some days. These immense parties are to me by no means agreable. I am not over fond of a croud on shore, and still less so for any length of time upon the water. A select society of attached friends, half a dozen, for instance, has in my opinion more charms beyond comparison. Yet vanity is gratified by parade, and even men of superior understanding are too prone to be dazzled by mock pageantry. In England it answers very well with the common people, and points have often been carried by imposing upon the vulgar with pomp and show. In this country it may have a still greater effect, as the lower class of people think less. I am therefore in a certain degree an advocate for state where it can produce a beneficial effect, but in the instance that calls forth these remarks I can see no possible benefit to be gained, and cannot help feeling mortified when I see a much valued friend and most worthy man so lavish of expence to answer no one good end or purpose unless it be the ridiculous and unjustifiable one of attempting to feed the follies and gratify the consummate vanity of an inconsiderate woman. You, as a lady of superior prudence, a virtue I fear not often met with in your sex, will, I am convinced, be of my way of thinking, and would prefer, did an opportunity offer which should afford a prospect of returning in a few years to your native country, the living at a moderate expence to an absurd profusion which might detain you many years longer in India. You must perceive that at present I have no cause to complain of being solitary, as we set down at table every day twenty in number and our time glides on very agreably. Still, I wish to be at home, though I may be disappointed in my expectation of being happier there, as the learned seem to have agreed that happiness is ideal, and that consequently we may be so in any place if we can but make up our minds to it. But begging their worships' pardon, according to my notion of things, this is not so easily done, and if I am not much mistaken the most sanguine supporters of the doctrine would have felt as much, if not more, in our old friend Robinson Crusoe's situation than he did. You were, I hope, prodigiously amused at the Assembly. Being the first, I presume it was consequently brilliant, and I doubt not the Stewards did everything in their power to give general satisfaction. As many spinsters were on that evening to make their debut in white, I think it would have been obliging in the gentlemen to have allowed them to adopt the colour of their dresses to their complexions, but I am told a *Favour* would be deemed sufficient. Your superior taste in dress is so universally admitted that it is doing you no more than justice to conclude that yours was the most elegant, if not the most costly, in the room. I hope on some future night to have the honour of being in your suite ; to be your beau I cannot have the presumption to aspire to, being an old married man, which is no recommendation to the ladies. You must know I am become quite sober and sedate, like some other folks, too, I am kept in admirable order. You will be convinced when you see me again that I want nothing but a full-bottomed wig to complete the gravity of my demeanour. With or without a peruke, I am at all times your *tres* humble *serviteur*. My Rib desires her best respects to you, and I beg mine to Mr. Hickey.

    I remain, with real regard, my dear madam,
        Your very sincere and obedient servant,

                    A. HESILRIGE."

                  " AUGURDEEP,
                      *Sunday.*

" May I trouble you to send a servant with the enclosed to Mr. Sherburne. It is to request him to send my phaeton to Cosspore for us next Sunday evening. Adieu."

    The writer of the foregoing letters succeeded his father as a baronet, shortly prior to which his wife had been obliged to return to Europe for the recovery of her health. During her absence he became so greatly embarrassed in his affairs that one of his principal creditors, a native, arrested him, whereupon he, very properly resolving not to pay one to the prejudice of the rest, upon the return of the writ surrendered himself in discharge of his bail and went to prison, where Mrs. Hesilrige, upon again going to India, found him. This mortifying circumstance, added to her health not being perfectly restored, preyed so much upon her as to produce a decline, which in about eight months terminated in her death. Shortly before that event, however,

Mr. Hesilrige had obtained his liberty. Soon after his coming to the title he was so inconsiderate as once more to engage in the holy state of matrimony, marrying a wild and giddy girl of fifteen, daughter to Mrs. Grey, the sister of Sir Home Popham's lady, Sir Arthur being then considerably on the wrong side of forty. From the variety of ill consequences arising from so foolish and unequal a match he was relieved by a bilious fever's taking him out of the world about five years ago, within six months after which event his wanton widow consoled herself in the arms of a handsome young lieutenant of infantry in the Company's service of the name of Wilkinson, who became her second husband.

# CHAPTER XIV

## THE DEATH OF CHARLOTTE

UPON my return from England in the year 1783 and again settling in Calcutta and resuming the practice of an attorney, I applied to those gentlemen that had been members of the committee for conducting the business of the petition to Parliament for trial by jury in civil cases to reimburse me the expences I had incurred in conveying such petition to England, etc., some of which gentlemen were well disposed to comply with my demand, considering the same as just and reasonable. At the head of those feeling and declaring their opinion thus stood my zealous advocate upon all occasions, Colonel Watson ; but Colonel Pearse, who had then just returned from the coast of Coromandel, Mr. Shore and others, opposing it, not, as they declared, from any personal enmity towards me, but from conceiving they were not individually liable to be so called upon, the just intentions of Colonel Watson and those equally well disposed were frustrated. Two of my warmest friends also were lost to me, Mr. Cottrell being dead and Mr. Higginson embarked for Europe.

Thus situated I was driven to the necessity of applying to the Supreme Court for redress, but previous to so doing I prepared and submitted my case to counsel, therein truly stating every particular relative to it, especially that of having not only given up my time and professional assistance entirely to the committee for more than two months prior to my sailing for England, but having likewise disbursed large sums of money in paying the Keeper of the Records and different officers of the Court for a great variety of copies of official documents which it had been deemed requisite to procure in the progress of the petition, and which had I made out a bill for as an attorney would have amounted to more than the sum I now demanded.

Upon this case I got an opinion most clearly and decidedly in my favour, saying I was indisputably entitled not only to a pecuniary remuneration for my personal attendance and services upon the committee as an attorney, but also a complete reimbursement of all sums of money I had expended for the advancement of the object in hand, but that as I had no written instrument to shew the nature of the contract subsisting between me and the committee I must necessarily have recourse to a Bill in Equity against those persons who had employed me, the prayer of which Bill must be to compel them to a specific performance of their parol agreement made with me. The opinion added that special care must be taken not to omit any of those names who ought to be defendants, otherwise I might be defeated by a demurrer for want of parties.

I accordingly prepared a Bill in Equity, laying the draught thereof before Mr. Brix, an experienced advocate of the Court, for his perusal and signature, who returned it the ensuing day without making the least alteration, accompanying it with a complimentary letter, wherein he was pleased to say it was by far the ablest and best-drawn pleading that ever had been laid before him, to which therefore he affixed his name with peculiar satisfaction, feeling convinced I could not fail of obtaining that redress the hardships of my case so eminently called for. The Bill being engrossed was filed and a subpœna for the defendants to appear and answer issued.

Just at that time my dearest Charlotte's situation became more critical. I observed her daily becoming weaker. With anxiety inexpressible I summoned Doctors Stark and Wilson to meet at my house and consult upon her case. They did so. The result was their advising me immediately to take her upon the river for a few days and try what effect change of air might produce. I caused a large and commodious boat to be forthwith prepared. On the 7th of

December, carefully conveying her on board, we proceeded to Budge Budge, where my valuable friend Major Mestayer received us into his hospitable mansion with all his accustomed and kind liberality.  During the first four-and-twenty hours of being there my dear woman became somewhat better, but then rapidly fell off and, expressing much solicitude to be at home, on the fifth morning we re-embarked and returned to Calcutta, where I landed her vastly weaker than when she left it and in every respect worse.  Still, neither of the medical gentlemen considered her as being in actual danger.

While I was at Budge Budge Mr. Morse had been appointed Sheriff, which office he was to enter upon the duties of on the 20th.  According to his promise he nominated me his Deputy or Under-Sheriff, but I was so engaged in watching my darling, whom I saw gradually and fast sinking, that 1 could think of nothing else.  She would not allow that she was at all worse, though compelled to admit she suffered greatly.  All patience and resignation, she bore a painful disease with a degree of fortitude unexampled, never when I was present uttering a complaint or even a sigh, lest it should increase my unhappiness.

On the 19th Doctor Stark, for the first time, told me he apprehended his patient in extreme danger, that so alarming a change for the worse had taken place in the preceding night he saw no hope left, and her death, even in a few hours, would not surprize him !  This was horrible tidings, nor can I attempt to describe the grief with which it overwhelmed me.  During the succeeding night I never for a moment quitted her bedside, though she repeatedly urged me in the strongest manner her enfeebled state would admit to retire and take some rest.  Rest, alas ! was wholly out of the question.  The 20th she continued nearly the same.  On that day I was under the indispensable necessity of going out to the gaol to receive charge of the prisoners, civil and criminal, examine the lists and state of the prison, etc., with the ex-sheriff.  Oh ! what a morning did I pass.  I scarcely knew what I said or did, and was in a constant tremor from the momentary expectation of the fatal event being announced.

The assignments and various deeds to which I was a party being executed, Mr. Morse considerately insisted upon my going home instead of to the Sheriff's office, and not to bestow a thought on business until Mrs. Hickey should be better. Alas : too sure did I feel that time would never arrive, for that I was doomed to the misery of losing her. Upon going home I found her nothing worse. On entering the room she languidly smiled, held out her emaciated hand, saying she was not in quite so great pain. I could perceive this was only said for the purpose of comforting me. Thus she continued four more days. In the morning of the 25th (a fatal Christmas Day to my happiness) after about three hours of perturbed, uneasy sleep procured from large doses of laudanum, she awoke, when seeing me hanging over her in an agony of grief she cast a mournful look upon me, then raised her poor arms and, drawing me towards her, kissed me with her almost clay-cold lips—such a kiss as I never can forget ! The effect of it is indelibly engraved upon my memory, never to be effaced ! In a faint and scarcely audible voice she bid me be comforted and submit to the fiat of the Almighty, said she had dreamt she was delivered of eleven children, the terror of which had awakened her, that she should soon be well and relieved from excruciating suffering. After a long pause she again entreated that I would not repine at what was unavoidable, adding, " God bless you, my dearest William, God bless you ! Oh, leave me, leave me ! " and fainted. The physicians entered at that moment, when Doctor Wilson exclaimed, " 'Tis all over. She's gone." This was the last I saw of her. They forced me from the apartment and the house. She continued to breathe, but without any other sign of existence, until ten o'clock at night, when with a gentle sigh she expired.

It is those only who have truly loved and survived to mourn the loss of all they held dear upon earth that can conceive the agonies I endured. My sorrow yielded not to the exhortations of numerous friends who with the most humane intention endeavoured to console me, bidding me reflect that she was released and happy! But such reflections had no power to conquer my regret or reconcile me to the sad event. On the contrary, they increased, they embittered, the severity of my pangs. In many instances did I verify the truth of the observation that "when we first conceive we clasp pleasure to our breast we in fact invite the stings of pain." Upon obtaining the uninterrupted possession of my adored Charlotte I thought of naught but supreme felicity, a felicity that proved of short duration, being checked almost every day of my life by an anxiety the most excruciating and distressing on her account. When the cruel hand of death seized upon her, then it was I felt, oh most keenly felt, the horror of my situation and the dismal loss I had sustained in being suddenly deprived of so much excellence. Safely may I say I truly, fondly loved her, loved her with an affection that every new day, if possible, strengthened. Our tastes were similar, our foundation of happiness depended upon each other; kindred feeling was the standard of both, and we were perfectly satisfied each with the other. Her funeral took place on the 26th, every respectful attention being shewn to her memory. Her remains were followed to its last sad mansion by a host of friends of both sexes, who sincerely loved and respected her living and truly mourned her dead.

After shutting myself up entirely secluded in a room at Tolfrey's, Mr. Morse, and some others equally attached to me, entered the apartment and in a great measure forced me to join them in the hall. They next urged me to leave Calcutta, where every object I saw continually reminded me of the irreparable loss I had sustained. The idea of change of scene was at least soothing, and I resolved to follow the well-intended advice.

Amongst the earliest of those who offered their condolence upon my domestic misfortune was Robert Pott, who recommended my directly proceeding to him at Burdwan, where every person of his family would unite in endeavouring to alleviate my grief. On the 30th (of December) I therefore set off, reaching his house to breakfast the following morning.

Whilst his guest I derived a melancholy satisfaction in expressing my grateful acknowledgments to the medical gentlemen who had with unremitting zeal attended and exerted their skill, though unhappily without success, to save my lamented love, likewise in addressing those friends whose kindnesses were unceasing, and as my recent heavy loss rendered me indifferent to all worldly matters I at once acceded to an offer that had been made a fortnight before, through Mr. Petrie, to leave the question between me and the committee for the petition to Parliament to the arbitration of two friends, one to be chosen by them, the other by me, or, if I chose it, both to be of my nomination. I accordingly wrote to Mr. Petrie to that effect, who answered me thus :

" DEAR SIR,

I have this moment received your favour of this date, and do not hesitate to own that I am well pleased for many reasons that the affair has now taken so amicable a turn, and will be settled without any further trouble to either party. I cannot deny that I was hurt at some things that had passed, because I was not conscious of meriting them as an individual, and because I would willingly have given twenty times the amount demanded had I seen it in the light you did, rather than have refused under a conviction of your right to it.

Every person pretending to humanity must have felt your late misfortune and have pitied you under the severest of human woes. To offer consolation whilst the heart yet bleeds would be fruitless, but we may be permitted to observe that giving way to unavailing grief is both sinful and unmanly. May God comfort you.

Your sincere and obedient servant,

JOHN PETRIE."

*Friday Evening.*

" I will endeavour to see Major Metcalfe who has consented to act as one of the arbitrators, and get him to fix a time for meeting Mr. Morse, whom you mention as the other."

The following was Mr. Morse's answer to an application I made to him to be my arbitrator :

" MY GOOD FRIEND,

I will act as an arbitrator with all my heart. Never think of the sheriff's office until you feel fully equal to the attendance. In the interim I can manage very well, or if I should want assistance can call upon Stackhouse Tolfrey, who has more than once tendered his services to act for you. I beg you will try to bear your misfortune with fortitude. The recollection of her great goodness ought to be a source of consolation to you. She is now happy, and it is all in all better that you are thus early separated than after twenty years' experience of her merits.

Believe me at all times,
Yours very faithfully,
R. MORSE."

Captain Serocold of the *Tortoise* addressed me in these words :

" MY DEAR SIR,

I can easily imagine the very great distress you must undergo from the heavy loss you have sustained in the death of that worthy and affectionate woman, your late wife. I heard of her decease with heartfelt concern, for I believe her to have been as excellent a creature as ever lived. The less said on this distressing subject the better. I am obliged to go down to the *Tortoise* to-morrow, on my return I shall make a point of seeing you.

With sincere regard,
I am ever yours,
WALTER SEROCOLD."

Mr. Frushard wrote thus :

" MY DEAR SIR,

Mrs. Frushard's heart smote her for so unwarily bringing you into company last night. You will, I am sure, do her the justice to believe it was not her fault. She had desired to be denied to all visitors, but the stupid servants misunderstood her.

I very readily conceive that it is yet too early days for you to attend to the dictates of philosophy or to listen to the soothings of friendship. Still, I wish you not to forgo them altogether. You should embrace a seasonable amusement sometimes, and allow me to assure you that when you do feel yourself strong enough you will make us particularly happy in being one with us. That comfort may be given you from whence alone it flows is the ardent prayer of,

My dear sir, your sincerely affected

And obedient servant,

JAMES FRUSHARD."

The following was from the clergyman who performed the funeral service :

" SIR,

  I was favoured with your obliging and affecting letter on Saturday evening, but was so particularly engaged as to be unable to write in the way I wished, for yours spoke the genuine language of the warmest sensibility. The extraordinary duty I had yesterday, with some unforeseen engagements afterwards, must apologise for my not doing it before this morning. In reply, my good sir, I can only say that you have been too kind in your acknowledgment for what was only my duty, and under that idea I wished to have returned what I found enclosed, but concluded that I was not sufficiently acquainted with you to be convinced, or even to suppose that such a measure would be so agreeable to you as my acceptance of it. Be pleased, sir, to accept my most sincere condolence, and believe me when I assure you that I had long a desire to become acquainted with the late Mrs. Hickey and yourself, but a variety of circumstances obliged me to defer being introduced until my return from a five weeks' trip with my young ladies towards Patna, and soon after such return I heard of the good lady's indisposition. When you shall have begun to receive the visits of your friends I intend myself the satisfaction of paying my respects to you,

And am with real esteem, sir,

Your most obedient humble servant,

T. BLANSHARD."

Doctor Wilson's :

" DEAR SIR,

Permit me to return my sincere thanks for your kind present. Be assured I shall always consider myself the more obliged to you for the high sense you must have had of my attention in sending me the very handsome ring with Mrs. Hickey's hair, and I beg you to believe my not having called upon you arose from no other cause than my being so truly hurt at the irreparable loss you have sustained.

I am, my dear sir,<br>Your obliged and obedient,<br>JAS. WILSON."

Doctor Stark's :

" MY DEAR SIR,

I have received your very genteel present and return you many thanks. It is perfectly sufficient for every purpose, and I only regret that my best exertions were attended with so little success on behalf of an object so deservedly dear to my friend, and so much to be lamented by all those who had the happiness of her acquaintance.

I am, my dear sir,<br>Ever yours,<br>JAMES STARK."<br>" Monday."

The arbitrators to whom my demand on the committee was referred made the following award :

" Thomas Theophilus Metcalfe and Robert Morse having met as Arbitrators to determine upon a case in dispute between certain gentlemen of Calcutta, known by the name of the committee appointed for certain purposes, on the one part, and William Hickey on the other, and read and examined with attention the several papers laid before us, do determine that the said committee shall pay to the said William Hickey the sum of sicca rupees three thousand, and order their agents in England to cancel his note to them for one hundred pounds, and that the said William Hickey shall execute a full and complete general release to the committee aforesaid. Given under our hands and seals this 16th day of January, 1784.

THOMAS T. METCALFE.
R. MORSE."

Sealed and delivered in the presence of

J. HENNES.
R. PHILIP WESP."

The above sum I immediately received, and so ended the business of the petition to Parliament for trial by jury in civil cases, as far as it related to me individually.

Pott exerted himself in various ways to make me forget my misfortune. He carried me about to the different gentlemen of the neighbourhood and to a beautiful hunting seat he had built about twelve miles distant from his house at Burdwan, thus varying the scene as much as possible. His family then consisted of his cousin, George Cruttenden, and Messieurs Trant and Ley. Whilst at Burdwan I received a most kind and affectionate letter from my old friend and shipmate Mr. Jacob Rider, who then resided at Luckipore as Commercial Chief, to which part of the country he warmly invited me to go and pass a month, or as much time as I could spare.

Conscious that my absence from Calcutta must be attended with much inconvenience to Mr. Morse as Sheriff, I determined to return, and on the 10th of January took leave of my sincere friend Bob Pott.

On my arrival at the Presidency I found full employment for every hour of the day, a fortunate circumstance as it prevented my brooding over my sad loss so much as I should had my mind been less engaged. The Sessions had proved uncommonly laborious from an immense number of prisoners in the calendar. Sir Elijah Impey had embarked for Europe on the 3rd of the month, Sir Robert Chambers, as senior puisne judge, thereupon officiating as Chief Justice, a change that was severely felt by the public, there being a tiresome and disgusting frivolousness of manners and conduct about the latter that rendered him extremely unfit for such a station, the contrast appearing more forcibly from his succeeding a man of first-rate talents, which Sir Elijah Impey undoubtedly was, who had always been indefatigable in the execution of the duties of his office and particularly punctual with respect to time, taking his seat upon the Bench precisely at nine o'clock in the morning, whereas Sir Robert Chambers, on the contrary, seldom made his appearance before eleven, and I have known him to be so late as half-past one, thereby keeping everybody waiting to their great prejudice and unnecessary waste of time.

# CHAPTER XV

## DROWNING SORROW

ON the 14th of January a native of the lower order in Bengal was tried for the murder of a child of six years of age, who he decoyed from the door of his parent, a wealthy Hindoo, into a private lane or passage hard by, where he cut its throat, casting the mutilated body into a tank, or pond, with a weight fastened to it to keep it at the bottom. The sole motive for this barbarous act was a desire to get possession of some gold ornaments the little creature wore round his ankles and wrists, according to custom in Asiatic families of opulence. Upon his being arraigned for this enormous offence he pleaded guilty, when Sir Robert Chambers, from a mistaken delicacy, pressed him not to do so, but take the benefit of having the case fairly discussed, and availing himself of any favourable circumstances, if any such there were. The prisoner being repeatedly urged to the same effect at last, though evidently with reluctance, and in an impatient manner said, " Well, if you will have it so, *not guilty.*"

A jury being empanelled, the trial was proceeded in, and the atrocious deed established beyond all possibility of doubt. The culprit being then called upon for his defence readily answered he had none, coolly adding, " What should I say ? I murdered the boy, and was compelled to do it by the devil. I am not to blame ; it was my fate, and that I should be hanged for it I know. It is all very right ! "

Upon the usual question being put to him by the Clerk of the Court of " What have you to say why sentence of death should not be pronounced upon you ? " he without the least embarrassment replied, " What should I have to say when I told you this morning that I took away the child's life ? I have told you so again and again. I have nothing more to say. You insisted upon my telling a lie, and have chosen to give yourselves (looking round the Court) a great deal of unnecessary trouble. It was your own doing and no fault of mine. I am very tired of being in this little box."

The trial was not over until near midnight, chiefly owing to the tediousness and trifling of Sir Robert Chambers, who spent half the time arguing with the interpreter upon the spelling of the witnesses' names, or the different meaning of particular words used by them in their testimony.

On the Monday following this ignorant and unfeeling wretch was executed. Mr. Morse wishing me to accompany him to see the sentence of the law fulfilled, I accordingly did so. At the fatal spot, when under the gallows and whilst the executioner was arranging the halter, etc., the Sheriff from a motive of compassion asked the malefactor " Whether he had anything to say or any particular wish to make," when the callous brute answered, " Yes, I am very hungry, having been kept in prison with hardly any victuals." Confounded at so strange a speech at such a moment, Mr. Morse could not for some time reply. At last he remarked to the man it was most extraordinary that at such an awful crisis, when in a few minutes he must quit this world and be launched into eternity, he should think of eating or feel a sensation of hunger ; that however much he (the Sheriff) might feel disposed to comply with his desire, unaccountable as it was, there was no possibility of procuring food at that place, whereupon the miserable creature, with the utmost composure, said, " Pray, don't give yourself the least trouble about me ; it is a matter quite indifferent whether I get a dinner or not. I am very hungry it is true, yet I should not have mentioned the circumstance at all if you had not so particularly asked me whether I wished for anything." The matter of the eating being thus finally settled in five minutes afterwards the cart drove from under him leaving him suspended.

In the month of February of this year the Governor-

General's lady, *ci-devant* Madame Imhoff, left Calcutta and embarked on board the Company's ship *Atlas*, Captain Cooper, for Europe.

In March my namesake, Mr. Thomas Hickey, the portrait painter whom I left in Portugal, arrived in Bengal with an intention of following his profession, and afterwards did so with considerable success. The first sight of him renewed my grief in all its force for the loss of my darling Charlotte by bringing to my recollection a hundred different circumstances that had occurred when we were living in the same hotel at Lisbon. Mr. Hickey took a large, handsome house in the most fashionable part of Calcutta. Soon after being settled therein he proposed painting a full-sized portrait of my lamented love, observing he thought he could execute it so as to gratify me, partly from the small picture done while we were at Lisbon but still more from his perfect recollection of her features and figure. He accordingly executed a whole length which, although undoubtedly a likeness was by no means a favourable or pleasing one. I paid him for it two thousand sicca rupees, or two hundred and fifty pounds sterling.

I now lived what is generally termed *hard*, that is constantly went to bed heated by wine, if not absolutely inebriated, being at first induced to commit excess in a hope of drowning reflection and brooding over my misfortune. This course of life too soon settled into habit; encouraged in it as I was by all the young men of the settlement at that period drinking very freely. Money came in tolerably fast, but not sufficiently so to enable me to pay off any part of my debts. It, however, sufficed to pay up all arrears of interest, and as I always found cash sufficient to answer present calls I continued to live as I had set out. My monthly expences upon an average amounted to three thousand sicca rupees. I kept one of the best tables in Calcutta, and always took special care to be supplied with the best French wines and the oldest madeira that could be purchased. Those hours that I felt the most miserable were from the time of awaking early in the morning until I got to business at my desk, more especially in the sitting down melancholy and alone to my solitary breakfast where every object in the apartment reminded me of my departed favourite. Finding this rather increased upon me than otherwise, I suddenly resolved to change my residence, and by paying my landlady a small sum as a premium she consented to relinquish the engagement I had entered into to keep the house a complete twelvemonth. I then went into a capital house situated within five hundred yards of the river and close to the Esplanade, the most airy and pleasant part of the town. I soon found the good effects of my removal in improved health.

In the middle of April a mandamus reached Calcutta for the examination of witnesses in a Cause instituted in England by the widow of Sir Eyre Coote (the circumstances of whose death and burial at Madras I have already related) against the executors, who doubted whether the testator intended two codicils he added to his will should have effect as to increasing the bequests to Lady Coote or not, their idea being that the second codicil was only meant to confirm and strengthen the first and not to add to what had previously been given. The gentlemen to whom the writ was directed as commissioners, at the head of whom stood the name of William Johnson of the Company's Civil Service, and who lately departed this life in England, did me the honour to nominate me to be their clerk. We met, I think, only five times, two hours each, when the evidence being finished which clearly established both codicils, making a difference of five thousand pounds to Lady Coote, the Commission was closed and returned, the day after which Mr. Johnson sent me one hundred gold mohurs (two hundred pounds) for my trouble, a liberal remuneration for a few hours' labour.

About this period Mrs. Pawson, with whom I had become acquainted at Lisbon, departed this life, a victim to one of those violent fevers so prevalent in the East Indies, and in six weeks after her death her husband was carried off after an illness of only four hours.

A great scarcity of European articles of eating and drinking now prevailed in Calcutta.  Ham and cheese were both sold at five sicca rupees per pound or twelve shillings and sixpence, claret scarcely procurable, and the little there was in the settlement sold at sixty-five sicca rupees a dozen. We, however, had a plentiful supply of that wine from Denmark, brought out by Captain Mercer in the ship *Resolution*, which, although admirable wine and wonderfully cheap, many people were afraid to drink from an idea that prevailed of the Danish merchants fining their wine with arsenic and sugar of lead.  As I conceived this to be a mere vulgar prejudice I tasted the claret, and thinking it uncommonly good I purchased two chests.

In the same month of April my *Plassey* shipmate and saviour from drowning, Mr. James Grant, returned to Bengal.  The night of his arrival I saw him at a splendid entertainment given by a club of gentlemen of which I was a member.  After what had occurred in London and his illiberal conduct towards me, I had no intention of taking the least notice of him, nor could I suppose he would court a renewal of acquaintance as I had spoken my opinion of him in very free and unqualified terms.  However, just before supper was announced he came up to me, and holding out both his hands said, " What ! my old friend and early companion still angry with me ! I do not deserve it, believe me ! You are under a mistake, for I am, as I always have been, very sincerely attached to you.  A common enemy to both deceived you and slandered me ! So come, shake hands. At any rate, I beseech you to forget and forgive.  Let us be reconciled."  This apparently open and ingenuous conduct at once disarmed me of all resentment, and though I knew how ill he had behaved I could not resist the acceptance of his proffered hand.  Thus were we again united in amity. I then invited him to dine with me on a subsequent day, and summoned all the bon-vivants of Calcutta to meet him. Amongst my party were the famous Colonel John Mordaunt, eldest natural son of the old Earl of Peterborough, the equally talked of Henry Fox Calcraft, son of the celebrated

Mrs. Bellamy, the actress, by Mr. Calcraft, the man who amassed an overgrown fortune as an army agent ; Messieurs John Haldane, Archibald Montgomery, Peter Moore and others of equal fame in the bottle way. For such a set I was anxious to obtain English claret, that is claret from London, and after much enquiry I discovered that Baxter and Joy's, who kept a Europe shop, had a small quantity which they reserved for favourite customers, and as I came under that description, and had therefore some interest in the house, I prevailed on them to let me have three dozen, they assuring me that was double what any other customer had been indulged with.

On the morning of the day the party were to dine with me I desired my *consumah* (steward) to give the wine that came in a day or two before, meaning that from Baxter and Joy's. During dinner the claret was greatly admired, and much surprize expressed by the guests how I managed in such a time of scarcity to procure wine of so superior a quality. It had all along struck me as greatly resembling the peculiar flavour of the Danish batch, but still I thought it could not be it.

While the *consumah* was removing the desert I, in a whisper, asked if he had according to my order given the English claret, to which he answered, " No, master, I will give now done eating." Vexed at this stupidity of my servants, I merely mentioned to one or two of my friends near me that they would now taste a very different liquor to what they had been drinking. Baxter and Joy's was accordingly introduced, when a general exclamation took place of " Zounds ! Hickey, they have changed the wine upon us." " Well," replied I, " if they have I trust it is for the better." " No, by God ! " exclaimed some of my guests, " quite the contrary, it is from most delicious to execrable stuff." Knowing as I did how the matter stood, I entreated they would not decide hastily but give the wine last brought a fair trial, as I had abundant reason to think it was beyond all comparison better than what they had pronounced in favour of. A second trial thereupon took place ; it was again compared with the *Resolution's*, and again the party unanimously decided that what they had drank during dinner was infinitely the best, it being uncommonly high flavoured, delicious wine, whereas the other was abominable, not fit to be drank. Finding this opinion general, I told them I rejoiced to find they had such correct taste, especially as I could indulge them upon very easy terms, the wine they admired having cost me no more than eighteen rupees a dozen, while that they abused and rejected was at the enormous price of sixty-five rupees a dozen. To shew how little real judgment operates, and how few men are capable of deciding from their own palate, the moment I declared the vast difference in the prices several of the party began to change their tone, some of them observing, " There certainly is a delicacy and a flavour in the English wine which the other wants," and they stuck to it the remainder of the day, merely, as I firmly believe, because it cost sixty-five sicca rupees a dozen instead of eighteen. John Mordaunt, Peter Moore and myself drank the Danish from really considering it the best, as it certainly was.

Upon my return to Bengal in 1783 I immediately became intimate with Mr. Francis Rundell, who had, during my absence in Europe, come out as an assistant surgeon in the Company's service. He was a fine dissipated fellow, and although in years not more than twenty-five, in constitution he was double that from early and continued excess. Both his features and person were uncommonly fine, eyes more piercingly expressive than even Garrick's, with a voice of perfect harmony and great strength at the same time. Altogether, no man was ever more admirably calculated for the stage, and the possession of such qualifications probably first occasioned his turning his thoughts to the sock and buskin. He was greatly attached to everything theatrical, having performed several characters in England for his own amusement or to serve actors of his acquaintance. His family violently opposed his making the stage a profession to live by, in consequence of which he took up the study of surgery, to which he served under a man of eminence for several years.

At the time of Mr. Rundell's arrival in Calcutta there was a most capital and complete theatre supported by voluntary subscriptions. A schism had recently occurred amongst the gentlemen performers originating in a contention about filling the first-rate parts, each individual supposing himself the best qualified. This dispute had been carried to so great a length that some duels had been the consequence, and at last they could not muster a sufficient number to act any play, besides which from a general profusion and extravagance in fine dresses the theatre became involved in debt to the amount of upwards of thirty thousand sicca rupees.

Mr. Rundell in a few weeks after becoming an inhabitant of Calcutta made an offer to the proprietors or subscribers to undertake the sole and entire management of the theatre on his own account, agreeing to find performers and get up plays at least once a week during the months of November, December, January and February. He further proposed, provided the proprietors would allow him to receive the admission money of one gold mohur each person, or for a box ticket, which was the price that always had been paid, and eight sicca rupees for the pit, he would bind himself to pay off the whole amount of debt due from the theatre, and never to call upon the proprietors for any supplies of cash under any pretence whatsoever. A general meeting of the proprietors was thereupon summoned, before whom Mr. Rundell's proposal being laid, it was debated upon and finally unanimously accepted. A deed was prepared between the parties and executed, and Mr. Rundell forthwith put into possession of the entire premises. There was a very good dwelling-house upon the ground in which he resided.

The settlement soon found the advantages arising from this grant, not only in an increase of their favourite amusement, but also that theatrical performances were got up and acted in a style thentofore unknown in India. Mr. Rundell's convivial disposition, his uncommonly pleasing and conciliating manners and superior abilities rendered him extremely popular, so that everyone who had stood aloof under the old system were now ready and willing to come forward and lend their individual aid in the way best adapted to their capacities, of which the new manager was perfectly competent to decide, besides which these voluntary performers had the benefit of receiving his advice and instructions whereby the style of acting was greatly improved.

So pleased and gratified were the settlement at the extraordinary alteration that the house was crowded whenever opened, and Mr. Rundell soon found he was likely to have an admirable good thing of it. In the course of the first season he cleared off the whole of the debts due from the theatre, the subsequent profits going into his own pocket. The disbursements, however, were unavoidably very large, for Mr. Rundell prudently and sagaciously adopted every measure he thought likely to please and gratify those gentlemen who assisted him in " strutting and fretting their hour upon the stage." He not only paid without a murmur for whatever dresses they chose to make up for the different characters they represented, but on the nights of performance, after all was over, gave a splendid supper upon the stage, where claret, champagne and burgundy were most liberally dealt out, many of the guests continuing at table until daylight. I have known him more than once pay eighty sicca rupees a dozen for the champagne. As from long habit and a strong head he could bear a great deal of wine he always contrived to make his young heroes gloriously drunk, and by so doing became the most popular man in Bengal.

Mr. Rundell's talents as an actor were certainly of the first rate. Upon Mr. William Burke seeing him perform *Hamlet*, he declared to me he thought him quite equal to Garrick, a high compliment from a man of Mr. Burke's judgment and who had always been an enthusiastic admirer of our English Roscius. The fact is that really nothing could surpass Rundell's mode of acting several parts, especially those of Hamlet, Jaffier or Pierre in *Venice Preserved ;*

—

.

King Lear, Othello, Richard the Third, Orestes in *The Distressed Mother;* Leom in *Rule a Wife and Have a Wife;* and Lord Townly in *The Provoked Husband,* in all of which characters, except Othello, Mr. Garrick shone conspicuously.

Mr. Rundell, notwithstanding all his large drawbacks, finding that his emoluments far surpassed his most sanguine expectation, determined to send to England for some second-rate actors, both male and female, for thentofore all women characters had been filled by the male sex, and although there were two gentlemen, Mr. Bride and Mr. Norfar, who excelled in female parts, still the want of women was materially felt. He ultimately succeeded in getting three very tolerable female performers from London and some male understrappers.

My habits of life being congenial with Mr. Rundell's scarce a day passed that we were not together some part of it. In his drunken frolics he had met with various disasters, and at different times broken both arms and one leg.

My Irish friend, Captain Richard Heffernan, who, when I left India in 1779, commanded the *Nancy,* then one of the Bengal Marine, under the shabby Commodore Richardson, now arrived in Calcutta from Bombay, where he had been upon his own private affairs, and he frequently called upon me.

Freskini continued with me, proving a very attentive and useful servant, and beyond dispute I had the best-dressed head of any man in Calcutta.

Whilst in the first burst of grief at the death of my dearest Charlotte, after a sleepless night I had just risen from my bed between six and seven in the morning and was sitting in the verandah in a loose great-coat, when a servant said a gentleman below desired to speak to me. Finding it was a stranger, I ordered the man to tell him I was not well and could not receive him. The servant returned again saying the gentleman requested only three words and would not detain me half a minute. I thereupon went downstairs, where I saw an elegant-looking man in regimentals who, after apologizing for troubling me at so early an hour, civilly asked me if I could contrive to call at his house any hour that day to dress a lady's hair. From the question I discovered that he imagined he was addressing Freskini, and certainly my dress and appearance might justify the supposition. I made a cold, formal bow, saying I would direct one of my servants to call Freskini and returned upstairs. Within an hour I received a very handsome apology for the mistake in a letter signed " James Crockett," whom I recollected a dissipated London dasher. He had run through an independent fortune, being finally obliged, like many other spendthrifts, to seek refuge from his creditors' attacks by accepting a commission in the East India Company's service. I soon afterwards became intimate with him, and had some laughs at his mistaking me for an Italian hairdresser.

My namesake, who frequently called upon me, observed it was a pity the whole-length picture of Mrs. Hickey had not a companion. This I perfectly understood, but was determined not to take the plain hint. His persevering attention to his own interest, however, was more than a match for my prudential resolves. He at last in direct terms said I ought to sit for my own portrait to match the other, and I was blockhead enough to comply, paying another two thousand sicca rupees for my folly. He made a very correct likeness, with which everybody seemed pleased. When first hung up in my breakfast-room I took my *banyan* in to see it, asking his opinion. After looking very earnestly some time without uttering a syllable I again asked what he thought of it and whether he should have known it was done for me. After another pause, he in a hesitating, doubtful manner drawled out, " Yes, picture like master, but where watch ? " At that time I always wore a rather showy gold chain with several seals, which the artist had not introduced, an omission that struck the Hindoo so forcibly as to occasion the " but where watch ? " without which he seemed to consider the work incomplete. I am afraid there have been many equally ridiculous criticisms

made upon pictures in Europe, and by those who ought to
have known better.

A *fête-champêtre* announced as to be given by Mr. Edward
Fenwick, a gentleman high in the Civil Service, entirely
engaged the public attention and conversation during the
greater part of the month of May. It was intended to be
celebrated at his country house, situated upon the banks
of the river, in Garden Reach, about five miles from Calcutta, which thentofore had been the property and place of
residence of my esteemed friends Mr. and Mrs. Lacam.
The gardens were to be brilliantly illuminated with many
thousand coloured lamps ; an eminent operator in fireworks
had been brought down from Lucknow to display his talents ;
the company to appear in fancy dresses, those that chose
it to wear masks. Ranges of tents were fixed in different
parts of the gardens, wherein tables were laid covered with
all the dainties the best French cooks could produce, for
the accommodation of three hundred persons, besides which
every room in the house was stored with refreshments of
every sort and kind ; different bands of martial music were
stationed in several parts of the gardens, and also in the
house, with appropriate and distinct performers for the
dancers. The last two miles of the road were lighted up
with a double row of lamps on each side, making every
object clear as day. In short, nothing could exceed the
splendour of the preparations for this rural entertainment.

The evening appointed for the fête was beautifully serene,
and fortunately without the strong southerly wind that
usually blows at that season of the year. I, of course, with
every gentleman of the settlement, had a card of invitation.
Unluckily it happened that I had one of my parties to dine
with me that day ; the consequence was my getting sadly
intoxicated, in which state, contrary to the advice and
remonstrances of my guests, who entreated me to go in
my chariot (indeed, two or three offered me a seat in theirs),
I chose to mount my phaeton, and off I set full gallop
without either *sice* or *mussaulgee*. The road was crowded
with carriages, notwithstanding which I contrived to steer

clear of the many I passed from my superior velocity until
under the long wall of Colonel Watson's docks, when a considerate idea about my horses got into my head, and I
thought for their sakes of slackening my pace. I accordingly
put them into a gentle trot.

While proceeding at this moderate rate I observed an
open carriage with, as I conceived, two ladies and a gentleman in it, endeavouring to pass me. My politeness to the
fair sex therefore induced me to draw off to the left to give
them room, in doing which my wheels came in contact with
the root of a large tree growing out of an old wall, and over
I went like a shot. My head first reaching the ground, I
scraped the skin completely off one side of my face. The
quantity of claret I had swallowed rendered this a matter
of indifference. I therefore, in spite of my accident, determined to proceed, and without bestowing a thought upon
phaeton or horses I walked on towards Mr. Fenwick's.

My dress was a light blue silk domino, which from my
tumble into a deep brick dust, added to the blood streaming
from my lacerated face, was in a sorry condition. The
moment I entered the principal room at Mr. Fenwick's
every creature therein surrounded me, asking questions innumerable how I could have got into such woeful plight.
Too drunk to satisfy their curiosity, some of my friends at
length got hold of me and carried me into a private room,
where my wounds were washed, clean linen furnished, and
I was put into at least a more decorous state for the company of ladies. Great persuasions were used to induce me
to go to bed instead of joining the gay scenes, but that I
would not hear of, swearing I would not forgo the pleasure
of beholding the fine women for all the world. As I was
always cheerful and good-humoured in my cups I afforded
much laughter to my fair friends by the nonsense I talked.
With the kindest attention they exerted themselves to
prevent my drinking anything more, so that in three or
four hours the consequences of the excess I had committed
at home went off and I became reasonable.

At a late hour, upon enquiring amongst Mr. Fenwick's

servants, I learnt that my horses and carriage had been brought on by General Stibbert, who seeing it in the road overset, and no servants belonging to it, very considerately ordered some of his people to get it to rights and bring it on to Mr. Fenwick's, where he concluded the owner of it must be. In my fall from the carriage I came down with such force that a parcel of seals I wore were torn from the watch-chain. One in particular, being my coat-of-arms, I highly valued from being a present of my brother Joseph's when I was going out a cadet to India in the year 1768. It was admirably well engraved upon an uncommonly fine bloodstone ; this seal was broken short off from the lower part of the setting.

The company did not begin to depart from Mr. Fenwick's until after seven o'clock in the morning ; many stayed to breakfast, of which number I was one. About nine I stepped into my phaeton, which had sustained no material injury, to drive to town. When at the part of the road where I had the somerset I begged Mr. Bird, who was with me, to allow me to stop until the servants looked about to see if they could discover my seal, an idea that greatly amused my companion, who deemed it superlatively ridiculous to suppose so small a thing should be found in a road fifty feet wide, many inches deep in dust, and over which several hundred carriages had passed since the accident happened. Yet, extraordinary as it certainly was, we had scarcely been there a minute when one of my *kitmudars* picked up and gave to me what I imagined to be a small piece of brick or tile, but which upon clearing away the dirt that covered it, proved to be my seal, the stone of which was uninjured. I caused it to be reset and wear it at this present day.

Having from my earliest youth been of an amorous disposition I began to feel the effects of a long continence. I therefore one night sent for a native woman, but the moment I lay myself down upon the bed all desire ceased, being succeeded by disgust. I could think of nothing but her I had for ever lost, and the bitter recollection rendered me so miserable that I sent off my Hindostanee companion untouched. The same circumstance occurred to me three successive times. Nature, however, at last proved too powerful to be surmounted, and I subsequently ceased to feel the horror that at first prevailed at the thoughts of a connection with black women, some of whom are indeed very lovely, nor is it correct to call them black, those that come from the Upper Provinces being very fair.

In the month of June Mr. William Burke came from Madras with an intention to reside in Bengal. He had just received the appointment of Paymaster-General to the King's troops in India, an office that allowed of his fixing at whichever of the presidencies he thought proper, and as he preferred Bengal he shortly after his arrival purchased an excellent country house, beautifully situated at the head of Garden Reach, commanding an extensive and rich view both up and down the river, taking in Fort William, the range of houses, fairly enough termed palaces along the Esplanade and Chouringee, with an immense forest of masts of ships moored off the town of Calcutta, from which city it was distant four miles. Mr. Burke brought round with him from Madras two young men, one of them Ensign Davison, as insolent and good-for-nothing a fellow as ever lived, who has since made himself very conspicuous by various acts of enormity, for some of which he merited the gallows, but instead of meeting with his deserts from the hands of justice, he is at this day enjoying a pension from the East India Company, with the rank of lieutenant-colonel on their establishment of Madras. The other protégé was Mr. Michael George Prendergast, also in the Fort St. George army as an engineer officer, a very different person in every respect from Mr. Davison. I spent much of my leisure time at Mr. Burke's; indeed, had I done as he wished I should have taken up my abode altogether there, a commodious bed-chamber and dressing-room being set apart for my use, and always retained for me, although I rarely occupied them, preferring going home to sleep in my own bed.

In the same month of June Charles Chisholme, who was second mate of the *Plassey* at the period of my sailing on board her, arrived in Bengal, having the command of the *Gatton* Indiaman. Chisholme completely verified the prediction of my old blackguard friend, Sam Rogers, who often told him when boasting of the manner he would conduct himself in when in the command of a ship, that he would be the greatest *bashaw* and overbearing tyrant that ever got a command, nor would he ever have an officer that would sail a second time under him, nor a passenger that would give him a good word. In the *Gatton* he brought out many passengers : among them were Mr. and Mrs. Stephenson (the latter being now Countess of Essex), the famous Major Baggs of duelling and gambling celebrity, and some other equally conspicuous characters. Captain Chisholme's behaviour had been so disagreeable and so unconciliating as to offend every person at his table, so much so that during the last two months of the voyage no one ever spoke to him ; he was completely at Coventry. He had quarrelled with and broke his second and third mates, both of whom publicly avowed their intentions of prosecuting him for damages on their return home. He made several attempts to justify himself to me by throwing the blame upon the passengers, the whole of whom he asserted were biassed and prejudiced against him by Messieurs Stephenson and Baggs, but his own story did not tell well, and I could not help saying, " Come, come, my old shipmate, I can plainly perceive Rogers's discernment was greater than anybody allowed him."

Captain Chisholme had on board a large pack of remarkably fine hounds, then in great demand by the Bengal sportsmen, for which he was offered twenty times their supposed value, but he likewise had one hundred and fifty pipes of madeira wine, an article with which the market was so greatly overstocked there was no sale at all for. Captain Chisholme therefore, like a wily Scotchman, finding his dogs so much sought after, determined to make them the means of getting rid of his madeira. He accordingly made his purser give notice that any person taking four pipes of madeira at three hundred rupees per pipe should have two couple of hounds at the market price those animals then bore. The scheme fully answered, for he disposed of both wine and dogs at a profit of upwards of one hundred per cent, instead of being an immense loser as otherwise must have been the case, there being no sale for madeira but at a loss of sixty per cent upon the prime cost. Upon his homeward passage he caught a severe cold by continuing exposed day and night for nearly a week to dreadful weather they encountered off the south end of Madagascar, which fell upon his lungs, produced inflammation and carried him out of the world the same day that the ship reached St. Helena.

By the *Gatton* I received a letter from Fozard, the livery stable keeper, from whom I had purchased saddle-horses during my residence in England in the years 1780 and 1781, and with whom they always stood at livery. Although I never had, like Mr. Van, encouraged him to treat me with familiarity, this letter of his was couched in remarkably free-and-easy terms, quite as if we had been living upon an equal footing in society. It commenced by reminding me that in the *hurry* that always attends a person's leaving one country to go and reside in another it had escaped my recollection to discharge a small balance due to him of twenty-five pounds, for which amount he had drawn upon me at sixty days' sight in favour of "his friend William Petrie," and was sure I would duly honour the bill. This friend whom he spoke of so familiarly was then a member of Council in the Government of Madras, and in daily expectation of succeeding to the President's chair. To Mr. Petrie I accordingly remitted the sum drawn for. Having finished this little matter of business he proceeded to give me what he called the news of the day, that is an account of certain rogues and prostitutes whom he supposed I must be acquainted with, concluding his curious epistle thus : "Our friend Van is completely done up. He has finally and effectually dished himself by marrying a little strumpet he took from the theatre, without character, fortune, accomplishment of any kind, or even personal beauty. Poor fool, what an end! He was always shallow-pated, and yet I cannot help pitying him. His name stands deep in my books, and I fear not a guinea will ever be forthcoming!"

About this period my friend Mr. Rundell's health became so bad that his physicians advised him to go to sea, in consequence of which he took his passage on board a country ship bound to Pulo Penang, since called Prince of Wales's Island, and in a few days after so doing embarked and departed.

# CHAPTER XVI

## SIR ROBERT CHAMBERS AND MR. JUSTICE HYDE

ON the 10th of June the Sessions commenced with another numerous calendar. Eight o'clock in the morning was the hour named in the summons to both grand and *petit* juries to attend, and they assembled accordingly soon after that hour, but Sir Robert Chambers, according to his usual custom, did not make his appearance until near one, and when he did go into Court the swearing both juries and delivering his charge to the grand jury brought it to three o'clock, when the fiddle-faddle body declared it was too late to commence a trial. The Court was adjourned and thus one day lost.

The following morning Mr. Justice Hyde and Sir William Jones took their seats upon the Bench precisely at nine, had a jury called and sworn to try a prisoner they arraigned, and then sat with their hands before them waiting the arrival of the apathetic Sir Robert Chambers, it being a point of etiquette not to commence any trial until the chief or senior judge was present. At eleven, there being no appearance of his coming, Mr. Hyde grew angry and impatient. He therefore wrote a note to Sir Robert telling him Sir William Jones and he had been upon the Bench two hours, the grand and *petit* juries in attendance the same time, and requesting to know whether he meant to come into Court or not. This note he was in the act of folding up when Sir Robert came smirking and smiling upon the Bench, and seeing the note upon Mr. Hyde's desk facetiously said: " Brother Hyde, I'm glad I have just saved my distance and prevented your dispatching that memento of my sluggardness. I am, however, now here, so you may tear your note." " No, I won't," sharply replied Mr. Hyde, " it will do for to-morrow," a severe and cutting rebuke that was thrown away upon the callous knight.

Late as Sir Robert came, another hour was wasted in his copying the list of the jury into his private minute book, etc. He then objected to try the prisoner who had been arraigned and was in the dock, saying the day had been set apart for the trial of the housebreaker, who was accordingly ordered up. Being placed at the bar, the Judge asked him what his name was, to which the man, with a most tremendous brogue, answered *Pater Carl*. The word Pater occasioned a variety of questions and most ridiculous replies. His next question was, " What countryman are you ? " to which the prisoner answered, " Faith, I'm all the way from the county of Kilkenny its own self." " How do you spell your name ? " enquired Sir Robert. The prisoner could not satisfy the Judge, being so ignorant he knew not a letter of the alphabet. After much absurd questioning from Sir Robert without obtaining the least information, Mr. William Townsend Jones, an Irish attorney, offended at what he considered superlative stupidity on the part of the Judge, bounced up and said, " Indeed, my Lord, Carl is a very old and respectable name universally known throughout Ireland, for it is truly Milesian, the divil a better in the kingdom. I have myself the honour of being acquainted with several of the family." —

Sir Robert : " Then perhaps, Mr. Jones, you may know something of this person at the bar."

Jones : " I don't exactly percaive that that follows, my Lord, or that I'm bound to know all of the name becase I do some."

Sir Robert : " Pray, Mr. Jones, how is the name spelt ? I suppose it ought to be with a ' K.' "

Jones : " Why it ought to be with a ' K,' my Lord, I cannot conjecture. The fact, however, is that the family who probably best know their own name spell it with a *say* (" C "). The prisoner nevertheless, my Lord, will be greatly obliged to you to prove they are all wrong and that it should be a ' K,' becase in that case he must be acquitted upon a misnomer."

Sir Robert : " I shall be obliged to you, Mr. Jones, to tell me how the name is spelt in Ireland."

Jones : " Indeed, and that I will most willingly, my Lord. ' C ' (which he again pronounced like " say ") ' A ' (like ah) ' R,' double ll."

Sir Robert : " What ! two ' r's,' Mr. Jones ; that's odd."

Jones (with much contempt) : " No, not two ' r's ' at all, but ' C ' (say) ' A ' (the first letter of the alphabet, call it how you plase) ' R,' double ll."

Sir Robert : " Oh, thank you, Mr. Jones. Very well now, I have it written down properly. Pray, Mr. Jones, do you speak Irish ? "

Jones : " By my soul and that I do, my Lord."

Sir Robert : " Then pray inform me, Mr. Jones, what Carl is in Irish."

Jones (with evident surprise at the question) : " In Irish, my Lord ? "

Sir Robert : " Yes, in Irish, what does it mean ? "

Jones (with ineffable contempt) : " Why the man's name, to be sure. What else could it mane ? "

This created quite a shout of laughter from the auditors, and Sir Robert asked no more questions, but, after looking over his book for some minutes he leaned over towards Mr. Justice Hyde, to whom he said, " This is the 16th (sic) of June, the very day on which Westminster and most of the great public schools in England break up for the holidays." Mr. Hyde, with a sneer, very expressive of his feelings, replied, " Is it indeed ? I cannot but wonder at your recollecting the circumstance."

It is scarcely to be credited that a man could so far forget the dignity of his station to act thus weakly at any time, more especially at the moment a fellow-creature was standing at the bar arraigned for his life. Yet with all this frivolousness of manner Sir Robert Chambers was a deeply read and very learned man who had passed through the

University of Oxford with peculiar éclat, and at the time of his being appointed to a seat upon the Bench of the Supreme Court filled the office of Vinerian Professor. So whimsical and yet so precise was he in the execution of the most trifling matter, that even in writing a common note he always first made a rough copy, using various words that expressed the same meaning. These words he placed one above another ; he then referred to Johnson and other authorities for the purpose of ascertaining which of the selected words would be the most correct to use, and adopted one accordingly. A cynical acquaintance of his, old Mr. Fowke, being one of a company where the character of Sir Robert, in point of literature and general science, was discussed, sarcastically but accurately enough compared his knowledge to a dictionary with the leaves misplaced or headed with wrong letters, where although eminent learning was contained in the work, you never knew how to get at it.

Mr. Justice Hyde, notwithstanding the glaring blemishes in Sir Robert Chambers as a public magistrate, was wonderfully attached to him, and had the highest opinion of his integrity, as well as of his talents, which was not exactly the case with people in general. Mr. Hyde himself was as high-minded and good-hearted a man as any in the world, yet he also had his failings and infirmities, being at times strangely petulant, and though possessed of good, plain sense, sometimes acted with so much impetuosity and intemperateness as to render that sense extremely doubtful. Hospitable to the greatest degree, his table, which was always profusely covered with the best of viands and choicest liquors, was free to every person that had the slightest acquaintance with him, and not a few were there who two or three times a week availed themselves of his liberal hospitality that would otherwise have been in want of a dinner. This sort of open table greatly increased upon Mr. Hyde returning to England, which bad health rendered necessary while I was in Europe. The number of pensioners he had was incredible, allowing them from one hundred rupees a month down to two and three rupees, according to their respective and relative situations in life. It is not, therefore, at all wonderful that his income of near eight thousand pounds sterling a year, which from the rate of exchange the Judges' salaries were paid at, it amounted to, proved inadequate to defray his expenditure. At the end of ten years' residence in India he found his debts so considerable as to be under the necessity of drawing upon his attornies in England for a lac of sicca rupees, or twelve thousand five hundred pounds, which was to be remitted from the produce of his paternal estate. I will now briefly relate some anecdotes that equally shew his philanthropy and oddity of temper.

It happened that Mr. Thomas Motte, who for several years had been one of the greatest merchants in Asia, from having embarked large sums of money in a speculation that turned out unluckily, became embarrassed in his circumstances, and finally was compelled to seek refuge from a prison by going to reside at the foreign settlement of Fredericksnagore under the Danish flag, upon which unpleasant event six of his most intimate and attached friends agreed to subscribe a monthly sum for his maintenance and support. His brother-in-law, Mr. Peter Touchet, at the desire of Mr. Justice Hyde, undertook to arrange the matter. He conceived that six hundred rupees per month would be an ample provision. He put opposite his own name one hundred rupees, Mr. John Haldane did the same. The subscription paper next went to Mr. Hyde, who put down his name with two hundred rupees. Mr. Peter Speke, who was in no way behind Judge Hyde in general benevolence or in acts of private liberality and munificence, thereupon made a remark upon the margin of the subscription paper, in the civilest language, saying that as the original intention was for six friends to subscribe the same sum for the distressed individual, he hoped Mr. Justice Hyde would not be displeased at being requested to reduce his monthly quota to one hundred rupees, that each might pay alike. Mr. Hyde, however, was not only displeased at being desired to lessen the amount, but extremely indignant at Mr.

Speke's presuming to dictate to him or to restrict the quantum of his donation. When, therefore, Mr. Touchet brought back the paper with Mr. Speke's remark upon it, Mr. Hyde pronounced him "an ass" (a favourite epithet of his to those who in any way offended him), adding, " You may go, sir, to this same Mr. Speke and tell him, if you please, from me, I think he has taken a liberty he is not warranted in. I trouble not myself as to what he does with his money ; he may squander it upon his women, as I believe he does, or throw it into the Ganges, I care not which, but I am quite clear he has no sort of right to inter- fere with me, or with the sums I choose to give away, no matter to whom." And taking the subscription paper to his writing-table he altered the figure of 2 to a 3, thereby making his monthly subscription three hundred instead of two hundred rupees, which sum he continued to pay until the time of his death.

With all his good qualities, and no man had more, he often suffered his petulance and irascibility to lead him into awkward situations, and more than once into a serious scrape. Polite and attentive as possible to those who visited him as a gentleman, he was, on the other hand, deficient in common civility when anyone, even if an intimate and personal friend, went before him in his judicial capacity, or upon any kind of business whatever, upon some of which occasions I have seen and heard him behave excessively rude. Whilst engaged upon any part of his duty he never asked a gentleman to sit down, nor did he ever then acknowledge an acquaintance. A captain of an Indiaman, who was well known to the Judge, went before him to swear an affidavit. While the Judge was perusing it the Commander sat himself down in a chair, whereupon Mr. Hyde, looking fiercely at him, said, " I didn't invite you to that freedom. Stand up ! " He then angrily questioned him relative to his Christian name (being sub- scribed " J. Price "), saying, " Pray, what is J. Price ? Is it Jacob or James, or Jeremiah, or Jonathan, or John, or what is it ? It is most extraordinary that people are thus

to be set a-guessing about your name." " My name, sir,"
replied the Captain, " is John, and that is the way in which
I have written it all my life." " Is it ? " rejoined the
Judge, " then it is a very foolish way, and you have been
doing foolishly all your life. The sooner you leave it off
the better." During this speech he signed the jurat thus,
" J. Hyde," upon which Captain Price rather flippantly
observed, " And, pray, who is to know what J. Hyde is,"
to which the Judge replied, " You are an impertinent cox-
comb. Go along out of the room. Do you pertly conceive
there is no difference between one of His Majesty's Justices
and the Captain of a merchant ship ! "

Mr. Hyde had a great dislike to any person's wearing a
scarlet coat that was not in the army. A thick-headed
Portuguese clerk to an attorney went before him to swear
to the service of some notice in the progress of a cause, as
a mere matter of course. Before the Judge began to question
him at all the fellow said, " Yes, my lord." " Yes, my lord,"
repeated the Judge in a muttering tone, " you are a prodigious ass." " Yes, my lord," said the writer. " Humph,"
grunted out Mr. Hyde, adding, " Now, Mr. Redcoat, I shall
ask you one question, to which I desire a plain and direct
answer." " Yes, my lord," said the writer. " What !
before you hear it ? " asked the Judge. " Yes, my lord."
" Pray now, Mr. Yes-my-lord, did not your master desire
you to say ' yes, my lord ' to every question I should put
to you ? " " Yes, my lord," replied the Portuguese. Whereupon the Judge in a violent rage threw the affidavit in his
face, ordering the servants to kick the stupid rascal downstairs.

Previous to the establishment of a regular police in
Calcutta it was customary for a judge to sit at chambers,
situate in the Lol Bazaar, for the purpose of transacting the
daily business of the town, also of adjusting any little
matters of dispute that might arise between the natives
not of sufficient magnitude in itself, or the parties too poor
to enter into a legal contest. Upon an occasion of this sort
two men of some consequence amongst the Hindoos appeared

before him relative to a very narrow slip of ground to which both laid claim. After hearing the statement of each Mr. Hyde recommended their leaving the question to be decided by arbitration, each party to name an arbitrator. One of the two readily consented, but the other, though with great respect, begged to decline so doing, saying he should prefer a decision by the Court. Mr. Hyde strongly urged him to arbitrate, which the man persisted in refusing to accede to, observing that he conceived the law to be clearly and indisputably with him, and he could without a doubt establish his claim by incontrovertible evidence, why then should he risk the caprice or prejudice of any individuals operating against him, which must be the case of an arbitration. He further remarked that both himself and his antagonist were opulent men, possessing abundant means to try their rights in the regular and common manner ; that to his lordship's opinion when delivered from his seat on the Bench he should bow with the most respectful deference and submission.

"And so you won't do as I advise and arbitrate, hey ? " said the Judge. "No, my lord," humbly replied the man, "I had rather not." "You had better," added the Judge. "Pray, my lord, excuse me and let me humbly entreat that the Court may determine between me and my opponent." The Judge angrily said, "No, I won't, and I give you five minutes to determine whether you will arbitrate or not." The Hindoo with great composure answered, "My lord, I require no time whatever. My resolution is formed. I do not choose to leave the point to arbitration, but to the decision of your lordship and the other judges in Court." "Oh! mighty well," said Mr. Hyde, "then I'll convince you that I can be just as obstinate as yourself," and he actually ordered one of the clerks of the office to fill up a commitment, which being done he sent the man off, guarded by peons, to the Calcutta gaol.

While the warrant was filling up a servant belonging to the Hindoo ran to the house of his master's attorney, Mr. Fairfax Moresby, who lived within a few yards, and informed him of what was going forward, whereupon Mr. Moresby instantly went to the Judge's chambers. Mr. Hyde seeing him enter, and probably suspecting the occasion of the visit, petulantly asked, " Pray, what do you want ? What has brought you here this evening ? " (The Judge had a particular dislike to any person's attending out of mere curiosity, and more especially to an attorney's being present.) Mr. Moresby replied, " My lord, I have taken the liberty of coming to speak on behalf of a client of mine who has just sent a servant to acquaint me that he has been ordered into confinement without any cause whatsoever."

The Judge here interrupted Mr. Moresby with, " You have taken the liberty of coming, and you say very truly it is a liberty, and an unwarrantable liberty. I wonder at your doing it, Mr. Moresby. The shorter your stay the better. Let me advise you to leave the room." Mr. Moresby, instead of doing so, said, " My lord, the man you have committed is a Hindoo of the highest rank and consequence. He is likewise a Brahmin, and as such will be disgraced by being confined in a prison with felons and persons he cannot associate with. I am ready to give bail for him to any amount required, and humbly conceive he has not been guilty of any offence for which bail can be refused." " I neither want your security nor panegyric upon the fellow respecting his caste, his wealth, or his high connections. Go about your business, sir, you have none here." To this Moresby replied, " My lord, it is my duty, without intending you the slightest offence thereby, to inform you that I shall forthwith apply to another judge for a writ of habeas corpus that the cause of my client's strange imprisonment may be enquired into."

This put Mr. Hyde into a violent rage. He roared out, " What ! do you presume to threaten me with your writs, or think to intimidate me by your impertinence ? Go along, sir. Get out, I say, or I'll send you after your rich Hindoo, and then you may include yourself in your habeas corpus." Mr. Moresby bowed and retired, when Mr. Hyde, recollecting himself, and the violence as well as the illegality of what he had done, instantly ordered a *hircarrah* to run as fast as he could to the prison with a release. The *hircarrah* did so, reaching the gaol before the Hindoo had left the outer lodge.

The house wherein the judges thus sat in rotation to transact the police business in an evening was hired by the Company, the upper part being occupied by the clerk, who was also an attorney of the Court. From the crowd that daily attended these chambers, of the lowest order of people, the house had been facetiously christened "Ragamuffin Hall," a name that Mr. Hyde was much displeased at, nor could anyone offend him more than by so calling it in his presence.

When sitting at these chambers the judges would execute any common matters for the practitioners of the Court and receive affidavits as the foundation for different processes issuing. Some matter of that sort had taken me there one evening, and while waiting for what I wanted, Mr. Solomon Hamilton came in accompanied by a client about to apply for letters of administration to the estate of a person deceased, named Huggins. The petition stated the applicant to be a nephew and next-of-kin, and that he had recently arrived in Bengal from Europe. It then prayed that former letters granted to a creditor might be recalled and cancelled and fresh ones granted to him.

It appeared to me that this nephew, whose name was likewise Huggins, was abominably drunk, and I could not help thinking his proctor guilty of a glaring impropriety in bringing a man in that disgraceful state to take an oath of so important and serious a nature as that of administrator. Some doubts arising in Mr. Hyde's mind relative to the propriety of the mode of application for recalling letters already issued, he desired the clerk to hand him the Charter and Act of Parliament under the authority of which the Court was constituted. While referring to those documents, the staggering drunkard muttered out, "And so I am to be kept waiting here whilst you are rummaging

among your damned old musty law books, am I ? Very
pretty, by God ! " This strange and coarse speech, although
delivered in a low under-voice, nevertheless drew the
attention of Mr. Hyde, who after attentively eyeing Huggins
for a minute said, " The fellow's intoxicated. Take the
filthy beast away." Hamilton, with difficulty, got him out,
he cursing and swearing at the " damned old quiz, in his
stiff formal perriwig, with his confounded folio volumes of
chicanery."

A few evenings after the foregoing scene had occurred
Hamilton again attended with Huggins, the attorney having
previously taken care to ascertain that his client was sober.
The moment the Judge saw the petition he recollected the
former circumstance, and, addressing Huggins, said, " So !
you have again made your appearance. Are you now in a
fit state to take a solemn oath and to engage to do your
duty with fidelity should you obtain what you apply for ? "
Huggins with respectful humility answered, " Yes, my lord,"
to which Mr. Hyde replied, " I have my doubts about it."
Having, however, administered the oath and signed an
order for the citations, he said, " There, I have done it,
notwithstanding I strongly suspect you to be unworthy of
the trust. Prove that I wrong you, and when you have
obtained letters of administration do not rob the children
of your late uncle of their property."

The following is another proof of his warmth of temper,
but equally so of his genuine sensibility. A man of the name
of Sherif had acquired a handsome competence in the
situation of an assistant extra clerk in the Calcutta treasury.
This Mr. Sherif debauched a young orphan girl, who thenceforward had cohabited with and been faithfully attached
to her seducer, in the period of seven years bearing three
children by him. At the end of that term he became
enamoured of another woman who was obtainable only
through wedlock. He therefore proposed to her, was
accepted, and became a husband, upon which event he
most ungenerously not only refused to make any provision
for his former favourite and mother of his children, but

called upon the faithful and ill-used girl to give up a gold watch, with various other trinkets and ornaments of the person which he had presented to her at different times whilst residing with him. The poor creature's remonstrances against so illiberal and base a measure were unavailing. She therefore made a representation of her case in writing in the form of a petition, and delivered the same to Mr. Justice Hyde, praying his lordship's interference to procure her redress and relief.

The humane judge felt keenly for her and was indignant at the vile conduct of her miserly betrayer ; still he was conscious that the law did not authorize or warrant his compelling that betrayer to provide for the unhappy woman, or even make him restore the articles he so meanly took from her unless she could have established by witnesses that they had been actual gifts, which she candidly declared she could not do, having no such proofs within her power. Mr. Hyde, however, resolved to try the effect of endeavouring to shame the man into an act of common justice, with which view he issued a summons in the usual form requiring Sherif to appear before him to answer a complaint made against him by the ill-treated woman, upon receiving which summons Sherif immediately took it to his lawyer to consult with him thereon, and having thus ascertained that the Judge could exercise no power over him upon the present occasion he went upon the day specified to the Judge's chambers, where Mr. Hyde civilly told him the reason of his summoning him, expressing at the same time his hope that what was stated had been exaggerated, and that he could not have behaved so cruelly to an unprotected female.

Sherif, presuming upon what his lawyer had told him, haughtily replied he did not consider himself bound to answer interrogatories, nor to reply to *extra judicial questions.* The latter phrase raised the Judge's choler, and he had, in consequence, recourse to his usual and favourite epithets of " impertinent blockhead and stupid ass." After a few seconds he thus addressed Sherif, " Do you not think, sir, such conduct will deservedly render you contemptible in the eyes of every person of feeling, and an outcast from society ? "

Sherif : " No, I do not, nor do I see the least reason why it should have any such effect."

Judge : " Then you are wilfully blind and callous, for are you not a robber of the worst kind ? Did you not plunder this poor destitute girl of the only patrimony she possessed, her chastity, and after so doing have you not basely and infamously abandoned her to want and misery, and yet you have the effrontery to say you are not unworthy the society of honest and honourable men ! "

Sherif : " I am the best judge of what is right to do and how to govern myself in matters which belong to me alone."

Judge : " I do not think so. You are upon the present occasion, and I lament that such is the case, beyond the reach of law. I possess not the power of compelling you to be commonly just, much less generous, but such grovelling, disgraceful sentiments as you have avowed must, I think, speedily bring you within the clutches of the law. I shall soon see you in a criminal court and will bear you in remembrance."

Sherif : " If to vent your scurrility is all you summoned me for I am not bound to wait for a continuance of it, nor will I."

Judge : " Oh, you won't ! Then ere you depart let me ask you one question, which if you refuse to answer I will answer for you. What are you, or what do you call yourself ? "

Sherif : " A gentleman ! "

Judge : " Oh ! a gentleman. What, you wear shoes, I suppose ! Every fellow that wears shoes in this country dubs himself gentleman. Got money, too, possibly, Mr. Gentleman, a man of fortune ? "

Sherif : " Yes, I have ample fortune."

Judge : " How much may you be worth ? "

Sherif : " Upwards of two lacs of rupees ! "

Judge : " Upwards of two lacs of rupees, hey ? And that you imagine constitutes a gentleman ? Why, you despicable wretch, an hundred lacs would not make you a gentleman, no wealth, no sum, no circumstances could do it. Go along. Get out, you contaminate the place. Take care of the approaching sessions. Get out, I say, vile wretch!"

Sherif seemed glad to obey the rough order and retired. The worthy Judge being thus foiled in his benevolent object, privately gave directions to his agent to pay the girl fifty sicca rupees every month without letting her know from what quarter it came, and to make the first payment that very day. This was actually done regularly for fifteen months, when the object of his bounty having discovered from whence the supply flowed, one morning called at his house, and with her eyes swimming in tears of gratitude, blessed and thanked him for his noble generosity, of which she was no longer in need, a reputable and opulent trades-man of Calcutta, who was perfectly well acquainted with her private history, having proposed marriage, and pre-viously to settle thirty thousand sicca rupees upon her, an offer she had accepted, and therefore had no longer occasion to trespass upon his bounty, a grateful remembrance of which would remain indelibly fixed in her mind while life remained. Nothing distressed this excellent man more than his acts of benevolence becoming publicly known, for ostentation had nothing to do with his innumerable charities.

I will mention two other rather laughable circumstances that occurred to this truly estimable man.

On his way home from Ragamuffin Hall one night his palankeen was stopped in the street by a young European woman, who with bitter cries and lamentations called upon him to do her justice, upon which, with his usual philan-thropy, he desired her to come to his house the following morning, and he would hear what she had to complain of. The girl, instead of waiting until the next day, instantly followed the Judge home. Upon her being announced, he ordered her to be conducted upstairs where he and three other gentlemen were just sitting down to supper. Upon her entrance, the Judge, to the great entertainment of his guests, rose and handed her to a seat at the table, urging her to partake of the fare, but the poor girl's heart was too full to allow of her eating, seeing which Mr. Hyde filled and made her drink a large glass of madeira, which materially relieved her. The cloth being removed, he, with the utmost mildness, asked who and what she was, though from her dress and the situation he had first seen her in it was pretty evident what her occupation was. She began a piteous tale, stating that she was of a good family in Scotland, her name Dundas, had two brothers, the eldest a captain in the army, the other a lieutenant in the Royal Navy ; that when scarcely fourteen years of age she had been seduced by a young cavalry officer, with whom she abandoned her father's house and protection, accompanying her favourite to various quarters in England, and finally, upon his regiment's being ordered to the East Indies, embarked with him for Madras. After being there a twelvemonth he lost his life in a battle with a detachment of Tippoo's troops, whereupon, being poor, friendless, and unknown, she proceeded to Bengal, and for upwards of a year had resided in the house from whence she ran that evening upon his lordship's passing, the owner, a Mr. Middleton and his wife, having treated her with great cruelty, although she paid them exorbitantly for her board and lodging ; that this couple daily got intoxicated and frequently when in that state beat her ; that they had that evening been more savage than ever, and she verily believed had she not made her escape into the street they would have murdered her.

This little narrative was given in a peculiarly feeling manner, accompanied by floods of tears, and being a fine young woman with a sweetly interesting countenance, the Judge's humanity, which was always uppermost, led him in strong terms to express his concern for her untoward fate, and to add something must be done in order to extricate her from the disgraceful state she was then living in. He then recommended her to return home for that night and he would send a servant with her, with a summons for Middleton and his wife to appear before him in the morning, when he would severely censure them for their misconduct, but against ever more entering their doors she strongly protested, declaring she would rather remain in the street. Finding her thus averse to returning to Middleton's, he summoned his sirdar bearer and asked him if he could not get a bed prepared in a spare room, to which the man replied there was not one in the house, Mr. Wroughton (who lived in the Judge's family) having the preceding day sent three cots to Bareset for the use of himself and two friends during the race week.

Old Billy Pawson (of whom I have already made some mention as the admirer of the widow Smith, now Lady Metcalfe) who was present, thereupon facetiously said, "I am afraid, sir, there is no alternative but Miss Dundas's taking half your bed, which fortunately is sufficiently large to accommodate a partner." This speech greatly offended Mr. Hyde. He told Mr. Pawson he was an impertinent and stupid old blockhead. Still, he was at a loss how to dispose of his new protégé for the night, from which dilemma he was relieved by her observing she could easily get a bed at one of the taverns, though at the first mention of such a retreat he did not seem to approve it. Mr. Motte, however, assuring him there were two houses of that description kept by orderly and discreet persons, he made no further objection, and ordered his palankeen to be prepared, bidding his chief *chubdar*, with some *hircarrahs*, accompany it, and upon no account to leave the lady until she was comfortably and safely lodged. He then handed her to his palankeen, which was thus seen parading through the public streets of Calcutta with one of the most notorious courtezans in it, to the infinite entertainment of the wits and wags of the place. But governed solely by benevolence, the Judge was indifferent as to all the ludicrous remarks made upon the occasion, nor would he retire to rest until the palankeen returned and the *chubdar* assured him they had left the Bibee Sahib (lady) safely housed at a respectable tavern, the mistress of which consented to receive her in consequence of her coming recommended by his lordship.

The other anecdote was this : An acquaintance of Mr. Hyde's who was stationed at Rungpore sent him a bag of walnuts, then considered a rarity, as they grew nowhere within the Province of Bengal except at Rungpore, and even there only one tree.  Mr. Hyde being particularly fond of that nut, conceived he had given very precise directions to his *consumah* about preserving them and sending a part to table daily as long as they lasted.  He had a peculiar way of speaking without raising his head from the book he was reading or the paper he was writing on, and his voice being low it was difficult to understand what he said unless to those accustomed to his delivery.  Having desired the walnuts might be boiled in milk, the outer skin taken off, and a plate of them put on the table with the dessert, he proceeded to order a mango pudding, a dish he also admired. The *consumah* heard something about boiling, peeling, milk, and pudding, and being aware how much his master disliked being obliged to repeat any orders relative to dinner, he without requiring any further explanation chose to judge for himself by concluding the walnuts were to be made into a pudding.  He accordingly so applied the whole quantity ! Dinner being served, after the viands were done with, the dessert followed, when the *consumah* placed a most enormous pudding at the head of the table before Mr. Hyde, who all astonishment exclaimed, " What the dickens have we got here !  I never beheld anything like this.  Surely it must have been prepared for the whole garrison of Fort William.  Pray, Mr. Consumah, what in the devil's name is the meaning of this outrageous dish, and what may you be pleased to call it ? "  " Walnut pudding, my lord," answered the *consumah*, with his hands closed together, a position of respect when addressing a superior.  " Walnut pudding !  Walnut pudding !  what does the brute mean by walnut pudding ? " angrily asked the Judge.  To which the *consumah* replied, " My lord, order walnut to boil, and peel, and milk, and pudding, so, my lord, I make pudding for my lord according order."  The Judge quite confounded and almost bursting with rage, which was not decreased by the whole party's laughing most immoderately, looked up in the *consumah's* face, saying, " You unaccountable beast, you brute without parallel ! " Then alternately addressing his guests and the terrified *consumah*, he continued, " A walnut pudding, gentlemen ! the first, I believe, that ever was made ! Oh, you cursed fool, you abominable stupid ass ! Any gentleman choose a bit of walnut pudding ? Oh, curse you ! A bit of walnut pudding, sir ? Damn you, you beast ! " and thus he continued, upbraiding and ironically recommending the novel sort of pudding for some minutes, his guests being almost convulsed with laughter. One of them then proposed tasting the extraordinary performance, which having done he pronounced it excellent, and that it was an admirable way of serving up walnuts though upon rather too profuse a scale ! The gentleman's facetious re marks entirely failed to restore the Judge's good-humour ; he remained much out of humour the rest of the day, nor could he with any patience hear a walnut spoken of for a long time after.

# CHAPTER XVII

## THE GOVERNOR GENERAL MR. HASTINGS AND OTHER OLD WESTMINSTER SCHOOL BOYS

IN the month of July a house upon the Esplanade, the most airy and best situation in Calcutta, becoming vacant, I had the good fortune to procure it, and immediately took possession. The building itself was very old and in a decayed state, but the beauty of the view from it and its vicinity to the Court-house made it a most desirable residence for me.

In the same month my friend, Robert Pott, accomplished his great object by obtaining the appointment of Resident at the Durbar of the Nabob of Bengal, at the City of Moorshedabad, which was at that time considered as the most lucrative office in the Company's service, the whole stipend or salary allowed by Government to the Nabob passing through such Resident's hands, in which channel a considerable portion of it always stuck to his fingers. He had likewise the further advantage of purchasing and paying for every European article the Nabob wished to have. The Resident also always held the advantageous post of collector of the customs for Moorshedabad and Cossimbuzar. Pott, however, did not attain these enviable situations without paying exorbitantly for them.

As I have before stated, Pott, through the interest and influence of Lord Thurlow, then Lord High Chancellor of England, had been nominated to the reversion of the Residency by the Court of Directors during his stay in London, and it was generally known that Sir John D'Oyly, the holder of the place at the time of Pott's return to India, intended to resign the service and leave Bengal at the end of the then current year, notwithstanding he gave out that he would remain two, if not three, years longer, and this he said in order to induce Pott, who he knew was impatient to be in possession, to bid money as a consideration for an earlier resignation.

Pott had been cautioned by several friends not to fall into this snare and so expend his cash unnecessarily, but such was his eagerness to get the offices that without a pause he at once entered into a negotiation with Sir John D'Oyly upon the subject, which ended in the baronet's screwing him up to the hard terms of paying no less a sum than three lacs of sicca rupees, which he pretended was very inadequate to being an equivalent for the early vacating the posts he filled. Sir John, however, was not contented with even the usurious conditions Pott had yielded to, for he further compelled him to take a parcel of trumpery old furniture at a valuation to be fixed by Sir John's own agent, Mr. John Burgh, who took care to value them high enough. Thus had Pott the further sum of ninety odd thousand sicca rupees to pay for articles he would not have accepted as a present, and the greater part of which he ordered to be thrown away the moment they became his property.

Exorbitant as the terms were, Pott was delighted, and with inexpressible satisfaction took possession of the house at Afzoulbang, distant about four miles from the City of Moorshedabad. Magnificent as this mansion undoubtedly was, it did not come up to the still more magnificent ideas of my friend Robert, who forthwith began to alter the whole plan, laying two rooms into one, building several additional apartments and erecting an entire new staircase, making it altogether by far the most splendid thing in India. Certainly no man living was better qualified to do so than himself, having uncommon taste in everything relative to houses and grounds, a qualification that cost him dear wherever he went. Even at Burdwan, although he knew he should continue there only a few months, he expended no less a sum than thirty thousand rupees of his own money in embellishments upon the house, not one rupee of which was he ever reimbursed.

About this time a circumstance occurred that for a time occasioned me much anxiety and uneasiness of mind. Having one day had company to dinner I, according to custom, drank too much claret. The party breaking up before dusk, Colonel Mordaunt, who was one of them, asked me to take him an airing. I therefore ordered my phaeton and away we went as fast as the horses could gallop. Unfortunately the Colonel expressed a wish to go through the fort, and I accordingly took that direction. The road was so narrow, especially in approaching to and upon the drawbridges, as to require a good coachman, and many accidents had happened by carriages meeting in those parts. I not only drove at an immense rate, but took the wrong side. After a sharp turn, and when actually upon one of the drawbridges, I encountered a post-chaise coming out of the fort. How we passed each other without our wheels coming in contact was marvellous, there literally not being an inch spare space between the two carriages, nor from the iron chain outside each of us. Luckily the post-chaise was driven by a steady European postilion, who, deeming a crash unavoidable, wisely stood still in order to lessen it as much as possible, and I shot by him like an arrow out of a bow. Had there been a *sice* with me on either side he must have been demolished.

It was now growing dark, yet I continued my career at the same pace through Fort William, when, turning a corner, the pole met the breast of a soldier at that moment crossing the road, and knocked him flat down, the horses apparently trampling upon him and the wheels passing over his body. Drunk as I was I instantly endeavoured to stop the horses, when Colonel Mordaunt roared out, "Zounds! what should we stop for? Clearly the man must be killed, but as it is so near dark perhaps we may not be known, so go on as fast as possible." I continued my course, and we soon cleared the fort and immediately drove home, where I sat down every moment expecting to have it announced to me that the man was dead. The evening, however, passed without my hearing a word about him or the accident. The next day the same, through the whole of which I was extremely unhappy, yet anxious to learn some tidings of the unfortunate creature I had grievously maimed, if not killed.

The second morning, as I still remained ignorant of his fate, I determined to know the worst and to make some enquiries about him, for which purpose I went into the fort and called at my friend Doctor Wilson's quarters, he then being garrison head surgeon. After chatting upon common topics for some time, I ventured to ask whether any accident had recently happened within the fort, to which the Doctor answered, "Yes, a very extraordinary one occurred two evenings ago, a private soldier of His Majesty's 73rd Regiment having been run over by Colonel Hampton's coach and four. The fellow was taken up and carried to my apartments. I found him insensible and, as I then really thought, irrecoverably gone, concluding the pole of the carriage had struck him in the breast and proved fatal, but upon examining the body I could not discover any mark whatsoever, nor even the smallest appearance even of a bruise. Upon putting my hand to his wrist I was agreeably surprized to find a strong and quick pulse. I therefore deemed it prudent to draw a quantity of blood from the patient, for which purpose I opened a vein in his arm, and within an hour afterwards he so far recovered as to be able to bear a removal to his barrack. He then positively asserted that Colonel Hampton's coach and four had run over him."

From this account of Doctor Wilson's I took it for granted there had been two disasters of the same kind, but was soon set right in that respect by Wilson's adding, "The man, it seems, was so excessively intoxicated that he saw more than double, for instead of a coach and four it was, as I have since been informed, a phaeton and pair, the horses in which had run away, so that the gentleman who was in the carriage had no sort of control over them, nor could he with all his exertions stop them after the accident had happened, they running at full speed out of the fort at the Plassey Gate.

The soldier had been accustomed to see Colonel Hampton pass about dusk to take his airing and therefore concluded it to be his coach, but it so happened that he did not use his carriage that day, not being quite well." I then with much solicitude asked him how the poor man was, and had the supreme satisfaction to hear he had not received any very serious injury ; that he was sore from the fall and still confined to the garrison hospital, but would be discharged therefrom the next day, and return to his duty in two or three.

Upon this pleasing news I told Doctor Wilson the circumstances and that I was the disastrous wight that had done the mischief, when he congratulated me upon having escaped so well. The alarm it occasioned me had the good effect of breaking me of the foolish habit of driving out when inebriated, and I rarely ever did so afterwards when at all in liquor, and never went without *sices*, nor drove at such a furious rate as thentofore. I requested Doctor Wilson to send the man to my house as soon as he should be well enough that I might make him some pecuniary compensation for the injury I had done him.

Three days after this interview with the Doctor the man brought me a letter from Captain Macdonal, who commanded the regiment, and with whom I was intimately acquainted, he, as well as myself, being a member of a very jovial society called the Bachelors Club. In this letter Captain Macdonal told me that having heard of the accident that had happened, and knowing the liberality of my disposition, he took the liberty of requesting that instead of giving money to the person I had unluckily run over, who, if I did so, would only get into further scrapes from it by intoxicating himself, that I would send the amount I proposed giving him to his wife, an industrious, worthy woman, who had with infinite credit to herself brought up and educated four fine children. He also observed that the man was one of the best soldiers in the regiment when sober, but if liquor came in his way he had no command over himself, constantly getting immoderately drunk. Upon this representation I took my friend's advice by sending this exemplary wife and mother a handsome sum of money for the use of herself and children, contenting myself by giving the man a couple of gold mohurs, previously exacting from him his honour as a soldier that he would not spend it in liquor. He willingly gave me the promise, which he rigidly adhered to, but feeling doubtful of his own fortitude he prudently resolved to place himself out of temptation, and actually gave the two gold mohurs to his wife, who purchased a small hog, a goat, and some other trifling domestic articles for her young family with the amount.

Captain Macdonal, who I have just mentioned, afterwards became a Lieutenant-General and Commander-in-Chief of the Army upon the coast of Coromandel, in which elevated post he became involved in a serious controversy with that contemptible upstart wretch, Sir George Barlow, the Governor of Madras, which arose to so great a height as finally to induce the General to resign his command and take his passage for Europe on board the *Calcutta* East Indiaman, which unfortunate vessel, together with three others of the same fleet, went to the bottom in a gale of wind off the south end of Madagascar, and every soul on board perished.

Upon my return from Mr. Burke's one day, I found Mr. Macleod, a gentleman in the Company's civil service on the Madras establishment, waiting at my house to see me, accompanied by a stranger whom he introduced to me by the name of Harpur, observing he was a nephew of our common friend, Mr. Francis Rundell, who had come to India as an Assistant-Surgeon in the said Company's service, expecting to be received by his uncle. "Now," continued he, "as our friend Frank is absent, and myself no more than a visitor in Calcutta, you, Hickey, must receive and entertain Mr. Harpur until his uncle returns to the Presidency." Thus Mr. Harpur became my guest. In our first *tête-à-tête* he told me that he had been bred a surgeon and had acted in that capacity for several years in a regiment of light dragoons, when finding the pay inadequate to defray the expence, the style of living of the regimental mess being extravagant, he found it prudent to accept the appointment he then held in Bengal, which Mr. Pickett, the great jeweller and silversmith upon Ludgate Hill, procured for him, Mr. Rundell, another uncle (the brother of my friend Francis) then being a partner of Mr. Pickett's.

I early discovered that Mr. Harpur was a man who, if he lived, must succeed in India ; his own interest always appeared to be uppermost, and he shewed an attention in all money matters such as I never saw surpassed by the oldest stagers, and this was the more extraordinary, Mr. Harpur not being more than three-and-twenty years of age. Two days after he became an inmate in my house, while we were sitting at the breakfast table, a native silversmith, whom he had desired one of my servants to bring, came in. Harpur then produced a parcel of old silver, consisting of broken buckles, pieces of spoons, and various other articles of that metal. After shewing the whole he asked the man if he could work them into some particular things which he specified. The silversmith answered, certainly he could. The next question was how much he would require for so doing. The man said that Europeans always charged four annas in the rupee, to which Harpur observed, " But as you are a Bengalee and not a European I want to know what you will work for." The man replied he could not do it under three annas. After disputing and cavilling for upwards of an hour Harpur beat him down to two annas, at which price the bargain was made. To my great surprize Harpur then went to his room from whence he returned with weights and scales.

After ascertaining the quantity of silver to the utmost nicety, Harpur desired the man let him know what loss would arise from the melting and reworking. The native answered that he could not possibly fix it, as it must principally depend upon the alloy that was in the different sorts of silver. This answer, reasonable as it was, by no means satisfied Harpur, who declared unless the loss was previously settled he should not have the job. Disgusted

at the fellow's sordid disposition and contemptible meanness, I told the native, in Moors, which language Harpur
did not understand, to take care and allow for the greatest
loss that possibly could happen, as it was evident he was
dealing with a most determined Jew. The workman then
fixed the wastage, of which Harpur made a memorandum
in writing.

In about a week afterwards the work was finished and
brought home, when I was suddenly alarmed by a voice
crying out piteously, "Dhoye, Sahib! Dhoye, Sahib"
(Justice), the clamour coming from my guest's room. I
thereupon went into his chamber, where I saw Harpur and
the silversmith over the weights and scales, the latter still
roaring "Dhoye." Upon my enquiring into the cause, Mr.
Harpur told me the rascal wanted to cheat him, which he
was determined not to submit to, that although the rogue
had himself fixed the loss in reworking he now pretended
it amounted to a rupee and a quarter more than he had
calculated it at. I could not help saying, "My God! is it
possible, sir, you can enter into such a discussion and make
so serious a matter about so very trifling a sum?" He replied
that he never would with his eyes open yield to imposition,
and he actually deducted the rupee and a quarter from the
amount due to the silversmith, who went away bitterly
complaining of the injustice he had met with. Such shabbi-
ness gave me a very despicable opinion of my guest, and
I am sorry to add a long subsequent acquaintance afforded
me no reason ever to change it for the better.

Mr. Macleod, whom I have just mentioned, was a remarkably clever and accomplished young man. He was
an excellent draughtsman and painter, a proficient in music
and dancing, by no means an indifferent poet, and a capital
actor, especially in genteel comedy. No wonder, therefore,
that his society was much sought after, and that he was
somewhat vain of his talents. About three years after the
period I am now speaking of he married a younger sister
of the famous Mrs. Bristow,[1] Miss Wrangham, born upon

[1] See p. 377.

the Island of St. Helena, who brought him a numerous family of children. His father formerly commanded an East Indiaman, in which line he acquired a noble fortune, and retired from the boisterous seas to enjoy himself in ease and splendour on shore. He settled in the country and kept a truly hospitable house.

Mr. Hastings, the Governor-General, being a Westminster, he annually gave a dinner to all his schoolfellows resident in Calcutta, and very pleasant those meetings were. At the first I attended at the Government House I was agreeably surprised to meet my old sailing friend, Colonel Cooper, who seemed equally gratified with myself at our once more getting together. We sat next each other, and during the dinner he told me that having had a cursed hard run of bad luck at the hazard table through a whole winter, he lost, not only his cash, but everything he could raise money upon, and was ultimately reduced to the dire necessity of selling his company in the Guards in order to discharge his debts of honour ; that being thus completely ruined in point of fortune, he had availed himself of an offer of a friend in the India direction to send him out a cadet to Madras where his friend, Lord Macartney, was Governor, who might be able to promote his interest ; that upon his arrival at Fort St. George Lord Macartney candidly told him he could do nothing for his advantage, but strongly advised his going on to Calcutta, where he (Lord Macartney) had many friends in whose power it would be to serve him (Cooper). "This," continued he, "is the way of the world. Men in power are civil and attentive to me in this part of the world, not from any merits of my own, but because I am known to be a natural son of Lord Holland's, the same influence having allowed of my still being Comptroller of Chelsea College, a place that yields me four hundred pounds a year, and Lord Macartney's letter to Mr. Hastings has fixed me in the latter's family, which not only furnishes me an excellent table and apartments free of all expence, but gives me eight hundred sicca rupees as one of his aides-de-camp."

The Colonel dined with us as a Westminster, for the rest of the family who had not been brought up at that school were obliged either to dine out or in a private room upon every Westminster meeting.    Mr. Hastings, who was by nature uncommonly shy and reserved, always unbent upon these occasions and became playful as a boy, entering with great spirit into all the laugh and nonsense of the hour, himself reciting a number of ridiculous circumstances that occurred in his time.    His health being precarious, he was necessarily abstemious both in eating and drinking, and therefore when he was obliged to preside and give toasts, had a mixture of weak wine and water prepared for himself, with which beverage he went through all the ceremonies, announcing the standing toasts with great regularity and precision.    After filling the chair until past midnight, by which time a majority of the company were incapable of swallowing any more wine, he vacated his seat and retired unnoticed, leaving a few of us to continue our orgies until a brilliant sun shone into the room, whereupon we rose, staggered to our palankeens, and were conveyed to our respective homes.    In the early part of the day of this meeting at the Governor-General's, I invited the same company to my house that day fortnight, when they all promised to attend except Mr. Hastings, whom etiquette did not allow to accept of any private invitations, or to dine with any but the members of Government or Judges of the Supreme Court.

On the day appointed, at two o'clock, the following party sat down to as good a dinner as could be provided, myself being in the chair.    Upon my left sat the Reverend Mr. Owen, a pedantic, methodistical parson, then recently arrived from England as a chaplain in the Company's service, next to him Mr. Edward Hay, the Chief Secretary ; Mr. John White, Mr. George Purling, Mr. Robert Adair, Mr. Stephen Bayard, Lieutenant Lewis, Mr. John Wilton, Mr. John Buller, Captain Gascoigne, Colonel Capper, Mr. George Arbuthnot, who acted as Vice-President ; Mr. Cornelius Fryer, Mr. Peter Touchet, Mr. John Chauvet, Mr. Charles

Sweedland, Mr. Francis Pierard, Captain Francklin, Mr. Walter Fawcett, Mr. Christopher Meyer, Mr. John Bourdieu, Mr. Robert Samuel Perreau, Mr. Samuel Adams, Colonel Cooper, and Mr. William Burke, making our number twenty-six. We got through the dinner admirably, my guests being delighted with some champagne of a very superior quality which I had provided for them.

The same company as were at my house met at Mr. Burke's a fortnight subsequently. At this meeting a proposal was made, and unanimously assented to, to send a gold cup to Doctor Vincent, then head master of the school, as a mark of respect and attachment. An appropriate complimentary inscription in Latin was prepared by some of the gentlemen, I really do not recollect whom, but clearly I had nothing to do with the composition, having entirely lost the small portion of classical knowledge I acquired while at Westminster. Be it as it may, the event proved the work did the producers no credit. The cup, which was very splendid, being finished, was forwarded to Doctor Vincent by an old Westminster returning to England. Eighteen months elapsing without any acknowledgment of the receipt of it, the subscribers were greatly surprized thereat, and were thinking of making enquiries as to the cause of this extraordinary silence, when a young lad recently from the school arrived in Bengal, who told us that the Doctor was delighted at receiving such a token of remembrance from his former scholars until upon perusing the inscription he found a false concord, at which he was excessively hurt and offended, observing he never could receive as a compliment bad grammar from those professing to express their gratitude for the education they had received under him as their head master. Yet with this correct feeling he nevertheless kept the cup ; at least, we who sent it never heard anything more about it.

# CHAPTER XVIII

## A PERVERSION OF JUSTICE IN AN EXTRAORDINARY CASE

ON the 22nd of October the fourth term of the year commenced, when having much business both in the Sheriff's and my own office it became prudent to lead a more regular life than I had done for some time before, to effect which purpose I refused several invitations to tavern dinners. Having a cause of importance for trial on the 29th I was fully occupied the whole of the preceding day preparing the papers, and had ate a fowl quietly at home and alone, then while at table I received a note from my friend, Mr. George Tyler, requesting me to come to him immediately upon an urgent occasion. I accordingly went directly to his house and found him in great agitation, though by nature he was one of the mildest men that ever lived. There was with him a Captain Griffin, of the Madras native cavalry, who was upon a visit and had resided with him several weeks. I likewise saw standing in the room one of my myrmidons, a sheriff's officer named Frederick Deatker, by birth a Dane, a daring, savage kind of fellow, whom from a ferocity of manner and being remarkably ill-looking, I had always greatly disliked, and from some irregularities I had detected him in would long before have dismissed him the office, but that in those days we found it extremely difficult to procure any description of European to act in the capacity of bailiff. He was also a constable, and considered the best of the whole set, which made him a favourite·with the judges, and more especially so with Mr. Justice Hyde.

Upon my reaching Mr. Tyler's, both that gentleman and Captain Griffin complained to me in the strongest terms of

Deatker's impertinent conduct.  They told me that while they were sitting at dinner Frederick Deatker, accompanied by another man whom they afterwards learnt was his brother, attended by at least a dozen dirty black fellows, burst violently into the room, ran about opening every other door that was not locked, and appeared resolved to ransack the whole house.  The gentlemen at first imagined the party were thieves, come to rob them, and under that idea Captain Griffin seized and drew his regimental sabre which was laying upon a couch.  He had actually raised his arm to make a cut at Frederick Deatker when he cried out that he was a sheriff's officer in the performance of his duty, having a writ to execute for a large sum of money.  Captain Griffin thereupon desired to see the writ, which being produced proved to be against a Mr. Barnet (this writ had come to the office two days before, when I made out a warrant upon it, which I delivered to the bailiff with orders to be careful and endeavour to find the defendant, the sum sworn to being upwards of a lac of rupees).  Mr. Tyler asked Deatker what he could mean by thus riotously and forcibly entering his house at the head of an armed mob in search of a person who did not reside there, adding he certainly would prosecute him for it with the utmost rigour of the law, to which Deatker replied he knew very well the defendant Barnet was concealed somewhere in that house, and by God ! he would ferret him out.  He then made an attempt to force a door that was locked, whereat Captain Griffin, with his sword in his hand, called upon him to desist, saying, "That is my bed-chamber in which is deposited property of mine to a large amount.  If you presume to force the door or attempt so to do, be assured I will cut you down."  Deatker made use of the most scurrilous and abusive language, swearing he would not leave the house until Barnet was delivered up to him.  He, however, desisted from any attempt to break open the doors.

In this stage of the business Mr. Tyler had dispatched a servant to summon me, as his attorney.  The moment I

entered the room Frederick Deatker cried out, " Sir, there
has been a rescue of a prisoner from me by these two gentlemen." Mr. Tyler and Captain Griffin replied that the
charge was false and unfounded, assuring me that Mr.
Barnet was not in the house at the time the people entered.
I told Deatker he certainly should be turned out of the office
for his violent and unjustifiable conduct, and that I would
also cause him to be dismissed from the situation of constable by representing his behaviour to the judges. He
then walked off, muttering about not being supported, and
how hard it was that he should be condemned for his zeal
and wish to do his duty.

Peace, as I imagined, being restored by the scoundrel's
departure with his followers, I returned home, but about
six in the evening I was once more hastily summoned
to Mr. Tyler's, his servant telling me that both his master
and Captain Griffin had been seized by Deatker and a
large party of sepoys with fixed bayonets. I forthwith got
into my palankeen to go to Mr. Tyler's, at whose door I
found two sepoys standing sentry, with their firelocks and
bayonets fixed, a large mob being collected in the street.
Upon enquiring of the sepoys the cause of their being thus
hostilely stationed they said they had been placed there
by Mr. Deatker, and their own sergeant, a European,
having orders not to suffer any person whomsoever to pass
out from the house without Deatker's orders and permission.

Upon my going upstairs I saw the sergeant, and Deatker
standing by him. Of the former I asked the reason of this
unusual and extraordinary appearance, to which he answered that Mr. Deatker had a warrant from the Honourable
Mr. Justice Hyde to arrest the two gentlemen, both of whom
were charged with rescuing a prisoner from the custody
of the sheriff's officer whom they had also violently assaulted.
I then proceeded to an inner apartment, where Mr. Tyler
and Captain Griffin were surrounded by sepoys with fixed
bayonets. I demanded a sight of the authority under
which they acted, upon which Frederick Deatker took

from his pocket the same, delivering it to me, and I found it actually bore Mr. Hyde's signature, being addressed to Henry Grace, head constable, and to all other peace officers, directing them, or any, or either of them, to take the body of George Tyler, and any other person or persons who should be pointed out by Frederick Deatker as having committed a breach of the peace, and bring his or their body or bodies before him at his chambers, at eight o'clock that evening.

Here was a general warrant with a witness ; one that beat Lord Halifax's in Wilke's case quite out of the field. Surprized at the Judge's thus trespassing the bounds of propriety and of law, I expressed my sentiments upon it in pretty strong terms, telling Deatker that as far as he had been a party concerned I would visit him with the heaviest weight of law, at which he insolently laughed, directly observing to the European sergeant that as it yet wanted nearly two hours of the time at which the prisoners (for he had seized Captain Griffin as well as Mr. Tyler the moment he entered) were to appear before his lordship he should convey them to a place of more security than that house, and accordingly, notwithstanding my repeated cautions and threats of the consequences, and also of all the sergeant could say to dissuade him from such violence, the latter observing "the gentlemen were perfectly secure where they were, nor did they betray the least disposition to oppose the law," he obstinately persisted, and as the sepoys who belonged to the town guard were, as the sergeant knew, particularly instructed upon all occasions to obey the orders of peace officers who sent for them, he (the sergeant) could not effectually oppose it, and Mr. Frederick Deatker actually marched off the two gentlemen under the guard of sepoys, still with fixed bayonets, through the streets of Calcutta for near a mile to a miserable little hole of a lower-roomed building, used as a lock-up house, where drunken seamen or others found guilty of riotous behaviour during the night were confined, until they could be taken before a magistrate.

Having seen them thus infamously lodged, I went as

fast as my bearers could carry me to Mr. Hyde's, where the servants informed me he was in his bed chamber taking his afternoon's nap. I, however, prevailed upon his sirdar bearer, in consequence of the peculiarity of the case, to call him. Being admitted, I stated my business, when, as he always was if he conceived his authority called in question, he appeared distant and haughty at first, but soon relaxed. He said Mr. Tyler had committed an offence that would subject him to very severe pains and penalties. To this I replied I was sure he had been misinformed and deceived by Deatker, for, from my knowledge of Mr. Tyler, I could take upon me to say he was incapable of doing anything ungentlemanlike or violent. The Judge then produced his minute book in which was entered the grounds whereon he had granted the warrant. These were the deposition upon oath of Frederick Deatker, who swore to a positive rescue. He stated that upon his entering the room where Mr. Tyler *and others* were sitting at table, one gentleman, whom he verily believed to be Mr. Barnet, the person against whom he had a writ of Capias, rose from his chair and ran into an adjoining room, to which he (Deatker) attempted to follow, but was instantly prevented by Mr. Tyler ; that he strongly remonstrated, again telling Mr. Tyler he had a writ against that person, at the same time producing it, whereupon another gentleman who was present, a stranger to him dressed in the regimentals of a cavalry officer, jumped up, seized a broad sword which lay upon a couch, drew it from the scabbard, flourished it over the deponent's head, swearing if he did not instantly leave the room and the house he would cut him to pieces, accompanying the threat by making a violent blow at him with such sabre ; that thinking his life in imminent danger, he suddenly quitted the room, running downstairs as fast as he could and going into the street, where he was standing when he saw the under-sheriff, Mr. Hickey, arrive in his palankeen, with whom he returned into the house and again went upstairs ; that to his surprize Mr. Hickey, instead of supporting him as he expected he would have done, being the acting-sheriff, began to abuse him grossly, saying he (Deatker) should be turned out of all his places and be utterly ruined.

I assured Mr. Hyde that the material facts thus sworn to were gross and infamous falsehoods, and I then related to him the very impertinent manner in which Deatker had conducted himself, especially his dragging Mr. Tyler from his house, together with Captain Griffin, conveying them like felons through the public streets of Calcutta in broad daylight, and locking them up in a wretched dungeon, where I had left them. The Judge thereupon sent off a *chubdar* with me, desiring the gentlemen might be immediately brought before him. They accordingly came with several servants who had witnessed the whole transaction, upon hearing whose evidence Mr. Hyde released Messrs. Tyler and Griffin, I undertaking to appear for them to any prosecution that might be commenced against them or either of them.

This matter made a great noise in the settlement, and became the subject of conversation in all companies. I put my threat into execution by turning Deatker out of the office, and endeavoured to persuade my friend, Mr. Morse, to take from him the constable's staff, which he declined, from apprehending it might be deemed disrespectful to the judges, or as interfering with their privileges, they, from the courtesy of the sheriffs, having always been paid the compliment of appointing constables.

Mr. Tyler and Captain Griffin, having resolved to make a public example of Deatker for his violence, directed me to commence two different actions against him of trespass, assault, and false imprisonment. This being done accordingly, in due course the causes came to trial, the defendant having to each filed a plea of justification in which he insisted that he acted as a peace officer, merely performing his duty as such by executing and endeavouring to execute processes that had been issued by a competent magistrate, etc. etc.

The cause in which Mr. Tyler was plaintiff being the

first called on for trial, we fully and completely established the facts, as I have above stated them, by a variety of witnesses, all consistent, respectable, and uniform, the European sergeant of the town guard proving the fact of the plaintiff's being unnecessarily forced from his house and confined in a loathsome prison, a proceeding he (the witness) had endeavoured to prevent by every argument in his power, but to which the defendant paid not the smallest attention. The defendant, on the other hand, called his brother and three other vagabond fellows whom no person in Court knew anything of, who swore they were present at the whole that passed, and point blank contradicted what our witnesses had deposed. So barefaced and flagrant was young Deatker's falsehood and prevarication that the Chief Judge, partial as he shewed himself, was compelled to put his testimony aside, declaring no reliance could be placed upon a single word he had said. Mr. Hyde's warrant and the offices he held, as well as those of the defendant Deatker were likewise proved.

The evidence and arguments of counsel on both sides being closed, the Senior Judge, Sir Robert Chambers, observed, "There unfortunately being a difference of opinion upon the Bench, the Junior Judge will, according to the established practice, deliver his first." Sir William Jones then, in a speech of two hours, in the most pointed, elegant, and nervous language reprobated the conduct of the defendant. He said it appeared to him to be a case of greater enormity, of more gross, wanton, and outrageous oppression than had ever come to his knowledge as having occurred within the British Dominions ; that the magnitude and atrocity of the offence called upon the Court, indeed, he conceived it was their bounden duty to shew this defendant that he had transgressed in a manner that called for the highest degree of reprobation. He further observed that throughout his public life he had been a strenuous advocate for the rights of Britons and liberty of the subject, and trusted his principles would remain the same to the last hour of his existence ; that if such persons as the

defendant were permitted to act in the shameful way he
had done with impunity there was no saying to what extent
the evil might not be carried. No man would be secure
either in person or property if such a wretch, such an
abandoned, unprincipled profligate was allowed to range
uncontrolled over Calcutta under the mask of being a public
peace officer, a fellow who had availed himself of the mistaken privilege allowed him of ordering a body of sepoys
wheresoever he pleased, who at his word were to carry into
effect all sorts of tyranny and oppression, and this, too,
where a Supreme Court of Judicature was established to
which every individual might with the utmost ease have
recourse ; that his blood boiled at hearing the facts proved
in this case, and still more at the base attempts to meet an
unanswerable case, as he considered it, by, he was sorry to
say, not only perjury, but subornation of perjury ; that in
a case of such unparallelled outrage, so uncommon a trespass
upon everything like law or justice he felt disposed, as far
as his single and humble voice went, to visit the aggressor
with the heaviest hand, so heavy a one that though short of
imprisonment for life, should still hold him up a terrible
example of the consequences of attempting to violate the
mild and benign laws of that country he was living under
the sanction and benefit of. He, therefore, was of opinion
there ought to be a judgment for the plaintiff to the full
amount of the damages laid in the declaration.

Mr. Justice Hyde spoke next. In a few words he said he
felt rather delicately situated from the warrant that had
given rise to the action having been issued by him, but as
in his conscience he gave credit to the witnesses that had
appeared on the part of the defendant, and those witnesses
established the plea of justification, a judgment for the
defendant must necessarily follow. Sir Robert Chambers
delivered a long and incoherent rhapsody upon the case.
He agreed with his brother Hyde that the weight of evidence
was with the defendant. In the course of his speech, which
no person present could make head or tail of, he chose to
be severe upon me by remarking, " Much of the evil in this

case has arisen from the impetuosity and intemperateness of the plaintiff's attorney. Nothing serious had occurred, nor appears likely to have occurred, until the arrival of Mr. Hickey, who, probably heated by wine, or influenced by some unknown motive, by the violence of his language and conduct irritated the defendant, which was the more unbecoming from his at the time filling the important situation of sheriff, or, at least, deputy, executing all the duties of the office."

Indignant at this unhandsome attack upon my character, unfounded, too, as it certainly was, I instantly said in a loud voice, "Your sitting upon that Bench, Sir Robert Chambers, does not entitle or justify your thus infamously aspersing and libelling me. You are a contemptible animal!" A look of surprize pervaded the whole Court, which was uncommonly crowded, and I believe the auditors expected to hear and see me committed for a contempt. The despicable Judge, however, took not the least notice of what I said. A judgment for the defendant followed, and pursuant to an Act of Parliament that applied and which was made in support of magistrates and their subordinate officers when in the exercise of their duty, treble costs were awarded to the defendant, Deatker. The leading counsel then turning to me said, "I presume you will let a judgment go against your client in the other case, of course," to which I replied, "You certainly do presume in that opinion, for I shall do no such thing. You must have a very strange opinion of me and my clients to suppose they will tamely submit to the decision of this Court. Most assuredly a reference will be made to a higher tribunal." Captain Griffin's cause was then called on, and nearly the same evidence given on both sides, ending with a similar judgment. The Senior Judge, Sir Robert Chambers, merely saying, "There must be a judgment for the defendant with treble costs, as in the last case." Whereupon Sir William Jones said he could not let such a judgment be recorded in silence, nor appear to have the sanction of his approbation, which undoubtedly it had not, very far from it. He then with increased energy and severity commented upon the shameful misconduct of Deatker throughout the whole transaction, finishing a most eloquent speech by saying in his opinion there ought to be a judgment for the plaintiff to the full amount laid in the declaration.

Captain Griffin appeared to feel these judgments in a vastly greater degree than his friend, Mr. Tyler, did, swearing he would publish the trial and send it home for circulation throughout the Kingdom of Great Britain, that every person might see in what manner the administration of justice was perverted and disgraced in the Supreme Court of Calcutta. He further resolved, if possible, to punish the sepoys for the part they had taken in the seizure of his person and conveyance of him to prison, and accordingly exhibited his charges against them in a regular way to the adjutant-general, which public officer in the usual routine of business laid the said charges before the commander-in-chief, who forthwith ordered that a general court martial might be assembled to try them, in consequence whereof the whole party were put under arrest. The Judge Advocate-General at that time was Lieutenant Henry Piercy Monck, who having summoned the number of native officers requisite to form a Court, deemed it necessary to subpœna Mr. Justice Hyde, myself, and some of the servants who had been present at Mr. Tyler's, as witnesses, in pursuance of which we attended at Barrackpore, where the court martial sat at the quarters of the commanding officer, who happened to be a particular friend of mine, Colonel Knudson. The first witness called was Mr. Justice Hyde, for being in the middle of a term his absence from the Presidency was a public inconvenience. While the Judge was under examination relative to the warrant he had issued against Mr. Tyler and under which Captain Griffin had also been seized and imprisoned, one of the number of the court martial, with the utmost composure, belched, making a loud noise in the operation, whereupon the Judge Advocate, vexed at what he considered disrespectful if not an absolute insult to one of His Majesty's Judges, rebuked the black officer in pointed terms for his breach of good manners, finishing his censure by asking him how he could be guilty of so indelicate and rude an act, to which the native officer with great sang-froid and indifference replied, "To ease my stomach," an answer that set the auditors in one general roar of laughter. The censure of the Judge Advocate was delivered in the Hindostanee language, as was the man's ridiculous though natural answer. Indeed, it was highly absurd in Mr. Monck to notice the circumstance, because from his experience and knowledge of Asiatic customs he perfectly well knew that so far from thinking it a breach of good manners to break wind *upwards*, the natives of India, high and low, consider it a compliment in a guest to do so, as showing that he has completely filled his stomach, nor do they ever check an inclination to belch any more than a European does to sneeze, and like us, who usually say, "God bless you" to the person sneezing, they have a compliment ready for the belcher signifying, "Much good may it do you."

The moment Mr. Hyde had finished his evidence he made his bow, and set out on his return to Calcutta.

The case on both sides being closed, the members of the court martial retired, or rather, sent all the strangers from the Court, in order to deliberate upon the evidence and determine the sentence. At the expiration of an hour we were readmitted, when the Judge Advocate announced an acquittal of the prisoners, adding, however, and, as he said, by the express desire of the native officers who composed the Court, that they had so acquitted the prisoners because they were satisfied from the evidence that they had done nothing deserving of blame, having acted in obedience to the orders of those they were told and understood it was their duty to obey, but the President and members in general hoped that after what had appeared upon the occasion that the Governor-General would in his wisdom give such orders as should in future prevent the company's sepoys being employed upon such degrading and improper service. Myself and several friends after the court martial was over were most sumptuously entertained by Colonel Knudson, at which dinner the health of Sir William Jones was drunk with three times three.

Soon after the extraordinary decision upon this very extraordinary case Captain Griffin was obliged to join his regiment upon the coast, it being ordered upon service. Previous to leaving Bengal he called upon me to say that whatever measures Mr. Tyler adopted in future upon the business he also wished to be pursued on his behalf, and he would defray the consequent expences by advancing any sum of money that should be requisite upon application to him. As I did not entertain a doubt but that Mr. Tyler would appeal to the King in Council from two such infamous judgments, especially when encouraged thereto by the strong dissent of that great and able Judge, Sir William Jones, I prepared the petitions of appeal, the draughts of which I took to Mr. Tyler for his perusal. Not having heard anything from him respecting them during a fortnight, I called twice or thrice at his house without meeting him at home. I therefore wrote a note to say the limited time for filing the petitions was near expiring, and I therefore wished him to return the draughts that they might be laid before counsel, to which he answered, by letter, that after mature consideration, and having already suffered so much uneasiness about the business, he had rather not proceed any further, but let it drop ! Equally surprized and vexed, I immediately went to him to urge the propriety of his appealing, the defendant's senior counsel having admitted to me privately he thought the judgments so barefacedly wrong, and so opposite to the evidence of the plaintiff's witnesses that he was convinced they must be set aside upon appeal. But all my arguments were unavailing, my friend pertinaciously refusing to follow my advice. I then offered to proceed myself for the sake of public justice, and that I would not call upon him for a single sixpence in the progress of the appeal, but still he resisted, entreating the matter might drop. It accordingly did so, and thus was the infamous Dane allowed to exult and triumph in his undeserved success.

Captain Griffin when informed of Mr. Tyler's supineness upon the occasion was excessively offended, and instantly wrote to me to request I would, at any rate, appeal his cause, as he would much rather expend five thousand guineas in law than submit to such injustice from two of the Judges of the Supreme Court, but as the six months allowed for filing petitions of appeal had elapsed before I received his instructions I could do nothing for him.

Mr. Tyler, as I have already, I believe, observed, was a determined philosopher, and possessed a most uncommon command of temper. Nothing that could occur ever deprived him of his suavity or composure.

Mr. William Burke was much attached to Mr. Tyler, who often visited him and was invited to all his parties. They frequently played backgammon for two or three hours of a morning. Mr. Tyler, from his not being expert at the game, nor playing with luck, generally lost, yet his antagonist's success did not prevent him from abusing Tyler for moving his men unskilfully, so that it was no credit to beat him. Even the uncommon gentleness of Mr. Tyler at last gave way to these attacks, and upon Mr. Burke's one day cursing and swearing at him for his vile play, and that, too, after he (Tyler) had lost three or four gammons from the mere power of the dice, he very gravely laid down the box, saying, " I know, sir, I am a bad player, no way equal to encounter you, but allow me to ask if it is not rather hard to be thus treated ? I do not like the game, and sit down to it only to accommodate and please you. I constantly lose my money and get scolded at and abused into the bargain." In consequence of this speech the table was instantly shut, soon after which Mr. Burke came up to me and asked if I had heard what George Tyler said. I said I had. "Then," added he, " my dear William, it is so strictly true that I can never play with him again ; it would, and justly, be considered equal to picking his pocket were I ever more to invite him to it. No ! no ! I never ought, or can."

Mr. Burke upon leaving Bengal to go to the coast, ap-

pointed Mr. Tyler his deputy to pay those regiments that
remained upon the station, a trust he executed with the
same fidelity that pervaded every transaction of his life,
yet Mr. Burke, who was himself not only the most inatten-
tive, but the most ignorant man that ever lived in public
life as to all pecuniary matters, upon the accounts being
furnished and delivered to him whereby he found that
nothing remained in his deputy's hands flew into the
most unbecoming passion, swearing outrageously that Tyler
had robbed and cheated him to an enormous amount. Poor
Mr. Tyler, sadly vexed and annoyed at so unjust an accusation, immediately waited in person upon Mr. Burke, taking
with him the whole of his books and vouchers for every
pagoda or rupee disbursed, and with a diffidence more
suited to a knave than to integrity personified, which he
undoubtedly was, humbly entreated him to allow of his
endeavouring to convince him that the accounts were
strictly correct, which he thought he could do would he
but compare the items with the vouchers. Upon this Mr.
Burke at once declared that he never thought otherwise,
making a thousand apologies for any unguarded or hasty
expressions he might in a moment of disappointment have
made use of, and he requested no more might be said upon
the subject. Still, Mr. Tyler urged him to go over the
accounts with him, which would be a mutual satisfaction,
but Mr. Burke persisted in declining to do so, very truly
observing he knew nothing of figures ; he was no arith-
metician. Upon Mr. Tyler's continuing importunate as
to his at least comparing the vouchers with the sums paid,
he begged to refer him to Mr. Thomas Redhead, to whom he
would speak, and had no doubt but he would inspect them
on his behalf. This being done accordingly, Mr. Redhead
found and reported to Mr. Burke that instead of there being
any balance due to him, Mr. Tyler had actually disbursed
from his own cash fifteen hundred rupees, which sum
remained due to him, and that, too, independent of all
commission, no charge whatever having been made by him
for the trouble he had bestowed upon the business.

# CHAPTER XIX

## WILLIAM BURKE'S TROUBLESOME PROTÉGÉ. LORD MACARTNEY AND COLONEL WATSON.

IN the month of November my respectable shipmate, Mr. Tilghman, who had in the year 1780 proceeded to England with his kinsman, Mr. Francis, with a view to getting appointed into the Civil Service of the Company, having succeeded therein by being appointed a writer on the Bengal establishment, he returned to India, but at the time of his arrival it gave me much concern to see he had suffered very seriously in health and was deprived of the use of his limbs. This malady had come on very suddenly and without any known cause, the complaint not yielding in the least to medicine, nor to all the exertions and skill of the physicians. They recommended him without further loss of time to leave India and again resort to a cold climate, as the only chance of a complete recovery. He accordingly followed the advice, embarking with Captain Urmston of the ship *Francis*, who had brought him out. This ship, homeward bound, touched at Madras, where, after a stay of only eight days, she proceeded on her voyage towards England, poor Mr. Tilghman dying two days after she departed from Fort St. George. This able and worthy man was a public as well as private loss. Had he been spared he would have proved equally an ornament to his profession and to his country.

Mr. William Dunkin, whom I found was always pitted against Mr. Davies as an advocate, shewed me particular attention and we lived much together. He was a native of Ireland, of an old and most respectable family. He inherited an estate in the northern part of the island of about fifteen hundred pounds per annum, but having been too profuse upon his accession to his fortune he had encumbered it.  Being married and having a numerous family, he went to India to practise at the Bar of the Supreme Court, under a hope of thereby bettering his fortune.  Mr. Dunkin and Mr. Stephen Casson, also a young Irish barrister, kept house together, and a very hospitable one it was.

In the month of December Captain Henry Mordaunt, who from the period of my arrival had been upon duty in the Upper Provinces, came to the Presidency.  He not only did me the honour to visit me, but expressed an earnest desire to renew our intimacy, and that we might be as good friends as formerly.  As I never liked to reject a proffered kindness from anyone I readily acceded, and invited him to dinner.

Towards Christmas Mr. Foxcroft, the Governor-General's attorney, called upon me by desire of his client, Mr. Hastings, to say that as the Governor was upon the eve of returning to Europe he should, previous thereto, release Hicky, the printer, from gaol by prevailing upon the judges to remit the fines for the non-payment of which he was then detained a prisoner, of which compassionate intention he requested I would in the capacity of under-sheriff inform Hicky.  This I accordingly did, and in a few days afterwards that turbulent man was once more at liberty.  From that time he became a warm and zealous defender and panegyrist of Mr. Hastings and everything he had done while at the head of affairs, forgetting how he had formerly bespattered and abused him.

In the month of January, 1785, Mr. Hastings embarked on board Captain Cotton's ship for Europe, being accompanied by Mr. John Shore, who suddenly and most unaccountably from an inveterate and bitter enemy became that gentleman's sworn bosom friend.  From whatever cause this change arose it proved a fortunate one for Mr. Shore, and was the foundation of his subsequent wonderful success, as through Mr. Hastings' influence alone he first procured a seat in the Supreme Council, then the dignified station of Governor-General with the rank of baronet, and ultimately was created an Irish peer by the title of Baron Teignmouth. So much for the consistency of politicians !

Mr. Hastings was succeeded in the Government by John Macpherson, Esq., who was shortly afterwards created a baronet.

The Reverend Robartes Carr, who had been a playfellow of mine when we were boys together at Twickenham, arrived in Bengal the latter end of the year 1784, as one of the chaplains of that Presidency, having been removed at his own request from a similar situation on the Island of St. Helena. My house was one of the first he came to, and and I made several pleasant parties for him. At one of these dinners where there were present Captain Ulysses Brown, Mr. Rundell, Colonel Cooper, and Captain Cairnes, the last-named being a fine high-spirited fellow who, having been in the army from the early age of thirteen, was greatly attached to the life of a soldier. At a late hour in the evening, but whilst we were yet at table, Mr. Davison came in. He had evidently been drinking and appeared more violent and savage than usual, throwing the wine about the room in all directions. As he had never been a favourite of mine, and I had only kept up the acquaintance out of respect to my friend, Mr. William Burke, which Davison very well knew to be the case, I consequently felt his impertinence the more, and without hesitation told him in plain terms he had no right so to misconduct himself, that if he could not behave with more propriety I should wish him to leave my house. To this he made a saucy answer, but still from an earnest desire to avoid a fracas arising at my own table I curbed my rising anger and made no reply. Not so Mr. Carr who, disgusted at his brutality, expressed his opinion of his improper behaviour very pointedly, whereupon Davison without further ceremony threw a glass of wine in Mr. Carr's face. This act of indecent violence was not to be endured ; I instantly rose from my seat and going up to Davison told him he was not fit company for gentlemen and I insisted upon his quitting my house. He also rose, putting his hand to the hilt of his sword, which upon his attempting to draw I knocked him down. Upon his getting up he made a blow at me, which I warded off. A scuffle ensued, but my friends interfering separated us, and they bundled him downstairs. They all agreed that I had behaved with the utmost moderation until his outrageous act to Mr. Carr induced me to treat him as he deserved.

Upon the party's breaking up Captain, or, rather, Major Cairnes, for he had obtained that rank by brevet, remained after the rest had departed to say that as he concluded Davison, blackguard scoundrel as he certainly was, would call upon me to give him satisfaction for the well-deserved chastisement I had bestowed upon him, he (Major Cairnes) would, if I wished it, accompany me to the field, for which kind offer I felt extremely grateful and thankfully accepted.

The following morning Mr. William Dunkin who, as well as his namesake, Mr. James Dunkin, had been of my party the preceding day, called to enquire whether I had heard anything of or from Davison, and added that he had been round to a majority of those gentlemen who were present the evening before and had witnessed what passed, who were unanimously of opinion that under such extraordinary circumstances I ought not to risk my life in a personal contest with such a fellow. Mr. Dunkin therefore entreated that in case of Davison's sending any hostile message I would not accept it. In order to get rid of him I promised that I would not take any step without previously consulting my friends.

Mr. Dunkin had scarcely left my door when Ensign Bradford, who was a great crony of Davison's, was announced. After the customary salutations he said it was with infinite pain that he waited upon me on so unpleasant an occasion, but that he had undertaken the ungracious office chiefly from a hope of being able to accommodate matters without proceeding to extremities. He then observed that Mr. Davison considered himself as having been extremely ill-treated, and that however improper his own conduct might have been in the first instance nothing could justify my striking him, yet as he was conscious all parties were heated by wine at the time he would be satisfied with my making an apology for giving the blow, and this he (Ensign Bradford) trusted I would agree to, as he really thought I ought.

I told him I was obliged by the kindness of the motive that had, as he assured me, alone influenced him to interfere, but that any apology from me was entirely out of the question, the behaviour of Mr. Davison having been so outrageous, so brutal and ungentlemanlike in every respect, from the moment he uninvited entered my house, that in my opinion the most abject and unqualified acknowledgment on his part was indispensably necessary, more especially so for the wanton and gross insult offered by him to a highly respectable clergyman. Mr. Bradford observed that was a question between Mr. Carr and Mr. Davison, having nothing to do with the indignity the latter had suffered. I replied it certainly had to do with it as it arose out of his unmanly violence, and which called forth my resentment just the same as if he had struck a woman in my presence. As we could not by any means agree upon this point, the conference ended after fixing a meeting for the following morning. I wrote to inform Major Cairnes of what had occurred and to say I would call upon him in the evening.

Major Cairnes was an Irishman, very well connected, and inherited a fortune of about six hundred pounds a year. When just turned of twenty-one years of age he married a young countrywoman, the daughter of a gentleman who resided in the neighbourhood, by whom he had a numerous family of lovely children.

Having taken an early dinner alone, I went out to Major Cairnes, who then resided about three miles from Calcutta. After chatting a little with Mrs. Cairnes and noticing the children, we retired to his study, where he shewed me a pair of pistols, which he observed had already more than once performed their duty admirably, and he sincerely hoped they would not prove less decisive upon the present occasion. He promised to be at my door rather before gun-fire to attend me. These points being arranged, we rejoined Mrs. Cairnes and soon after sat down to supper. We were talking over our wine, Mrs. Cairnes having just retired for the night, when a servant who spoke some English entered the room, saying there was a European enquiring for me. The Major was greatly alarmed at this notification, for having been threatened by two or three importunate creditors he apprehended it might be a bailiff come to arrest him. I instantly made him pass through an inner passage, desiring he would lock himself into the next chamber. I then went to see who wanted me, and really thought my friend's fears were too well founded when I saw one of my own myrmidons. I directly addressed him, saying, "Major Cairnes is not at home. He dined and supped in town and is not yet returned." The bailiff, with much humility and many bows, replied he did not want Major Cairnes, his business being with me, and pulling a paper from his pocket presented it to me. Conceiving it to be some document from the office that wanted my signature, I opened it. Upon perusal, to my inexpressible surprize, I discovered that it was a warrant from Mr. Justice Hyde, requiring my immediate attendance before him, being charged upon oath with an intent to commit a breach of the peace.

After going in to allay the Major and Mrs. Cairnes's fears, I returned to the bailiff and told him I would obey the order by waiting upon the Judge early in the morning. The man, with the utmost respect, said no doubt my word might at all times be safely relied on, but on the present occasion I must excuse his entreating me to accompany him to his lordship, who had told him he should not go to bed until he had seen me, no matter how late in the night it might be.

Upon hearing this, I ordered my palankeen and went with the bailiff to Mr. Hyde's. Upon entering his room he began a lecture upon my rashness and the impropriety of a man holding the office I did of deputy sheriff pre-meditatedly going to commit the most outrageous breach of the law. He further assured me that the judges had resolved to treat with the utmost rigour any and every person, no matter what his rank might be, who was brought to the bar of their Court, as a murderer, for nothing short of that title did the person deserve who deliberately went out determining to rob a fellow-creature of life. He added that I ought to feel truly grateful for being prevented executing my savage purpose, and then called upon me for security to keep the peace. I observed that at so late an hour my friends were probably all in bed, but that I would give the requisite security the next day if he would have the goodness to allow me until then. Mr. Hyde replied it could not be ; that justice must be administered with an equal hand to the high and low, the rich and the poor. " But this I will do," said he. " I will wait until you can by letter summon two securities to become bail, as you are now actually in custody and cannot be released before that be done." I therefore wrote and sent off to Mr. William Dunkin and Mr. Geo. Tyler. The latter living close to Mr. Hyde's was with me in a quarter of an hour, Mr. Dunkin within the hour, when the Judge took my recognizance in forty thousand sicca rupees that I would keep the peace, and each of the bail in ten thousand, and I was then discharged. The following morning, as I understood, my intended antagonist, Mr. Davison, was also taken upon the Judge's warrant while on his way to the ground where we were to have fought. Being conveyed before the Judge, he was obliged to give the same amount of security I had done, after which he was permitted to depart.

In a day or two afterwards I learnt that this had been brought about by Mr. James Dunkin and Mr. Burke. The latter having heard of the quarrel and conjecturing that a hostile meeting must ensue, he resolved to prevent its taking place, for which purpose he called upon Mr. James Dunkin and easily prevailed upon that gentleman to attend him to Mr. Justice Hyde to request his interference, which he readily did by issuing his warrant upon Mr. Dunkin's making affidavit it was the intention of the parties to commit a breach of the peace by meeting to fight a duel.  Thus was I prevented from, in all probability, taking the life of my adversary or of losing my own.  I took it for granted that Mr. Davison, with his usual impetuosity and violence, would assert that I had for the purpose of being interrupted communicated to some friend the time and place agreed upon for the meeting, but in that suspicion I did him injustice and was agreeably surprized to find that he publicly declared it was no fault of mine and arose entirely from the mistaken zeal of Mr. Burke and Mr. James Dunkin.

About this period Lord Macartney, who had been appointed by the Court of Directors to succeed to the office of Governor-General, arrived in Calcutta, though not with an intention to avail himself of the compliment paid him, for he declined accepting the situation.  His lordship took up his abode with Mr. William Dunkin, who was an old friend and fellow collegian.

Lord Macartney came to Bengal greatly prejudiced against the European inhabitants for indulging themselves too much in what he considered extreme indolence and luxury, by constantly going about in carriages or palankeens instead of making use of their legs, as the less assuming residents of Fort St. George did, and always had done.  Another instance he gave of the Bengal gentlemen's unnecessary extravagance was their using punkahs or hanging fans, suspended by ropes to the ceiling, to cool them while eating their meals.  In vain was he assured that walking could not be adopted in Bengal, the sun most certainly having an effect it had not upon the coast of Coromandel, or in other parts of India, and that no European could expose himself to its meridian influence without feeling the ill-effects and suffering materially in health.  This he asserted was a mistaken and absurd prejudice, which, at any rate, he would not give in to.  He accordingly sallied forth on foot, without either palankeen or a bearer with a *chatta*, contenting himself with carrying a small one in his own hand without deigning to open it.  He was, however, soon compelled to do as other people did.  By thus setting the sun at defiance he lost his appetite, had frequent headache, a pain he never had previously been subject to, and one day in particular returned from one of his walks with a considerable degree of fever upon him, all which evils the physicians assured him arose from exposing himself to the burning rays of the sun. Being convinced of his error, he ceased his walks and speedily recovered his health.

In the month of February, 1785, my friend, Colonel Watson, resigned his post of chief engineer, with the intention of going home, being succeeded by my good-humoured shipmate, Major Mestayer, who thereby obtained the rank of lieutenant-colonel. After holding the situation only one week, he also vacated it, and engaged a passage for Europe in the same ship with Colonel Watson, as did also Major Metcalfe and his wife, likewise my brother Westminster, John Scawen, whose object was to get himself confirmed in the office of military auditor-general, to which he had been appointed by the Court of Directors, but could not get possession, the Government of Bengal not choosing to turn out the gentleman who at that time executed the duties thereof much to their satisfaction.

Colonel Watson was so greatly attached to Bengal that he never would have quitted it had not his health failed. He was a convincing proof of what I have already remarked as to the injurious effects of the sun in Bengal, as he for many years thought exactly as Lord Macartney did on that subject ; he was constantly out from morning till night in it, and though he had several fevers in consequence, never would allow that they were brought on by the sun. At last, however, his original vigorous constitution was so seriously impaired that he was driven to the necessity of trying the effect of change of climate.

The whole party embarked on board the *Deptford*, commanded by Captain Gerard. After they had been two months at sea Colonel Watson became so much worse he could not leave his bed, and his death was hourly expected. About a week previous to their reaching the Island of St. Helena he was pronounced by the doctor to be at the last gasp. Perfectly conscious of his dangerous state, although his intellect remained strong, he determined to make a new will, not having then made any provision for his wife. For this purpose he requested Messieurs Mestayer and Metcalfe to meet in his cabin and commit his wishes on that head to writing. They accordingly went, when after he had stated to them the heads of his intention, he became languid, seeming to have an inclination to sleep, upon which Major Metcalfe said they had better postpone any further proceeding until the evening when he would be rested. To this the Colonel assented, remarking, however, to the two gentlemen that the framing of his will could not occupy many minutes of their time, as his instructions to his executors would be that whatever property he died possessed of should be divided into three parts, one-third to be paid to his natural daughter, then residing in England, one-third to his wife, the remaining third to be applied to the prosecution of his claims upon the East India Company, and when those claims should have been established and the amount recovered by his executors to pay over the same to his said daughter as her sole property. "However," added he, "we will arrange all circumstances and nominate executors after your dinner."

The gentlemen then left the cabin and the Colonel fell into a profound sleep in which he continued until a late hour in the evening, and nothing further was done that day respecting the will. The next morning, to the surprize of the doctor, and every person on board, he was infinitely better, and continued improving in health until the ship's arrival at St. Helena. Upon landing on that salubrious spot he continued to mend, so that no more was said about the will. Between St. Helena and England he again declined, gradually becoming weaker and weaker, so that it was scarcely expected he would live to reach England; his friends on board therefore several times reminded him of the propriety of making a will, which he always declined, saying he was sure he should survive, and would prefer doing it on shore where he should be more at ease. When the *Deptford* arrived off Dover he lay in a state of insensibility. He was, however, carefully conveyed on shore, put into comfortable lodgings, and every degree of care and attention shewn him. On the second morning after his thus being landed he departed this life.

Upon examining the Colonel's private papers a will was found bearing date in April, 1777, which he had made while we lay windbound at Portsmouth when going out to India in the *Sea Horse* (Captain Arthur). By this will he bequeathed the whole of his fortune both real and personal of every description, and wheresoever it might be, to his natural daughter, she being at that time at a school in the country, and no more than six years of age. Thus was his unfortunate widow left nearly destitute, as almost all he possessed was personal, consequently there was nothing for her to expect dowry from except the dock lands in the neighbourhood of Calcutta. The daughter thus came into a fortune of upwards of three hundred thousand pounds. A few years after her father's death she married Lord Carbery, an Irish baron.

In the year 1786 Mrs. Watson went out again to Bengal to try what could be done relative to the landed property. She was advised to apply for administration, and having obtained the same received a very considerable sum as commission upon sale of an immense quantity of naval and other stores, but what ultimately turned out of much more advantage to her, she became acquainted with Lieutenant Nowell, of the Company's military service, who shortly afterwards quitted the army to engage in making indigo, by which he amassed a prodigious fortune, married her, and they are now enjoying themselves amidst the highest degree of splendour in England.

My friend Scawen having accomplished the object of his trip to England, resolved to return to India on a French ship, he being very partial to that nation. After only a few months' stay in London, he set off for L'Orient, taking Paris in his way to that port. While residing in the French capital he met with two young ladies he had known in

England, the daughters of a Mr. Kilpatrick, a celebrated gay and dissipated London beau and sportsman. These girls Scawen prevailed on to accompany him to the East. Scandal gave out that during the voyage he enjoyed all the privileges of a husband without the solemn tie with the eldest, a very charming creature. Be that as it may, they arrived together in Bengal, where she continued under Scawen's protection. Soon after Mr. Davison's coming to Calcutta he was struck with the beauty and accomplishments of Miss Kilpatrick and proposed marriage. As she did not like him, on the contrary avowed an utter detestation, she peremptorily refused his offer. He, nevertheless, persevered in his attentions, following wherever she went, and as he gained over Scawen to his interest the fellow had frequent opportunities of persecuting her with his love. Mr. Burke likewise became a strenuous advocate for his protégé, so that the poor girl was tormented in all directions.

After being persecuted for several months Miss Kilpatrick, in sullen despair, yielded to the importunities of her supposed friends, and was led a miserable victim to the altar. Just before the sacred ceremony was to commence she fell upon her knees to Davison, beseeching him with floods of tears not to render her and himself wretched by forming a connection she could not think of with any other sentiment than horror and disgust ; that having no human beings in India to look up to for protection, advice, and support except her sister and Mr. Scawen she had, contrary to her own inclination, yielded to their solicitations. Still, she hoped he would not force her into a state from which nothing but misery could arise, for she actually hated and detested him. Davison continuing inexorable to her prayers and supplications, the ceremony went on, during which something extraordinary seemed to be working in her mind. When finished (although she had not made one of the responses) the husband appeared quite happy. With a free-and-easy air he approached, offering to salute her, whereupon she pushed him from her, and turning to her sister, Mr. Burke, and Scawen, she thus addressed them in the tone and accent of despair : " I have yielded to your cruel persuasions, for I was a poor forlorn, helpless creature, without one human being with compassion enough to befriend or protect me. What your object has been in such tyranny is best known to yourselves. In my sister it was natural for me to look for consolation and support, but she chose to join my persecutors and condemn me to death. God forgive her. For you, sir," said she, turning to Mr. Davison, " who have thus ungenerously and basely forced me to become your nominal wife, I here swear," and she dropped upon her knees, " by the great and almighty God you never shall know me as such, never pollute my person by your loathed embrace, nor will I ever be more your wife than in the accursed name, so help me God, in my last moments which are fast approaching."

The brutal husband thereupon, with the ferocity of a tiger, seized her by the hair of her head and forcibly dragged her into the adjoining chamber. The party were thunder-struck, nor did anyone offer to interfere until Mr. Burke, shocked at her piercing cries, followed them. Upon seeing Davison with one hand fixed in her beautiful tresses and beating her with the other, he attempted to lay hold of him, when the monster quitted his unhappy wife, and seizing Mr. Burke by the throat would soon have strangled him had he not been rescued by his servants, aided by Mr. Scawen and the clergyman who had performed the marriage ceremony.

Altogether there never was so extraordinary a scene ; the poor girl lay in a fainting fit, while Mr. Burke ran about the house like a maniac, crying, " Murder ! Murder ! Get a constable, get a constable." In about an hour the wife recovered, and with much difficulty Davison was prevailed upon not to molest her. Retiring to her bedchamber she there locked herself in. Rigidly did she adhere to her resolution of not allowing him to touch her. Three days after the wedding the ill-suited pair embarked for Madras, and upon the passage the miserable girl departed this life,

III.—T

most certainly dying of a broken heart. The unfeeling savage of a husband directly returned to Bengal, where it might reasonably have been supposed he never would have wished to shew his face again ; but what is more strange and unaccountable Mr. William Burke once more received him into his house, seeming as much attached to him as if nothing had occurred to render him unworthy his intimacy or acquaintance.

# CHAPTER XX

## A VISIT TO BOB POTT IN HIS PALACE

IN the month of April Mr. Benjamin Mee arrived from England. This gentleman was the only son of a very respectable merchant of the City of London, who had for many years been an active director of the Bank of England. Mr. Benjamin Mee was brother to Lady Viscountess Palmerston. He had led a gay and extravagant life which, added to some speculations he engaged in turning out unluckily, so far involved him in debt that upon a final settlement with his creditors little of his property remained. Being, however, of an active mind and in the prime of life he did not despond. Some of his city friends advising him to try India, he accepted the appointment of a cadet for Bengal, not with any intention of continuing in the army, but merely to get to the East Indies with the sanction of the Company. He was a man of the most insinuating and engaging manners. I was early introduced to him, and from that day we became sworn friends.

Immediately after Mr. Mee's arrival in Calcutta he resigned his cadetship and entered into the firm of the Bengal Bank, the other partners then being my two friends Mr. Jacob Rider and Major Metcalfe. The emoluments of the business were immense, their notes being as current as cash all over the British territories in Asia, and in circulation to an amount almost incredible. But as men do not always act wisely or attend to what is, in fact, their own interest, these gentlemen instead of minding their bank and that only, as they clearly ought to have done, embarked in a variety of different schemes, some of which failed,

hurting their credit, involving them in disputes and litigation, and finally, at the end of some years, completely
ruining the bank.

In the same ship with Mr. Mee there also came out Mr.
Thomas Henchman, one of the most clear-headed and
shrewdest men the East India Company ever had in their
employ. After a residence of several years in Bengal,
during which he had been a contractor for supplying piece
goods for the Europe market on account of the Company,
he himself returned home to recruit his health, which being
completely restored in the course of three years he at the
end of that term again visited the East, and was immediately put into the important and high situation of Military
Paymaster-General, that office becoming vacant by the
resignation of Mr. Claud Alexander, afterwards created a
peer by the title of Lord Caledon.

My friend, Bob Pott, now consigned to me from Moorshedabad a very pretty little native girl, whom he recommended for my own private use. Her name was Kiraun.
After cohabiting with her a twelvemonth she produced me
a young gentleman whom I certainly imagined to be of my
own begetting, though somewhat surprized at the darkness
of my son and heir's complexion; still, that surprize did not
amount to any suspicion of the fidelity of my companion.
Young Mahogany was therefore received and acknowledged
as my offspring, until returning from the country one day
quite unexpectedly, and entering Madam Kiraun's apartments by a private door of which I had a key, I found her
closely locked in the arms of a handsome lad, one of my
kitmuddars with the infant by her side, all three being in
a deep sleep, from which I awakened the two elders. After
a few questions I clearly ascertained that this young man
had partaken of Kiraun's personal favours jointly with me
from the first month of her residing in my house, and that
my friend Mahogany was fully entitled to the deep tinge of
skin he came into the world with, being the produce of their
continued amour. I consequently got rid of my lady, of
her favourite, and the child, although she soon afterwards

from falling into distress became a monthly pensioner of mine, and continued so during the many years I remained in Bengal.

Major Russell having been much indisposed during several months with dysentery which he could not get rid of, was recommended to try the effect of change of air. He, in compliance with that advice, proposed proceeding up to Pott's at Afzoulbang, pressing me to go with him, which I agreed to do. A noble pinnace being prepared, and abundance of provisions and liquors laid in, we embarked and had a very pleasant voyage, stopping to take a look at Plassey House, and the famous plain where Lord Clive many years before fought a great and decisive battle, obtaining a complete victory over the Nabob's army. In eight days we reached Pott's residence at Afzoulbang, beautifully situated on the banks of the Cossimbuzar River, distant about three miles from the military cantonments of Berhampore and two from the city of Moorshedabad, or, as the natives pronounce it, Muxadavad, in which city the Nabob of Bengal usually resides.

Pott's house, or, rather, palace, for such it might fairly be called, was most splendidly furnished, everything being in a style of princely magnificence. He received the Major and me with the cordiality and warmth of an old and attached friend. I had a suite of apartments allotted to me of the completest kind, with warm and cold baths belonging exclusively to them, and every other luxury of the East.

The morning after our arrival Pott proposed taking me in his phaeton to Berhampore, when to my utter astonishment upon descending the grand staircase, which was lined on both sides with servants, all of whom respectfully salamed him as he passed, and going into the courtyard, I saw a party of light horse drawn up, dressed in rich uniforms and mounted upon beautiful Arabian horses. The men upon our entering the carriage saluted with their sabres. Upon my enquiring in a low voice of Pott the meaning of this, he laughingly replied they were part of his bodyguard, consisting of sixty, and that he never moved from home without their attendance. When Pott took hold of the reins two of the troopers immediately preceded us, ten others following us. Thus escorted away we dashed to Berhampore, where we visited Colonel Forbes, the Commanding Officer of the station, Colonel Brisco, the second, and other officers of rank.

After inspecting the barracks for the soldiers, both European and native, and other public buildings, we went to pay our respects to my old friends, Mr. and Mrs. Keighly, at Cossimbuzar, of which factory he was chief. On our way home we stopped to see Mr. Edward Fenwick, the gentleman who gave the famous *fête champêtre* at his garden near Calcutta, of which I have before made mention. He was now Commercial Resident at Moorshedabad. We also left our names at the houses of several other gentlemen who held civil appointments in that part of the country, after which we returned home to dress for dinner.

At two o'clock we sat down to a sumptuous entertainment with nearly thirty persons. Mr. Pott's inmates at that time, besides Major Russell and myself, were Mr. and Mrs. Burgh, Mr. and Mrs. Lindsay, The Honourable David Anstruther, who commanded the Nabob's bodyguard, his lady, Miss Donaldson, Mrs. Anstruther's sister, and Mr. Farrington, the landscape painter.[1] His own immediate family consisted of his cousin, George Cruttenden, Mr. Trant, Mr. Ley, and Doctor Glass, surgeon to the Resident at the Durbar. Every individual in the house ordered carriages or saddle-horses as they pleased, to take the air morning and evening, Pott's head coachman always taking care to retain some particular vehicle for his master's use, generally a phaeton.

Upon my first arrival at Afzoulbang Pott announced to all his company, both male and female, that as the duties of my profession made it impossible for me to be long absent from the Presidency he should during my stay at his house

---

[1] Probably the artist, George Farington, a brother of Joseph Farington, R.A., the landscape painter, whose diary is now in course of publication. George died at Moorshedabad in 1788,—ED.

attend to me exclusively, and take me out constantly in order to shew me all that was worth the inspection of a stranger, and this he adhered to faithfully, daily varying the direction of our drive. Thus time glided away almost imperceptibly. Amongst other excursions he took me to the Nabob's palace in the city, having the evening before sent word to His Highness that he should the following morning bring the most particular friend he had in the world to breakfast with him. The Nabob received us with the utmost politeness and affability, giving an excellent breakfast, quite in the English taste, after which he took me round his noble suite of apartments, his gardens, menagerie, aviary, and stud of horses. Upon our departure he presented me with a pair of beautiful shawls.

During our drive to Afzoulbang I observed a mendicant at the side of the road. He appeared to be a cripple, and made a prodigious noise, accompanied with much gesticulation. Pott, in passing, threw him a rupee, of which the fellow took not the smallest notice, continuing his clamour with a volubility I never heard equalled. Pott, seeing me look surprized, asked if I understood what the man said. I answered that I did not know one word he uttered, but from his manner I should have supposed him angry at something. Pott then told me he was abusing him, as he always did, for giving so little, saying, "Aye, you Haramzada! you consider yourself a charitable man! A Behaudur, a Ballattee Behaudur. You pompously throw me down a pitiful rupee and think yourself wonderfully munificent! But what is a rupee? You ought to give a hundred! Have you not built for yourself a splendid mansion, whilst I am grovelling on the bare earth? Have you not a swarm of servants watching your wants while the flies and insects are eating me up! You have carriages and you have horses with troopers galloping at your heels to raise the dust and choke poor men like me, and with all that you think much of bestowing a dirty rupee upon a Brahmin who is your superior! Fie upon you! Will such charity give you a passport to the regions of bliss? No, I tell you, no. You'll go where all such Behaudur haramzadas ought, to the devil, who will reward your pomps and your state with stripes out of number !"  "But how is it possible, my dear Robert," asked I, "that you can have heard all this flying by at the rate we did ?"  "Oh," replied he, "I have stopped more than once for the express purpose of ascertaining the words that accompanied his furious action, and found them invariably to the same purport, and always gross abuse, and this would be the case were I to pass him ten times a day."

Three days after we had been to the Nabob's he came in great state to return the visit, when he invited the whole of Pott's party to a supper and display of fireworks the following evening, to which we went and were magnificently entertained.

Our next excursion was to see a herd of monkeys or baboons to the amount of several thousands.  They inhabited a mango grove about five miles from Moorshedabad, are of an immense size, at a short distance excessively like a parcel of Bengalees assembled together.  From the frequent visits made to them by strangers they are become familiar, and came round us quite close in vast numbers, grinning, chattering, and making a variety of strange noises and contortions.  In fact, I by no means relished their proximity, nor could I entirely divest myself of an apprehension that they would attack us.  I was, however, informed there was not the least danger, and that their apparent anxiety and the hideous noises they made only shewed their desire to partake of the cakes and sweetmeats they knew we had, according to custom, brought for them.  These articles Pott's servants had, but were ordered to keep out of sight in order to shew me their vehement impatience.  The cakes, etc., being produced and delivered to the leaders of the band, for leaders or chiefs they undoubtedly have, and none others presumed to touch a single thing, they went off to their respective trees, making an abominable yell as they scampered away, not very unlike what I remember in Westminster School upon an unexpected holiday, or as it is there called "An early play."

Having spent a very agreeable fortnight at Afzoulbang, I took my leave, my companion upwards, Major Russell, intending to remain there some time longer, and after supper on the 1st of May I got into a buggy of Pott's and set off, he having sent on two horses to convey me to Plassey House, where my palankeen and dawk bearers were, into which I stepped. Many, indeed most, men can sleep in their palankeens, but as that was not my case that mode of travelling was exceedingly disagreeable and irksome to me. The bearers usually move, including change of men, at the rate of four miles an hour, proceeding by night even faster than in the day, which makes travelling tolerably quick, *bangys* carrying the baggage, which, of course, is always as little as possible. After going two stages, each stage being about eight miles, from some mistake, which rarely occurs, there were no fresh bearers, and those who carried me thither declared themselves totally unable to go any further, the weather being most oppressively hot. Unfortunately, too, the then next stage was an uncommonly long one, being full ten miles.

I was set down in a village with a hope that fresh bearers might be looked for every moment, but after waiting more than an hour, I became very uneasy. At length, by means of bribery, which operates alike upon all men in all climates, I prevailed upon the same set to go on. They took up the palankeen. Their pace, however, was uncommonly slow, rough, and tiresome. After carrying me six miles they set me down in the middle of an immense plain where not a tree was to be seen in any direction nearer than two miles, the sun being actually like a furnace. Here they declared their incapability of going a yard further. All my remonstrances, entreaties, and promises were equally fruitless ; they would not budge a foot. After talking together some minutes in their own unintelligible jargon off they all ran in a body, leaving me under the influence of such heat as I never before experienced, nor shall I ever forget it. I really thought I must have ended my life on the burning plain of Mirzapore.

With a sorrowful heart I looked after the bearers, who I saw running towards a tope or grove about three miles off! What to do with myself I knew not ; my mouth and throat were parched almost to suffocation ; not a morsel of victuals or drop of water to allay my dreadful thirst, and this in a heat no one can have an idea of except those unhappy men who were shut up in the Black Hole in Calcutta in the year 1757. Yet in this horrid situation was I doomed to remain, nor was the prospect of approaching night very consoling, as that part of the country abounded with tigers, which animal as soon as it became dark generally forsook their thick jungles to search for food in more open parts. Nor could I attempt to proceed on foot, being utterly at a loss which way to bend my course, and having no one object in sight to direct me. In a state little short of despair, I lay myself down in my palankeen.

At the end of two tedious hours I had the inexpressible satisfaction to see several persons approaching. They proved to be my bearers, who returned apparently much recruited in spirits. They told me they had found themselves so completely exhausted from the intense heat that to proceed was not in their power, therefore they went to a tank which they knew was within about two miles and a half, where they had recruited their strength by bathing and eating mangoes, afterwards laying down under the shade of the trees and sleeping an hour. They therefore said they could now carry me the rest of the stage. Never in my life was I more rejoiced than at getting over that abominable sultry plain. At the first village I came to I procured a water-melon, which, insipid as that fruit is, I found the most delicious thing I had ever tasted.

At four in the afternoon I reached Hooghly, thirty miles from Calcutta. Here Mr. Kinloch, a friend of mine, resided, and I determined to stop at his house to get some refreshment. Upon calling at his door, I learnt from the servants that their master had been out three days upon a hunting party and was not expected back until the end of the week. Observing I looked fatigued, the *consumah* invited me in, saying he would get me some dinner as quickly as possible. He kept his word, for in less than an hour I sat down to an excellent dinner, with a bottle of capital good claret, made cold as ice. Most perfectly did I enjoy the meal. My friend the *consumah* then shewed me into a handsome bedchamber, which he pressed me to occupy, saying his master would be very angry with him if he let any guest leave the house to travel until properly rested. I thanked the man for his attention, but being anxious to reach home, I resumed my seat in my palankeen about seven o'clock in the evening and continued my journey. A little after two in the morning I was on my own bed in Calcutta.

Upon rising to breakfast I found, amongst various other notes of invitations to dinner parties, one to a Westminster meeting to be given by Mr. Hay the following week. At this I attended, and a very jovial day we had. Conversing over our wine one of the party mentioned " Poll Puff," a well-known and interesting body to us all. This Madam Poll Puff every morning at the opening of the school took her station at the great gate with a deep basket filled with most exquisite apple puffs, from which she derived her name, the price of each being threepence ; but she would divide one, of course, the charge being three-halfpence. This occupation she had followed upwards of thirty years, becoming grey in the service. Mr. Wilton proposed a subscription to enable her to live with comfort when age and infirmity should render her unequal of attending to her business. He mentioned one hundred pounds as a proper sum to present her with, to which some of the gravest and most considerate gentlemen present objected, for that if she was not more prudent than persons in her line of life usually were it might prove her death, and thus we should be killing her with kindness. After much discussion and debate as to the best plan to be adopted for her benefit, a majority voted for purchasing a small annuity (twenty pounds per annum was finally agreed upon) so as to provide the necessary comforts for her in old age and yet not encourage the vice of dram drinking to excess, to which she was known to be addicted.

The requisite sum was immediately raised, and the amount remitted to Sir Elijah Impey in London, accompanied by a letter from his brother Westminsters of Calcutta, requesting him to direct his attorney to purchase the annuity.   This commission the Judge kindly executed, and if the poor woman be still in the land of the living she enjoys the benefit of her former youthful friends' recollection of her.

One would hardly have thought that an act like the foregoing could have been disapproved of by any man, or set of men, especially as it was so much within bounds and unostentatiously moderate, but within three months after the donation a paragraph appeared in one of the daily newspapers published in London, in the severest terms, reprobating the general propensity to folly and extravagance betrayed by every East Indian or *Nabob,* as they were designated, whose sole object, the ill-natured writer observed, was to squander the enormous wealth acquired by plunder and extortion in every species of absurd profusion, in proof of which, and to satisfy the public that it was not an unfounded or illiberal accusation, they could confidently assure their readers from undoubted authority that a set of men residing in Bengal, at a loss how otherwise to expose their prodigality had actually lavished a very large sum of money in the purchase of a handsome annuity for an old pie woman, of whom they had occasionally bought a penny tart when schoolboys ! So much for the base perversion of a meritorious action.

Upon Mr. Hastings quitting the President's chair to return to Europe he turned over my friend Colonel Cooper to the protection and patronage of his successor as Governor-General, John Macpherson, Esq., who, in consequence, continued him in the situation of an aide-de-camp, an absolute sinecure, the Colonel never attending except when he heard there was likely to be a pleasant party at the Government House.   Colonel Cooper resided in a commodious bungalow on the opposite side of the river to Calcutta, where he kept a beautiful Hindostanee woman to whom he was greatly attached, and who returned his kindnesses by every degree of respectful attention in her power to bestow, the most important part of which was her zealous endeavours to wean him from the destructive and baneful practice of drinking brandy or other spirits profusely, and even in the morning. This she in some measure succeeded in, though it was only effected by locking up the liquors and peremptorily refusing to let him have any except at meals.

The Colonel and I being engaged to dine with Mr. Woolley, of sporting celebrity, we agreed to go together in the Colonel's boat, Mr. Woolley's residence being at the lower end of Garden Reach. Colonel Cooper, according to custom, got excessively drunk with his favourite wine, champagne, and as usual when in that state had no inclination to leave the bottle, although the rest of the gentlemen had long before departed. As I considered myself in some measure bound to see him safe home, I reminded him it was getting late and we had better move. It was, however, near midnight ere I could prevail upon him to stir, when with the assistance of the servants we got him into the boat.

In our way up the river we passed the Honourable Mr. Charles Stuart's house, then a Member of the Supreme Council. Colonel Cooper, perceiving lights in the hall, insisted in spite of my most violent remonstrances, and my stating the unseasonable hour, that he would pay him a visit, for which purpose he ordered his *mangee* to steer to the shore. Upon reaching the bank I, at first, determined not to leave the boat, but seeing he could not walk, and he begging me to go in with him only for five minutes, I consented. Upon entering the supper-room we found a large party of ladies and gentlemen who had spent the day there, and who had just given directions for their carriages to be prepared. Mr. Stuart, who was one of the best bred men, appeared much distressed at Colonel Cooper's coming in so disguised in liquor, and appeared at a loss how to act. Cooper seeing amongst the company Mr. Titsing, the Dutch Governor of Chinsurah, staggered up to him to shake hands and soon proposed " A glass of Hollands." While they were taking it Mr. Stuart attended his female guests to their carriages. Upon his return Mr. Titsing whispered him to leave Cooper to his management and go to bed. This he did, apologizing to me who he saw was not so much intoxicated as my friend.

The moment Mr. Stuart was gone, Mr. Titsing, drawing his chair close to Cooper's, said with his foreign accent and delivery, " Come, Co–lo–nel, you and I shall drink anoder glass of de Yin (for gin)," and he filled his own and Cooper's glasses. This was exactly what Cooper liked, and he chucked off the contents. In half a minute Mr. Titsing again said, " Come, anoder glass, Co–lo–nel," filling both as before. These were as quickly swallowed as the former. In an instant Mynheer proposed and filled *anoder :* Cooper stared, but after a little pause drank the contents, when Mr. Titsing once more replenished the glasses, whereupon Cooper hiccupped out, " Zounds ! " to which Mr. Titsing answered, " This is noting, noting at all. It is waters to me ! Come, Co–lo–nel, anoder." With a sudden effort Cooper rose from his chair ; he would, however, have fallen had I not caught hold of him and proposed re-embarking, to which he made not the least objection.

Had it not been for this considerate interference of the Dutch Governor, who literally could drink gin like water, the Colonel would have sat at table and annoyed Mr. Stuart until morning, for when once he became intoxicated there was scarce a possibility of getting rid of him. I have more than once been obliged, with some degree of violence, to have him carried bodily away by the servants in the very chair he sat upon.

About the time I am now writing of I became subject to dreadful attacks of spasm in my stomach, which greatly alarmed the medical man who attended me. I fancied that bleeding would be of service, though so great a prejudice prevails against taking away blood in India that it is scarcely ever done. Upon my first requesting to try the effect upon me, he exclaimed, " Not I, indeed. Do you think I'm mad ? " These attacks were constantly attended with faintness, with the most distressing depression of spirits and violent cold sweats. Doctor Wilson therefore expected to find a languid, feeble pulse, but upon feeling was astonished at my having a very full, strong, and rather quick pulse, and he said, " With such a pulse as you now have I shall not object to your losing a little blood, because it possibly may give you ease and I am clear can do you no harm." I accordingly had half a pint taken from my arm, and either actually was, or fancied myself, better after it. I continued the practice occasionally for about eighteen months, when being once under the operation I suddenly fainted, and a considerable time elapsed before I recovered, after which Dr. Wilson never would bleed me again.

# CHAPTER XXI

## LORD CORNWALLIS AS GOVERNOR-GENERAL, AND MORE OF BOB POTT

IN August of this year (1785) two gentlemen were added to the society of Calcutta, who became great acquisitions thereto. These were Doctor James Hare, a physician from Scotland, a man of eminent skill and deep erudition, and Robert Ledlie, Esq., a barrister-at-law, coming to practise in the Supreme Court. I had long known him by sight as a gay London man whom I frequently met in public places. Upon comparing notes, I found we had as common acquaintances many celebrated persons of both sexes, respecting whom we afterwards often spoke, making mutual communications of interesting anecdotes that had occurred.

At this period I was balloted for, and chosen a member of, the Bachelors Club, so-called because when any one of it married he was obliged or at least, it was customary to send in his resignation. The members at the time of my election were limited to twenty. From the nature of such a society as that of Calcutta this club necessarily fluctuated much in members, and the changes were frequent. It nevertheless subsisted for upwards of twenty years with the highest éclat.

In the beginning of September, 1785, Earl Cornwallis arrived in the *Swallow* packet, his lordship being appointed Governor-General and Commander-in-Chief, the first and only instance of those two elevated stations being united in one and the same person. Lord Cornwallis brought out with him as his staff, Colonel Ross (his private secretary), Captain Madan and Captain Harry Haldane, his aides-de-camp, two high-spirited and amiable men. Soon after their arrival they both became members of the Bachelors Club, as likewise did Mr. David Ross, who arrived at the same time with his lordship, being on board the *Ravensworth*. Mr. Ross I also well knew as a dashing London buck.

On the *Ravensworth* came two Miss Philpotts, the eldest of whom some time afterwards married Mr. Harington, now Sir John, having succeeded to a baronetage, the other about the same time became the wife of Mr. Calvert. Both these ladies have been many years in England, their respective husbands having acquired large fortunes in the Company's service. In the same vessel came Charles Fuller Martyn, Esq., a barrister, who called at my house to tell me Mr. Carter was a shipmate, and as he had often during the voyage mentioned his intimacy with my family he (Martyn) thought I might be glad to hear of his arrival. This young gentleman I had known at my father's in the latter end of the year 1780. He was then quite a boy, had recently arrived from Ireland, and was under the immediate protection of the Earl of Inchiquin ; common fame, indeed, made him his natural child, but his history, shortly, was this : Lord Inchiquin knew his parents, who were tenants of his. Having a numerous family, with very slender means of providing for them, his lordship undertook the education of one of the boys who happening to have an uncommon fine voice he had him taught music, and when yet a child he used to astonish the congregation at an Irish cathedral by his extraordinary powers. Lord Inchiquin brought the boy over to England with him, where he was received most kindly by Mr. Burke's family, my father's, and all of his lordship's friends. His vocal powers were of so superior a kind that Lord Inchiquin determined to send him to Italy in order to let him have the advantage of the best possible instruction. After astonishing the audience at the Opera House by singing a single Italian song, and the same with Miss Linley at the oratorios, he was sent off to Naples, with the strongest letters of introduction to Sir William Hamilton, the British Ambassador, and his lady, in the middle of the year 1781. Upon his reaching Italy Lady Hamilton made him quite

III.—U

her pet, settled him in her family, and her delight was making him from morning to night sing little plaintive English ballads, at the head of which stood " Sally of our Alley." But in this love of that style of singing the object of his visit to Italy was lost in a great measure, dissipation and an uninterrupted course of company necessarily interfering with his musical studies.

Thus matters went on when one morning after passing the greater part of the night singing to his elegant and engaging hostess, and a numerous party of persons of the first rank in Naples, assembled at her palace, to his inexpressible surprize and mortification the boy found he could not utter a single note. From that moment his original voice was completely and for ever gone. The period of his puberty had arrived and the above change was the consequence. He, however, afterwards by habit and superior genius acquired the talent of singing in a feigned voice very sweetly. At the end of another year he took leave of Italy and returned to England, soon after which some person suggested to his patron, Lord Inchiquin, the probability of his turning his acquirements to advantage by visiting the East, and as he liked the plan himself he was forthwith fitted out and dispatched to Bengal.

Upon thus hearing of his arrival from Mr. Martyn, I immediately went in search of him, with a view of asking him to my house, which I did in compliment to my much-respected friends, Lord Inchiquin and the Burke family, who I knew were his patrons and protectors. Upon going to the tavern, I saw in the large hall, amongst many strangers, an uncommonly vulgar-looking little body, whose face I thought I had seen before. His dress was not more elegant than his person. Enquiring if a young gentleman of the name of Carter was in the house, this person came forward, and with a terrible brogue declared his name to be Carter. I then asked him if he recollected ever to have seen me before in London previous to his going to Italy. He answered he did not, being then " mighty small ! " but he " belaived from my faytures I must be Mr. William Hickey."

Having procured a palankeen and bearers, I took him home with me, and from that hour he continued my guest during his residence in Bengal. He soon informed me the object of his coming to India was to teach music and singing, in consequence of which I spoke to all the ladies of my acquaintance in his behalf, and although I did not find any of them disposed to put themselves under his tuition, one and all declared their readiness to promote his success. Some of the fair ones recommended his establishing a subscription concert, which they would patronize. This scheme meeting his approbation was adopted, and answered so completely that he cleared upwards of fifteen hundred sicca rupees, which set the little fellow quite agog and half mad with joy at his wonderful success.

I introduced Carter at the Catch Club, the leading members then being Messieurs Playdell, Golding, Haynes, Salt, Messink, and Edmondstone, all of whom had fine voices, with considerable taste, which was greatly increased by the superior skill and judgment of Carter. These gentlemen and many others occasionally made Carter handsome presents, and as my little paddy was of the same disposition as Mr. Harpur in the love of money his cash rapidly accumulated, especially as he had no disbursements except for clothes, in which he was far from extravagant !

Amongst those who benefited from Carter's instructions none did so in so great a degree as Miss Prince, now Lady Popham, being the wife of Sir Home. This lady possessed uncommon powers of voice without knowing what to do with it or how to avail herself of the advantage Nature had blessed her with. Under Carter's management she became a proficient, and had candour enough to admit how greatly she had benefited by his advice and directions.

Mr. Calvert, who married the youngest Miss Philpott and who, as I before stated, acquired a large fortune in India, was a man of not very elegant manners nor person. Shortly after the sisters arrived he made his proposal in form, and the lady, without the least hesitation, gave him a flat and positive refusal, but as diffidence or bashfulness was not amongst his failings this rejection did not reduce him to despair. He continued his assiduities and attentions to her. Amongst various other stratagems to catch her by an affectation of liberality and show, he purchased a splendid English post-chaise for which he got four beautiful horses, driven by two postillions in rich liveries. In this equipage he made his appearance upon the race-course where the belles of Calcutta usually took their station for half an hour in the cool of the evening, there stopping to give breath to their horses and to chat a little with their male acquaintances.

Mr. Calvert upon seeing his enamorata drove close up to the phaeton she was in. After the common salutations, finding she took not the least notice of his dashing equipage, he significantly asked her what she thought of his *love trap*. "Elegant, upon my word," replied the lady, "quite magnifique." "And what think you of the *bait* within it?" enquired he. "Do you mean to speak in French or English?" maliciously asked Miss Philpott. This severe witticism quite confounded the poor lover and raised a general laugh from all who heard it, at his expence. The prudent damsel, however, within a month from that time accepted of Mr. Calvert for a husband.

The supercession of Mr. Macpherson by Lord Cornwallis reduced the former to the situation of a private gentleman in the settlement he had been at the head of, Sir Robert Sloper, the late Commander-in-Chief, being in a similar predicament, and as it was not the season of ships sailing for Europe they were under the disagreeable necessity of remaining in Bengal during several months, the inhabitants in general continuing to shew them every mark of respect in their power.

Soon after Lord Cornwallis's arrival Mr. William Burke invited his lordship and suite to dine with him at his gardens, which was accepted. I had the honour to be of the party, when I found our new Governor-General of most engaging manners and great affability. After a very cheerful dinner, a good deal of wine being drank by all present, Mr. Burke, about eight o'clock in the evening had occasion to leave the room for a few minutes, when Lord Cornwallis availed himself of his host's absence to order his carriage, into which he was just stepping to go to town when Mr. Burke reappeared, and endeavoured to prevent his progress, violently opposing so early a breaking up. His lordship remonstrated, begging and entreating to be allowed to go, declaring he had already drank too much, indeed more than he had done for years ; that having much business of importance to transact the following day he must not run the risk of incapacitating himself.

Mr. Burke, not choosing further to urge his lordship, suffered him to seat himself in the coach, but upon Colonel Ross's attempting to follow Mr. Burke seized him, saying, " No ! no, Colonel, you stir not yet, I assure you. Although Lord Cornwallis must be permitted to do as he pleases I will not part with you," and he pulled him back. Lord Cornwallis, anxious to get away himself, was glad to compound by the detention of his secretary, calling out, " Aye, aye, Burke, that's right, that's right. Keep Ross. I don't want him, nor any one of the family. Keep them all, Burke." And away he drove alone, without any troopers, or even a single servant behind the carriage, nor did he during his residence in Bengal, except on occasions of state, ever suffer a soldier to follow him.

Colonel Ross being thus brought back to the party continued at table drinking bumper toasts until one o'clock in the morning, by which hour everyone present was satisfied with the quantum of wine, the Colonel, with the aides-de-camp, staggering off in high glee. I often heard Colonel Ross declare that Burke's dinner was the only time he ever committed a debauch in India, and Lord Cornwallis also observed that even retiring as he did he found he had taken quite sufficient claret, being, if not actually tipsy, very little short of it.

The *Swallow* packet was now to be dispatched for Europe, and to convey thither Lord Macartney. His lordship accordingly embarked, having a short passage, but just

as they entered the British Channel encountered a severe
gale of wind, the weather being so extremely dark, and the
wind dead on shore that Captain Anderson became somewhat alarmed for the safety of the ship.  Reckoning himself within a few miles of the Islands of Scilly, he was
poring over his chart, marking  bearings  and distance,
when the only sail out blew to shivers, rendering the situation still more critical.  Lord Macartney chose that unlucky
moment to ask the Captain, "What port he expected to
make ? "  " Hell, my lord ! " roughly replied the Commander, " if the weather does not change within a very few
hours," which it fortunately did.

Lord Cornwallis entertained most hospitably, having
daily a party of from twenty to twenty-five.  After his
escape, as he termed it, from Mr. Burke's he determined
never to dine from home, except at the Chief Justice's, or
places of equal ceremony, which etiquette made it necessary
he should do once a year.  From my intimacy with the
members of his lordship's family I generally received an
invitation once a week.  Dinner was served with a scru-
pulous exactness, the hour being four during the hot months,
and three in the cooler.  He sat at table two hours, during
which the bottles were in constant circulation.  If any one
of the company, from being in conversation with his neighbour or other cause, inadvertently stopped their progress,
or what was quite as serious an offence, passed them without
putting in the corks, his lordship instantly attacked the
defaulter in the first instance, calling out sharply, " Pass
the wine, Mr. ——" and in the latter, " Fie, fie ! sir, how
can you omit to put the cork into the bottle before you
pass it ? "

Mr. John Lewis Auriol (my little ungrateful boy Nabob's
master) a foolish, weak, chattering blockhead, though sharp
and acute enough where his own interest was in any manner
concerned, had come to the Presidency from his station
up the country in order to be introduced to the new
Governor-General, after which ceremony he, of course,
had an invitation to dine at the Government House, re-

turning from whence to the house of Thomas Dashwood, Esq., where he resided upon his occasional visits to Calcutta, Mr. Dashwood being married to a sister of his, Mrs. Dashwood asked him how he liked Lord Cornwallis. To which "Jacky," as he was by many contemptuously called, answered, "Oh, vastly indeed. I never saw so well-bred a man in my life. He was exceedingly polite and attentive, and during dinner spoke to me at least thirty times." "Did he?" dryly asked Mr. Dashwood. "Then I dare conjecture that fifteen of those times were to pass the bottle, and fifteen to pass the cork."

The *Walpole* Indiaman having arrived from Europe, Mr. Richard Birch, whose sister was married to Captain Churchill, the Commander, brought that gentleman to my house to introduce him to me, observing that his brother-in-law, besides being desirous of the pleasure of my acquaintance, wished to consult me upon a matter of business, the nature of which he stated as follows : Mr. Robert Pott, seeing by the annual list that the *Walpole* was to be one of the Bengal ships that season, had written to him (Captain Churchill) in London strongly soliciting him to take out a considerable quantity of plate therein particularly specified and described, on his (Pott's) account. It was to be made at Grey's in Bond Street, Churchill to pay for it upon delivery and Pott to repay him the amount one month after the *Walpole's* arrival in Bengal, with the addition of fifty per cent thereon as a compensation for his trouble, the interest of his money, and freight of the goods. Pott was also to insure the same from London to Calcutta. To these terms when proposed Captain Churchill acceded, and actually fulfilled his part of the contract.

Upon Captain Churchill's arrival in the River Hooghley he directly addressed a letter to Pott at Afzoulbang, enclosing him one of the bills of lading, together with Grey's bill and requesting his directions as to forwarding the plate up to him, to which letter Pott answered that the articles specified had been ordered by and were intended for the Nabob, who, having changed his mind, did not now want them ; that he (Captain Churchill) must therefore look to His Highness for payment.

Captain Churchill, naturally displeased at such treatment, replied that he knew nothing about the Nabob, nor ever before heard his name mentioned or alluded to in the transaction ; that he, Pott, had ordered the articles according to his drawings or plans, from his own silversmith, had made the agreement in his own name without the most distant allusion or reference to the Nabob, and as he (Captain Churchill) had bespoke the articles in obedience to such desire of Pott's, at his (Pott's) workman's, had paid for the same when delivered, and brought them out to India, he could not consider it either handsome or fair treatment to be now referred to the Nabob for payment, consequently he should look to him (Pott) and to him alone for the amount due.

Captain Churchill then told me that Pott persisted in his refusal to pay. " I must therefore," he said, " request the favour of you, Mr. Hickey, without loss of time to commence an action on my behalf against this Mr. Pott." To this I observed that I was so circumstanced with respect to Pott, with whom I had lived in habits of the strictest friendship since he was quite a boy, that it was totally impossible for me to pursue any legal measures against him, but that I should not only be glad, but consider it as a favour done to myself, if he would previous to issuing any process, wait the result of a friendly application from me to Pott, who I felt scarce a doubt would readily follow my advice. Captain Churchill very civilly and without the least hesitation complied with my desire.

I therefore wrote to Pott, stating the facts as given to me by Captain Churchill, and observed that if such statement were correct he (Pott) had not the shadow of a pretence for refusing to receive and pay for the plate. To my private letter Pott answered in his usual style of absurd ribaldry, overwhelming me with a rhapsody of nonsense he was fond of indulging himself in at times ; he concluded thus, " And now, my dear fellow, having nearly exhausted all my spleen against this dirty slush bucket, this half-payed, lousy tarpaulin of a skipper, this vendor of cheese, ham, porter, and other filthy articles for lucre of gain, this common driver of a stage coach, this contemptible Maître de table D'hote, I candidly, fairly, most gravely and most assuredly assure you, my much loved William Hickey, my highly respected and respectable attorney, my very able, learned and diligent solicitor, proctor, etc., that I will not pay one single pucka pice. Therefore, without cavilling defend, defend my cause, most sound and profound lawyer."

After such stuff as this, and Pott's affecting to make a joke of the business, I could do no more than inform Captain Churchill I had been disappointed in my hope of prevailing upon Pott to settle without litigation, and he must therefore pursue whatever steps he thought right. Captain Churchill, finding I would not act for him, went to another professional man, who commenced an action, whereupon I again wrote to Pott, entreating him to pay the demand without wildly and unnecessarily increasing the evil by a heavy expence, besides incurring the stigma of contesting against a fair and just debt. This produced another strange and incoherent epistle from him, wherein he asserted that Churchill was told the things for which he gave the order were for the Nabob who was to pay for them ; that he (Pott) was no more than an agent in the transaction, except that from his having some acquaintance with Churchill he wished to get him an advantageous and lucrative commission. He at the same time admitted he had no proofs whatever to support his case, but continued, " Pay I will not, my dearest Bill, until old hemp and tar has the sanction of a judgment of the superior big-wigs in his favour, which if he can let him obtain, and much good may it do him." It is scarcely necessary to add a judgment was obtained upon as clear a case as ever came before a Court.

Vexed at my friend's obstinacy and folly, I communicated the result in somewhat angry language, for which he only laughed at me. Having enclosed a draught for the amount of the judgment and costs upon his agents in Calcutta, payable at sight, he once more indulged in his rhodomontade, " And so, my friend William," said he, " you pretend to be offended and petulantly ask what in God's name I could mean or what could be my drift in resisting the payment of as fair and just a debt as ever man owed.  I'll tell you then, William, what my drifts, for I had more than one, were :  imprimus, to vex a pompous, coxcomical, impertinent hound of an East India Captain, the whole race of whom I abhor and detest, and so ought you, Master William, were it only for that abominable vagabond, Baker's sake. .  My next drift was to distribute a little of my superfluous cash amongst my acquaintances of the long robe, and pray let me enquire if there were not here and there a few such obstinate, wrong-headed fellows as your humble servant, what would become of the honourable band of attornies, advocates, special pleaders, and hangers-on innumerable of the law—how would the poor, miserable dogs exist ?  Hey, William, answer me that.  As to my morality or character being called in question, I say fudge, William, errant fudge !   At any rate, should I lose my present character, a fair chance would offer of finding a better."

# CHAPTER XXII

## SIR JOHN AND LADY DAY. CELEBRATING
## YOUNG RICHARD BURKE'S BIRTHDAY

EARLY in December I was surprized by a visit from Sir John Day, who was profuse of civil speeches and professions of regard and attachment, which led me to conclude there must be a motive ! and so it turned out. After telling me he was about to leave India, having engaged a passage on board the ship *Resolution*, which belonged to and was commanded by Captain Mercer, he went direct to his point, saying, " You must, I presume, Mr. Hickey, have heard that the Governor-General and Council some time ago presented me with the sum of thirty thousand sicca rupees over and above my salary, as a complimentary as well as substantial return and acknowledgment of my indefatigable zeal and attention, which they admit I have always shewn for the interest and welfare of my honourable employers, the East India Company. But those paltry shabroons of Leadenhall Street—I allude to the Court of Directors—with that meanness peculiar to them, have lately sent out orders to this Government to call upon me forthwith to refund the said thirty thousand sicca rupees, together with interest at the rate of eight per cent per annum from the date on which I received it, up to the day on which it should be repaid into the Treasury. As this certainly is the most cruel, the most unjust and illiberal measure that ever was adopted, I therefore intend to try my influence in person with those said Directors, and trust my eloquence and powers of persuasion will be sufficient to induce a revocation of their order, but to effect this it may become requisite to prove to them the eminent services I have done them as well as that I have during my sojourn in Bengal given up my time wholly and solely to their benefit, which the Governor-General and Council were so sensible of they had voluntarily, without application, presented me with the remuneration I have mentioned. I think it prudent likewise to be armed with proofs that I rejected much private business and large fees that were at different times offered to me by individuals, because I would not have my attention in any manner diverted from their particular affairs."

Sir John then pulled from his pocket and delivered to me a written paper, to which he requested I would fix my signature. Upon perusal I found it was a certificate, couched in the most unqualified terms, stating that to my knowledge he had repeatedly sacrificed large sums of money offered to him in his capacity of a British barrister from his determination not to let any private business draw off his attention from the interests of the East India Company. I observed to him that this paper went much farther than I could think of sanctioning with my signature ; that true it was I perfectly recollected having upon two occasions, and no more, offered him fees with professional papers, which he declined accepting, assigning as a reason that until his dispute with the Chief Justice relative to his right to appear and plead at the bar of the Supreme Court whenever he pleased without taking any oaths was decided, he could not go into Court upon any account. Notwithstanding this remark from me he still pressed for my name to the paper, observing no injury could ever arise to me or to anyone thereby, whereas much advantage would accrue to him if I consented, and that several other attorneys would follow my example and sign. I persevered in refusing to certify beyond what was within my immediate knowledge, viz. that I had twice offered him fees as a lawyer which he declined to accept. Finding all his eloquence fruitless, he at last accepted the certificate in the terms I proposed.

The circumstance of these rejected fees were as follows : Soon after my arrival in Calcutta, wishing to serve Sir John Day as an old acquaintance, as well as being a person for whom I knew my father had a regard, I sent him a case of very great importance, in which some nice questions of law were involved, with a fee of fifty gold mohurs, and a further one of an hundred gold mohurs, as a retainer in a cause intended to be instituted on the equity side. This case having remained with him a month my client, a native of high rank, became anxious to have it answered in order that he might commence his suit. I therefore applied several times to the Advocate-General for his opinion, who at last returned it unanswered, saying he could not bestow the requisite time to it. But I firmly believe the true reason was he did not feel himself competent. As he took no notice of the retainer, I wrote to him again to ask whether he meant to give his assistance in Court, as if not, I should be obliged to give my client credit for the amount. To this he replied, " His duty to the East India Company would make it impossible for him to attend to any cause in which they were not either parties or in some way interested, he therefore returned the retainer." But how did he do this ? By a draught upon his agents at three months' sight, whereas I had paid it to him in hard cash !

That Sir John was a man of talents and finished scholar there was no doubt, equally certain it is he was no lawyer, nor had he at any period of his life endeavoured to make himself one by study or attention to the profession. He and his lady were in some respects well matched, both being full of vanity and pompous folly, both, too, being alike fond of courting great people, and boasting of their intimacy with their Majesties and the whole of the Royal family, as with half the nobility of the realm ; yet her ladyship's origin was not of the most elevated kind, she being a daughter of Mr. Ramus, a favourite servant of the King's, and for many years page of the back-stairs at St. James's Palace, her paternal uncle being a respectable cheesemonger at Charing Cross, and purveyor of that useful domestic to His Majesty, as announced upon the sign of a Cheshire cheese placed over the shop door.

But this odious and stinking trade of cheese selling was a

sad annoyance to the female Ramus, and especially to Lady Day after she became dignified with the title of " lady-ship." She was sadly ashamed if ever seen visiting at this uncle's, but as he was known to be rich, and from having no children of his own would probably leave his fortune to those of his brother, self-interest made her so far sacrifice her feelings as sometimes to honour him with a call. Her ladyship, one morning, not very long before she was to embark for India, ordered her smart coach to Charing Cross in order to pay her respects to the wealthy uncle, taking care, however, to go at so early an hour that it was unlikely any of her fashionable acquaintances would be abroad. Upon reaching the house she observed the street door open, a fortunate circumstance as she thought. Calling to her footman to let her out, she darted from the carriage with great alertness, when oh ! shocking to relate, just as she had entered the passage leading to the stairs, a vile female domestic who was in the act of washing the same, presented her mop plump to her ladyship's face in order to prevent further progress, accompanying this hostile salutation with, " No, no, miss ! you don't pass this way, I assures you. If you must come in, pray go round by the shop as you used to do." The indignant lady had nothing for it but compliance ! What a mortification to a silly woman !

In due time the arrogant couple embarked for Europe, giving themselves such intolerable airs on board the *Resolution* as disgusted everybody except Captain Mercer, who was greatly diverted at their ridiculous behaviour. Being a man of considerable humour, he was constantly playing some joke to render the knight's absurdity more palpable, of which the following is a striking instance :

As the ship approached England nothing was talked of by Sir John and Lady Day but their speedy meeting with the King and Queen, how rejoiced their Excellent Majesties and every branch of the Royal family would be to see them once more, when no doubt some new honour, some special mark of favour and attention would be conferred ! About a week before making the land the *Resolution* in the middle of the night fell in with a small brig, only a few days from Plymouth. Soon afterwards it fell calm, continuing so for some hours. At daylight the captain of the brig hoisted out his boat and went on board the *Resolution*. Captain Mercer could not resist so fair an opportunity of putting a hoax upon the learned Advocate-General. He therefore gave the visitor his cue by making him acquainted with Sir John Day's foible. As he happened to be fond of a joke, he at once entered into the spirit of the thing and engaged completely to effect Captain Mercer's object.

The plan was immediately arranged between the two Commanders. Sir John's apartment being half the round house, he was early awakened by a bustle made on the poop on purpose to rouse him. Ringing his bell to know what occasioned so much more noise than usual, his servant told him a strange vessel was close alongside and the captain of her on board, whereupon, dressing himself as quickly as possible, he went upon deck, with much stateliness making his bow to the stranger, enquiring whence he came and what news. The Captain having related some trivial circumstances, Sir John next asked as to Indian politics, and whether Lord Cornwallis's dispatches had been long arrived. The answer to this was, " His lordship's first dispatches reached London three months ago, and about a week before I left Plymouth, I heard a second packet had arrived which had occasioned great alterations in India, for his lordship having soon after he got to Bengal been attacked with a dangerous illness, thought the climate would not agree with his constitution ; he therefore resolved not to stay long in it, and had sent home to request a successor might without loss of time be sent out, in consequence of which his desire had forthwith been complied with, and one of the fastest sailing frigates in the navy left Plymouth the day before my brig did, carrying the nomination of Governor-General to a gentleman who has been some years in Bengal, whose name I do not recollect but who filled a high situation in the law, was a *Sir*, and now created a Peer." " Then," observed Sir John, " it must be either Sir Robert Chambers or Sir William Jones." "No," replied the Captain, "I do not think it was either of those names ; I rather think it was *Knight*."

Captain Mercer who had joined the two gentlemen during their conversation, now exclaimed, "I'll be hanged if I don't believe you are yourself the man, Sir John Day, the Captain here only mistaking your title for your name." "Upon my word, sir, you are right—Day was the name I perfectly well recollect, and, moreover, that he was called something General." "Aye, to be sure," said Mercer, "Advocate-General." "Yes, Advocate-General it certainly was," answered the Captain. "God bless me," said Sir John, "can it be possible ! Good God ! who could have imagined such extraordinary honours would thus early have been heaped upon me. It is scarcely to be believed it is too much ; I could not expect such elevation," and away he darted into his cabin, crying out to his wife, "Well, my dear, now you are indeed a lady, nothing less than a peeress of the realm. His Majesty, God bless him, has been graciously pleased in his goodness to call me up to the House of Peers, and not only so, but likewise in his bounty to confer upon me the dignified situation of Governor-General of all the Indies. It is wonderful ! I never could have thought myself deserving of such kind remembrance by their Gracious Majesties, for I am sure that worthy Queen of ours has had her share in obtaining these undeserved honours for us ! Well, my dear Lady Day, this will make our immediate return to Bengal indispensably necessary. I am bound as much by duty as inclination to give my humble aid to promote the British interests in India, and undoubtedly will do so during my Government, the arduous task of performing which will call for all my abilities as well as all my zeal. We shall barely have time to throw ourselves gratefully at the feet of their Majesties, there humbly offering our unfeigned thanks for their unexampled kindness, and once more embark for Asia."

A breeze springing up about ten o'clock, the Captain of the brig took leave, proceeding to his vessel to continue his voyage, which was to North America, first touching at the

Azores or Western Islands.   After this nothing was talked of by the proud knight and supposed new peer but the great importance of the office he was destined to fill, though he could not avoid lamenting that his necessary residence in the East would, for some years at least, prevent exercising his duty in the House of Lords.

Captain Mercer finding Sir John so elated, talking of nothing but himself and the material changes for the better he would make as Governor-General of India, began to hint at the probability that all that had been related might be premature, if not altogether fabricated, remarking that the Captain of the brig had avowed himself an American, and that all of that country were the most notorious liars in the world, indeed there was no relying upon what one of them ever said.   To this Sir John replied it was utterly impossible the man could be mistaken upon this occasion from the very precise and particular manner in which he stated the facts. " Well," said Captain Mercer, " we shall ascertain whether it be true or not in four-and-twenty hours."

How the disappointed pair felt upon their arrival in England and finding Sir John still remained a simple knight and nothing more, nor that any change had taken place in the Government of Bengal, may easily be conceived from the characters I have already given of them.   Sir John probably consoled himself in the idea of the many enjoyments he should have from the ample fortune he had acquired in the East.   But if such thoughts did occupy his mind, he was there equally disappointed.   Shortly after his return home he became hypochondriacal, that grievous malady increasing so much as to amount nearly to insanity.   At the end of six years he actually fancied he should live to want a morsel of bread, that all mankind were leagued together to plunder and cheat him, and that every bank-note that came to his hands, no matter from what quarter, was forged.   Fully possessed with this notion, he used to run about to his banker and to every common friend he had to shew the note or notes he had received and ask if they were not palpable forgeries, nor had any assurances they gave to the contrary

the least effect in changing his opinion.   In this miserable
condition he continued a couple of years, then dying a
martyr to his unfounded anxiety and alarms.   He left his
widow handsomely provided for, who survived him only
four years.

In December Sir John Macpherson (the Minister, as some
sort of recompense for superseding him in his Government,
having made him a baronet) and Sir Robert Sloper took
their passages for Europe.

It having always been the custom for the members of
Government and the principal persons of the settlement to
dine together at the Court-house on Christmas Day, followed
by a ball and supper for the ladies at night, the same took
place on the 25th of December this year, although somewhat
against the inclination of Lord Cornwallis, who expressed
his disapprobation, as according to his idea the day ought
to be celebrated rather as purely religious than in feasting
and mirth.   The dancing he particularly objected to, and
from that year no public dinner or entertainment of any
kind has ever been given on Christmas Day in Calcutta.   At
this dinner Lord Cornwallis, as Governor-General, presided.

In the month of January, 1786, a very unpleasant part of
Lord Cornwallis's duty was promulgated and carried into
effect.   This was an order he had brought out to commence
prosecutions against a number of the senior servants of the
Company who had either themselves been contractors, and
in the execution of such contracts had been guilty of gross
frauds, or had from the influence of their offices joined the
contractors in robbing and cheating the Company.

The granting of contracts of every description, with the
terms or conditions of them, had for several years rested
solely and entirely with the Board of Trade, which Board
consisted of a President and eleven other members, generally
consisting of the senior civil servants, as they rose to it by
their standing, though the term "*rising*" to it was ill-
adapted to the case, it frequently happening that men were
called from situations of immense emolument to take their
seats at the Board of Trade where the avowed allowance

was the comparatively pitiful sum of eleven hundred rupees per month. It was, however, a well-known fact to every man in India and to every director in Leadenhall Street that the members of the Board of Trade made up the deficiency or difference between this awkward *kick upstairs* to a seat at the Board and the lucrative situations they had been taken from by either themselves having a share or proportion in each contract they granted, or else making the contractor allow them a certain commission for the granting such contracts, a circumstance so public that no member of the Board ever considered it necessary to make a secret of it. It was therefore pronounced unjust in the extreme thus suddenly, unexpectedly, and without the smallest previous intimation, to construe into a legal offence what had been openly and avowedly the practice of the service at all times, for was it to be supposed the Company's oldest servants were to rise to posts that could not defray their current domestic expences. Yet unjust as the measure indisputably was the Directors accepted it, and Earl Cornwallis was made the instrument of its being effected. The first step was a proclamation issued by order of the Governor-General, stating " the high displeasure the Court of Directors felt upon *discovering* that various enormities, peculations, and frauds had long been committed by their Board of Trade upon them in Bengal in connivance with the contractors, which iniquitous practice they were determined not only to put a stop to and prevent the commission of in future, but upon the delinquency being brought home to any individuals to punish them with the utmost severity and inflict the full penalty of the law, for which purposes they had directed Lord Cornwallis to file Bills in Equity, or take such other steps as the Law Officers might advise, against all those persons standing in such predicament."

Lord Cornwallis had from the time of his arrival in Bengal been, by means of secret agents, endeavouring to ascertain the names of the parties and the special facts upon which they were to be attacked, an employment deemed somewhat derogatory to the rank and character of his lordship.

It may, however, be fairly presumed that his lordship did
not so consider it, otherwise he would not have undertaken
the business.   The gentlemen pitched upon to be prosecuted
were Mr. Aldrassey, who had been President of the Board
of Trade, but then resided in England, Mr. Davies, who
succeeded him, then also at home, Mr. William Barton,
President of the Board at the time of Lord Cornwallis's
arrival, Mr. Rider, Mr. Rooke, Mr. Bateman, and Mr.
Keighley, all at different periods Members of the Board, and
charged with being themselves the real contractors, although
the'contracts were made in other and fictitious names, and
lastly, Mr. Thomas Fleuchman, who being himself a contractor had joined with the Board of Trade in defrauding
his employers to a great amount.   Against all these gentlemen the Company's Attorney was instructed to proceed ;
Bills in Equity were accordingly prepared and filed against
each separately, praying an account and that the defendant
might be decreed to pay back with interest, all sums thus
dishonestly acquired from the complainants ;  against Mr.
Barton, who was more deeply involved than the rest, there
were no less than four Bills, all of great length, being for so
many specific acts of tergiversation.   Scarcely had these
Bills been put, upon the file ere Lord Cornwallis by the
arrival of a packet received a new and peremptory order
from his *Honourable Masters* that the hour the prosecutions
should be commenced, he must dismiss the respective
defendants from the posts they held and suspend them from
service until the final issue of the Cause and the pleasure of
the Court of Directors should be made known ;  thus rendering several of their oldest servants destitute, and in fact pre-
judging them, by punishing without a defence or a hearing.

I was congratulated by my friends as being in the direct
road to fortune by the increase of business these prosecutions would give me.   Of the unfortunate gentlemen attacked, I was employed by Messrs. Barton, Rider, Bateman,
Keighley, and Fleuchman.

Mr. Barton at first talked boldly, and swore stoutly, but
soon finding that Government were armed with stronger

evidence against him than he had expected they could have found, and that if he abided an issue to the Causes there must be Decrees against him to the amount altogether of one hundred and fifty thousand pounds he, without saying a syllable to me of his intention, suddenly decamped bag and baggage to the Danish Settlement of Scranpore, from whence, in a few months afterwards he proceeded to Europe on board a Danish East Indiaman. He fixed his residence in the City of Copenhagen, purchased the rank of nobility, and after living a few miserable years in Denmark departed this life.

Messrs. Bateman and Rider each candidly admitted the facts charged by the Bills, to a limited extent, but urged the notoriety of such practices and insisted that when adopted they did not consider themselves as acting dishonourably or unfaithfully to their employers and that even with the douceurs then allowed to the contractors they had been material losers by rising to seats in the Board of Trade. The Court of Directors admitted the force of this argument and those two gentlemen being involved in a trifling degree comparatively to Barton and others, they were restored to their service without being compelled to return the sums so improperly received.

Mr. Keighley gave determined opposition, fighting his way inch by inch. After ably contesting the matter during fifteen months in Calcutta, his health became so much impaired that the physicians recommended change of climate as his only chance of recovery. He therefore applied to Government requesting that they would allow the further legal discussion of the question between him and the Company to be referred to the Court of Chancery in England, which request was granted ; he soon after sailed for Europe in the ship *Rose*, Captain Gray. I gave him letters of introduction to my father and brother, who for some time acted as his Solicitors, but difference of opinion arising in the progress of the Cause, my father not approving of some steps Mr. Keighley wanted to be taken and refusing to execute them, he took his papers away and went to another Attorney.

After a most expensive litigation during several years, he in a great measure succeeded against the Company, but being obliged to pay his own costs as well as part of theirs it so involved him that he ultimately was arrested by some of his creditors and sent to the King's Bench prison where, I rather believe, he ended a worthless life.

Mr. Fleuchman alone stood his ground in Bengal. He answered the Bill most completely, justifying everything he had done as a contractor. Upon this Answer coming in, the Advocate-General moved to dismiss the Bill without costs. The latter part Mr. Fleuchman resisted, but after arguing the point a whole day the Court decided against him and he was consequently obliged to pay his own costs. He was then restored to the Service, but he immediately sent in his resignation declaring that he would no longer serve under such a set of illiberal men as the then Court of Directors, who had by their shameful conduct rendered themselves unworthy of the labours of any man possessing the feelings or sentiments of a gentleman. It is almost superfluous to add that previous to such resignation he acquired a large fortune. Upon his return to England he became an eloquent and popular speaker in the general Courts of Proprietors, invariably attacking, and with considerable success, the measures and conduct of the Directors.

The above-mentioned Equity Suits were in a progressive state during the period of sixteen months, proving so advantageous to me that I was enabled to discharge nearly half the amount of my debts ; the remainder continued a heavy encumbrance from the high rate of interest, which was twelve per cent. My domestic expences were also very great, sometimes exceeding 4000 rupees each month, and never less than 3000. Exorbitant as this rate of living may appear, I could not lessen it, keeping as I always did throughout my residence in India the best company in the Settlement.

Mr. William Burke always celebrated his young friend Mr. Richard Burke junior's birthday which was the 9th of February. This gentleman was the only son of Mr. Edmund

Burke.  On the above day of the year 1786, we sat down to
a splendid dinner, consisting of turtle, venison, and every
rarity that was procurable.  The party consisted of one
hundred and twenty persons, accommodated in a suite of
three rooms.  Lord Cornwallis, who with the rest of the great
people was invited, pleaded indisposition, and sent an
excuse, but the whole of the staff attended ; it turned out
as usual a drunken business, attended with some unpleasant
disputes from the brutal violence of my old antagonist
Davison, though nothing serious arose from it.  When the
company at a late hour was reduced to about a dozen, Mr.
William Dunkin attacked Mr. Burke for his total neglect of
a Colonel Wray, an Irish gentleman whose family had
all been particularly intimate with every branch of Mr.
Burke's, and who were near neighbours of Mr. Dunkin's in
the North of Ireland.  This Colonel Wray was stationed at
the Presidency and left his card at Mr. Burke's house upon
his first arrival, but had never received an invitation to any
one of his parties.

In answer to Mr. Dunkin, Mr. Burke hiccupped out, " Oh,
damn the Irish beast, he and all his race are yahoos.  I
never desire to have anything to say to him, or his damned
clan, besides I understand the fellow will blow out the brains
of any person the shape of whose face, or the size of whose
nose happens not to meet his approbation.  Oh, no !  damn
the Irish spalpeen, I'll have nothing to do with him.  He
shall not come into my house, by God."  Mr. Dunkin defended his absent friend, and although obliged to admit that
he had been unlucky enough to be involved in more than
one cause, zealously justified him in them all.

After a noisy, drunken discussion of the Colonel's merits
and demerits for more than an hour, the contest ended by
Mr. Burke's good-humouredly saying, " Well, after all,
perhaps I may have formed a wrong opinion of this Irish
Colonel, whom I really do not know, but you do, friend
Dunkin, and entertain so high a regard for him that you
may as well, in my name, invite him to dine here this day
fortnight, when the Governor of Chandernagore and some

other Frenchmen of fashion are to be here, and previous to that day I will call at his house and leave my card."

Colonel Wray, accepting the invitation, was on the appointed day received by Mr. Burke with the most polite attention, he lamenting that he had not earlier had the honour of being made known to him. Mr. Burke happening to have a severe cold complained a good deal, observing "he was so ill as to be unfit to preside at the head of his table."

There was present at this dinner Monsieur Le Comte de Montigny, the Governor, and four other French officers from Chandernagore; Colonels Fullarton, Cockerell and Pierce, with several civilians, forming altogether a party of twenty-eight. The foreigners were, of course, placed on each side of the host, Colonel Wray being nearly opposite to him. Some time after the cloth was removed the topic of conversation unluckily turned upon the relative situation and clashing interests of the King's and Company's Officers when upon service together. Several of the party (though there were some of His Majesty's Army present) spoke upon the subject, observing how unjust as well as unpolitic it was to put quite boys of King's Officers over the heads of veterans of the Company's, as frequently was the case upon the detached commands; amongst others, Colonel Wray with much mildness and moderation gave his sentiments thereon. This most unaccountably roused Mr. Burke, who with the gestures and manners of a lunatic attacked the Colonel. In a few seconds he had worked himself into a paroxysm of rage, actually screeching out the following rhapsody, which he accompanied with violently striking his clenched hand upon the table, and rising from his chair upon his feet. "God damn my blood if I ever heard such low, blackguard, grovelling sentiments coming from the mouth of a person calling himself a gentleman! You, Mr. Major, Colonel, What's-your-name—damn your name! I never wish to know your name nor have anything to do with a fellow capable of making such dirty, illiberal comparisons," and down he sat, a profound silence with looks of the utmost astonishment pervading the whole party, which was not lessened by Mr. Burke's again rising and with extreme agitation addressing Colonel Wray, saying, "Sir, I beg your pardon. Sir, I beg ten thousand pardons, Sir, of you and of the company, every one of them, I have thus wantonly offended. I have behaved shockingly, I am ashamed of myself, I know not what possessed me; forgive me, Sir, I beg," and bursting into tears he dropped into his chair apparently near fainting.

All eyes were turned to the Colonel, who it was feared by those who had heard he was an irritable, quarrelsome man would commit some act of violence upon receiving so extraordinary a provocation, instead of which, with the utmost command of temper and placid manner, he replied, "To prove, Mr. Burke, that I feel not a particle of resentment, I shall be glad to drink a glass of claret with you; and as you before dinner complained of a severe cold, of being languid and beyond measure low-spirited, I sincerely hope that this little exertion will have had a good effect and set you quite to rights." This truly considerate and temperate behaviour of Colonel Wray's deservedly gained him the approbation of the party, as well as of all who heard it spoken of. It fixed Mr. Burke as a zealous friend and admirer. He ever after treated the Colonel with the most marked attention and respect.

In March I was deprived of the professional assistance of my esteemed friend Doctor James Wilson, he being appointed Surgeon to the Presidency of Radshy, and therefore obliged to depart for that station. In point of talent, however, his loss was not so materially felt, from there still remaining at the Presidency two very able men, Doctor Charles Allen and Doctor James Hare, both of whom occasionally attended me.

Having during my residence amongst the French at Trincomalay found how highly they respected the fraternity of Freemasons, and the advantage it would have been to me had I at that time been of the Order, I determined to become a "Brother" at the earliest opportunity. Upon my arrival at Bengal Masonry happened to be much in fashion, there being several Lodges that met, the one distinguished by the title of " Number Two " being considered the most select.  At this therefore I was proposed, and after the usual examination and ceremony of " making," as it is termed, the mummery and absurdity of which by the way greatly offended me, I became a member.  In a regular way I rose to the degree of Master, soon after which I filled the high office of Senior Warden.

# CHAPTER XXIII

### A RIVER EXCURSION. THE FRATERNITY OF BUCKS. A DREADFUL HURRICANE

THE remainder of the year passed without any material happening. I at times had attacks of spasms; probably increased if not actually brought on by living too free. As I had been strongly recommended to use the exercise of riding, I purchased two capital saddle-horses, one of them having been a famous racer that had won several plates and matches. He was called Momus, the property of a Mr. Richardson, a keen sportsman, from whom I purchased him, and who felt rejoiced at getting a kind master for an old favourite. For about six months I rode generally about twice a week; at the end of that time I grew tired from the very early hour at which it was necessary to ride, and I gave it up though I continued to keep my horses. My little Irish guest, Carter, was prodigiously fond of riding: he never missed a morning and was particularly pleased with Momus, always speaking of him as the pleasantest horse he ever mounted.

Towards the end of the year my shipmate, Mr. Humphry Howorth, who had acquired a large and rapid fortune of at least forty thousand pounds, from getting a slice of the opium contract, determined to return and enjoy it in England. Soon after he reached home he purchased my father's house in St. Albans Street, became a regular frequenter of Newmarket, and kept racers.

At this period, I lost a steady friend in Mr. Harry Vansittart, who was carried off very suddenly, as is too often the case in the burning climate of Asia. Having heard he was indisposed, I stopped at his door on my way to Mr.

William Dunkin's, where I was going to dine about one o'clock in the afternoon, and was told he was extremely ill. Between five and six, the same day, being on my return home, I again stopped at the invalid's house, where I was greatly shocked at being informed that he was dead and the corpse gone about half an hour to be buried. This is quick work and appears horrid to persons recently from Europe, yet it is often indispensably necessary from the body's becoming putrid nearly as soon as the breath leaves it.

Just after the remorseless tyrant Death had thus deprived the world of one of its brightest ornaments, which Mr. Vansittart certainly was, Mr. William Dunkin was attacked by a violent and dangerous fever, in which the doctors Fleming and Allen had for several days scarce a hope of saving him. The indefatigable kindness and attention, however, of Doctor Allen, who never left the house day or night, fortunately preserved him to us, but the disease left him so reduced and languid it was deemed necessary to change the air, in consequence whereof he expressed an earnest desire that I would accompany him upon an excursion up the river for a month or six weeks. Being particularly desirous to oblige one who had been unremitting in his acts of kindness to me, I agreed to make one of the party.

On the 1st of February the requisite boats being prepared, Mr. Dunkin, Doctor Allen, Mr. James Dunkin, Mr. Stephen Casson, and myself embarked at Calcutta, Mr. Casson undertaking the management of the provisions and everything respecting the table. As I was better acquainted with the disposition of the natives than he was, I advised that the pinnace on board which Mr. Dunkin was and in which we were to mess, should not stir from the Ghaut until the Bobbachee Khemsah, or cooking-boat, as well as the *Consumah* and servants' boats with the live-stock preceded us, for if they were not well looked to we might be left in the lurch for our dinner. Mr. Casson, not liking my interference, coldly observed I need be under no alarm he having taken the precaution to put a *hircarrah* into each boat, to see that his orders were strictly adhered to.  Notwithstanding Mr. Casson's confidence, I still suggested the propriety of at least seeing the boats ready to start before we moved, which Mr. Dunkin likewise wished, observing that as his appetite was just returning he should not like to be disappointed of his dinner.  Mr. Casson repeating his assurances that there was no danger of that kind, my opinion was overruled.

At ten in the morning the different pinnaces left Chaundpaul Ghaut with a fine southerly breeze at a strong springtide, carrying us at the rate of full nine miles an hour.  By half-past eleven we were off Seranpore, when Mr. Dunkin expressed a wish to have something to eat, but not a morsel was to be secured, everything being in the small boats of which there was not the least appearance.  I therefore proposed stopping at Seranpore, either to procure victuals or wait the coming up of the said boats.  Again I was overruled and petulantly begged not to be so impatient.  On we stood, passing Chandernagore Chinsurah, Hooghly and Baudel, above which latter place there is no town near the river for many miles.

Our hour for dining had been fixed for two o'clock ; it was now past three, yet no appearance of the boats.  Mr. Dunkin complained much of hunger and began to upbraid Mr. Casson for so obstinately and pertinaciously adhering to his own opinion instead of following the prudent advice I had given.  Finding fault, however, or grumbling would fill no empty stomach.  At five Doctor Allen observed to Mr. Dunkin that if he could eat curry he thought he might procure some from a small budgerow that was in company, on board of which were two children (the Doctor's daughters) with their mother.  Mr. Dunkin instantly answered he would give the world for anything in the way of food.  Heaving to, therefore, the Doctor took our attendant rowing-boat and went to his family's budgerow, from whence he in a few minutes returned with an excellent curry, plenty of well-boiled rice and a loaf of bread, upon which we fell to and soon devoured the whole.  Between five and six o'clock it becoming dusk we brought to for the night, a little above Sooksangor.

At nine at night the servants joined us, each laying the blame upon the other. One had forgot his hubble-bubble, another his tobacco. Then Mr. Dunkin's barber detained them till he got his master's razors sharpened. At length when the servants were assembled they found the mangee of the cooking-boat absent and had to wait his coming. In short, from a variety of frivolous wants, as is always the case with Bengallees when leaving the place of their usual residence, they did not start for full three hours after us. Upon this specimen of Mr. Casson's management and arrangement, on the outset, the party—especially Mr. Dunkin—were disposed to put him out of commission; whereupon I tendered my services, which were accepted conditionally, that is, that I must at least for two hours every morning play picquet with Mr. Dunkin, during which time if anything was wanted Doctor Allen agreed to officiate as *maître d'hôtel* in my stead. From thence forward we had an abundant and well-furnished table.

As we proceeded upward we found great impediments from the freshets in the river, which in some parts ran with such force we could not get on for hours together. At one bluff point in particular, just within the entrance of the Cossimbuzar River, the wind having died away nearly to a calm, the Dandies could not with every exertion move the pinnace, which was of the largest size, a single inch ahead. After toiling in vain for three hours the whole fleet were obliged to bring to, when the Dandies of them all came to assist us, and by their united exertions dragged us to a stream that ran like a sluice. But in effecting this, we lost an entire day, in fact we had begun to despair of ever getting round this tremendous point.

On the seventh day after leaving Calcutta, late in the evening, we reached Massey House, under the bank of which we secured our boats and had just ordered tea and coffee when Mr. James Forbes, an Attorney of the Supreme Court, entered the cabin, bringing with him some prodigious fine wild hog and a quantity of different sorts of game which his people had killed during the morning. Mr. Forbes had been cruising about the river a month in the hope of recovering his health, after being dangerously ill with the liver. He had his wife with him. This lady had recently arrived from Scotland, the place of her nativity, in consequence of Mr. Forbes requesting she would do so, when he left Edinburgh fifteen years before. He was attached to her, and so long a residence in India not abating the fervour of his love, he wrote to invite her : but alas, upon beholding her, oh what a falling off was there ! She, whom he had left a blooming stout lass, had become a wrinkled, wretched-looking old woman, so dreadfully altered as to create disgust instead of creating desire. Yet such as she was, he considered himself bound in honour to fulfil his engagement to her and therefore married her. Upon first seeing her he disclaimed all knowledge of her, gravely insisting he had never before set eyes on her ; but she soon found means to identify herself, which having been done beyond all doubts she, in her broad Scotch dialect, observed that " verily her gude mon, her dear Jammy, was somewhat the worse for wear as well as hersel."

On the 9th we arrived off Afzoulbang, where I was in the act of writing a note to my friend Robert Pott, when the very man himself came alongside our pinnace in a magnificent boat of his own building, attended by a swarry of at least fifty persons. Our approach had been announced to them the previous evening by some of the Nabob's native officers stationed at Cossimbuzar. Pott insisted upon our immediate landing and taking up our abode in his house, which we did, being received and entertained during the ten days that we stayed with the utmost hospitality and in his usual splendid style. Two of the days of our sojourn we dined with Mr. James English Keighley, the gentleman whom I have already mentioned, and by anticipation given some account of. He was Commercial Chief of the Factory, besides which he carried on extensive business in raw silk whereby he acquired an immense fortune. He lived with a degree of pomp and extravagance little short of Pott. We also had one very cheerful day at Mr. Edward Fenwick's (of *fête-champêtre* fame), another with the Nabob, and the following one with the Commanding Officer of His Highness's bodyguard, the Hon. David Anstruther, who resided about two miles from Afzoulbang. This gentleman, although accomplished in many respects, was very vulgar and brutal in his behaviour to women, especially to those of his own family. He married in Bengal a Miss Donaldson, daughter of a needy tradesman in a country village of Scotland who, upon finding one of his girls well disposed of in India, sent off to the same destination two more who had arrived at their sister's, Mrs. Anstruther, only a few days previous to our visit. The youngest of these girls, Miss Moggy, became the ill-treated wife of the wild and profligate Mr. Holt ; in point of fact, she was one of the loveliest creatures I ever beheld.

Messrs. Dunkin and Casson, as well as myself, being desirous of reaching Calcutta by the opening of the Term, which was to commence on the 1st of March, Mr. Dunkin's health and strength being perfectly re-established, on the 19th we took leave of our Afzoulbang host, and embarked, our fleet gently gliding down the stream to Cossimbuzar, where the party had promised to spend a couple of days with Mr. Keighley, who received and entertained us most hospitably : on the 21st we proceeded towards the Presidency. The Cossimbuzar River in particular spots being very low we experienced considerable difficulty in getting over the shoals, sometimes sticking fast when all the people were obliged to jump overboard and force the boats off. On the 23rd, we once more got into the Hooghly, and arrived at Calcutta on the 27th, having passed a very pleasant month.

At the end of March my drunken friend, Colonel Cooper, embarked for England, from whence he had received letters informing him that his creditors had signed a letter of licence allowing him three years for payment of their respective demands, but upon his arrival in London he had the mortification to find that two of those tradesmen, to whom he was largely indebted, had refused to execute, declaring that if he made his appearance they would arrest him and consign him to a prison, to avoid which he forthwith crossed the British Channel, taking up his abode at Boulogne, where a few years after he breathed his last.

In May I received a visit from my friend, Mr. Stackhouse Tolfrey, who called to announce his approaching marriage with Miss Messink, one of the most beautiful young women of Bengal, and to invite me to the wedding, which I attended accordingly, having the satisfaction to see a worthy man made completely happy.

In the same month, being summoned to a party at Mr. William Burke's garden house, where I met Mr. Benjamin Mee, Major Macdonal, and several other sporting men, in the evening hazard was proposed. Mr. Burke well knowing that I never played, whispered me to request I would that night sit down and play for him, for he had a presentiment I should prove successful. I therefore took my seat, and at the end of three hours rose a winner of upwards of three hundred gold mohurs. This was the only time in my life I ever made one at a hazard table.

Having several friends to dine with me, the conversation happened to turn upon the subject of the fraternity of Bucks, when some of the company expressed a wish that a Lodge might be established in Calcutta, and I was requested to ascertain whether there were a sufficient number of that Society to form a Lodge.

About this period Mr. John Scawen, who went to Europe in the same ship as Colonels Watson, Mestayer, Metcalfe, and others, returned to Bengal, having succeeded in the object of his voyage by getting the Court of Directors to appoint him Military Auditor-General, an Office he would have undoubtedly enjoyed but for his own folly, for instead of making the best of his way to India, he trifled away his time in Paris, and in running over the Continent, during which the Government of Bengal put Colonel John Murray, now Sir John Murray McGregor, Bart., into the situation, and were so pleased at the correct manner in which he performed the duties of the office that when Mr. Scawen did at last arrive they peremptorily refused to displace the Colonel, nor could all the memorials and protests of Mr. Scawen induce the Governor-General and Council to alter their resolution : he was therefore obliged to submit to act in the capacity of deputy, with a comparatively trifling salary of one thousand sicca rupees per month.

The result of my enquiries respecting the Bucks was that there were besides myself five other gentlemen residing in Calcutta who were members of that Society. Their names were Francis Rundell, Phinehas Hall, Arthur Mair, Robert Haldane, and William Golding, and as four were fully competent to form a Lodge it was immediately determined to set it on foot, and as a great number of gentlemen had entreated to be admitted a meeting was summoned at my house of the original members, for the purpose of framing rules and establishing all requisite preliminaries.

I have already mentioned the circumstance of a quantity of plate having been brought by Captain Churchill for Pott, and the lawsuit consequent thereto, which plate, by the decision of the Court, Pott was obliged to receive and pay for. As it consisted of articles for which he had no occasion, he resolved to dispose of the whole by a raffle, making four prizes. The number required being soon obtained the subscribers threw. I was fortunate enough to gain the second prize, which consisted of a splendid epergne, with the usual accompaniment of hanging saucers, etc., for the centre of the table. The charge made by Grey for this article was two hundred pounds.

On the 2nd of November this year (1787) a most tremendous hurricane occurred. The weather at that period is generally settled and serene in Bengal, the north-east monsoon being then considered as completely set in towards the northern extremity of the Bay, though by no means so to the southward ; this year, however, it had been rainy and bad for some days. Having a business of importance coming on that morning in Court, I rose earlier than usual.

At seven o'clock I went in to my office when the rain was descending in torrents with a strong wind from the eastward, which by nine had greatly increased, and before ten it blew what my *Plassey* shipmate, Doctor Court, would have denominated " a mere fright." The house I then inhabited being very old shook so violently that I really expected it to come tumbling about my ears. My guest, little Carter, was quite alarmed, and at each gust exclaimed with his accustomed brogue, " Auch, my dear Sir, surely then we will all be buried in the ruins of the building ! Auch, how it shivers and shakes ! "

In the height of the tempest I was obliged to go to the Court which, with the utmost difficulty, I reached, the bearers supporting the palankeen on each side ; so severe were the gusts that I was upwards of half an hour getting a hundred yards. From the Court I beheld one general scene of distress and havoc, especially amongst the small craft on the river. Even the largest ships were put into violent motion, pitching as if in an open ocean. Had I not been an eye-witness, I should not have believed any power of wind could have so agitated such a comparatively small body of water as the Hooghly at Calcutta. The *Britannia*, a fine vessel of four hundred tons burthen, then laying at anchor off the town, was obliged to cut away her masts to prevent her over-setting, which from her being nearly empty she certainly would have done. The *Comet* packet that had arrived from Bombay only the preceding day, was in imminent danger of foundering, being nearly full of water. The wind roared in so unusual and extraordinary a manner as to render it utterly impossible to see to business, the judges not being able to hear a word. There we all remained, therefore, most anxiously looking out of the window towards the river, expecting every instant to see the *Comet* go to the bottom.

The hurricane continued with unabated fury until noon when it suddenly, in a moment as it were, fell absolutely calm, leaving the most awful appearance in the sky I ever beheld ; the rain ceased with the wind, but the whole atmosphere was more depressed and heavier than I ever felt it : the clouds all round became of the deepest and dismal copper colour.  During this calm some of us went to the top of the Court-house to view the devastation both on the river and shore ; the latter, as far as the eye could reach, was covered with the wreck of boats and small vessels ; eight large ships had broke from their moorings and were laying in various positions upon a sand-bank and upon the shore opposite Calcutta.  Whilst contemplating the scene of desolation, I observed the line of the sky towards the south-west rapidly changing from copper to a still darker purple, the clouds rolling about with uncommon velocity, and evidently rising fast, whereupon I remarked to my companions that we were certainly going to have a repetition of the storm from a directly opposite quarter.  We therefore descended, and had scarcely reached the Court-room when the tempest recommenced from the south-west with such a tremendous crash as made us think everything must yield to its force.  There was no rain, yet a darkness prevailed so as to appear like night ; the wind roared as loud as thunder, the scene altogether forcibly bringing to my mind the monsoon hurricane I had encountered with my ever-lamented Charlotte five years before.  The second blast continued for four hours when it decreased to a strong gale and heavy rain then fell, attended by severe thunder and lightning.

I had invited a large party to dine with me that day, only three of them, however, ventured to leave their houses. Upon returning home from Court, I found Carter in a great fright, and he told me that in the whole course of his life he never had passed so dismal a day, every moment expecting to be demolished by the downfall of the mansion.

On the 3rd the sun rose in all its majestic splendour without a single speck of cloud in the heavens, and a more beautiful morning was never seen, but the dreadful devastation that met the eye in every direction was truly lamentable.  Women and children were wailing the loss of husbands or fathers, and parents that of their young ones ; the variety of distressing objects that presented themselves in all directions is not to be conceived; the surface of the water was covered by floating wrecks, while the land was strewed with the ruins of fallen houses and trees; of the latter some of an immense size were torn up by the roots, laying across the most public roads and streets. An avenue of fine full-grown timber-trees, consisting of at least a hundred, which led from the outer gate up to the house door of Mr. Hardwicke at Barrypore, about fourteen miles from Calcutta, were, with the exception (I think) of six, every one blown down by the first gale from the north-east and lay upon the ground in the direction the wind blew from until the change to the south-west, when many of them were actually forced round to a different position. Incredible as this appears, it is an undoubted fact, ascertained by the whole of Mr. Hardwicke's family and by many of his friends.

The 10th of November being the day previously fixed upon the five original Bucks met at my house, when Mr. Mair and Lieutenant Golding, who had every particular as to the form to be observed in constituting a Lodge within their recollection, as also the ceremony of making or admitting a new member, committed to writing every circumstance, which being read and approved were adopted. Mr. Mair likewise undertook to bespeak and superintend the making of the different jewels and regalia worn by the Officers; at the express desire of the party present I consented to be at the head and was immediately nominated "Noble Grand," my supporters being Messrs. Rundell and Hall. Mr. Mair accepted the troublesome office of Secretary. Among our rules and regulations it was determined to limit the number of members to twenty-five, as being likely to render the Lodge select and respectable as well as to make it the object of pleasant men to become members. Upon comparing the lists of friends each of us had who were desirous of belonging to the Society, we found considerably more candidates than were required to fill the Lodge; the gentlemen, I as Noble Grand proposed, were George Elliot, Michael George Prendergast, John Addison, Stephen Bayard, John Wilson and John Melville.

Mr. Stackhouse Tolfrey having acquired an independent fortune took a passage for himself and his handsome wife on board one of the Company's ships, and early in the month of December they sailed for England. I availed myself of that opportunity to send as a present to Mrs. Burke the handsome epergne of Pott's which I won in the raffle.

Captain Gerard, of the Company's ship *Deptford*, who was then in Bengal, having been educated at Westminster, took the opportunity of giving an entertainment to all of the School then resident in Calcutta. Upon our assembling at his house, I greatly admired four landscapes that were hanging in his dining-room. Captain Gerard told us they were the property of a very worthy young man, the second mate of his ship, who being a friend of Mr. Farrington, the painter,[1] employed him to paint them in the hope of their turning to account in India, but instead of his expectation being realised no person had hitherto offered half of what they cost him, which was £200, and he greatly feared his young friend would be a material sufferer upon the occasion. Upon this representation one of the company immediately proposed adding one hundred per cent to the cost price, and at that amount raffling them. This suggestion was forthwith adopted, the list being filled by the party present, dice were produced and we proceeded to determine who was to possess the pictures. The gentlemen having all thrown except me and Captain Gerard, who held two chances, I took the box and threw fifty, being the highest number. Captain Gerard threw only thirty-six, but on his second chance also threw fifty ; we were left therefore to determine the tie. I again took the box and threw the uncommonly low number of eighteen, concluding Captain Gerard must be the successful person, when to the surprize of us all he threw but seventeen, his first being three aces and his second deuces, the third a six and a deuce. Thus the pictures became my property for three hundred rupees, the sum paid for each chance, this prize, with the silver epergne, being

---

[1] Probably Joseph Farington, R.A., as his brother George was in India at this time.—ED.

the only instances of good fortune I have ever met with, either in lottery or in raffle, during my long residence in India, although in that period I had tried my luck in many score, both of the one and the other.

Mrs. Cairnes being now attacked with a severe fever, was so much debilitated and reduced by it that Major Cairnes resolved to make her change the air. They therefore embarked for the Upper Provinces, and I saw no more of them for a considerable time. My guest too, Mr. Carter, had frequent slight attacks of liver, which convinced me that the heat of India would not allow of his remaining long in it. As he found that every week seriously affected him he prudently determined to content himself with a small independency he had acquired of nearly four thousand pounds, and returned to England. I had the further satisfaction of securing for him a passage, free of every expence, on board the *Lord Camden*, commanded by my excellent friend Captain Nathaniel Dance.

I had often admired a lovely Hindostanee girl who sometimes visited Carter at my house, who was very lively and clever. Upon Carter's leaving Bengal I invited her to become an inmate with me, which she consented to do, and from that time to the day of her death Jemdannee, which was her name, lived with me, respected and admired by all my friends by her extraordinary sprightliness and good-humour. Unlike the women in general in Asia she never secluded herself from the sight of strangers ; on the contrary, she delighted in joining my male parties, cordially joining in the mirth which prevailed, though she never touched wine or spirits of any kind.

About this period two artists of splendid talents, the Messrs. Daniell, uncle and nephew, arrived in Bengal ; and as I was always as great an encourager of merits as my humble means would allow, I not only subscribed myself but procured many other names to a work they commenced upon of drawing and engraving in *aqua tinta*, twelve views of different parts of Calcutta ; they completed them within a twelvemonth, but being the first attempt they proved very inferior to many subsequent performances.

# CHAPTER XXIV

### THE DOWNFALL OF ROBERT POTT. DAVISON'S DUELS
### WITH WILLIAM BURKE AND PRENDERGAST

IN February, 1788, I had the pleasure of receiving letters from my family, which were brought out by John Royds, Esquire, an intimate friend of my father's and eldest sister's ; he was a gentleman of accomplished and elegant manners who had spent his time in the best company in England ; formerly he possessed a handsome estate in Yorkshire, but by living rather too profusely had injured it so much as to make it necessary for him to leave England, and like many others in similar situations, try what Asia would do for him. Having when a young man, though without any thought at the time of ever following the profession of the Law, been called to the Bar, he now came out to Bengal with the intention of becoming an Advocate in the Supreme Court. As he had always been a gay man of pleasure, he had not bestowed much of his time in studying Coke, Salkeld, or Ventries, consequently could not be a profound lawyer, but to society in general he was a great acquisition : he constantly made one of my parties, as well as those of Mr. William Dunkin, who shewed him the utmost attention.

In March, I received a kind and grateful letter from Mr. Carter, from Bombay, the *Camden* having been sent to that place to convey a cargo of cotton from thence to China, where she was to be filled with tea for London. Indeed, it was owing to this circuitous route of the ship that I was able to get him a passage gratis, for had she gone home direct from Bengal, I neither could have asked or expected such a favour as she would have been crowded with passengers. By Carter's letter, I learnt what I had before had some suspicion of—his being seriously in love with Miss Prince, now the wife of Sir Home Popham. He not only avowed the attachment, but acknowledged that he had proposed and been positively refused, which disappointment he said operated more to prejudice his health than the climate, and that not being able to endure the sight of her he so much loved, notwithstanding her proud rejection, had induced him to take my advice and leave India. In the course of a long voyage little Paddy's love cooled, and by the time he reached England he had so far gotten the better of it that he soon after his arrival married a Miss Wills, a smart and rather good-looking girl, who in due time bore him a son, who has grown up the exact counterpart of his father. The following year produced a daughter, after which she had no more children, and in about eight years after his return he died from a severe attack of liver.

In the same month of March Mr. John Shee, now a baronet, left India. About the same period my friend Pott had a violent quarrel with his head assistant, Mr. John Addison, who, from having been in the same situation with Sir John D'Oyly, was extremely jealous and offended at Pott's superseding him by stepping into the posts of President at the Durbar and Collector of the Customs. He, in fact, became a most inveterate enemy of Pott's, suffering his personal dislike to carry him so far as to accuse his principal of various frauds and peculations. Pott recriminated, and so rancorous were both parties that at length the attention of Government was drawn to their dispute, in consequence of which an enquiry into the conduct of Mr. Pott was directed ; in the discussion thereof, Pott and Addison were so eager to ruin each other that a number of facts were established against both, whereupon they were removed from their situations, too fatally effecting their object of ruining each other. From that time to the day of his death Pott remained out of employment ; nor did his antagonist, Addison, get any situation until sixteen years after.

My friend, Mr. William Dunkin, now began to talk of returning to England for the purpose of trying to obtain a seat upon the Bench, a report then prevailing that an impeachment had been voted in Parliament against Sir Elijah Impey, which would of course do away his Chief Justiceship.

In April Mrs. Rider, the wife of my friend and *Plassey* shipmate, Jacob Rider, with her daughter, a smart showy girl of about seventeen, arrived from Europe in a French ship. Having resided the last four years in Paris, they brought out the latest fashions, setting all the women wild to procure the same sort of cap or hat as worn by them. In consequence of this increase of family, Mr. Rider was obliged to take a large house in Calcutta and greatly add to his establishment of servants.

Mr. Keighley upon the suit in equity being commenced against him was deprived of his situation at Cossimbuzar. He therefore, after leaving an agent at that place to carry on the business of his filatures or silk manufactories, took his family to reside at a capital mansion belonging to him at Russassugly, five miles to the southward of Calcutta. Mrs. Keighley was one of the prettiest as well as the cleverest women in India, for both which reasons she was envied and detested by her own sex, most of whom were illiberal enough to propagate ill-founded scandal respecting her moral conduct. This she herself treated with the most sovereign contempt, but being a great favourite of mine, I always defended her character when I heard it attacked by any of my female acquaintances.

I generally passed Saturday and Sunday at this place Russassugly, but having a particular dislike of sleeping out of my own bed, I returned to town after supper on Saturday night, driving out again early the next morning to breakfast. Mr. Keighley drank very hard and with such an example as he constantly set it was difficult to avoid committing excess. One of the greatest debauches I ever witnessed occurred at his house with about a dozen sad fellows. In the midst of our Bacchanalian rioting one of the party recollected that the new church which had just been erected was to be consecrated and opened for Divine service the next day, under the direction of the Rev. Mr. Johnson,

Senior Chaplain of the Presidency. It was instantly determined by the drunken set that we should all attend the religious ceremony. It was then about two o'clock. I therefore suggested the propriety of retiring to bed, as otherwise we might render ourselves wholly unfit to appear in a place of Divine worship. My considerate proposal was scouted, and instead of it a motion of Mr. Keighley's to continue at the bottle until it was time to go to church was carried by acclamation. We accordingly remained pouring down claret until eight in the morning (Sunday), when the gentlemen staggered to their respective rooms to put on clean clothes. Having dressed we reassembled at the breakfast-table, trying how far strong coffee would operate towards sobering us. I then found the zeal for going to church had considerably abated. At nine three carriages being announced ready, upon mustering the party no more could be prevailed upon to proceed than five, these were Mr. Keighley, Colonel Mordaunt, Mr. Shearman Bird, Dr. Bailey, and myself, who all stepped into Mr. Keighley's coach and were rapidly conveyed to the church, the steps of which we were only able to ascend by leaning upon and supporting each other. It may easily be believed that in such a state we sadly exposed ourselves, drawing the eyes and attention of the congregation upon us as well as that of the clergyman, who took occasion to introduce into his sermon a severe philippic against inebriety, against indelicate behaviour in a sacred place and Sabbath-breaking, and directing those parts of his discourse pointedly to the pew in which we sat. I have often thought since of that profligate scene with shame and contrition.

A few weeks after the above disgraceful circumstances, I had as usual spent Saturday at Russassugly. At one in the morning I was mounting into my phaeton to go to Calcutta, when Mrs. Keighley came to the door, and as she had often done before, upbraided me for the folly of not sleeping where I was instead of going such a distance. I pleaded how much I felt the want of a night's rest, which was invariably the case if I attempted to sleep in a strange bed ; that the drive after supper was far from unpleasant, and I would certainly be at Russassugly again before she was up ; whereupon she gave me a hearty shake of the hand, saying : " Well, you must do as you please ; so good night, God bless you ! "

On Sunday morning whilst dressing I was told that Mr. Chapman, who had been at the party the preceding day, and whom I had left at Mr. Keighley's, wished to speak to me.  Upon going to him, I said, " I suppose you are come for a seat to Russassugly ; I see my phaeton is at the door, so come along."  To this, with a very melancholy face, he replied, " It is all over with Russassugly.  No more mirth and jollity there for, alas, poor Mary Keighley is dead." Confounded at such unexpected information, I asked the particulars, when he said, he had been awakened by one of his servants at 5 o'clock in the morning running into his room and crying out that Mrs. Keighley was dying.  Upon which he instantly rose, and going to her chamber found she had already expired.  Mr. Keighley informed him he had not been more than an hour in bed when he was called by a female servant, who said her mistress was dreadfully ill ; that upon going to her apartment (for they did not sleep in the same chamber) he found her laying in a state of insensibility.  Dr. Bailey, who was in the house, being summoned, opened a vein ; this with the application of powerful volatiles restored her and in a few minutes she appeared materially better, recovering her speech and recollection, when she said that upon falling asleep she dreamt a similar hurricane arose to that of the 2nd of November, that the windows were burst open by the violence of it and in the same moment one side of the house fell down burying her in the ruins, after which she knew no more ; scarcely had she related this extraordinary dream when she suddenly fell back in a second fit from which she never recovered.  About half-past three with a deep groan she breathed her last.  At five in the evening of that very day, instead of partaking of her kind and cheerful hospitality, as I had done the preceding one and expected to have often repeated, I attended her lifeless body to its sad last mansion. These are awful lessons and must cause a serious impression for a time at least even upon the most thoughtless.

Mr. Keighley, although in some respects what is termed a fashionable husband, had, notwithstanding, always lived happily with his wife ; he appeared deeply afflicted by his loss : for several days was *inconsolable :* and at the end of a fortnight took unto himself another spouse, marrying a Miss Peach, of whose delicacy I could not entertain a very high opinion, as I conceived no female possessing a particle of feeling could have consented to unite herself to a man who had only been a widower a few days. I was invited to the wedding dinner, where a circumstance occurred that if I had before had a doubt of the bride's want of judgment and understanding would have decided the point. In the middle of the dinner she suddenly burst into a most violent fit of crying, and rising from her seat ran out of the room ; her husband instantly following her. The company imagined she had been attacked with some sudden illness, which for my part I could not help supposing arose from a stroke of conscience, a compunction at so rapidly filling the place of a former wife. A few minutes relieved us from our different conjectures, Mr. Keighley returned laughing immoderately, and told us the occasion of her distress and so suddenly leaving the room was her discovering that the party present consisted of the ominous number of thirteen ! Could anybody have expected in these enlightened times so silly a creature to exist in the rank of a gentlewoman, yet so it was. The morning after this hasty wedding I received from a jeweller a mourning ring, as one of the pall-bearers at the funeral of the late Mrs. Keighley !

In the middle of the year (1788) my health became worse than ever, scarce a week passed without a violent spasmodic attack in my stomach which always greatly alarmed the medical men who attended me. Several of my friends conceiving I lived too freely, especially when I had parties at home, advised me to leave off drinking claret. In compliance with their wishes I did so, Mr. Dunkin, who had not a high opinion of my resolution or that I should adhere to the determination of abstaining from *Lol Shrob*, insisting upon clogging me with a penalty. For this purpose he gave me twenty-five gold mohurs, and I was to pay him one hundred the first time I should be seen intoxicated ! I rigidly kept to my plan for several months though without deriving any material benefit therefrom. Dining one day with a very jovial party at Mr. Dunkin's, having drunk my two or three glasses of madeira, I sat dejected and out of spirits, when Mr. James Dunkin suddenly exclaimed, " By God, Hickey, if you persevere in this vile, abstemious existence for another month you will send yourself out of the world. Take my advice and drop it. Come, begin immediately by taking a bottle or two of claret, which I will answer for it will do you more good than all the doctors." To my great surprize, Mr. Dunkin joined his namesake, saying, " Come, William, as the sober plan seems to be universally reprobated, and certainly has not been attended with the hoped-for success, let us drop it, and return to generous red wine. As to our agreement, let us agree to waive it ; for myself I, in the presence of these respectable witnesses, undertake not to exact the penalty of your drinking too much." He then filled me a very large bumper of claret, the whole party drinking to my speedy restoration to health. I drank at least three pints, went to bed, slept better than I had done for a long time, and rose the following morning quite a new creature. Of course, I made no more experiments as to leaving off wine.

About this period accounts reached India that an impeachment by the Commons of Great Britain had been commenced in the House of Lords against Mr. Hastings for malpractices during the time he filled the situation of Governor-General, in which business my greatly esteemed friend, Mr. Edmund Burke, took a very active part, by doing which he created to himself a number of very bitter enemies in Bengal, in which part of the world Mr. Hastings had a host of enthusiastic admirers.

Our Bucks Society went on famously and was so popular

that our Secretary's book was filled with the names of candidates for admission. We therefore, after some debate upon the point, extended the number of members to thirty-five ; this increase, with the departure of several of the Brothers from the Presidency, made the number to be elected nineteen. Amongst the candidates was that trouble-some fellow, Davison, who Mr. William Burke still continued to patronise and support, notwithstanding he, from his intemperate behaviour, was in perpetual controversies and broils. What that worthy and truly respectable man found to admire in him no one could discover, his manners towards everybody being supercilious, insolent and overbearing. Their acquaintance first arose out of an extraordinary circumstance. Mr. Burke and this young man, who was then only twenty years of age and an ensign in the Company's service at Madras, happened to meet at the same party at dinner, where in the evening box and dice being produced they set to at hazard. In the course of play a dispute arose about a bet between Mr. Burke and Davison, when the former told the latter he was an impertinent and silly cox-comb and puppy, for which Davison sent him a challenge. They met the following morning, exchanged a brace of pistols when, through the interference of the seconds, the matter was accommodated, Mr. Burke embracing his antagonist, declaring he was a very high-spirited, noble boy. From that day they became sworn friends, and Mr. Burke upon all occasions supported and defended him in his follies and extravagancies, not only paying his debts, which amounted to a considerable sum, but supplying him with cash whenever he chose to ask for it. To such an extent was this carried that Mr. Prendergast assured me that within eighteen months Mr. Burke had disbursed above four thousand pounds upon him.

After my quarrel with Davison and our being mutually bound to keep the peace no intercourse took place between us for several months, nor did we in any way notice each other if we casually met, until I was one day infinitely sur-prized by a visit from him, when he declared that he entertained a very sincere regard for me, exceedingly lamented what had occurred, and begged my pardon for his violent behaviour, which he said was entirely ascribable to his being drunk : he therefore earnestly entreated that we might be reconciled. Such humility in so haughty a man astonished me, but as I did not see how I could with propriety reject his advances we shook hands. After which he called daily at my house, frequently asking permission to dress there when engaged to dine in Calcutta as Mr. Burke had no house in town. Of course he had the use of a chamber, but he behaved so outrageously, beating and otherwise ill-treating my servants, that after remonstrating with him in vain, I forbid him my house. Still he used to persevere in frequent calls.

Upon the establishment of the Bucks Society, Davison expressed an earnest wish to belong to it ; for some time I parried his applications to me by telling him I had already the names of more friends to bring forward than could come in turn for a long time. Yet he persisted in saying he was sure I could secure his election if I chose it, that he knew he was unpopular, that unless he had my avowed support he should never succeed, and that if I proposed him the Lodge would, in compliment to me as their President, elect him ; in short, he continued so importunate that I at last consented to propose him ; however, I am free to confess that I did so from a conviction that his universal bad character and his being detested by all who knew him, must effectually bar the possibility of his being elected. Having ascertained from the Keeper the day he was to be balloted for, he had the presumption to go to the house we had taken and fitted up for the sole use of the Society, saying he was certain that from my having proposed him he should be elected.

It so happened that every individual member then in Calcutta attended the meeting, which I concluded was for the purpose of black-balling Davison, and I fully expected that he would not have had one single vote for him except my own and Mr. Mair's, who seconded me on the nomination. Upon inspecting the box there were only two black balls, these, however, being sufficient to exclude. I apologised for leaving the chair a few moments, thinking it would be civil to communicate the result to Davison myself. Whilst talking to him upon the subject one of the members came out and calling me aside requested I would not send Mr. Davison away, but return to the Lodge. This I did, when the Secretary told me he had good reason to believe that the black balls were put in by a mistake ; the gentlemen, therefore, wished to ballot again. Although I felt this was said in compliment to me, I did not wish to avail myself of the civility, yet knew not well how to decline it. A second ballot then took place, and the candidate was unanimously elected. Nothing was left, therefore, to me but to receive the newly elected Buck. Mr. Rundell afterwards told me that upon my leaving the room, Mr. Hall had addressed the Lodge, expressing his concern at a candidate being rejected who was proposed by their Noble Grand, and as such a circumstance was unprecedented, he trusted those brothers who had inadvertently put in a black ball would correct their error. The proposal was instantly adopted and Mr. Davison elected. The very day that he thus became one of the Society he made himself conspicuous by moving that the Lodge should give a ball and supper to the Settlement ; several persons present opposing this wild scheme, he insisted upon taking the sense of the Lodge at large ; his motion was thereupon balloted for when not a single member, except himself, voted for it. This raised his ire exceedingly, and from that time he began to speak disrespectfully of the Society wherever he went.

The election for Noble Grand being annual, and my year drawing towards the conclusion, I directed the Secretary to issue notices to every member to attend for the purpose of choosing a new Noble Grand. Upon the day appointed every member in Calcutta attended except Mr. Davison ; the balloting-box being opened, it was found that every gentleman present had voted for me, there being no other name in it but that of Mr. Rundell, which was put in by me. The Secretary in declaring upon whom the election had fallen, was pleased to pay me some high compliments : thus I became a second time the President.

Mr. Davison, although every person seemed disgusted at his doing it, continued to abuse and ridicule the Bucks. Mr. Prendergast being in a large company where Davison was very bitter in his remarks upon the Society, remonstrated upon the indelicacy and impropriety of his conduct, but his interference only increased the acrimony of Davison's language, who ended his vulgar attacks by saying none but blackguards belonged to it.

Mr. Prendergast the next morning, accompanied by a friend, went to the house of Major Hervey, where Davison was then upon a visit, with a fixed determination to make the latter apologise for the coarseness of his speech the preceding evening. Being shewn into the room where Davison and some ladies and gentlemen were sitting, Prendergast desired to speak to Davison apart, who accordingly followed him into the garden ; when there Prendergast reminded him of the offensive expressions he had used, adding that he was come to demand an apology or that he would give him satisfaction. Davison said he would neither : that he saw no occasion for apologising and certainly would not involve his bail for keeping the peace in a scrape by going out to fight. Prendergast told him the security given had reference only to keeping the peace towards Mr. Hickey and had nothing to do with any other individual. Davison, however, persisted that it was general, whereupon Prendergast said he was a pitiful scoundrel, and immediately gave him a severe horsewhipping. The same evening a gentleman carried a challenge from Davison to Prendergast, in consequence of which a meeting was fixed for the following morning at the Dutch Settlement of Chinsurah, where the parties, each with a friend, attended accordingly, their weapons being pistols. Dame Fortune, like the fickle jade she sometimes proves herself, favoured the worthless, for Davison at his second shot lodged a ball in his antagonist's thigh, who was carried off the field in a dangerous state. The surgeons put him to extreme torture in their fruitless

endeavours to find and extract the ball.  For several days
his life was pronounced as irrecoverably gone, but the wise-
heads proved mistaken, the ball did not touch any vital part,
and after enduring much pain the wound healed and he
recovered.

The first time that Prendergast attended the Lodge after
the above duel he stated every particular of the transaction,
commenting upon the persevering brutality of Davison in
refusing to apologise for the unwarrantable and opprobrious
epithets he had applied to the Society in general.  A member
then observed he should submit two motions to the serious
consideration of the Lodge, and immediately moved that
the statement just communicated by Mr. Prendergast should
be entered upon the records, which being unanimously
agreed to, he next moved that under the circumstances
of the case, established by Mr. Prendergast, Mr. Davison
was unworthy of remaining upon the list of Bucks, that his
name therefore be expunged and he expelled with ignominy.
This motion also passed *nem. con.*, several of the members
in forcible terms reprobating Davison's illiberal conduct ;
the Secretary was directed to communicate the result to
Davison, at the same time acquainting him he had been
ignominiously expelled by thirty-two members, the whole
number present.  The fellow was vexed to the soul at this
issue of the business, his mortification being increased at
finding that the whole Settlement pronounced him egregiously
in the wrong—not a single person but condemned him,
except Mr. William Burke, from whom I received a letter
upon the subject couched in the most extraordinary terms,
vindicating his protégé and as inconsiderately censuring the
Society for their violent measure.  His intemperate epistle
concluded by calling upon me in rather dictatorial terms
" *instantly to cause the disgraceful and illegal vote to be
rescinded,*" which was (he said) the only reparation we could
make an English gentleman.

This curious letter I endeavoured to answer with temper
but firmness ; I recapitulated the behaviour of Mr. Davison,
contrasting his indecent language with the mild and correct

lines pursued by Mr. Prendergast until driven to the necessity of chastising him ; I lightly touched upon the favourable opinion the Settlement at large entertained of Mr. Prendergast, whilst Mr. Davison was universally detested, despised, and by a few feared. I further observed that any effort on my part to get the vote rescinded was quite out of the question. The measure had not been hastily or intemperately adopted, but after a candid and full investigation it had resulted from the cool and unbiased judgment of every gentleman present, thirty-two in number ; all men of as nice honour and independent principles as any in the world : I concluded by expressing my earnest hope that the evident partiality he betrayed to Mr. Davison would not interrupt the friendship he had honoured me with from my earliest infancy. To this I got no reply ; Mr. Burke, however, marked his feelings by increasing, if possible, his attentions to Davison, whom he carried with him wherever he went, carrying his partiality so far as to urge many families who had been disgusted with the overbearing conduct of Davison and wished to drop his acquaintance, not only to forgive his improper conduct, but to invite him to their best parties.

A few days after the foregoing letters had been exchanged I met Mr. Burke at the Bengal Bank, when I perceived that he would not acknowledge me. I nevertheless addressed him as if nothing had happened to interrupt our familiarity, but in return only got a cold, formal bow. I therefore determined to drop all intercourse with him, and as I was then indebted to him for four thousand sicca rupees, which sum I had borrowed upon an emergency to pay off a creditor who was becoming importunate, I immediately forwarded that amount with the following letter : " Dear Sir, Having now a supply of cash, I beg leave to return the four thousand sicca rupees you was so good as to advance me a few months ago, to enable me to discharge a debt that then pressed. I am, dear Sir, Your obliged humble servant, W. Hickey." To this I received a very angry reply, concluding, as I thought, in equivocal terms, as he said there was an account subsisting between us which until properly adjusted he should not receive any money from me; he returned, therefore, the four thousand rupees. I had at different times done business for Mr. Burke in my professional capacity, but certainly had no more idea of making any charge for the same than if I had been employed by my father, and the more so as the whole had been for conveyancing or similar matters in which there was no disbursement of cash. With this impression upon my mind, I conceived the words " properly adjusted " must allude to *interest* upon the four thousand sicca rupees, under which notion I calculated the exact sum due at the rate of 12 per cent per annum, again enclosing the principal with that addition, apologising for having omitted to send the interest before. To this letter also I received a very indignant reply, wherein amongst other strong expressions, he said, " Your father, sir, whom I have loved like a brother more than fifty years, would not have used me thus; when, sir, did you ever know of my receiving interest for a friendly loan or why do you insult me by offering it? I am your debtor to a considerable amount for much business done on my account; when it suits your convenience to see what it amounts to, should any balance remain due to me, I must of a course accept it and you will be pleased to pay it into the Bengal Bank to my account. I mean this so far as relates to principal but no further. In the interim, I take leave, sir, again to return a sum as not belonging to your most obedient servant, W. Burke."

Upon the receipt of this letter, I immediately paid the whole amount into the Bengal Bank on Mr. Burke's account, and there the matter rested between us, except that Mr. Mee subsequently often told me Mr. Burke positively refused having anything to do with that money, actually scratching the item out of his bank-book in which he had been given credit for it. He therefore advised me to draw upon it, which I as pertinaciously refused.

# CHAPTER XXV

## FAMINE IN BENGAL. A DISPUTE WITH THE FRATERNITY OF MASONS. AN ACQUISITION TO THE BAR

IN December, 1788, Mr. William Dunkin took his passage for Europe on board the *Phœnix*, Captain Gray, in the ensuing January. I accompanied him a few miles down the river to the country house of Mr. Farquharson (thentofore Sir John Macpherson's) where we dined. In the evening he embarked in a pilot's schooner that was to convey him to the ship. The being deprived of his society was a serious loss to me and I felt it acutely.

In February we lost Mr. Jeremiah Church, an advocate of the Supreme Court, a good-humoured, pleasant man of considerable talents, he was taken off very suddenly with one of those violent fevers so prevalent in Bengal.

My friend Pott, soon after being deprived of the lucrative situation he held, in which, however, he had not saved a guinea, married Miss Cruttenden, a first cousin of his own, a very charming woman who was universally admired and respected and who proved an exemplary wife.

Mr. Philip Yonge, a barrister, having suffered in health, took his passage for Europe, by whom I sent as a present for my brother twelve views of different parts of Calcutta, drawn and engraved in *aqua tinta* by Messrs. Daniell.

The house I inhabited upon the Esplanade now became so bad as to render it dangerous, being liable to fall every north-wester. I therefore gave my landlord notice I should quit it at the end of the month. He thereupon called to say he found me so excellent a tenant, he wished to retain me, and if I would go into another mansion of his he would pull down the house I left and rebuild it according to any plan

I chose.  I accepted the offer by inhabiting a very capital house belonging to him in Council House Street.  The very day I left the old one he sent in workmen to commence pulling it down.

The letters I received in April gave me every reason to suppose my favourite sister, Ann, had serious thoughts of coming out to me, but however much such an event would contribute to my comfort, I could not for a moment think of advising or permitting it, because I felt sure from all accounts I had received of the sad state of her nerves and her general health, that the climate of India would be destruction to her.  I therefore wrote in the strongest terms to prevent her carrying such intention into execution.

This year a dreadful scarcity of grain prevailed, the crops having failed throughout the Provinces of Bengal and Behar, from which circumstance the laborious poor became distressed for food to supply their families.  In consequence of this the British inhabitants of Calcutta, with their accustomed benevolence, entered into a voluntary subscription for their relief, whereby so large a sum was raised as to enable them to feed upwards of twenty thousand men, women, and children daily.  Six different stations were fixed upon in opposite directions for delivering out rice, ghee, and other articles of provisions, two English gentlemen attending at each station to superintend the proper distribution ;  this continued about four months when such immense crowds of miserable creatures were drawn to the Presidency by the hope of relief that Government became alarmed and were under the unpleasant necessity of issuing orders to stop the further delivery of rice, etc., after a certain day therein specified, of which public and written notices were proclaimed and stuck up all over the country and every possible precaution was taken to prevent a further influx of people to the Capital ;  but nothing could stop the unhappy, famished wretches from rushing in crowds to Calcutta, the neighbourhood of which became dreadful to behold.  One could not stir out of doors without encountering the most shocking objects, the poor, starved people laying dead and dying in every street and road. It was computed that for many weeks no less than fifty died daily, yet this patient and mild race never committed the least act of violence, no houses or go-downs were broken into to procure rice, no exclamations or noisy cries made for assistance ; all with that gentle resignation so peculiar to the natives of India, submitting to their fate and laying themselves down to die. Everything in the power of liberal individuals was done for their relief; indeed, one must have been less than man, absolute Buonapartes, to have witnessed such horrible scenes of misery without feeling the bitterest pangs and exerting every nerve to alleviate them.

A rumour now prevailed in Calcutta that the noble Governor-General, Lord Cornwallis, had thoughts of taking unto himself a wife, the lady destined for him being a Miss Philpott, sister to the lady who after exercising her wit upon Mr. Calvert, married him. The report, however, proved unfounded, for while the peer was expected daily to announce his intention, the fair one as suddenly and unexpectedly became the wife of Mr. Harrington, a gentleman in the Company's Civil Service, now a baronet.

Another report was that Sir John Macpherson was again appointed Governor-General, and actually on his voyage out to relieve Lord Cornwallis, while private letters from England to individuals in Bengal asserted that Philip Francis, Esquire, would be his lordship's successor.

Mr. George Wroughton, the Company's attorney, having determined to leave India, called upon me earnestly to recommend my forming a connection in business with Mr. Benjamin Turner, who for several years had the entire management of his office, conducting the same with equal ability and integrity ; being a man of extraordinary mildness he was a prodigious favourite amongst the opulent natives. I readily agreed to follow Mr. Wroughton's advice, requesting he would undertake to arrange the matter between us. This he set about with such zeal that in three days Mr. Turner and myself executed a Deed of Partnership, but as he was not at that time admitted an attorney, the business continued in my name alone. I found him in every respect a vast acquisition, active and clever, with indefatigable assiduity and a perfect master of his profession ; Mr. Wroughton turned over all his best clients to our office, giving us ample employment ; my house was crowded from morning till night by natives flocking to Turner with their different causes. I therefore wished him to assign some part of them to me, to which he said there was no occasion ; that he had long given himself up to the desk, the labours of which had become habitual ; that he had no acquaintances to lead him abroad and preferred giving up his whole attention to business to any sort of amusement, besides which he knew I went much into company, and had frequent parties at my own house ; he therefore entreated that I would continue to live as I had been used to do, and he should do very well leaving me to see to the European clients. He further undertook upon my declaring my utter ignorance of arithmetic to keep the office accounts himself. In consequence of this arrangement I ceased to fag as theretofore, becoming comparatively a man of pleasure.

Mr. Burke left Bengal for Madras, the duties of his office of Paymaster-General to His Majesty's troops requiring his presence at the latter place. Major and Mrs. Cairnes also went at the same time. Lord Cornwallis having written to Lord Clive, then Governor of Fort St. George, to request he would give the Major a Company in one of the King's regiments upon the coast, Lord Clive did so immediately, but from anxiety and fretting Major Cairnes's health was so much undermined he was not able to join his regiment, gradually grew worse and in about ten months departed this life, leaving an amiable widow with a large family of children entirely unprovided for. The usual liberality of the East corrected the evil, a large sum was collected by subscription for the benefit of the widow and children which was paid into the hands of trustees.

Previous to Mr. Burke's leaving Calcutta our mutual and kind and considerate friend, Mr. Benjamin Mee, successfully exerted himself in bringing about a reconciliation between him and me. We met at dinner at the Bengal Bank, shook hands very cordially and to my great gratification parted upon good terms. Mr. Burke took his protégé, Mr. Davison, with him to Madras, continuing to patronise and support him.

I shall here state a ridiculous dispute I got into with the fraternity of Masons. The Lodge No. 2, in which I had been made, had belonging to it several of the tradesmen of Calcutta ; also two or three vagabond attornies, to neither of which description of person did I ever speak, and was therefore considered by them as extremely proud. A new Lodge having been established, consisting of the principal gentlemen of the Settlement, I sent in my resignation for No. 2, and was elected a brother of the new Lodge. This gave great offence to those I had left.

About two months after my change, I received an official letter from the Secretary of my first Lodge, calling upon me in very peremptory language without loss of time to pay the sum of one hundred and fifty sicca rupees, stated to be arrears of fees due from me to the Lodge. As I did not approve of the manner in which this demand was made, though indifferent about the amount claimed, I wrote an answer without using the fraternal address, and began with a simple " Sir." I observed upon the impertinence of the demand, which I denied the justice of, and although I might have probably paid had it been civilly asked, I would not yield to the insolence of any low-bred fellow tacking to his signature the title of " Secretary." My letter being laid before the Lodge, the Master and his Warden took the matter up with much warmth ; another epistle was addressed to me expressive of his surprize my unmasonic letter had created, and requiring an explanation for such conduct. I remained silent. A second and a third was written to me which I treated with the same silent contempt. I was then threatened with a complaint against me to the Provincial Grand Lodge which had no more effect than the preceding addresses.

During these letters I was elected Senior Warden of the new Lodge, which had become extremely popular, so much so that at every meeting we had from eight to a dozen brothers proposed. This success added to the irascibility of the first Lodge : they actually did represent my conduct to the Provincial Grand Lodge as being scandalous and derogatory to the character of a Mason. Mr. Edward Fenwick, of whom I have before spoken more than once, being then the Acting Provincial Grand Master, called upon me to admonish me privately as a friend, and advised my settling the business by apologising to the Lodge I had insulted for my intemperate language. This I refused to do, whereupon I received an elaborate address from Mr. Fenwick, assuring me my contumacious treatment of the Lodge I had belonged to must and would be taken up very seriously, and if I persisted in refusing to apologise, I should soon have occasion to repent my obstinacy. At this I laughed.

A complaint was regularly made to the Provincial Grand Lodge, where a difference of opinion prevailed amongst the officers, some of them thinking that the Grand Lodge had no right to take cognisance of such a complaint, my letter being a private one from one individual to another in no way to be considered as masonic. I had a strenuous advocate and supporter in Mr. Hugh Gayer Honeycomb, the Junior Grand Warden, who upon finding the Grand Master and several members were for expelling me, insisted upon the question being referred to the Grand Lodge of England for their decision. This after a long debate was voted for, unless I should upon more mature consideration see the propriety of apologising. Mr. Fenwick, too, made another attempt to work upon my feelings, in an address consisting of *eight sheets* of paper, containing an elaborate dissertation and panegyric upon Masonry, followed by a strong censure of my contumacious behaviour towards the Secretary of the first Lodge, whom I had wantonly and unlike a Mason offended and grossly insulted, for which offence, if I did not satisfactorily apologise, the consequence must inevitably be that *I should be deprived of all the benefits of Masonry and no longer be considered a brother*. To this grave and voluminous philippic I wrote a concise reply, saying, I had received his (Fenwick's) letter, and notwithstanding the *dreadful anathema* it contained certainly would not make any apology either to a set of or an individual blackguard. This drove the Provincial Grand Lodge gentry half crazy from conceiving their dignity attacked, though I had not addressed or signed my letter as a Mason. The Acting Provincial Grand Master immediately issued an order to the Master of the new Lodge to elect a new Senior Warden in the stead of William Hickey removed for contumacious and unmasonic conduct. The Master of the new Lodge refused to obey, but not liking to enter into a personal altercation upon the question, resigned his chair, as did his Junior Warden ; thus was a serious schism created amongst the fraternity in Calcutta.

To finish this *important* matter at once. A reference upon it, with all the circumstances, being made by the Provincial Grand Lodge to the Grand Lodge of England, the Grand Master and his Council returned for answer that the Provincial Grand Lodge of Calcutta had no right to take up the business in the way they had done, and had committed a gross error in removing the Senior Warden of the new Lodge, whom, therefore, they ordered to be immediately restored to his situation. The letter concluded by an expression of surprize at the Provincial Grand Master and his Officers being so ignorant of what their duty was. This was a matter of great triumph for me and my friends ; the Provincial Grand Secretary sent me an official notice of my restoration, and I was much importuned to resume the station I had held, which, as I had never been very fond of the Order, I persisted in declining, and from that time to the present day have never been within a Mason's Lodge.

My friend, Mr. Jacob Rider, having disposed of his daughter in marriage to Mr. Richard Comyns Birch, and his saucy helpmate, Mrs. Rider, being tired of the sameness of a Calcutta life, once more departed to take her share in the more exhilarating scenes of London and Paris.

Mr. William Burke, upon his leaving Bengal to go to Madras, presuming he should no more return to Calcutta, presented me with an admirable bust of Mr. Edmund Burke, a statuary of admitted merit and talent, executed by Mr. John Hickey brother to the portrait painter, Thomas Hickey. Unfortunately, this promising genius died in the prime of life.- Mr. William Burke also gave me a picture painted by Thomas Hickey, being small size whole lengths of Mr. Edmund Burke and Mr. Charles Fox, in which the former was represented as reading the famous India Bill prepared and brought into prominence by the latter. It was but an indifferent performance, yet valuable to me from the transcendent abilities of the two statesmen. This artist (Mr. Thomas Hickey), finding business upon the decline in Bengal, accompanied Mr. William Burke to Madras, where under that gentleman's patronage and warm recommendation he met with considerable encouragement.

In the hot weather of this year (1789) I suffered much from attacks of spasm in the stomach which the medical gentry pronounced unsettled gout. Be it what it might, nothing gave me relief except large doses of laudanum, having tried tincture of guiacum assafœtida, valerian, ether, and all the string of nervous medicines without the least benefit.

In July Lord Cornwallis gave a splendid entertainment to the whole Settlement, in consequence of His Majesty's recovery from mental derangement. Superb fireworks and illuminations were prepared, but it proving a wet evening, torrents of rain pouring down, totally prevented the intended exhibition. Upwards of a hundred thousand small coloured lamps were fixed on the southern front of the Government House.

Mr. Michael George Prendergast, who had been one of Mr. William Burke's protégés, having procured Lord Cornwallis's permission to settle at Dacca, went to reside in that city, where he commenced maker of fine piece goods and became a steady man of business.

Colonel Pearse, Commandant of the Corps of Artillery, died this month ; his remains were attended to the grave by Lord Cornwallis and all the Council. In less than a week afterwards Captain Dixon, who had been aide-de-camp to the Colonel, also died. He was a young man of great abilities. He was taken ill and died in three hours after he was first attacked. The season proved an uncommonly sickly one, fatal to many; amongst those carried off was Mr. Atkinson, a barrister of the Supreme Court, who had come to India by the advice of Mr. William Dunkin, that gentleman being an old and warm friend of Mr. Atkinson's father, a respectable apothecary in Pall Mall. Mr. Atkinson was taken ill in August, the symptoms being diseased liver; from the first he was uncommonly low-spirited, saying he was sure he would not recover. On the 31st of August I left town to spend a few days, as I frequently did, with my friend, Major George Russell, at Barrackpore, early in the morning of which day I called upon Mr. Atkinson, whom I found quite despondent; he cried bitterly, saying he felt himself that he never should leave his room. As I did not consider him in a dangerous state, I said all in my power to console him and encourage him, though without effect. Taking leave, I proceeded on my excursion, and on the 5th of September received intelligence of his death, and that by his will he had appointed me, jointly with Mr. James Dunkin, an executor.

At the period I am now writing of Major Russell, although he had attained the rank of a field officer, knew nothing of military tactics, never having done a day's duty or relieved a guard. He had acquired a very handsome fortune by building the Barrackpore barracks and other public edifices which, as already observed, he squandered away at the gaming-table in England, and then returned to India to endeavour to acquire a second independence. During my visit to him, Colonel Sir Alexander Mackenzie, the commanding officer of the station, left the place, whereupon the command devolved upon Major Russell, it becoming his duty to muster the troops on the second of the month. On the 1st the Major had a large party to dine with him. Amongst the company were Major Farmer, Major Sir Patrick Balfour, and Captain Norman Macleod, all of whom commanded battalions of Sepoys and were considered three of the best officers in the Company's service.

After dinner Major Russell, with much pleasantry, was laughing at his own ignorance in military matters, at the same time avowing his apprehensions he should commit some blunder the following morning. The guests encouraged him, observing that there was so little to do it would not admit of mistakes for that the troops would be all assembled in line under arms ready to receive him, the only motions being four, executed by beat of drum, ruffle and flam alternately, after which he would receive the returns from the respective officers, and there would be an end of the business. "Aye," said Russell, "but then depend upon it, I shall make them ruffle instead of flam, and flam instead of ruffle." "No," said Lieutenant Thomas, an admirable officer, who was Adjutant of Captain Macleod's battalion, "that cannot be, the drummers knowing their duty too well. However," continued he, "for your satisfaction, I will render any mistake impossible," and calling for pen, ink, and paper he wrote down precisely what the Major had to do, saying, "I, Sir, will attend you, and I'll answer for it no Commander-in-Chief could go through the ceremony better than you will." This created much mirth, Major Russell insisting that the same party should dine with him the next day to congratulate or censure him according to his deserts. We accordingly met, when the Major received the congratulations of the military men upon *the able manner in which he had performed his duties*. Never did a more convivial or merrier set get together than we were.

Towards the end of the year Mr. John Shaw arrived in Calcutta; he was a young man of high reputation as a scholar and lawyer, and being connected with the family of Mr. Davies, the Advocate-General, the latter gentleman received him as his guest. Contrary to expectation, Mr. William Burke again came to Bengal, and during his stay we were as familiar and friendly as we had ever been.

In November William Burroughs, Esquire, also a barrister, come out to practise in his profession, arrived, bringing with him letters from my father and sisters, to whom he was well known. He appeared, from the manner in which they mentioned him, to be a favourite. My sister Ann particularly expressed her wish that I would shew him every attention in my power. My father, too, spoke of him in terms highly complimentary : he observed that he was a gentleman who had pleaded with ability and considerable success at the Irish Bar, had married a young lady of beauty and merit, in right of whom he became possessed of a valuable estate, and of which he remained the possessor near twenty years when a new claimant to the property started up, instituted a suit at law for the recovery thereof, and after much litigation was finally successful, whereby Mr. Burroughs was reduced from affluence to merely what he made in his profession, the evil being increased by the heavy sum he was obliged to expend in carrying on the contest which involved him so deeply in debt that he was under the necessity of secreting himself to avoid a prison, so left Ireland and came over to England, where he resided under a feigned name.

Through the kindness of my father and other friends, Mr. Burroughs was enabled to make a small provision for his deserted wife and children and to equip himself for the East Indies, where he was desirous of trying his fortune. It not being the season of the Company's ships sailing he went across the Channel to L'Orient, at which place he engaged a passage on board a French East Indiaman ; very fortunately for him he met two other English gentlemen who had gone to France for the same purpose as he did, and took their passages in the same ship : these were Mr. Charles Purling, an old Civil servant upon the Bengal establishment, and Mr. John Palmer, a son of my esteemed friend, Major William Palmer. After a short and pleasant voyage they arrived safely at Pondicherry, the principal French Settlement on the coast of Coromandel, where upon landing Mr. Purling alone, whose rank had been ascertained, was treated with the utmost respect and attention. The Governor invited him to reside at his house, and several splendid entertainments were made for him, while on the contrary Messrs. Burroughs and Palmer were wholly neglected, or if mentioned at all it was by the contemptible title of "*Les Gens de petits Moyens*," in order to distinguish them from their more dignified countryman Purling ; this greatly hurt their pride and vexed them, but they were without remedy.

I found Mr. Burroughs a lively, sensible,' shrewd man, appearing to possess sound judgment, and a perfect scholar, at that time mild and unassuming. Such a man I felt happy to treat with every degree of kindness and attention in my power ; for several months after his arrival at Calcutta he took no step whatsoever, whether material or immaterial, without previously consulting me. One day, chatting over the business of the Court and discussing the characters of the different practitioners, he laughingly observed that since his arrival he had heard of nothing but the transcendent abilities, the wonderful acuteness and talent of Mr. Davies, the Advocate-General, who was said to monopolise all the business of the Court, but, continued he, this surprising genius cannot be on both sides at once, and certainly I shall not have the least objection to meet him in the field, and try what my, perhaps, weak exertions can do against him. I liked this spirit in him, and upon his enquiring how Mr. Davies had obtained the degree of weight he possessed, I gave him all particulars I knew.

Mr. Burroughs candidly informed me of the precise state of his affairs and the circumstances under which he had left England, expressing himself very gratefully for the extraordinary kindness my father had shewn him in the time of his distress ; that, situated as he was, his inclination and attachment to his family equally induced him to save every sixpence that was possible : that should he be successful in his profession, he was resolved not to expend one rupee more than was unavoidable. To this I answered that, praiseworthy as such an intention certainly was, yet the nature of the climate and the execution of the duties of a laborious profession made it indispensably requisite to have certain comforts, or what perhaps might be by some persons deemed luxury, for the preservation of health : such as a good habitation in an open, airy part of the town, a saddle-horse for the sake of exercise, and above all other things never to drink bad wine. To all this he objected, saying the smallest house he could procure would suffice, horses he would have nothing to do with nor any expensive European liquors. In spite of my strongest remonstrances, he hired a wretched little hovel in a narrow, dirty back lane, furnishing it with a bed and a few chairs and a table. But notwithstanding so miserable, so parsimonious an outset, I lived to see this very man the most ostentatious and in some instances the most extravagantly expensive man in Bengal, his manners altering as much as his mode of living ; from being the most humble he became insolent, overbearing and arrogant, so as to be universally despised and detested.

# CHAPTER XXVI

UPHOLDING THE RAJAH OF TRAVANCORE.
COMMODORE CORNWALLIS AND THE ANDAMANS.
SIR PAUL JODDREL AND MISS CUMMINGS

IN the first term of the year 1790, I had a question of considerable importance and agitation in Court. It was a matter of account between an eminent Mogul merchant, named Hadjee Mahattee, and his agent, a European, the merchant accusing the said agent with having committed a variety of frauds and having cheated him to an amount of £50,000, which sum he sought to recover ; the agent denied the charge *in toto*, and to law they went with mutual acrimony and vehemence. I was the solicitor for Hadjee Mahattee, Mr. William Dunkin his leading counsel, Mr. Davies being engaged on the part of the European agent. We filed a Bill in Equity for discovery and an account, to which the defendant demurred, and it was this demurrer that stood for argument soon after Mr. Burroughs' commencing business in the Supreme Court. I was perfectly aware that Mr. Advocate-General felt confident of success and that he should establish his demurrer ; I laid the whole of the papers before Mr. Burroughs, with a fee of fifty gold mohurs, the largeness of which was an agreeable surprize, and made him sit down to the consideration of the case with the most earnest attention. At the end of a week, during which my client and myself had been often with him consulting upon the merits, he became quite master of the subject and told me he had not the least doubt but that he should be able to support the Bill, and compel the defendant to account, notwithstanding the brilliant talents of his adversary, Mr. Davies, which had been so thundered in his ears, and to the determined partiality and well-known prejudice of the Acting Chief Justice.

355

The demurrer being called on the Advocate-General in support thereof spoke with such force that the auditors one and all thought there must be an end of the complainant's Bill. Mr. Burroughs then rose, and in an elegant speech, delivered with great fluency and in the most correct language, faced the subject in a totally different view to what the defendant's counsel had done, commenting upon the various circumstances of the case with a clearness and perspicuity that delighted every person that heard him, except those directly interested upon the occasion. In a few minutes after he had begun to speak, I perceived that Mr. Davies did not feel himself so secure of success as he had previously expressed himself. My idea upon this was corroborated by his calling me and desiring I would instantly retain Mr. Burroughs for Breroo Dutt, who had a cause of great magnitude depending, I being his Attorney, observing also that he (Mr. Burroughs) was a man of superior ability. In half an hour more he expressed a similar wish respecting another client of mine, and before Mr. Burroughs finished he (Mr. Davies) desired Mr. Turner, my partner, to retain Mr. Burroughs in every cause in my office, wherein he (Davies) engaged for my clients, adding "That man will, I see, give me more trouble than the rest of the Bar united."

Mr. Burroughs proved successful, the demurrer being overruled. The new Advocate was highly complimented by both the Bench and the Bar on the eloquence as well as legal knowledge he had displayed. This commencement was, as he afterwards frequently declared, the foundation of his fortune. During three following days his study was filled with a succession of natives of rank and of attornies, all pouring in retainers, both special and general, to such an extent that he exultingly produced his book of fees whereby he shewed me that he had already received upwards of fifteen hundred gold mohurs. I never beheld anything equal to his joy and the expressions of eternal gratitude he used to me for thus early affording him an opportunity of publicly shewing his professional talent ; he professed himself to have been raised from the borders of despair to the very pinnacle of happiness entirely through me. While I remained with him he wrote to an Agency house to send him a remittance to England of one thousand guineas, which having received he again turned to me with tears starting into his eyes, and, taking my hand impressively, said : " All I possess in the world I am indebted to your friendship for, nor can I ever sufficiently make my acknowledgment ; I should have felt supremely blessed in the idea of being able to do as much as this for my family (pointing to the bills of exchange upon the table) at the end of twelve months instead of in a few days only after my arrival." I sincerely congratulated him, observing there could be no doubt of his future success ; but that in order to ensure a stock of health, so as to enable him to bear the fatigue both of body and mind in executing the duties of his profession, he must necessarily relax a little occasionally, and that he must get into a better house, purchase horses, a carriage, etc. To this he civilly replied that he had already found my opinion and advice so advantageous that selfish motives would induce him in future to follow it whenever I kindly gave it. So elated was he that he soon went from one extreme to the other, became intoxicated with his good fortune, proving how difficult a thing it is to bear success with moderation.

I derived much amusement from daily superintending the progress of my new house, in the building and completing of which Mr. Robertson, the proprietor, neither spared his own attention nor his cash, the bricklayers' and carpenters' materials all being of the best.

I had the pleasure to receive a letter from Mr. William Dunkin, written during his stay at St. Helena, at which island he was in perfect health, but said they had rather a long passage from Bengal to it.

In March, 1790, my new mansion being finished and very handsome, I removed into it. I furnished it in such a style as gained universal approbation and acquired me the reputation of possessing great taste. The principal apartments were ornamented with some immense looking-glasses, also with a number of beautiful pictures and prints, forming altogether a choice and valuable collection. The expence was enormous, but as I looked only to pleasant times, having no idea I should ever be able to lay up a fortune, I was indifferent about the price of things, purchasing every article I felt any inclination for. When completed my house was pronounced to be the most elegantly fitted up of any in Calcutta, and, in fact, there was no one like it. Some of my facetious acquaintances christened it " Hickey's picture and print warehouse."

I now felt another deprivation consequent on such a fluctuating society as Calcutta. This was the departure of Dr. Allen, who tempted by the prospect of great personal advantage was induced to leave the Presidency to settle at Dacca. His attentions to me as a physician had been unremitting. He had studied my constitution critically, and although he could not eradicate the complaints under which I suffered, he considerably lessened them, ascertaining, too, some points of importance, one of which was that mercury, no matter how prepared, always proved injurious if taken inwardly ; also that all powerful operating drugs did me harm. He therefore substituted a mixture, consisting of senna, manna, cream of tartar, and two or three other trifling ingredients that accorded better with my stomach and intestines than any medicine I had before taken, and which I continued to use successfully until my return to England.

I found very material advantage from occasional excursions from Calcutta, and frequently spent two or three days at a beautiful spot about thirteen miles from the Presidency, called Baraset, where Mr. Yates, a keen old sportsman who was well known upon the turf at Newmarket and elsewhere, had a delightful country seat, and where I was always sure of meeting a pleasant society ; the only drawback to these visits was the host's great love of wine, which he drank to excess, daily committing a debauch. Though as correct and well-bred a gentleman as ever lived when sober, in his cups he was far otherwise, being then petulant, irascible, and disposed to be quarrelsome. Nothing excited his ire more than refusing to follow his example by swallowing enormous quantities of wine ; I, however, generally contrived to steal off at a reasonable hour, and being considered an invalid the landlord would not molest me ; whereas if any other guest skulked or attempted to make his escape from the room Mr. Yates made a point of ferreting him out of his hiding-place and drenching him with penalty bumpers.

Mr. Yates was a Gloucestershire man, possessing a handsome estate in that county which he run out, and then like many undone heroes took refuge in the plains of Hindustan, being at that period at least forty-five years of age. In order to get to India, with the permission of the Court of Directors he obtained the rank of a cadet in their military service: Mr. Wheler, a member of the Supreme Council and at the time of Mr. Yates's arrival in Bengal, Vice-President, Mr. Hastings, the Governor-General, up the country upon business of importance, being acquainted with Mr. Yates's family and desirous of serving him, appointed him his aide-de-camp, and made him Persian translator to Government, he not knowing a single word of the language. From the emoluments of those two situations he saved during the period he held them upwards of twenty thousand sicca rupees.

The intense heat of the month of May this year proved more hostile to me than usual, having more violent spasmodic attacks than I had ever experienced. Dr. Hare, who had occasionally attended me with Dr. Allen for the two preceding years, became my sole physician, for I found no benefit from multiplicity of opinions. One day that I thought myself dying I sent for Dr. Hare who, after the common form of pulse feeling and asking various questions, said he would order me some medicine, for which purpose he called for writing apparatus. I then told him I had for some time been used to taking a prescription of Dr. Allen's, which answered every purpose and agreed perfectly well, neither producing sickness nor any disagreeable effect. Upon his desiring to know what this prescription was, I produced the original, whereupon he said, "Then by all means continue to take it. From seeing what it consists of,

I should have imagined it could not have answered the intended purpose, it appearing to me to be only fit for a child." Those ingredients I continued to take with every advantage until I left India, and occasionally whilst upon the voyage to Europe.

Tippoo Sultaun, son and successor to Hyder Ali, and a no less inveterate enemy to the English than his father had been, having wantonly and unprovokedly attacked the Rajah of Travancore's territories, as was conjectured merely because the Rajah was the steadfast friend and faithful ally of Great Britain, the Supreme Government of India determined to uphold the Rajah, and accordingly issued orders to the Governor and Council of Madras to send troops to his assistance ; but Mr. Holland, who then presided, appearing averse to do as directed, and the Governor-General entertaining some doubt of his integrity, his lordship determined to proceed to the coast, there to take the command of the Army upon himself, for which purpose everything was put in train, and he was upon the eve of departure when a dispatch reached Calcutta announcing the arrival of His Majesty's frigate, the *Vestal*, which vessel brought out the nomination of Sir William Meadows to the Government of Madras. Whereupon, Lord Cornwallis, knowing he might rely upon that gallant and experienced officer's executing any orders of his, relinquished the intention of going himself, and wrote to say what his objects were, to Sir William, at the same time informing him that men, money and stores should be furnished from Bengal. A large detachment, consisting of three companies of artillery with two of His Majesty's regiments, were accordingly embarked for the coast of Coromandel forthwith, and six battalions of native troops were likewise ordered to get ready with all dispatch for the same destination by land, the sepoys in those days not having conquered their religious prejudices so far as to consent to go on board ship as they have since often done, and that for considerable distances, which has proved highly advantageous to the East India Company. The Sepoy corps were to be under the command of Lieutenant-Colonel Cockerell, an officer of great judgment and experience, my friend, Major Russell, being second in command.

The *Vestal* brought us the first account of that most extraordinary and, as it has fatally turned out, dreadful and ever to be lamented event the French Revolution, the evils of which now seem to portend the utter ruin of the whole Continent of Europe, and, it is to be apprehended, ultimately of the island of Great Britain.

Commodore Cornwallis, Commander-in-Chief of the British Squadron in the Eastern Seas and brother to the noble Governor-General, though very unlike him both in person and manner, came to visit his lordship. The commodore was a living Trunnion, but more of a brute than Smollet made his hero. After a sojourn of three weeks in Calcutta, during which he abused or found fault with everybody and everything, he took his departure for a country better adapted to his rough temper and disposition, that is the Andamans, a cluster of islands situated in the Bay of Bengal, off the eastern coast of Pegu and Siam, and said to be inhabited by a race of anthropophagi or cannibals, described by some historian as being utterly incapable of civilization. Amongst this savage people did the valiant Commodore Cornwallis (and valiant he indisputably was, of which he gave abundant proofs) prefer living to that of a polished society of an English settlement. In common justice to him, however, let me add, that in his apparently strange attachment he had a particular object in view, that of forming a colony upon the grand Andaman, which island was well known to abound with forest timber of a fine quality and prodigious size equally well suited for ships or buildings. The grand Andaman had also one of the noblest and most spacious harbours in the world. In consequence of Commodore Cornwallis's strong recommendations, and the favourable representations he continually made respecting the national advantages to be derived from securing a permanent footing upon the Andamans, the Government of Bengal at last resolved to establish a settlement upon at least one of them, to execute which Major Alexander Kyd, an able Engineer officer, with the requisite assistants, artificers, a body of troops and stores of every kind, were dispatched from Fort William ; fortifications were constructed and other public buildings erected, everything going on as well as could be wished, when a stop was suddenly put to any further proceedings by orders from England, the Court of Directors having come to a resolution that Pulo Penang, now called Prince of Wales's Island, situate nearly at the mouth of the Straits of Malacca, should be the place for establishing a settlement upon ; in which determination every man of science and capable of judging upon such a subject pronounced the Leadenhall folks egregiously wrong ; their fiat, however, being irrevocable, Commodore Cornwallis's favourite plan was abandoned, the works and buildings which had been constructed upon the Andaman were demolished, lest any other European Power should land upon the island and be benefited from seeing such things ready prepared to fix themselves there ; thus was an enormous sum of money absolutely thrown away.

During Commodore Cornwallis's residence at Calcutta, I became acquainted with two very fine fellows belonging to his fleet, Captain Smith, an old post-captain, who commanded the *Perseverance*, a noble frigate, and Captain Delgarno, of the *Atlanta*, sloop of war. The latter, who was without exception the most drunken varlet I ever saw, was a prodigious favourite of the Commodore's, who had made him a master and a commander, intending further promotion for him when opportunity offered. For these naval gentlemen I made several jovial parties during their sojourn among us, always giving them champagne and claret to their hearts' content. At one of the dinners I gave them Mr. William Burke, Mr. Royds, Captains Rees, Smith and Gray, the three latter all commanding Indiamen, Captain Buchanan of the *John* packet, on board of which Mr. Royds had recently come passenger from England, Mr. Burt, chief officer of the *Dublin*, and others were present. After a sad debauch, about three o'clock in the morning, my party being then reduced to half a dozen, a variety of cold meats, grills, etc., which we had been eating of remaining upon the table, two favourite dogs of mine came to me when, as was my custom, I began to feed them with cold roast beef, which raised the ire of Mr. Burt, who abused me exceedingly, swearing I must be deficient in breeding or I should never have attempted to feed a parcel of damned dirty curs in the presence of gentlemen, and by God he would remain no longer in the house of a man guilty of so unpardonable a rudeness, and he instantly rose from his seat and staggered downstairs. Beastly drunk as he certainly was, and, indeed, I was myself far gone, I could not but be surprized at so strange and unexpected an attack upon me. But as I made great allowances to the state he was in and never was quarrelsome myself when in my cups, I was easily persuaded by Captains Smith and Delgarno not to take any serious notice of what Mr. Burt had said.

The day after it had occurred I was talking over the unaccountable violence of Mr. Burt with Captain Buchanan, when Mr. Burt was announced, who, accompanied by Captain Smith of the *Dublin*, had called to make every possible atonement for his abominable and outrageous conduct of the preceding night. Never did I behold a man more truly hurt and distressed than he appeared to be. It seems he had no recollection whatsoever of the circumstance, but when Captain Smith asked him about it upon first seeing him that morning, and telling him how shamefully he had abused me, he felt quite ashamed of himself, and could not rest until Captain Smith agreed to accompany him to my house, there to offer any sort of apology I might require. Mr. Burt and I shook hands, he expressing his grateful sense of my good-nature in so readily forgiving his improper behaviour.

Captain Delgarno was upon all occasions a zealous defender of Commodore Cornwallis, insisting that a great part of his roughness of address and manners was assumed, his natural disposition being far otherwise ; that the cause of the frequent quarrels he was said to be involved in arose from the want of consideration in the officers by either omitting to carry into effect the orders he gave, or impatiently replying to his complaints of their inattention. " I am certain (said Captain Delgarno) " that were I to be in the same ship there never would be an angry word passed between us, and if left to my own choice, I would prefer being his captain to any other man in the Navy." Captain Delgarno, however, verified the remark of its being much easier to preach than to practise, for shortly after he made the above speech he gained the rank of post and had command of the flagship given him, Commodore Cornwallis having then attained the rank of Admiral. Only three days did he serve under the man he had professed to know so well how to manage, ere a violent dispute occurred, in which Captain Delgarno, instead of yielding a jot to his commanding officer, strenuously opposed him, in consequence of which from being the warmest friends they became inveterate enemies, so much so as within the short period of two months to induce Captain Delgarno to resign the command of the Admiral's ship and take his passage to Europe on board an East Indiaman.

Charles Sealy, Esquire, a barrister of the Supreme Court, a man universally respected, who had been many years in Bengal, where he married one of the daughters of Captain Cudbert Thornhill, the master attendant, by which lady he had a numerous family, having the grievous misfortune to lose her after a short illness, became disgusted with the place, resolving to quit the country and go to pass the remainder of his life amidst his own relatives in England, where several of his children had already been sent for education.

All who knew Mr. Sealy were surprized at his determination of leaving India, for although he had acquired an ample fortune the habits and customs of the country seemed to have become congenial to him and he appeared so attached to them as to make his connections fear he would not be happy under the change to a European mode of life. He, however, thought otherwise, made the trial and fell a martyr to it, as he died whilst upon a journey to Salisbury, his native town, a few months after his arrival in England.

Just after my friend Mr. Sealy's departure, I had a trial to come on in which I felt a peculiar interest. My client, who was the defendant, was the editor of a Calcutta newspaper, the plaintiff being Sir Paul Joddrel, physician to His Highness the Nabob of Arcot. Sir Paul resided with his family at Fort St. George ; it consisted of himself, Lady Joddrel, a young lady of the name of Cummings, whom he introduced to everybody as his niece, and who appeared in all parties the companion of Lady Joddrel, and a female child who was supposed to be Sir Paul's by Lady Joddrel. After residing upwards of two years at Madras, mixing with the best society of the place, Captain Carlisle of the Artillery paid his addresses to Miss Cummings, and all matters were in fair train for their wedding, when an awkward report got about the Settlement that this Miss Cummings instead of being Sir Paul Joddrel's niece was, and long had been, his mistress, with which curious fact Lady Joddrel was well acquainted, and that the child which was supposed to have been Lady Joddrel's, was Sir Paul's by Miss Cummings. An intimate friend of Captain Carlisle's having heard this extraordinary rumour, thought it his duty to communicate the same to Captain Carlisle, in order to put him on his guard and afford him an opportunity of making some enquiries as to the truth or falsity of so uncommon a story. Captain Carlisle thereupon endeavoured to trace the report to its source, when he learnt that the circumstances had been first promulgated by a gentleman recently arrived from England, where he said the matter was publicly discussed and generally believed.

Miss Cummings was at this time upon a visit to my friend Mrs. Cairnes, the Major's widow, which lady upon the facts coming to her ears at once put the question to her guest, and to her great surprize Miss Cummings without the least hesitation acknowledged both charges were but too true. A meeting of the patrons and patronesses of the Female Orphan Society, of which Sir Paul was an active member, was thereupon summoned, and the unworthy knight's name immediately expunged from the list. The managers of the Public Rooms following the example thus set determined to refuse Sir Paul and his family all access thereto, to effect which they caused advertisements to be published in a weekly paper called the *Madras Courier*, stating the proceedings of the Asylum and Public Rooms managers, and the reason. These advertisements were afterwards copied into the Calcutta public prints, and my unfortunate client not content with merely copying them chose to animadvert in very severe terms not only upon the shocking depravity and immorality of such conduct, but the unparalleled impudence of a man who felt conscious of committing such enormity obtruding himself and his iniquitous associates into correct modest families.

For these observations and comments Sir Paul attacked the Bengal editor, although he had never attempted to do so by the Madras printer or editor, both of whom were well known, contenting himself as to them with violent threats of a prosecution, but instead of carrying such threats into execution, he and his precious family suddenly removed themselves bag and baggage to the French Settlement of Pondicherry, where they were out of the reach of the process of British Courts of Justice.

I had the good luck to secure the assistance of Mr. Burroughs for my client, actually meeting the plaintiff's attorney going upstairs to Mr. Burroughs' house to retain him as I was descending from having already done so. From the peculiarity of our case we could not think of justifying, neither had we any other evidence to give than that the obnoxious language had first appeared in the *Madras Courier*, and that the account was generally believed at that Presidency and publicly discussed, in consequence of which Sir Paul had abandoned his post and fled to a foreign settlement.

Mr. Davies, as counsel for the plaintiff, was very bitter in his statement. Anticipating what the defence would be he met the same with equally ingenious and powerful arguments, contending that the defendant shewed his malignant disposition by the grossness of his comment upon the conduct of an individual whom the liberality of the laws of his country considered innocent until otherwise determined by a jury. Mr. Burroughs made the most of our case, urging with much force and eloquence all the favourable circumstances. Sir Robert Chambers, in pronouncing judgment, observed that had the defendant contented himself with simply copying what had been published in the *Madras Courier* he should not have considered the plaintiff entitled to anything more than nominal damages, but the remarks and comments he had voluntarily and unnecessarily chosen to insert in his paper, in addition to the Madras advertisement, materially altered the case, and no legal justification thereof having been pleaded, the plaintiff must have a judgment. They therefore awarded Sir Paul Joddrel the sum of fifty rupees as damages ! Mr. William Burke was a strenuous and violent advocate of Sir Paul Joddrel, swearing the whole story was a base and infamous calumny, a fabrication, a conspiracy, a mere party affair, which the abandoned and profligate niece had from interested motives joined in, basely conspiring to stigmatise and destroy the character of a respectable and worthy member of society ! An unanswerable question did away with Mr. Burke's opinion. "Why then did Sir Paul secretly abscond and seek protection under a foreign flag ? If innocent, why not manly meet the charge which, if void of foundation, could easily have been refuted, at least so far as concerned the birth of the child, which he represented to be Lady Joddrel's ? "

# CHAPTER XXVII

### PURCHASING A GRAVE NEAR CHARLOTTE'S.
### A STRANGE STORY OF A CHAPLAIN
### AND AN UNDERTAKER

CAPTAIN Smith of the *Perseverance* brought Sir Richard Strahan, who commanded the *Vestal* frigate, recently arrived from Europe, to my house to introduce him to me, and I had the pleasure of his acquaintance during his stay in Bengal. He frequently did me the honour to dine with me. The second time of his doing so he brought with him a young midshipman belonging to his ship, Lord William Townshend, son to the Marquis of Townshend, about thirteen or fourteen years of age, who appeared to be a fine, pickle boy. He got excessively drunk, at which Sir Richard was highly offended, and he gave his little protégé a severe lecture, which appeared to be quite thrown away. Upon my inviting them again to dinner, Sir Richard only consented to his noble midshipman's being of the party upon my promising not to ask him to drink any wine, and he placed the young sprig of nobility next to himself at table in order to keep a watchful eye over him, a thing he knew to be necessary to prevent his committing excess.

This boy from infancy had a tendency to insanity. Some years after his being in India, he was travelling in England with one of his brothers in a post-chaise, when their conversation was whether life under all the evils that attended it was worth keeping ? After a long discussion they were both of opinion that the evils so greatly outweighed the blessings that existence was not desirable : they therefore immediately determined to withdraw themselves from it, and taking out a pair of pistols they had in the carriage they intended each to shoot the other, or each to shoot himself.

It was never ascertained which was the fact ; one shot took effect, proving fatal instantaneously, I do not recollect upon which of them ; the other pistol missed fire. The postilion stopping upon hearing the report, got off his horse and opening the door of the carriage found one of them fallen off his seat, weltering in his blood, the other sitting very composedly. Upon being asked what had happened to his brother he made no answer, nor would he ever state a single circumstance relative to the transaction. He has ever since been confined as a lunatic.

My health now became worse than ever, myself and friends thinking I was not long for this world. In a particularly violent spasmodic attack Dr. Hare gave me a dose of laudanum which although I swallowed as directed I did without any idea of its affording me relief, observing that I knew what it was from the smell and was certain it would rather increase than lessen my torment, laudanum having invariably done so. To this the doctor answered, " Possibly that may hitherto have been the case ; but my laudanum is very differently prepared to what you have been used to take and I am quite clear will be of service." This was about eleven o'clock at night. The doctor sat by my bedside to watch the effect of the medicine. For about an hour the pain decreased when the spasms returned with increased violence. He therefore administered a second dose, but without advantage. At half-past one in the morning he was summoned by a lady in a dangerous labour ; he therefore gave me another draught, desiring that if that did not procure me ease that I would at the end of another hour drink a large glass of brandy, as he could not venture to prescribe any more opium. Within the time limited I fell into a profound sleep, continuing so until late in the morning : upon opening my eyes, I saw Dr. Hare just entering the room. The spasms in my stomach ceased, but I felt dreadfully sick and faint with a severe headache. These complaints the doctor assured me would soon subside, being occasioned by the extraordinary quantity of laudanum, " For," said he, " in somewhat less than three hours you

III.—2 B

took two hundred and twenty drops ; your situation was extremely critical and required a powerful hand.  The fact is there is something peculiar in your stomach, for although strong medicines do not in general accord with it, there is undoubtedly an exception with regard to opium or laudanum, of which from the nature of your constitution large doses are requisite to produce a good effect, and it is evident to me the reason that you have hitherto found no benefit from that excellent remedy is that you never until now have taken a sufficient quantity.  Drs. Allen and Wilson, like the other practitioners of physic in Bengal, are too much afraid of that searching and operative drug :  they have been in the habit of prescribing twenty-five or thirty drops at most as a dose, whereas you require greatly more, and I gave you in the last instance one hundred drops, followed by eighty and lastly forty, making the whole two hundred and twenty, and be assured that in these spasmodic attacks you are so frequently assailed with, nothing less than one hundred drops will answer the desired purpose."  Dr. Hare was certainly right.

Notwithstanding that I was so often so dangerously ill, when not in actual pain my spirits were excellent.  Fortunately the violence of the spasms seldom continued above eight or ten hours ;  in my own mind, I had no doubt but that they would ultimately carry me out of the world, and that my bones would lay in the burial-ground of Calcutta, in which case I was desirous they should be deposited near those of my departed and much-loved Charlotte.  Calling one day at Stuart's, the coach-maker, to look at a new Europe-built chariot I had just purchased of him, I there met his partner, Maudsley, who besides being a coach-maker managed and conducted the very lucrative business of undertaker ;  of him I enquired whether it was possible to secure a particular spot in the burying-ground for that I found the graves multiplying so rapidly that the part in which Mrs. Hickey's remains lay was nearly surrounded quite close, and I was anxious, in the event of my dying in Bengal, to be buried near her.  To my enquiry Mr. Maudsley replied,

" Certainly, Sir, you may ; I have already prepared several vaults for families. It is by no means an uncommon thing." I thereupon desired him to do whatever was needful. About a fortnight afterwards he called at my house to say that he had executed my order, and he presented me with the following bill :

WILLIAM HICKEY, ESQUIRE. TO THOMAS MAUDSLEY.

*Dr.* 1790, June 19th.

To a grave built in the burial-ground at Chouringee ⎫ Sicca
of bricks and best stone chunam and materials ⎬ Rs.
—extent 10 ft. by 6 ft. 6 ins. and 7 ft. deep .. ⎭ 100.

Contents received. THOMAS MAUDSLEY.

This bill was accompanied by the following letter :

" SIR, I take the liberty of sending the bill for the grave you ordered, and beg leave to remark, Sir, that if you should have the misfortune to use it there would be a further sum of 100 rupees sicca to be paid to the clergymen of the Presidency for permission fees. I am, Sir,

Your most obedient Servant,

THOMAS MAUDSLEY, 1st July, 1790."

This permission fee, as the undertaker called it, had been just then for the first time demanded and generally considered an extortion, from the chaplains' salaries and perquisites being all fixed and settled by the Court of Directors. But as with respect to me it was a post-obit demand, as I conceived, I took no notice of Maudsley's letter. The priest, however, being resolved not to relinquish his rights, on the 7th day of August following caused his coadjutor, the undertaker, again to address me thus :

" SIR, By desire of the Reverend Mr. Blanchard, I take the liberty of sending the accompanying bill. I am, Sir,

Your obedient Servant,

THOMAS MAUDSLEY. 7th August, '90."

The bill was in these words :

"WILLIAM HICKEY, ESQUIRE.   *Dr.*   1790, June 19th.

To fees due to the Chaplains of the Presidency for their permission to make a vault of brick and mortar in the burial-ground of Chouringee—sicca rupees fifty.

N.B.—In the event of its being used as a foundation of a monument a further charge of fifty rupees will be then made.

Calcutta, the 6th August, 1790.

Received payment:     S. BLANCHARD."

This demand struck me as so blackguard and disgraceful in a clergyman to make, independent of its being unjust, that I had at first determined to resist the payment, but upon further consideration I did not think it was worth contending about, and therefore sent the fifty rupees required.  I, however, mentioned the circumstance to several of my friends, who all agreed in pronouncing it very disreputable in Mr. Blanchard, as a professional man, to act in such a manner.

A history now came out that made the indecorous conduct of the senior chaplain most palpable and glaring.  Maudsley, whom I have already mentioned, had purchased the situation of undertaker from a man of the name of Palmer, to whom he paid a large sum of money as a consideration for relinquishing the business in his favour.  Palmer was a great speculator and lost considerably by some shipping concern he had engaged in.  Upon his quitting the undertaker's line, the Reverend Mr. Blanchard called upon him for payment of a bond he held of his for five thousand sicca rupees.  Palmer insisted that by various documents in his possession he could shew that this bond had been more than fully liquidated, both principal and interest, by sums he, Mr. Blanchard, had at different times received which belonged to the joint stock, and, therefore, instead of requiring further payment he ought to deliver up the said bond to be cancelled.  He also positively asserted that upon a fair settlement of account a balance of several thousand rupees would appear to be due to him (Palmer). This statement the parson would not listen to, threatening, if the amount he claimed to be due upon the bond was not forthwith discharged, he would put it into the hands of his attorney for recovery. Palmer still resisting, Blanchard swore to the debt and caused him to be arrested ; Palmer put in bail for the action and immediately filed a Bill in Equity against the plaintiff at law, in which bill he stated a most disgraceful and iniquitous sort of partnership to subsist between him as undertaker and Blanchard as head chaplain of the Presidency, under which partnership Palmer, in consideration of Blanchard's empowering him alone to perform funerals, thereby making a monopoly in his favour, engaged to allow him, Blanchard, twenty per cent from the gross amount of all his bills for funerals.

In Palmer's Bill in Equity was also stated several letters of Blanchard to him of a most degrading nature. From one of these the following paragraph was extracted : and stated verbatim. "A bill of yours for the funeral of Mr. —— has been brought to me by the agency house of Fairlie & Co., with a complaint from them of its exorbitancy (and most exorbitant no doubt it is). What a blockhead you are ; how often over and over again have I desired you to be upon your guard, and am now obliged from your unceasing and inveterate stupidity again to desire you, cautiously to observe who the parties are that employ you, and from whom you expect payment, more especially to attend to the connection they stand in with respect to the deceased ; husbands and wives, fathers, mothers, affectionate children, and those kind of near and dear relations are the only proper objects to clap on upon, and you may always do it with perfect security ; too much cast down and afflicted by the death of those they love and were sincerely attached to, to examine or dispute the items of an undertaker's bill, no matter how much out of all bounds they may in their own minds pronounce it, they nevertheless order payment. But merely common, indifferent friends, and above all, your correct cold-blooded attorneys or agents who care neither for the living nor the dead are the sort of persons who will scrutinise the bill for a funeral more closely than they would that of a notorious thieving Bengallee tailor. With such sort of folks you ought to be extremely cautious in your charges. In making out the bill now before me you must either have been drunk or mad ; *seventy-two scarves and hat-bands !* To follow the corpse of a poor cabinet maker, and *five gold mohurs* with the use of the best black velvet pall ! What superlative folly ! These items are particularly and severely commented upon by the immaculate Fairlie. I have struck out sixty of the scarves and hat-bands, and the five gold mohurs altogether. Do, I beg you, Palmer, show a little more common-sense and mind what you are about. This foolish system, if persisted in, will not only cause ruin for yourself but to everybody that has to do with you." In another letter he says to the same Mr. Palmer, " You're egregiously mistaken in supposing that our profitable season is the hot weather or the Rajus; that is by no means the fact, November and the early part of December for me : that is the period of our harvest. Look over your memorandum book and you will easily ascertain that I am right, and find that during those two months there are at least three deaths for every one at any other part of the year."

Mr. Davies, the Advocate-General, was engaged as counsel for Palmer, the draft of the bill was therefore laid before him to revise and settle. That learned advocate having heard, in public conversation, of the strange demand made upon me for " permission fees," he requested to see the papers respecting it, which I shewed him, and he declared he would make use of them in the progress as evidence of the systematic plan of robbery and meanness practised by the head chaplain of the Settlement. But the priest had too much good sense to make a production of such documents necessary, for the very moment after he had perused his office copy of this remarkable Bill of Equity, finding himself in so tender and so vulnerable a point, and how impracticable it was to answer the charges satisfactorily, he at once and without hesitation, cried "peccavi," humbly entreating that his adversary would consent to an amicable adjustment of all differences, for which purpose he offered a carte blanche as to terms. Palmer thereupon required that Blanchard should cancel and deliver up the bond for five thousand sicca rupees which he had arrested him for, that he, Blanchard, should discontinue the said action at law and pay the full costs on both sides ; that he should likewise apply to have his, Palmer's, Bill in Equity dismissed upon the terms of his, Blanchard's, paying the full costs incurred by Palmer, to which Palmer would consent by his counsel, and finally that Blanchard should execute a general release to Palmer.

These conditions, severe as they were, Blanchard thankfully acceded to and fulfilled without loss of time, as he would willingly have done had Palmer even required him to pay him twenty thousand rupees as hush money, and in so yielding he only would have acted with common prudence, for had the suit in Equity been proceeded in he must have been alike ruined in fame as in fortune, besides being dismissed with ignominy from the East India Company's service.

Upon the circumstances of a grave being dug, pursuant to my orders as hereinbefore mentioned, Mrs. Hay, wife to the Chief Secretary, exercised her pleasantry by making and propagating the following story : " That in one of those hypochondriacal fits by which I was frequently attacked, imagining as usual that I was on the verge of departing this life, I sent for the undertaker, to whom I gave directions to make everything ready for my funeral, in obedience to which Maudsley forthwith caused a grave to be dug, sending a handsome coffin with appropriate furniture to my house : but as I had previous to his arrival got rid of my melancholy, I would not receive the coffin : that in two or three days afterwards the undertaker sent in his bill, which upon my refusing to pay, an action at law was threatened against me for recovery of the amount claimed ; that after much altercation and correspondence upon the subject the matter had been compromised by my consenting to pay half the sum demanded and relinquishing all claim to the grave." The first person who mentioned the thing to me was Mr. William Burke, who said Mrs. Hay had assured him she knew it to be an undoubted fact. Having related the real circumstances to Mr. Burke, I could only join in the laugh, and give the fair lady credit for her inventive genius and facetiousness.

After such an account as the foregoing of the Reverend Mr. Blanchard it will not surprize anyone to hear that he accumulated a large fortune, with which, accompanied by a sister who was as deserving a woman as any in the world, he, in about eighteen months after the undertaker's attack, embarked for Europe.

The contest with Tippoo Sultaun becoming every day more serious and doubtful Lord Cornwallis determined to take the field in person against him, for which purpose he made preparation for proceeding to the coast of Coromandel. His lordship also expressed his wish that Mr. William Burke would accompany him in his capacity of His Majesty's Paymaster-General. Mr. Burke in consequence equipped himself for an Asiatic campaign. Having been informed that he would frequently be under the necessity of riding on horseback, an exercise he had not been in the habit of taking for many years, he thought it a proper caution to practise a little previous to his departure, and accordingly purchased a tractable animal, which being caparisoned and brought to the door for a first essay, he boldly mounted to the infinite surprize of his servants, who were all collected in a body to behold so novel an exhibition as their master in the character of an equestrian. Being firmly seated in the saddle he turned to Samby, his favourite Madras man, exultingly saying, " There, Samby, what do you think of me now ? " To which Samby answered, " I think Master certainly got up, but I think Master too much fear come to make horse gallop." " Do you," said Mr. Burke. " Then you are mistaken, you damned, impudent rascal ; so here goes," and giving the horse a stroke with his whip off he went in a smart canter round the compound, in front of the house, whereupon the whole posse of attendants set up a loud huzza !

This season deprived Calcutta of one of its principal ornaments by the departure of Mrs. Bristow for England. She was a native of the little island of St. Helena, her maiden name Wrangham ; a fine, dashing girl, not by any means a regular beauty, but an uncommonly elegant figure and person ; remarkably clever and highly accomplished. Her natural flow of spirits frequently led her into extravagancies and follies of rather too masculine a nature ; instead of seating herself like other women on horseback, she rode like a man astride, would leap over any hedge or ditch that even the most zealous sportsmen were dubious of attempting. She rode several matches and succeeded against the best and most experienced jockeys. She was likewise an excellent shot, rarely missing her bird ; understood the present fashionable science of pugilism, and would without hesitation knock a man down if he presumed to offer her the slightest insult ; in short, she stopped at nothing that met her fancy, however wild or eccentric, executing whatever she attempted with a *naïveté* and ease and elegance that was irresistible. Upon her first arrival in India she had a number of suitors, from whom she selected Mr. John Bristow, a respectable character, high in the Company's Civil Service, but plain in features and in dress. He was generally considered as possessing immense wealth, an opinion strengthened by his settling the extraordinarily large sum of £40,000 upon Miss Wrangham when he married her. At the time she left India she had by him four lovely children, the proper education of whom was her chief motive for quitting her husband and embarking for Europe. She often declared that but for that object she should prefer residing in Bengal to any other part of the world.

In the middle of this year two old acquaintances of mine arrived in Bengal in the command of East India ships. These were Captain John Pascal Larkins, with whom I had been schoolfellow at Streatham Academy, who now com-

manded the *Warren Hastings,* and Peter Douglas, third
officer of the *Plassey* when I was in her, now commanding
the *Queen.* The latter gentleman had recently been at
Madras, and from him I learnt that Mrs. Cairnes, after having engaged passage for Europe on board the *Earl of Orford,*
Captain White, for herself and children, had suddenly
relinquished her apartments in the ship and paid forfeit.
The supposed reason was her being attached to Captain
Carlisle of the Madras Artillery, the gentleman I have before
spoken of as the professed admirer of the famous Miss
Cummings. Captain Douglas, however, did not think that
was the cause, but that her continuing in India was owing
to the disputes and litigation occasioned by Sir Paul Joddrel's
strange business.

In the midst of Mr. Burke's preparations for going to the
coast he met with an alarming accident. On the outside of
his house he had erected a staircase of wood, enclosing the
same with canvas, the intention being to give the servants
access to his bedchamber and private apartments without
passing through the body of the house. The platform at the
top of the stairs Mr. Burke used for bathing. Either the
water had rotted the planks or the builder had put in un-
sound wood, for one morning just as Mr. Burke had gone
there to bathe the flooring suddenly gave way and he was
precipitated to the ground, falling nearly fifty feet. That
he was not killed upon the spot was miraculous ; he escaped
without any fracture though wretchedly bruised, which
kept him to his room five weeks. During his confinement
Mr. Prendergast, his quondam protégé, lay dangerously ill
with a diseased liver ; an abscess having formed internally ;
for several days the doctors had no hopes of saving him. It
was proposed to him, quite as a forlorn hope, that he should
undergo the dreadful operation of cutting ; which he agreed
to, and it was performed successfully. He recovered, becoming as stout as he had ever been. While given over Mr.
Burke, though labouring under great pain himself from his
accident, expressed the utmost solicitude about him, sending
regularly twice a day to enquire how he was, but the moment

he heard he was likely to recover he took no further notice, nor ever had any intercourse with him.

Upon the Madras Army's first taking the field to go against Tippoo Sultaun the Commander-in-Chief (Meadows) issued a general order that became the subject of much discussion and difference of opinion. The object, evidently, was to inspire the troops with a determination to conquer or die, as it held out the dreadful situation they would be reduced to if taken prisoners by their savage enemy who had practised the most unheard-of cruelties upon all the unhappy Europeans who had been so unfortunate as to fall into his clutches. Some persons pronounced this address " a soldier-like, manly performance, well adapted to raise the energy of the private soldier," while others declared it " a melancholy, desponding harangue, calculated to excite no other sentiment than despair in the minds of the men to whom it was addressed."

/

# CHAPTER XXVIII

## WILLIAM CANE'S LETTERS FROM FRANCE

THIS season I received, nearly at the same time though of such different dates, the three following letters from my esteemed and valuable friend, William Cane, Esquire. They gave me real concern as recording the misfortunes of as worthy a man as ever lived and to whom I felt myself under the greatest possible obligations.

"My dear friend, a hard marriage settlement, some extravagance, and Mr. Stephen Popham, have forced me to quit my country perhaps for ever. I am, however, settled in a pleasant and healthy province, where I live upon three hundred pounds a year, and might be happy could I forget I had ever been more fortunate. Mrs. Cane's attachment to me and her love of retirement diminishes much of the unhappiness I should otherwise feel on her account, but to think my poor boy is to suffer in his education for his father's imprudence, and that born to better hopes he can now have but the unsubstantial tinsel of French breeding, are thoughts that sometimes overpower me, and I declare to you, as a man that knows me well and my way of thinking, that I should long since have ceased to live, and thereby have restored affluence to my family (as annuities form the whole of my debt) had not the certainty of the desolation my death would occasion to Mrs. Cane held my hand, and forced me to exist in spite of myself. I have been in Touraine nineteen months, have changed houses—the only dear article here—three times, and am at present fixed in one, as I have already observed in all probability, for the rest of my days. It is spacious and for a French place of residence commodious, only the air, which has a free circulation under every door and through every window, much displeases and annoys Mrs. Johnson (this lady was mother to Mrs. Cane), who has accompanied us. For my own part, I believe it infinitely more wholesome than the warm parlour of Berners Street. I have a garden of two acres which supplies me very abundantly with legumes, far superior in quality to the best in the London market, and an overplus for sale which more than pays five guineas, the gardener's wages. I have a vineyard which produces on an average twenty-five hogsheads of wine annually. But, alas! it is not drinkable, at least only by peasants in its original state or else distilled. I sold my *récolte* last year for thirty-six louis, this year I am determined to make brandy of it all (five hogsheads of wine make one of Eau de Vie) and keep it until that commodity grows dear, one bad *récolte* immediately doubling the price. I have ten acres of land in tillage, which produced barley last year to the amount of thirty louis, and this season will give me wheat for a year and a quarter, and the ensuing oats for all my horses for a period of three years. I have a verger that Mrs. Cane has decorated with numbers of beautiful balsams, flowers from England and all the gaieties of a parterre; its shade is formed by standard peach trees, nectarines, greengages, etc., which together with other fruit trees round and across my vineyard I sell after retaining what is necessary to the *ménage* for twenty louis. I have a meadow the grass of which added to that of my vineyard, produces about ten louis' worth of hay, and my mulberry leaves fetch five more, making in all an hundred and one louis. I pay an hundred and five rent and the expence of tillage, vignerons, etc., amounts to about thirty-five more; consequently I sit at nearly thirty-nine guineas rent, furniture included. For the first time in my life I keep a regular debtor and creditor account, and can tell to a sou how much I expend and the return. I firmly believe had it not been for the occupation at first and the amusement at last of my farm I should have sunk under the ennui of such a change of scene. I have cows, hogs, poultry of every kind almost for nothing, that is a couple of chickens whiter and fatter than those of Brentford from friend Miles, for ten pence English. I have a commodious chaise which holds four occasionally by means of a *strapontin*, and two handsome grey horses, which, though they are not Dumpling and Beauty (two favourite phaeton horses he drove in England), serve well enough. To dress them, a saddle-horse and myself, I have a *garçon* who outscrubs Scrub a bar's length. He cuts wood and brings it into the house, washes the two parlours and hall, cleans knives and plate, goes almost every day to Tours two leagues off on foot, rides postilion, and dresses my hair infinitely better and in half the time the coxcomb, Mr. Hook (his *valet de chambre* in England) took. His wages are six guineas a year! and he is always clean, neat, and good-humoured; neither am I in any danger of losing him, as my place is reckoned to be one of *very little work*, and I give a third more wages than the natives. Perhaps you will be at a loss to comprehend the first of these assertions, unless you suppose that in general they assist the oxen at the plough. Plato, I think it is, that says the lewd will be punished in another life by a continuance of their desires without a possibility of their gratifying them. Now, as whist was one of my original sins, I find myself a little in the predicament of Plato's culprit, being compelled to play dumbee every night with Mrs. Cane and her mother. Your old friend Tyger (an immense large Newfoundland dog), though an American, does not take kindly to the French. He is grown troublesomely fond of me and with his own good-will would never leave me night or day; but as the best of friends sometimes miff, so do we, upon which occasion he retires to his bed, a soft mattress in the passage, where he patiently waits until time has blunted the edge of my choler. I have more than once heard the servants, with the utmost gravity, assert that he knows more than he ought! and a century ago I fear the faithful beast would have stood a chance of being burnt for a witch. Gip (a favourite spaniel of Mrs. Cane's) was left behind, the ladies not being able to accommodate her in travelling to Dover. As for me, I had retired some days before, for having received information that Mr. Littlekales had taken out a writ against me, I immediately went privately to Billingsgate, there got into a wherry and proceeding down the river met Johnson off Limehouse, he being at the helm of that charming little vessel that we have sailed so many leagues together in, the *Congress.* As he happened to have but few passengers, I made them exchange into my wherry, and going on board hired him to run me down to Margate. I talked to him so much about the ports of Calais and Boulogne, though apparently without any object in so doing, that he was induced to propose the traject, not in the least suspecting the real state of affairs, until I myself informed him thereof when safely housed in Dessein's parlour at Calais. The grateful, poor fellow was greatly affected at the sad reverse in my fortunes ; he, however, gave me great credit for my sang-froid as we had been becalmed two days between London and the Nore ; I offered him a guinea for himself above the stipulated sum for the cutter's hire, but no entreaties of mine could prevail on the worthy creature to accept it. I felt a pang in going by Erith more easily conceived than expressed ; to pass as a fugitive a place where I had so long resided independent and so often rode triumphant over the little billows, where I had, too, spent many of the happiest days of my life—now, alas ! to return no more—was a soul-cutting reflection.

"To avoid suspicion, I was obliged to run into danger. Just as we arrived off Gravesend, the wind died away and the flood-tide setting in we were forced to let go an anchor. It was then eight o'clock on the evening of the 12th of August, 1777. Having no provisions on board, Johnson proposed my going on shore and that he would attend me in order to purchase some. Besides, as I had got into the cutter at half-past two he knew that I could not have dined. I accordingly landed, but not thinking it prudent to go to the ' White Hart,' where you and I always took our claret, and where everybody was so well acquainted with ' Squire Cane of Erith,' I entered the every way inferior Falcon Inn. I ordered a beefsteak to be dressed, of which with difficulty

I contrived to swallow a few morsels, for my heart was too full to have any great appetite. While at my solitary and miserable meal, I heard a violent noise upon the stairs; listening in order if possible to learn the occasion, I found that two officers of justice were arrived with a determination of taking somebody. I soon came to a resolution what to do. I had my sword on, which I drew, and taking the carving-knife in my other hand placed myself behind the door, determined should they attempt to enter the room to put them both to death, and trust to the generosity of the people present to allow of my escape to the boat. Thanks to fortune, I had no occasion to put it to the trial : after passing a full half-hour behind the door in a cold sweat, more from the horrible idea of using a knife than from any consequences arising from the sword, I learned that it was some other unhappy person whom they sought who had only a few minutes before crossed the river and made his escape into Essex ; I never did, and hope I shall never again, pass such another half-hour. Had I ever entertained an idea of such moments of exquisite misery when squandering away thousands, surely I should have held my hand, and if not turned absolutely a miser, should at least have commenced an excellent system of economy. Well, if I have hitherto failed in becoming an economist, I am so now. We are four in the parlour and seven in the kitchen, that is to say, lacquey, gardener, two *femmes de chambre, une fille de chambre, cuisinière*, and *une fille pour la basse-cour ;* for dinner I have two and two, besides a handsome dessert every day : drink six hogsheads of capital old wine a year, and have spent but £550 in nineteen months, of which my horses and carriage cost forty-five, cows and hogs twelve, linen twenty, and eight hogsheads of wine now all in my cellar forty, making altogether one hundred and seventeen. I dare say you spend thrice as much, and probably don't live half so well. In one article, however, you have greatly the advantage : firing, of which, I presume, a little goes a great way, but which costs me twenty-five guineas a year.

" Nothing hurt me so much at first as the base ingratitude

I experienced from several persons who were indebted to me in small sums, loans of friendship, and who never have, nor, I suppose, ever will, pay me. Kelly owes me one hundred and forty guineas, not a shilling of this shall I ever touch, I fear. There is another quarter from whence I met the same unkind usage. A quarter it will pain you to read of, but I think I ought to mention it. The night that I strongly urged your father to see and forgive you, the Burkes were present ; amongst many other arguments on your behalf I used this—if a reconciliation was only prevented by want of cash to fit you out once more, that should no longer be an impediment, as I would cheerfully advance any sum requisite for the purpose, which he might repay to me whenever it was convenient, until when I never would ask for it. When my accumulated distresses so rapidly and unexpectedly thickened upon me, I applied to your father, explaining every particular and requested that he would give me some sort of acknowledgment for the amount I had advanced, payable in two, three or four years, or at whatever period he chose. According to his usual custom, he began by turning my proposition into a joke, but ending with a flat denial to give me any acknowledgment whatever or to admit the debt at all. I afterwards got Dick Burke to speak to him on the subject, but all in vain. He said that if I was such a fool as to advance so considerable a sum of money without being properly authorised, I deserved to suffer for my want of common caution. It then occurred to me that soon after your return from the West Indies your brother Joseph had written me a letter, wherein he said that any money I would advance to you he would be answerable for. I thought it more just that a brother should suffer than I, who although a warm and sincere friend was no way related by blood. Besides, I knew that he was so necessary to your father that could I once obtain a verdict of a jury for the amount due to me, he would forthwith discharge it. I, therefore, under the advice of Mr. Greenland, the attorney, made the attempt, but failed. By way of comfort, however, this same Greenland tells me I may

III.—2 C

send out powers and sue you in the Court of Calcutta. Now that, my good friend William, is a measure that I am sure you know me too well to suppose me capable of were my circumstances far worse than they actually are ; yet there are two things that I do not scruple to recommend to your serious consideration, and as I really consider them reasonable, I have no doubt of your compliance. The first is that as soon as you are worth a little money you will make your will in all due form and thereby dispose of your effects in case of death in such a manner as that I may be paid principal and interest of your debt to me, and put in the name of James Adair and George Dempster as trustees for me. The other proposal is—if you are successful, when worth one thousand pounds clear and not before, to send me one hundred pounds, and the like for each thousand you make afterwards until the whole of my debt is liquidated. I think it is superfluous and unnecessary to tell you that had my circumstances continued as they were, I never should have thought of such a thing, but really and truly, my good William, at present a hundred pounds would comparatively be like Lord Clive's fortune to former times. Popham is, I am told, doing remarkably well at Madras ; he owes me upwards of four thousand pounds ; should he continue successful and deal honourably and fairly by paying me interest at 17 per cent, for I raised all the hard cash I could for him by annuities, and pay at that rate of interest myself, I might once more be set afloat and get into an English harbour again, but there are so many contingencies that I almost despair of such a pleasing event ever occurring.

" I believe I have already told you that Mrs. Cane's pin-money of two hundred pounds a year, and her mother, Mrs. Johnson's, one hundred, which she pays to me for her board and lodging, forms my entire income. When the half-yearly stipend arrives, as it is all paid in silver, I regularly spread the whole amount upon the floor, then lay myself down and roll on it. The thought did not originate with me, it is Charles Fox's, to whom ready money is as rare a commodity as it is to me. My old manservant Cook came with us at forty guineas a year and Mrs. Cane's maid at twenty-five, the latter speaking French inimitably well. I, however, soon sent them back to England, replacing Mrs. Cane's servant by one quite as good, if not superior, at six guineas a year. I also had with me a Mr: Watel, peruquier François, who did me the honour to accompany me at twenty guineas a year in capacity of interpreter, for you know full well I spoke not a word of French. After three months' residence in this country, I had acquired a sort of jargon sufficient to make myself understood, and then all my six servants cost me but twenty-three guineas a year. Thus have I filled this whole letter with accounts of my *ménage*, but as I am well convinced of your regard for me, perhaps it is the most agreeable subject I could dwell upon, as you will thereby perceive that if ever fortune should smile upon me again adversity will at least have done me some good by teaching me to proportion my expences to my income, and to have ascertained beyond doubt that a strict regularity in one's accounts is the only method of attaining it.

"Your old favourite, William, is really grown a remarkably fine boy. He speaks French like a native and I am brushing up my Latin that I may instruct him in that language myself. He was at a French school, but they taught him to lie and thieve with all the little evasions that attend auricular confession and mental reservation—I shall endeavour to bring him up *un honnête homme, mais ni juif—ni Mahomedan—ni——* Boyes says it is very difficult to pen a whisper, and I say there is much comprised in a dash, therefore instead of 'a word' I use a dash 'to the wise.'

"Mrs. Cane, who often speaks of you with great regard, has lost her love of the pleasing art of drawing. She is grown religious in proportion as I lose mine, and never prays less than an hour and a half night and morning, besides meditations '*pendant la journée.*' I had a letter not long ago from Peter Wybrants; he is well, quite as fat as when you last saw him, and I am afraid quite as idle. If such be the fact, I also fear that you and I have something to answer for by having lent our aid to make him so with our excursions to France, Margate, Weymouth, and so forth. Adieu, my dear Will, let me hear from you by every opportunity,

Yours most affectionately, WILLIAM CANE."


" MY DEAR WILL HICKEY.    Tours, May 29th, 1787.

" It is now two-and-thirty years since our acquaintance first commenced at Twickenham and Westminster School; and it is now eleven since with a well-founded confidence you came to me at Erith when on your return from Jamaica your father would neither receive nor see you. Had our situations been reversed, I should have experienced as much from you, and I will venture to assert been received with equal kindness on your part. The money I expended in fitting you out for the East Indies I did not feel the loss of at the time, and so little did I ever think of forcing you to pay me that I refused your proffered bond, contenting my-self with a simple acknowledgment of the debt in writing. After we had both quitted England, I tried to get my money from your father and brother as they were able and I con-ceived ought to have been willing to repay me, particularly as they were aware that at the period I so tried, I was in pressing want of it. I failed in my attempt, for Law and Equity are not always companions. But, my dear Will, with you I am persuaded I run no such risk. I have waited ten long years to give you time to acquire the means of acquit-ting a debt of honour and gratitude, and at present take the liberty of drawing on you for the amount in order to pay a debt of honour and gratitude likewise, for to supply some pressing wants which arose at that time, I borrowed of my old and true friend, Mr. Roger Wilbraham, three hundred pounds, all of which from the date of the generous loan I am still indebted to him. In order to discharge another meritorious call, I granted an annuity of six years' purchase to Messrs. Gemmel and Duncan Davidson. The principal part of my property they had sequestered in the year 1781, and are in possession of it at this day. The fact is, that by Christmas next I shall be seven hundred pounds out of pocket in consequence of my loan to you ; but I by no means desire you to pay me so much, all I require is the principal, being two hundred and forty-seven pounds and interest thereon at 5 per cent. As your circumstances better and you become opulent, I should receive kindly from you a pipe of madeira, to make up the difference between three hundred and eighty-one pounds, the sum I drew for, and seven hundred pounds, which as already observed I am really out of pocket. I trust, my dear fellow, that you will not disgrace me by causing the three bills to be protested, which for your accommodation I drew at one, two, and three months after sight. Their returning to Europe dishonoured might occasion my utter ruin by being prosecuted for them here, and as you know Bills of Exchange are recoverable in any country of Europe. I will also venture to add I think, in the event of your dying unmarried, you ought by some legacy to make up my loss to me ; observe, however, that should you have any family, I do not require such bequest, the pleasure of having contributed to your success in life being sufficient for your faithful friend, WILLIAM CANE.

" P.S.—Any letters or parcels may be addressed for me at Roger Wilbraham's, Esquire, M.P., St. James's Place, London. Lord Mansfield at the trial said I might sue you in India, where I should certainly recover ; such a measure will never be adopted by W. C."

" MY DEAR WILLIAM.      Tours, April 20th, 1789.

" Your returning all the three bills protested throws me into a situation the most deplorable. I paid them away to Mr. Wilbraham, being part of a debt due to him for money lent, and it is to his kindness only that I owe my not being at this hour in a jail. Should anything happen to him, I cannot expect the same indulgence from his executors or representatives. How terrible to think that my personal liberty is thus at stake; you must be well aware that a Bill of Exchange follows a man all the world over, you never can fly from it. Could I have thought when I advanced money for your outfit that you would have subjected me to what is worse than death; disgrace, and imprisonment. Surely in a place where you have resided eleven years you could not be so destitute of friends as not to have been able to get someone to lend you the money rather than thus unkindly treat me. I relied too much on the goodness of your heart and to your known high sense of honour not to make another attempt, though in a much smaller way and at a longer date. I therefore draw on you two bills, each being for fifty pounds, one of them at six, the other at twelve months' sight, confiding in your natural benevolence of disposition, the recollection of our long-established and strict intimacy, and your sense of my present embarrassed situation which is infinitely worse than when I wrote to you two years ago, as I declare before the living God, I am not in possession of the receipt of one shilling either of my own or of Mrs. Cane's fortune. In short, my dear Will Hickey, if what I have already stated has no effect nothing I can add will, but I have better hope, and trust that you will not so neglect your old steady and constant friend, WILLIAM CANE.

"P.S.—About six weeks ago my son left me to go to Ireland. Lord Earlsford gave me hope of procuring a commission for him. He is five feet ten inches in height, fences remarkably well, and draws in a superior style—an elegant dancer and altogether what the French term ' un joli Cavalier.' I believe he will not much longer remain in poverty, as I have all the reason in the world to suppose I have a stone in my left kidney. If I die before we settle, I heartily wish you success. Adieu!

"One word more, my dear Will, before I finish. I understand you acknowledged the debt to Mr. Dashwood of Calcutta except seventy pounds. There are now two years' more interest due, amounting to twenty-four pounds—in all four hundred and five pounds. Although there cannot be a doubt of the correctness or propriety of my former statement, yet for your accommodation I am willing to strike off the seventy pounds in question, provided you accept the two bills for fifty pounds each and give your bond to Mr. Dashwood, who is duly empowered to close the business for the remaining two hundred and thirty pounds, payable at whatever date you think it will be convenient to you to take it up. Do not suddenly refuse to do this, take time to consider of it, and when you recall every circumstance of our long friendship and intimacy, I rely upon it you will, in the manner least distressing to yourself, do justice to your old and now unhappily distressed friend, William Cane."

Never did I suffer more distress of mind than at not having it in my power to liquidate my respected friend Cane's debt at the moment of his first applying for it, feeling, as he very truly says, that it was a debt of honour and gratitude ; but, unfortunately, it came upon me at a time when I was harassed in two or three different quarters for the discharge of English debts of equally long standing, to arrange which I had been obliged to borrow money at the ruinous interest of 12 per cent, a rate that in itself was the source of destruction to several of my acquaintances, for the natives of India, not content with that exorbitant advantage, constantly insist upon those persons who are indebted to them settling annually, and if unable to pay in cash cancel the former security and take a new one, including the interest for the preceding year, by which means the debt accumulates so rapidly that few persons can withstand it. I have already observed that this grievance proved a very heavy load about my neck for many years. When I ascribe the above method of keeping accounts to the natives alone, I am wrong, having seen various instances of the same kind in British merchants ; indeed, it has become quite common with the different agency houses. I will just mention one example where a wealthy native was the creditor. It happened to Mr. Joseph Sherburne, a very old servant of the Company, who when in his writership, and upon his first arrival from England, borrowed from a Bengal sitcar nine hundred sicca rupees for which he executed a bond and warrant of attorney to confess judgment, payable in six months, and not having a command of money he continued to renew the security every six months ; I myself saw this gentleman prosecuted in the Supreme Court for fifty-eight thousand odd hundred rupees, to which enormous amount the comparatively trifling sum of nine hundred had swelled in the manner above mentioned.

Although I was unable to pay Mr. Cane, I exerted my utmost endeavours to assist him through other mediums ; with which object in view I addressed as affecting a letter as my pen was capable of producing to Mr. Stephen Popham, then residing in Madras, in which I represented the melancholy reverse of fortune our mutual friend had undergone, and without in the slightest degree insinuating that this reverse had been accomplished by the considerable sums advanced on his (Popham's) account and for his sole use and benefit, from an apprehension that such a memento might injure instead of promote my object, I merely stated that Mr. Cane had nothing to subsist on for himself and family except Mrs. Cane's pin-money of two hundred pounds a year, and therefore that a few hundreds from an old friend, either as a loan or as a present, would prove acceptable. I even condescended to flatter a man for whom I certainly felt nothing like respect, and blushed while I complimented. But I might have spared myself the ungracious task, for the unprincipled man did not give me any answer whatever, nor did he ever remit a single guinea to Cane who had acted so generously towards him.

Another attempt I made on my poor friend's behalf was not a jot more successful (though I am anticipating in point of time in mentioning it now). Mr. Burroughs, who found money pour in so fast as even to astonish himself, had not strength of mind sufficient to make him bear success with becoming moderation. I in common with the rest of his acquaintances observed a sudden change in his manner, also in his style of living, and I could not but despise him for betraying such weakness. When one day conversing with him upon the subject of cutter sailing, I purposely mentioned the name of William Cane, to whom I had heard he was distantly related, or was in some way connected with the family, upon which he said, " Do you allude to Cane of Berners Street ? " I replied that I did, he being an intimate friend of mine from early infancy. "And of mine likewise," replied Burroughs, " although, from residing in different countries, he being in England and I in Ireland, we for several years did not meet, and now you bring it to my recollection it must have been you I, at the desire of Peter Wybrants, and accompanied by him, called upon twice or thrice at a paperhanger's shop in St. Albans Street, where you lodged and at that time was going through a course of mercury. This was, I believe, in the latter end of the year 1776 or early in 1777, and I recollect you was in woeful plight." Upon his mentioning the latter circumstance, I perfectly remembered him. From this acknowledgment of Burroughs' knowing my distressed friend Cane, I augured favourably, and thought I had a fair chance of interesting the successful advocate in his favour. I likewise imagined nothing would be so likely to stimulate his liberality as a perusal of Cane's own statement of his situation, and therefore put his letters into my pocket when going to call at Mr. Burroughs' house. I told him I had recently received those letters from Mr. Cane and had brought them for his perusal, hoping he too would interest himself on behalf of a truly respectable and most worthy man. He affected to be rejoiced at hearing of his dear friend Will Cane, for whom he entertained the most sincere regard and to whose family he laid under great obligations, was in good health, adding that he would certainly write to him by the first ship that sailed. Then opening one of the letters I had given him, while perusing it I perceived his countenance altered ; he knit his brows, appearing at a loss what to say. After hastily running his eye over it he returned it to me, coldly observing, " Mr. Cane has always shown himself to be an inconsiderate, extravagant man, the inevitable consequence of which must be distress and embarrassment ; he has no one but himself to blame.  However (continued the insolent upstart), some of his uncles, who are all opulent, will no doubt come forward to aid him as to pecuniary matters, and indeed near relations are the fittest persons to be applied to." Considering the terms he had been upon with Mr. Cane, such behaviour struck me as even more unhandsome than Mr. Popham's silence, upon my application to him.  This feeling operating strongly upon my mind, I took up my letters from the table on which Burroughs had laid them, and without saying another word indignantly left his room and house. This was the first trait I had of the Irish gentleman's meanness, though subsequently I had innumerable instances of it. My manner towards him altered accordingly, cold and distant when we met in parties, nor did I ever go near him, except by special invitation, or upon matters of business.

· Though I had not the power, I had certainly every inclination not only to have repaid Mr. Cane the uttermost farthing but to have afforded him further pecuniary assistance, and I felt greatly at a loss how to answer his letters without remitting some cash.  The two first therefore remained unanswered, but upon receiving the third, enclosing bills for small sums and drawn at a long sight, I hesitated not a moment to accept them, and directly wrote to him, saying I had not only done so, but would in like manner liquidate the full amount, without deducting the seventy pounds I had previously objected to.  I likewise expressed myself in most affectionate and grateful terms, such as in fact and truth I really felt towards him, of which he seemed fully sensible.  '

**END OF VOL. III**

# INDEX

Gower, Sir Erasmas, 97
Gower, Captain, 102 *et seq.*
Grange, De, Mr., 92
Grant, Mr. James, 204
Grasse, Count De, 64
Gray, Captain, 309, 362
Greenland, Mr., 385
Griffin, Captain, 247 *et seq.*
Guiamara, Donna, 3
Guignace, Monsieur, 126

### H

Hadjee, Mahattee, 355
Haldane, Captain Harry, 288
Haldane, John, 205, 222
Haldane, Robert, 322
Halifax, Lord, 250
Hall, Phinehas, 149, 322, 337
Hallam, Captain, 89, 91, 94
Hamilton, Solomon, 146, 168–9, 180, 227–8
Hamilton, Sir William, 289
Hamilton, Lady, 289
Hammersley, Harriet, 4, 5
Hampton, Colonel, 239
*Hannibal, The*, 50, 57–8
*Hannibal, The Little*, 62–3, 81, 103, 110–1
*Hardi, The*, 76, 111
Hardwicke, Mr., 325
Hare, Dr. James, 288, 313, 359, 369–70
Harington, Sir John, 289
Harington, Lady, 289
Harpur, Mr., 241 *et seq.*, 291
Hastings, Warren, 160 *et seq.*, 181, 244–5, 262–3, 284, 359
Hay, Edward, 245, 283
Hay, Mrs., 375–6
Haynes, Mr., 291
Heffernan, Captain Richard, 209
Henchman, Thomas, 276
Hennes, Mr., J. 198
*Heros, The*, 50 *et seq.*, 57, 63, 67, 75 *et seq.*, 110, 112
*Hertford, The*, 95
Hervey, Major, 338
Hesilrige, Sir Arthur, 154, 174–5, 179, 181 *et seq.*
Hesilrige, Mrs., 154, 174–5, 179, 184 *et seq.*
Hickey, Ann, 343, 352
"Hickey, Mrs. William" (*see* Barry, Charlotte)
Hickey, John, 349

Hickey, Joseph (father of William), 96, 352
Hickey, Thomas, 202, 349
Hickey, William—
sets sail with Charlotte Barry in the *Raynha de Portugal* for the East, 1
anchors and goes on shore at Funchal, 2, 3
storms and gales, 6 *et seq.*
his concern for Charlotte, 10, 20 *et seq.*
his graphic description of a violent tempest, 18 *et seq.*
detained under suspicion at Trincomalay in the hands of the French, 34 *et seq.*
receives harsh treatment from the Governor's hands, 35 *et seq.*, 77
receives much kindness from Captain Gautier, 38 *et seq.*
anxiety during Charlotte's illness, 42 *et seq.*
entertained by Monsieur Chevillard, 45 *et seq.*
arrival of the French fleet, 50
goes on board the *Heros* to pay his compliments to Admiral Suffren, 51
states his case, 52 *et seq.*
discusses the English Admiral, Sir Edward Hughes, with Admiral Suffren, 55 *et seq.*
dines with the Admiral, 62–3
his high opinion of the Admiral, 66–7, 84, 109
the *Raynha de Portugal* detained as a prize, 68 *et seq.*
his appeal for release to the Admiral, 74 *et seq.*
farewells to French friends, 78 *et seq.*
on board the *Blake*, 80
anchors at Cuddalore, 82 *et seq.*
efforts to sail for Madras, 83 *et seq.*
hostile reception by Colonel Nixon, 85 *et seq.*
embarks for Madras, 88 *et seq.*
handsome presents from Admiral Suffren, 90
his tribute to the French, 92–3
arrives at Madras, 94
entertained by Mr. Popham, 94 *et seq.*

*Truth.*—" A happy find. He is as candid as Barry Lyndon and hardly less interesting. Indeed in one way he is more interesting. He gives you the vividest picture of the life of a fast youth in those days. He had a story of extraordinarily varied and stirring adventure to tell, and needed only a pen as lively as his life to make it as interesting as a novel by Smollett. Really it is hardly too much to say that the ' Memoirs ' have all the elements of such a novel in solution, and need only crystallisation to be another ' Peregrine Pickle.' I do not know where you could get a more dramatic picture of the haunts and habits of the fast youth of that disreputable day."

*The Athenæum.*—" One of the most interesting eighteenth-century documents that have appeared for some time. His narrative is marked by extreme simplicity, but shows no slight faculty for observation and considerable sense of humour. It gives the impression of an unstudied transcript of the life of a typical man of his time. We have touched upon scarcely a tithe of the entertaining matter contained in this volume and shall eagerly await the continuation."

*Birmingham Post.*—" These memoirs have much of the attractiveness of Pepys's diary. The book abounds in anecdote and incident."

*Sunday Times.*—" It is all in the true eighteenth-century style, the style of ' Roderick Random,' of ' Tom Jones ' : amusing, highly amusing these reminiscences most certainly are."

*The Outlook.*—" There is scarcely a phase in London life between 1760 and 1775 upon which this exceedingly amusing book does not throw some new and interesting light : these exceedingly entertaining and often exceedingly piquant reminiscences."

*The Scotsman.*—" However well the eighteenth century may be already recorded in books of memoirs there will always be room for so readable a book of autobiography as this."

*The Irish Times.*—" Related with Defoe-like fidelity."

*The Standard.*—" Gives a realistic picture of life about town in early Georgian days. The record is amazingly lively."

*The Sportsman.*—" Extraordinarily vivid and faithful, a marvellously interesting book, absolutely genuine and as such a more important human document than sees the light once in a generation."

*Daily News and Leader.*—" He describes his experiences in a lively and gay and at times rather scandalous style. It has some of the bad and good points of a Smollett novel : as an eighteenth-century human document it will by many readers be found absorbing."

*Daily Express.*—" It is one of the most absorbingly interesting books of recent times."

*Western Morning News.*—" In the annals of autobiography there is perhaps no book which is quite such a self-revelation as this."

*The Tatler.*—" We must ever feel grateful for a series of the most vivid descriptions of eighteenth-century life—bad, vicious, but somehow invariably picturesque."

*1*

and also in the frankest mood of self-revelation. One is charmed to follow him in his adventures. He was a keen observer of men and things, a shrewd judge of character : he associated with many people of worth and note and with few who had not some points of human interest."

*Westminster Gazette.*—" A remarkably frank and vivid picture of eighteenth-century life in London and abroad. A second volume which has made its appearance is no less interesting than the first."

*Daily Chronicle.*—" A genuine eighteenth century vignette, a human portrait of a man of fashion. He is perfectly frank about everything. His sprees, his amours, his debts are all entered and you learn to love him for his very failings."

*Scotsman.*—" Brings before one in a human document of uncommon frankness the figure of a roystering, buckish, fashionable, elegant and fast young man of the period of Smollett's novels ; his book must always remain one of interest and importance for a student of the English social atmosphere of the eighteenth century."

*Manchester Guardian.*—" A second instalment of a zestful book which has already caused critics to find analogies in Pepys, Fielding, Smollett, Defoe and Barry Lyndon : it is a lively performance."

*Daily News.*—" One of the happiest discoveries of recent years. Hickey's autobiography has been compared to Smollett and indeed in its breeziness and variety it deserves the comparison."

*Sunday Evening Telegram.*—" The first volume was rightly acclaimed as one of the biggest literary finds of modern days. The second volume is every bit as interesting as its predecessor. There is not a dull page, and the light shown on life in fashionable circles in the middle of the eighteenth century is as good as anything we have had since the great novelists of the period."

*Yorkshire Post.*—" About as lively as anything to be found in Fielding and Tobias Smollett. His adventures are related with droll humour."

*Sunday Times.*—" The second volume has as marvellous a resemblance to a Smollett romance as its predecessor—records irregular love intrigues a Peregrine Pickle never bettered, and has a wonderful study of almost insane jealousy."

*Sheffield Telegraph.*—" He has written so intimate a picture of the life of 1775 onward that his book will live in literature with some of the greatest autobiographies."

*Sportsman.*—" In writing these memoirs he did the world a service he can hardly have foreseen. They rank with the best extant, not only Pepys but Benvenuto Cellini's."

*Country Life.*—" The picture of London in the middle years of the reign of George III is inimitable."

*Outlook.*—" He is interested in everything and his interest makes every page interesting also."

*The Tatler.*—" This new volume is equally as delightful, as amusing, as interesting and (whisper it low) as indiscreet as the first volume."

*Land and Water.*—" As good reading as the first volume. Every line he writes has an interest : it is human and full of life, and much is of historical value. These fascinating memoirs."

Lightning Source UK Ltd.
Milton Keynes UK
UKOW03f2113130114

224541UK00006B/108/P